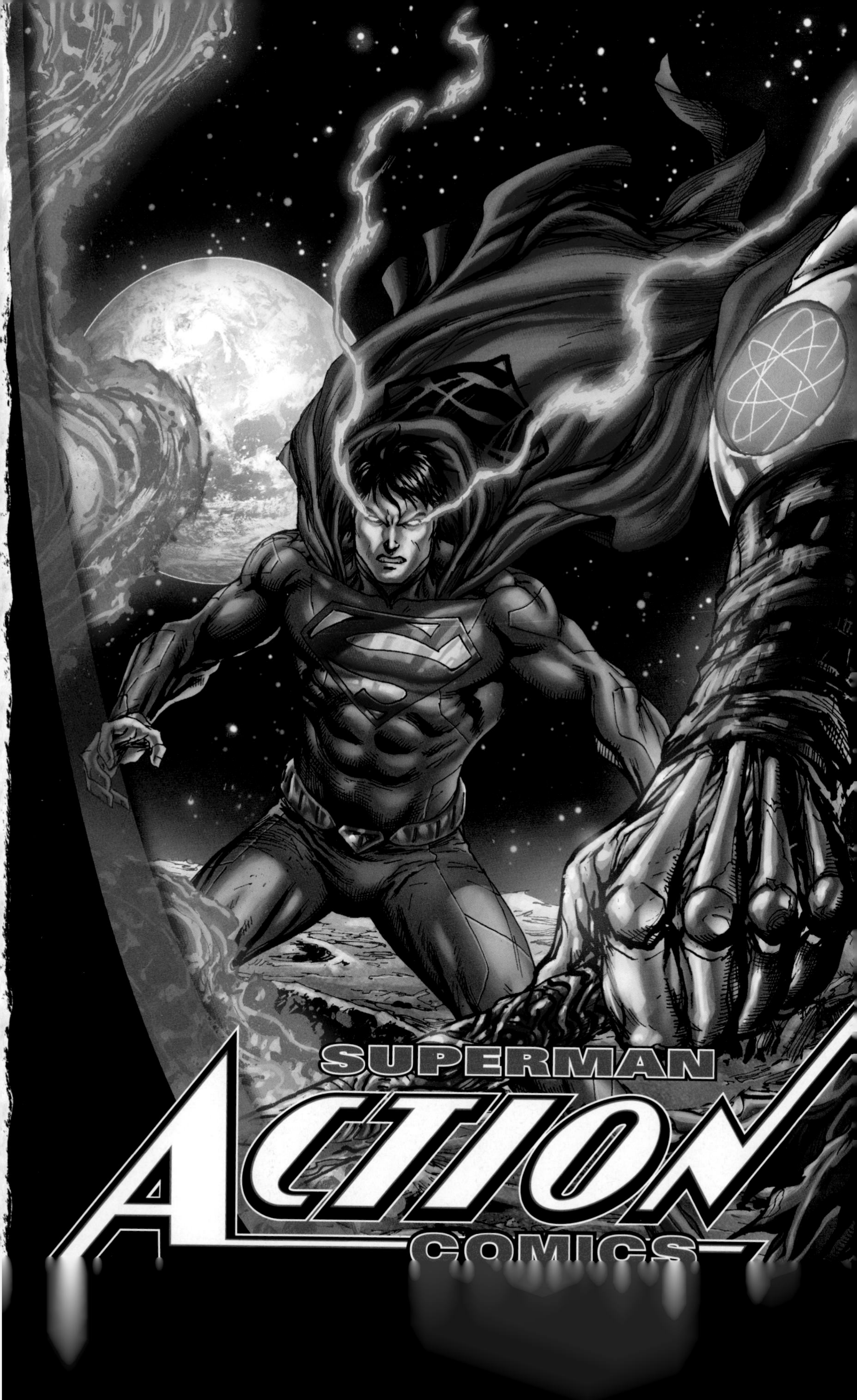
SUPERMAN
ACTION
COMICS

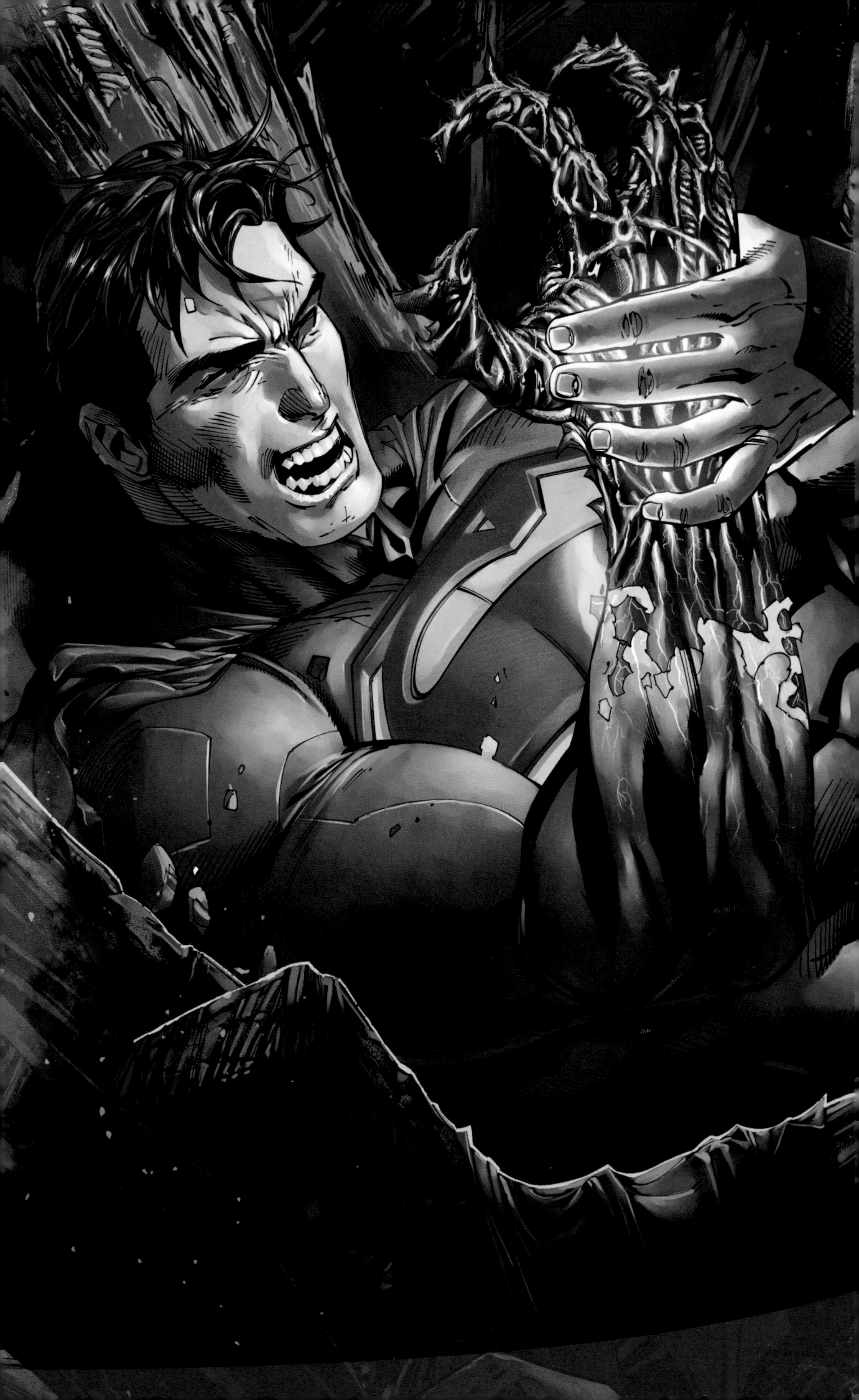

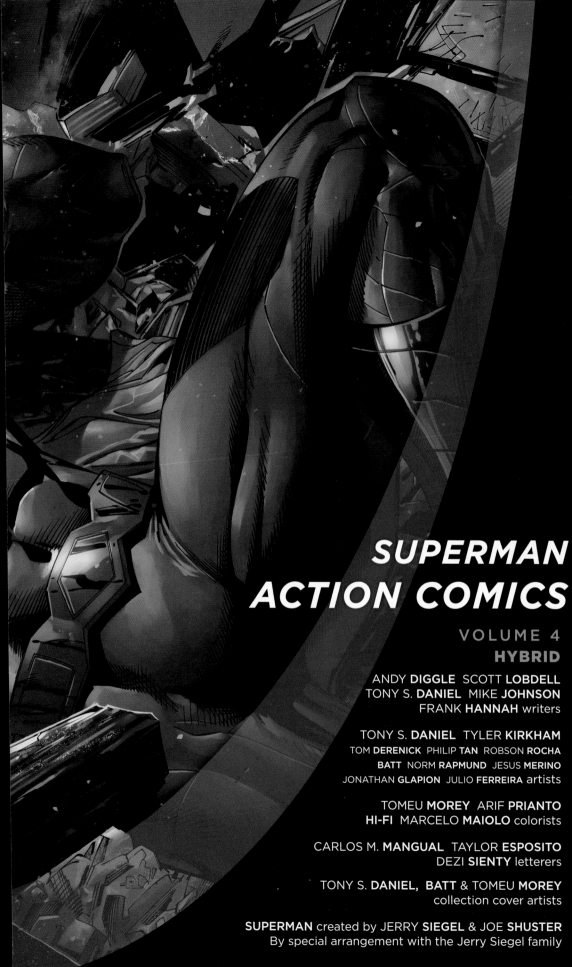

SUPERMAN
ACTION COMICS

VOLUME 4
HYBRID

ANDY **DIGGLE** SCOTT **LOBDELL**
TONY S. **DANIEL** MIKE **JOHNSON**
FRANK **HANNAH** writers

TONY S. **DANIEL** TYLER **KIRKHAM**
TOM **DERENICK** PHILIP **TAN** ROBSON **ROCHA**
BATT NORM **RAPMUND** JESUS **MERINO**
JONATHAN **GLAPION** JULIO **FERREIRA** artists

TOMEU **MOREY** ARIF **PRIANTO**
HI-FI MARCELO **MAIOLO** colorists

CARLOS M. **MANGUAL** TAYLOR **ESPOSITO**
DEZI **SIENTY** letterers

TONY S. **DANIEL**, **BATT** & TOMEU **MOREY**
collection cover artists

SUPERMAN created by JERRY **SIEGEL** & JOE **SHUSTER**
By special arrangement with the Jerry Siegel family

EDDIE BERGANZA Editor – Original Series RICKEY PURDIN Associate Editor – Original Series
ANTHONY MARQUES DARREN SHAN Assistant Editors – Original Series ROBIN WILDMAN Editor
ROBBIN BROSTERMAN Design Director – Books ROBBIE BIEDERMAN Publication Design

BOB HARRAS Senior VP – Editor-in-Chief, DC Comics

DIANE NELSON President DAN DIDIO and JIM LEE Co-Publishers
GEOFF JOHNS Chief Creative Officer
AMIT DESAI Senior VP – Marketing and Franchise Management
AMY GENKINS Senior VP – Business and Legal Affairs NAIRI GARDINER Senior VP – Finance
JEFF BOISON VP – Publishing Planning MARK CHIARELLO VP – Art Direction and Design
JOHN CUNNINGHAM VP – Marketing TERRI CUNNINGHAM VP – Editorial Administration
LARRY GANEM VP – Talent Relations and Services
ALISON GILL Senior VP – Manufacturing and Operations HANK KANALZ Senior VP – Vertigo and Integrated Publishing
JAY KOGAN VP – Business and Legal Affairs, Publishing JACK MAHAN VP – Business Affairs, Talent
NICK NAPOLITANO VP – Manufacturing Administration SUE POHJA VP – Book Sales
FRED RUIZ VP – Manufacturing Operations COURTNEY SIMMONS Senior VP – Publicity BOB WAYNE Senior VP – Sales

SUPERMAN – ACTION COMICS VOLUME 4: HYBRID

Published by DC Comics. Copyright © 2014 DC Comics. All Rights Reserved.

Originally published in single magazine form in ACTION COMICS 19-24, YOUNG ROMANCE 1, SUPERMAN ANNUAL 2 © 2013 DC Comics.
All Rights Reserved. All characters, their distinctive likenesses and related elements featured in this publication are trademarks
of DC Comics. The stories, characters and incidents featured in this publication are entirely fictional.
DC Comics does not read or accept unsolicited ideas, stories or artwork.

DC Comics, 1700 Broadway, New York, NY 10019
A Warner Bros. Entertainment Company.
Printed by RR Donnelley, Salem, VA, USA. 6/13/14. First Printing.

HC ISBN: 978-1-4012-4632-7
SC ISBN: 978-1-4012-5077-5

Library of Congress Cataloging-in-Publication Data

Diggle, Andy.
Superman - Action Comics. Volume 4, Hybrid / Andy Diggle, Tony Daniel.
pages cm. — (The New 52!)
ISBN 978-1-4012-4632-7 (hardback)
1. Graphic novels. I. Daniel, Tony S. (Antonio Salvador), illustrator. II. Title. III. Title: Hybrid.
PN6728.S9D54 2014
741.5'973—dc23
2014010810

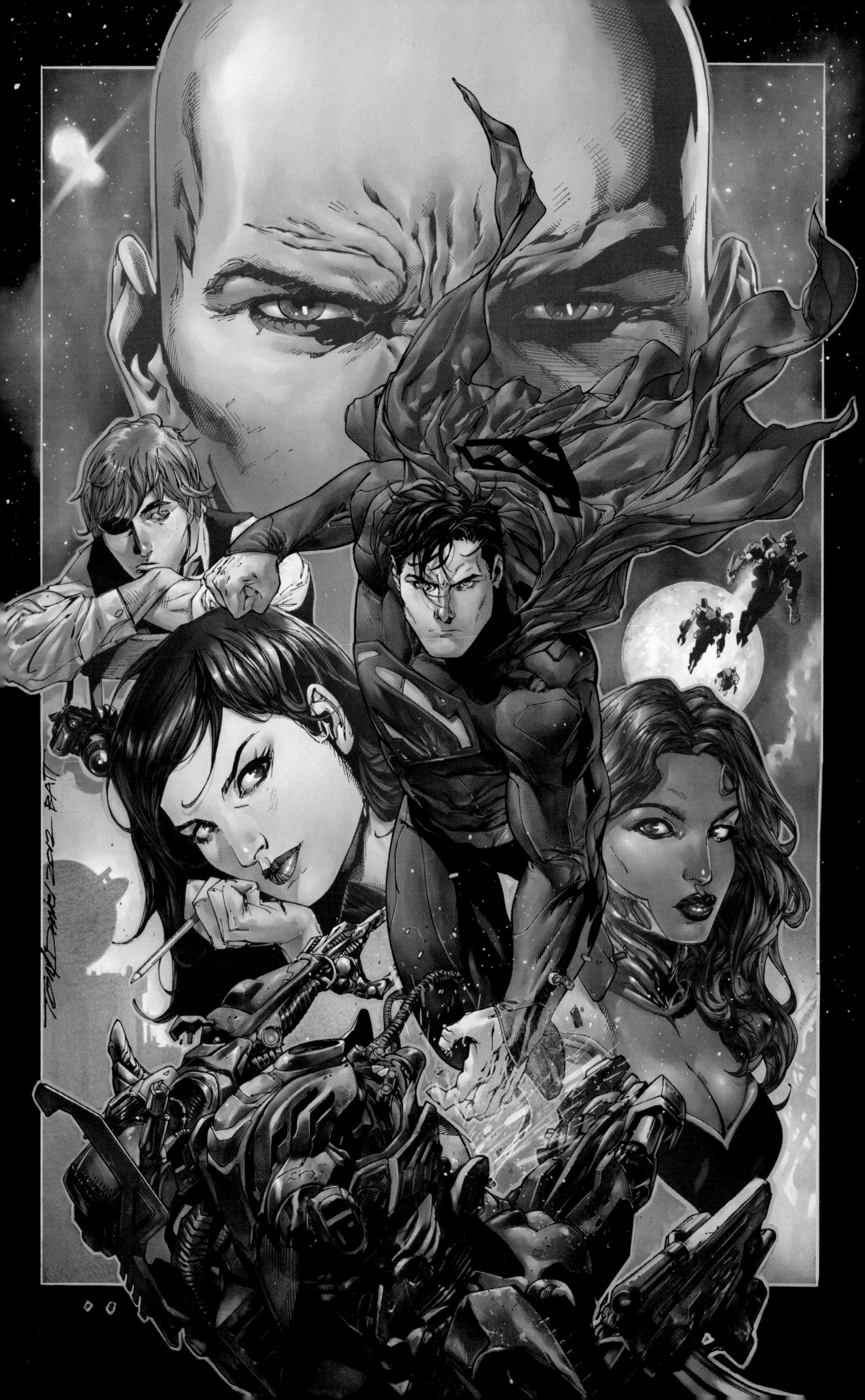

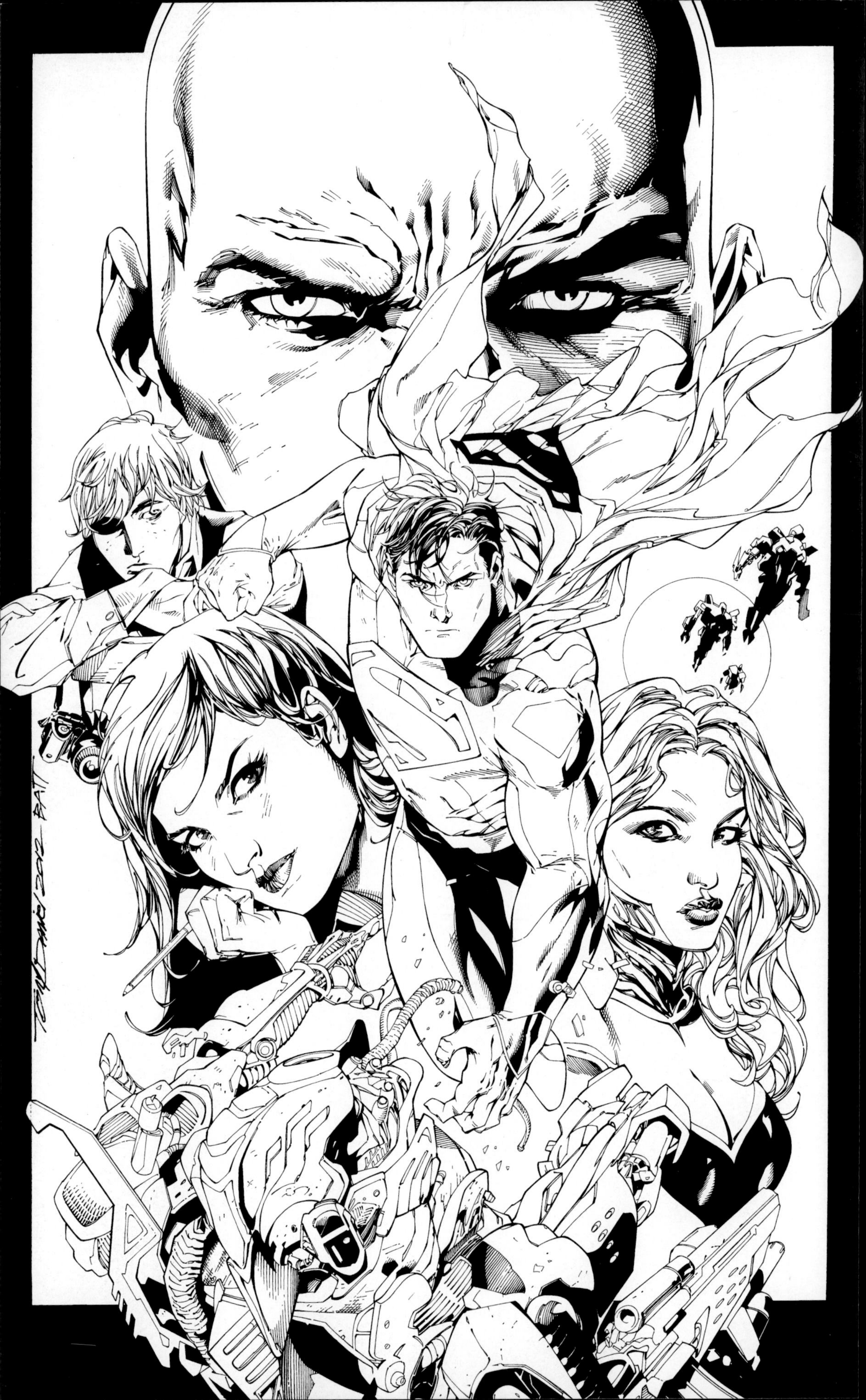

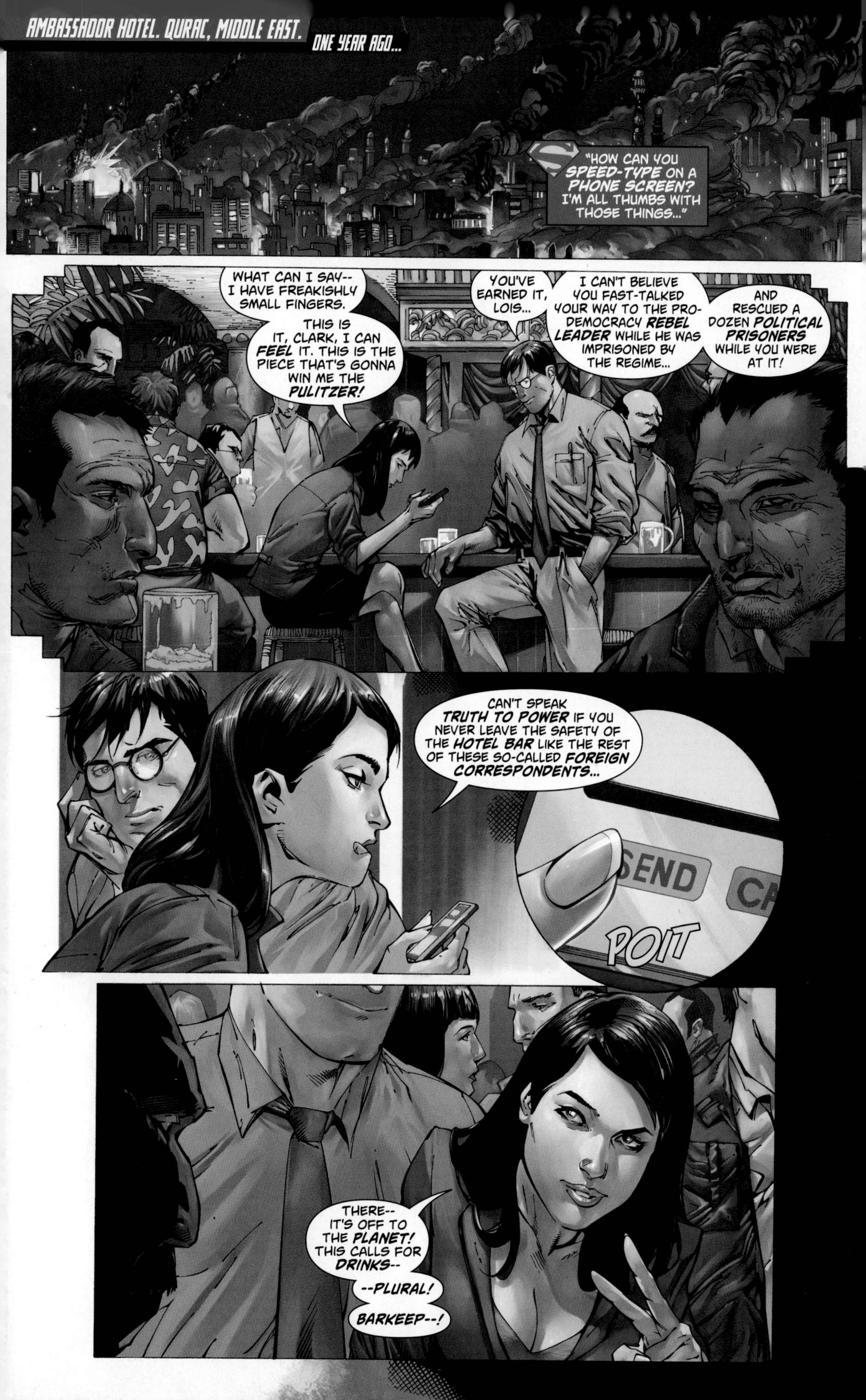
AMBASSADOR HOTEL. QURAC, MIDDLE EAST.
ONE YEAR AGO...
"HOW CAN YOU SPEED-TYPE ON A PHONE SCREEN? I'M ALL THUMBS WITH THOSE THINGS..."
WHAT CAN I SAY-- I HAVE FREAKISHLY SMALL FINGERS.
THIS IS IT, CLARK, I CAN FEEL IT. THIS IS THE PIECE THAT'S GONNA WIN ME THE PULITZER!
YOU'VE EARNED IT, LOIS...
I CAN'T BELIEVE YOU FAST-TALKED YOUR WAY TO THE PRO-DEMOCRACY REBEL LEADER WHILE HE WAS IMPRISONED BY THE REGIME...
AND RESCUED A DOZEN POLITICAL PRISONERS WHILE YOU WERE AT IT!
CAN'T SPEAK TRUTH TO POWER IF YOU NEVER LEAVE THE SAFETY OF THE HOTEL BAR LIKE THE REST OF THESE SO-CALLED FOREIGN CORRESPONDENTS...
SEND
POIT
THERE-- IT'S OFF TO THE PLANET! THIS CALLS FOR DRINKS--
--PLURAL!
BARKEEP--!

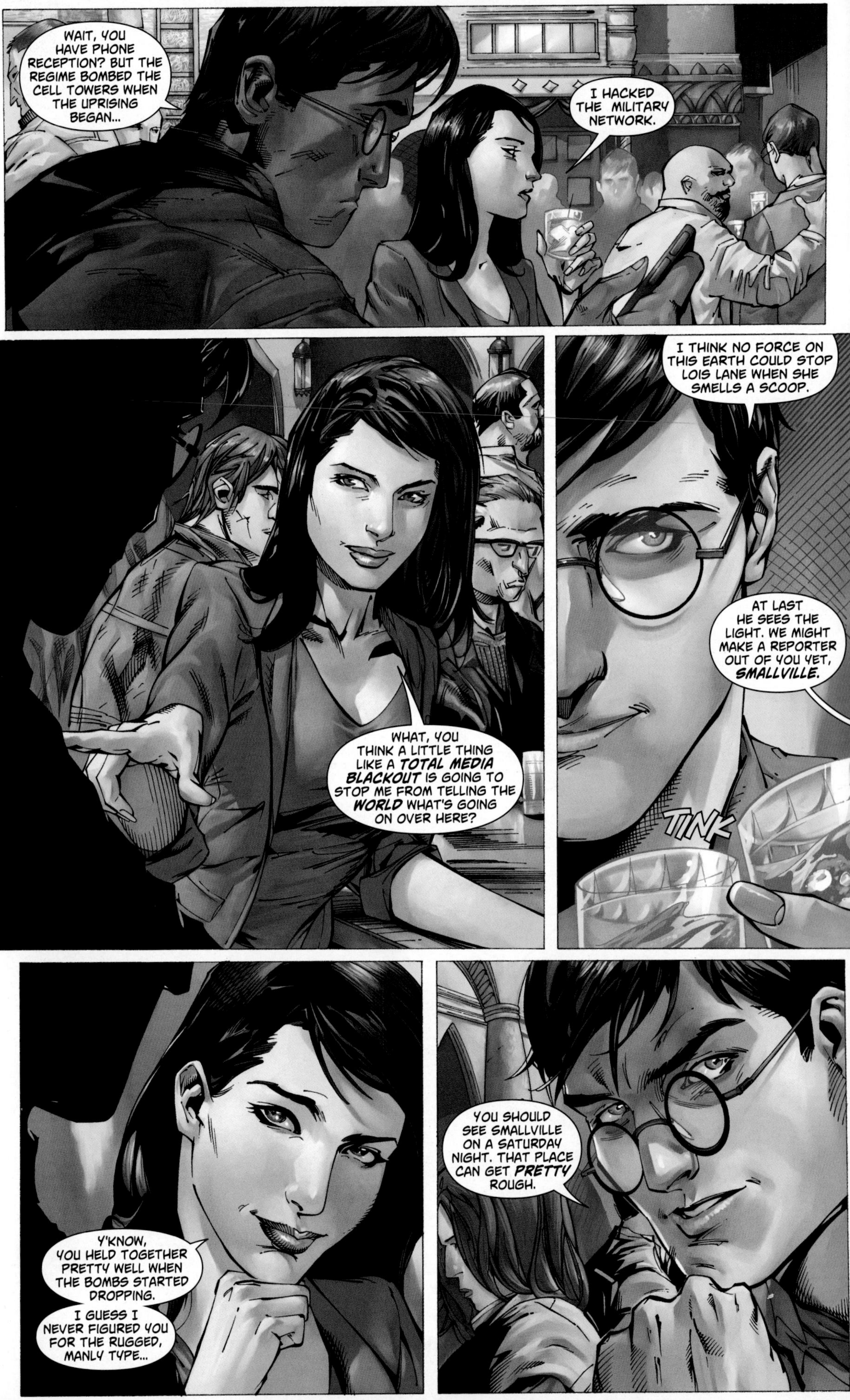
WAIT, YOU HAVE PHONE RECEPTION? BUT THE REGIME BOMBED THE CELL TOWERS WHEN THE UPRISING BEGAN...
I HACKED THE MILITARY NETWORK.
WHAT, YOU THINK A LITTLE THING LIKE A TOTAL MEDIA BLACKOUT IS GOING TO STOP ME FROM TELLING THE WORLD WHAT'S GOING ON OVER HERE?
I THINK NO FORCE ON THIS EARTH COULD STOP LOIS LANE WHEN SHE SMELLS A SCOOP.
AT LAST HE SEES THE LIGHT. WE MIGHT MAKE A REPORTER OUT OF YOU YET, SMALLVILLE.
TINK
Y'KNOW, YOU HELD TOGETHER PRETTY WELL WHEN THE BOMBS STARTED DROPPING.
I GUESS I NEVER FIGURED YOU FOR THE RUGGED, MANLY TYPE...
YOU SHOULD SEE SMALLVILLE ON A SATURDAY NIGHT. THAT PLACE CAN GET PRETTY ROUGH.

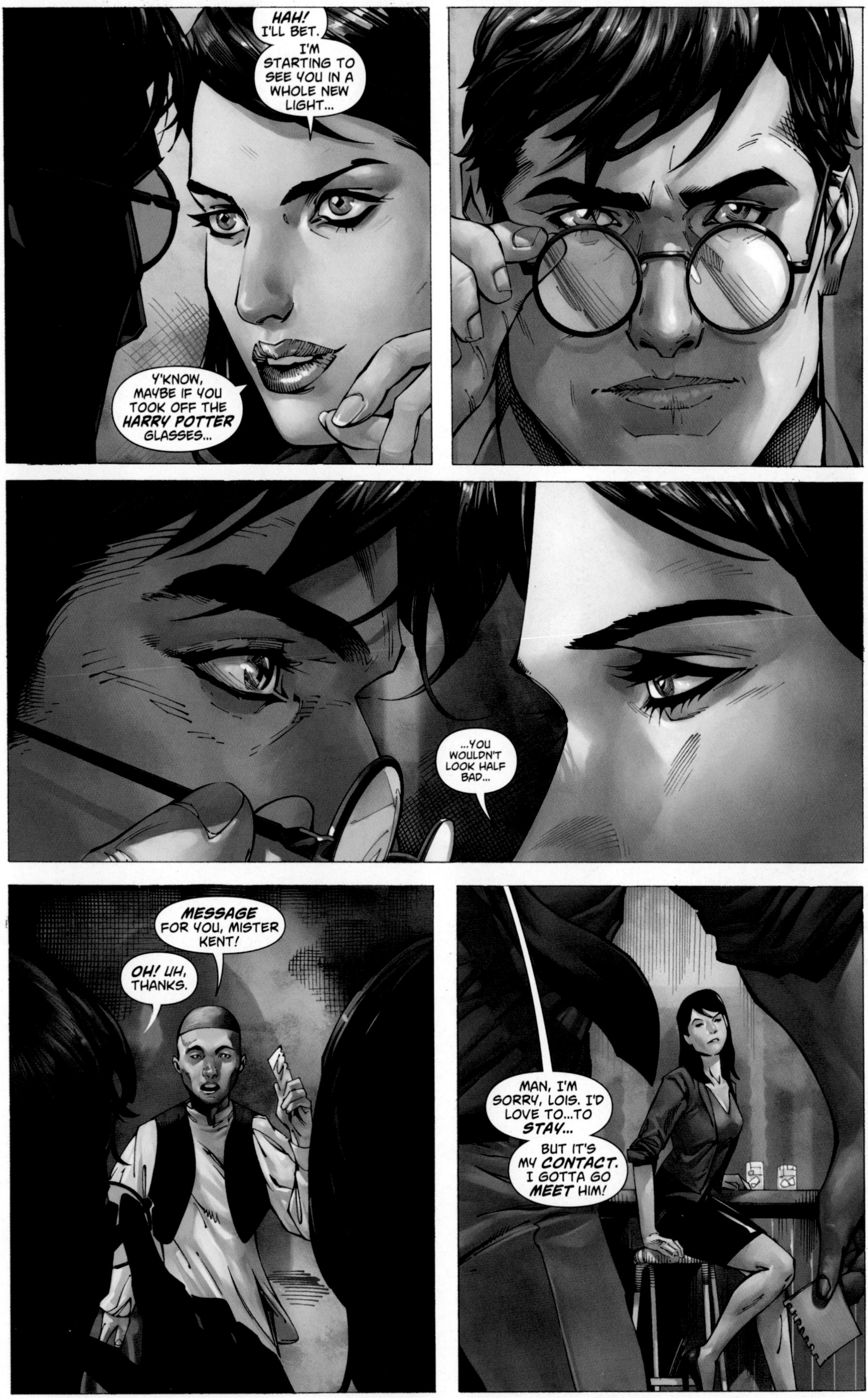
HAH! I'LL BET. I'M STARTING TO SEE YOU IN A WHOLE NEW LIGHT...
Y'KNOW, MAYBE IF YOU TOOK OFF THE HARRY POTTER GLASSES...
...YOU WOULDN'T LOOK HALF BAD...
MESSAGE FOR YOU, MISTER KENT!
OH! UH, THANKS.
MAN, I'M SORRY, LOIS. I'D LOVE TO...TO STAY...
BUT IT'S MY CONTACT. I GOTTA GO MEET HIM!

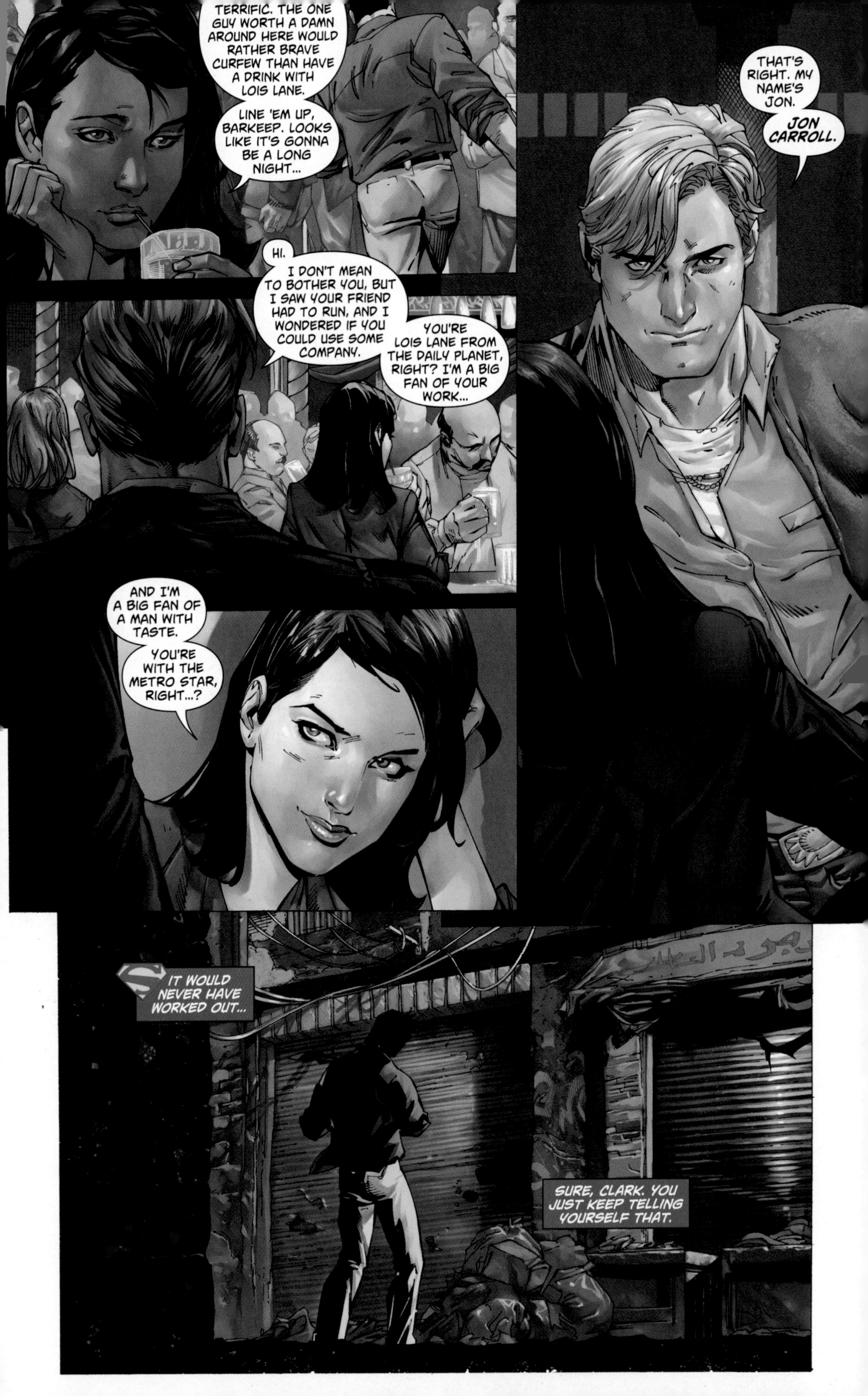
TERRIFIC. THE ONE GUY WORTH A DAMN AROUND HERE WOULD RATHER BRAVE CURFEW THAN HAVE A DRINK WITH LOIS LANE.
LINE 'EM UP, BARKEEP. LOOKS LIKE IT'S GONNA BE A LONG NIGHT...
HI.
I DON'T MEAN TO BOTHER YOU, BUT I SAW YOUR FRIEND HAD TO RUN, AND I WONDERED IF YOU COULD USE SOME COMPANY.
YOU'RE LOIS LANE FROM THE DAILY PLANET, RIGHT? I'M A BIG FAN OF YOUR WORK...
AND I'M A BIG FAN OF A MAN WITH TASTE.
YOU'RE WITH THE METRO STAR, RIGHT...?
THAT'S RIGHT. MY NAME'S JON.
JON CARROLL.
IT WOULD NEVER HAVE WORKED OUT...
SURE, CLARK. YOU JUST KEEP TELLING YOURSELF THAT.

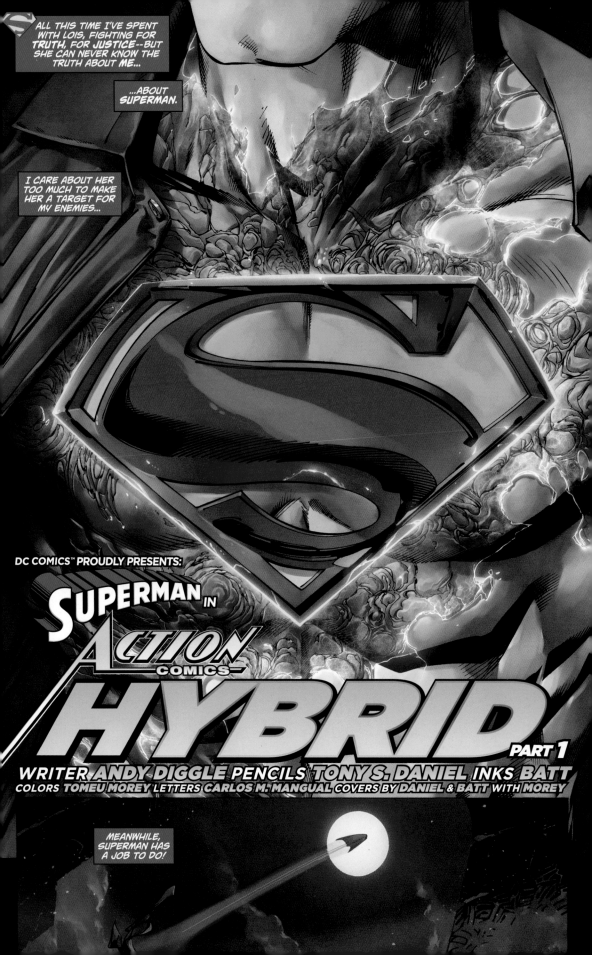

ALL THIS TIME I'VE SPENT WITH LOIS, FIGHTING FOR TRUTH, FOR JUSTICE--BUT SHE CAN NEVER KNOW THE TRUTH ABOUT ME...

...ABOUT SUPERMAN.

I CARE ABOUT HER TOO MUCH TO MAKE HER A TARGET FOR MY ENEMIES...

DC COMICS™ PROUDLY PRESENTS:

SUPERMAN IN

ACTION COMICS

HYBRID

PART 1

WRITER ANDY DIGGLE PENCILS TONY S. DANIEL INKS BATT
COLORS TOMEU MOREY LETTERS CARLOS M. MANGUAL COVERS BY DANIEL & BATT WITH MOREY

MEANWHILE, SUPERMAN HAS A JOB TO DO!

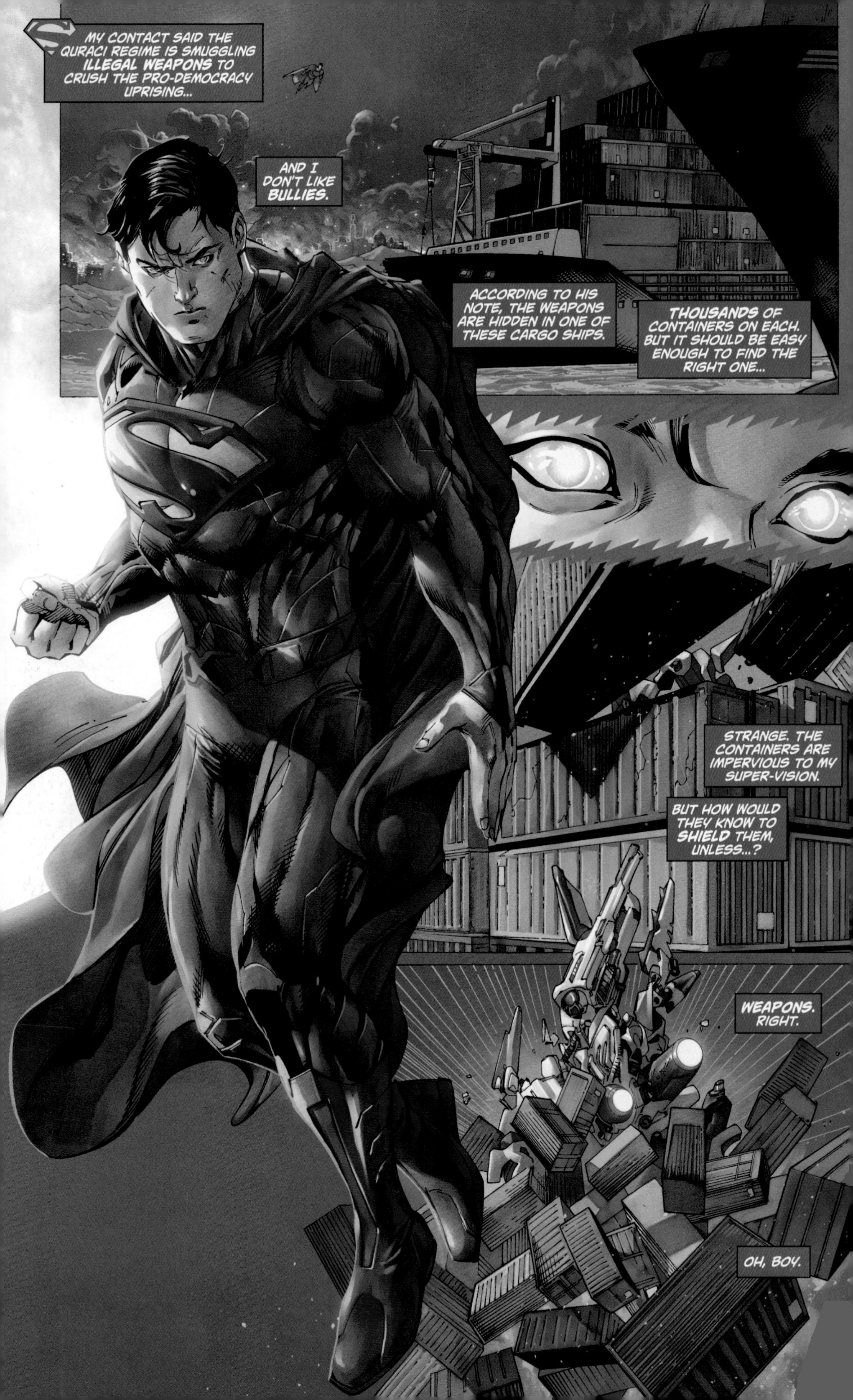
MY CONTACT SAID THE QURACI REGIME IS SMUGGLING ILLEGAL WEAPONS TO CRUSH THE PRO-DEMOCRACY UPRISING...
AND I DON'T LIKE BULLIES.
ACCORDING TO HIS NOTE, THE WEAPONS ARE HIDDEN IN ONE OF THESE CARGO SHIPS.
THOUSANDS OF CONTAINERS ON EACH. BUT IT SHOULD BE EASY ENOUGH TO FIND THE RIGHT ONE...
STRANGE. THE CONTAINERS ARE IMPERVIOUS TO MY SUPER-VISION.
BUT HOW WOULD THEY KNOW TO SHIELD THEM, UNLESS...?
WEAPONS. RIGHT.
OH, BOY.

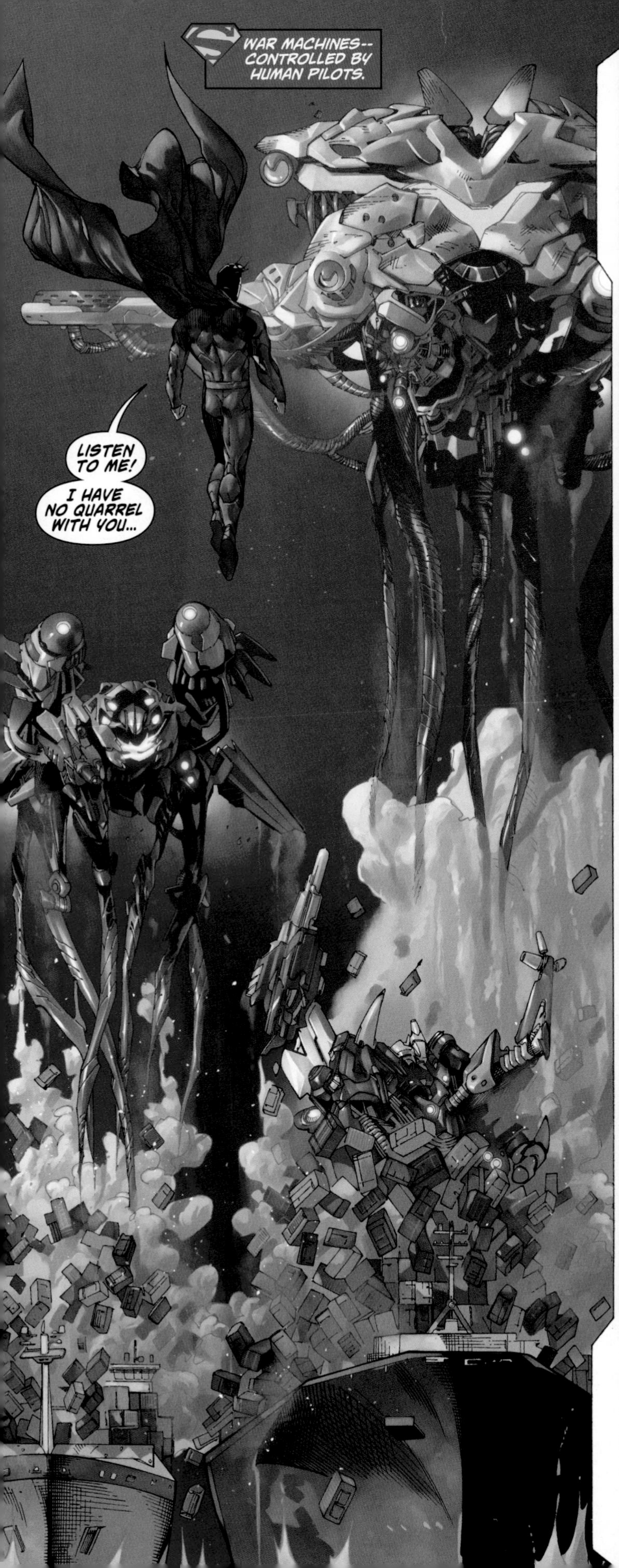
WAR MACHINES-- CONTROLLED BY HUMAN PILOTS.
LISTEN TO ME!
I HAVE NO QUARREL WITH YOU...

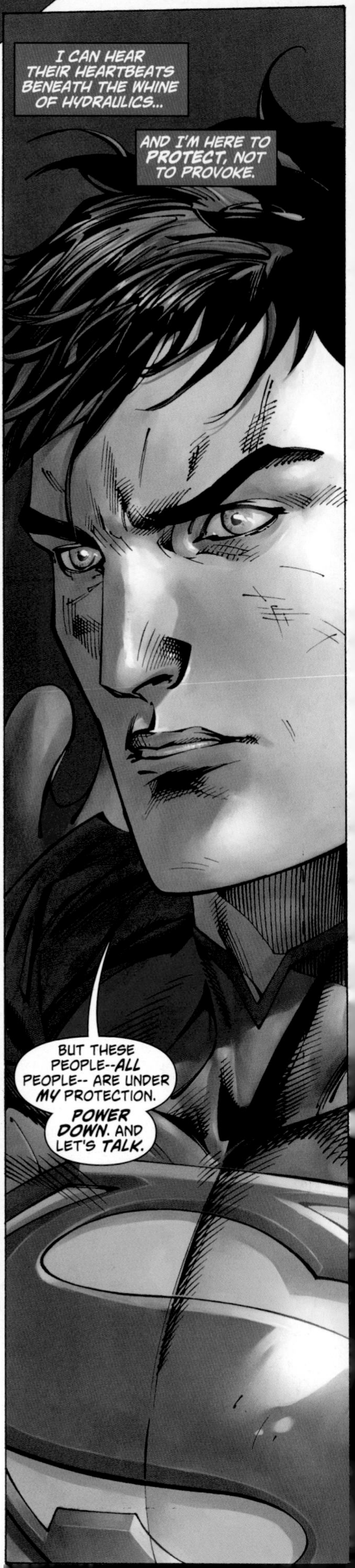
I CAN HEAR THEIR HEARTBEATS BENEATH THE WHINE OF HYDRAULICS...
AND I'M HERE TO PROTECT, NOT TO PROVOKE.
BUT THESE PEOPLE--ALL PEOPLE-- ARE UNDER MY PROTECTION. POWER DOWN. AND LET'S TALK.

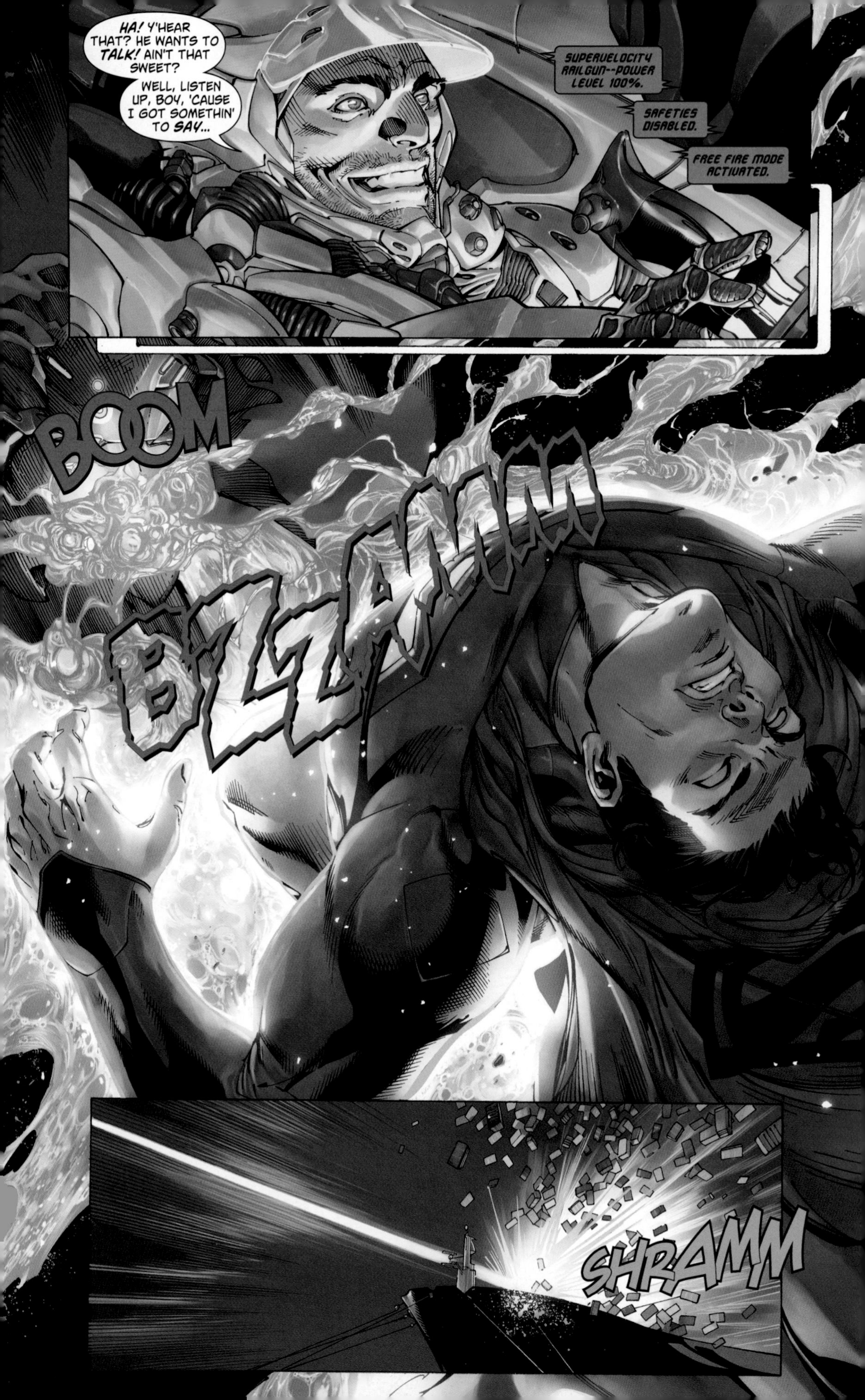
HA! Y'HEAR THAT? HE WANTS TO TALK! AIN'T THAT SWEET?
WELL, LISTEN UP, BOY, 'CAUSE I GOT SOMETHIN' TO SAY...
SUPERVELOCITY RAILGUN--POWER LEVEL 100%.
SAFETIES DISABLED.
FREE FIRE MODE ACTIVATED.
BOOM
BZZAMM
SHRAMM

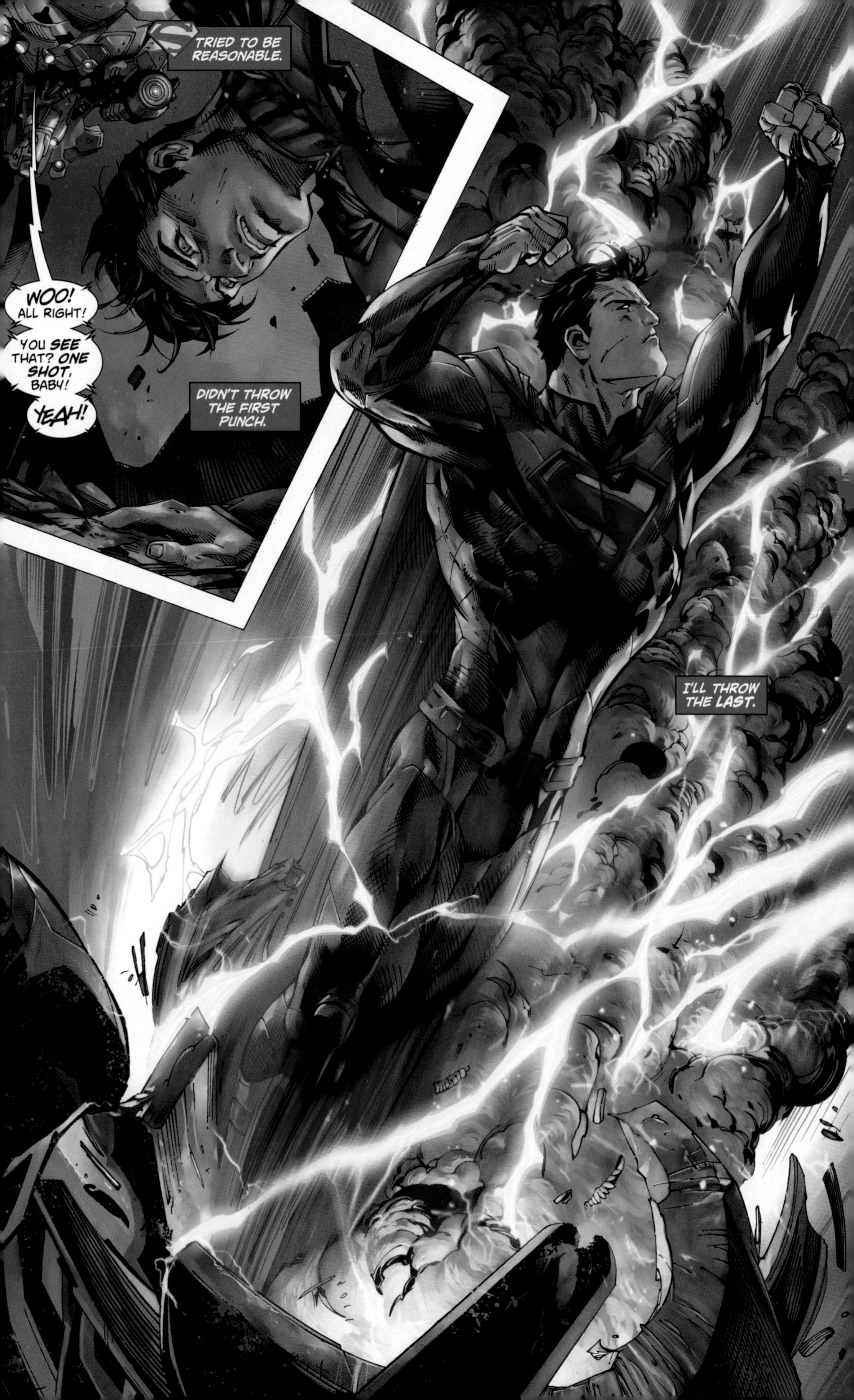
TRIED TO BE REASONABLE.
WOO! ALL RIGHT!
YOU SEE THAT? ONE SHOT, BABY!
YEAH!
DIDN'T THROW THE FIRST PUNCH.
I'LL THROW THE LAST.

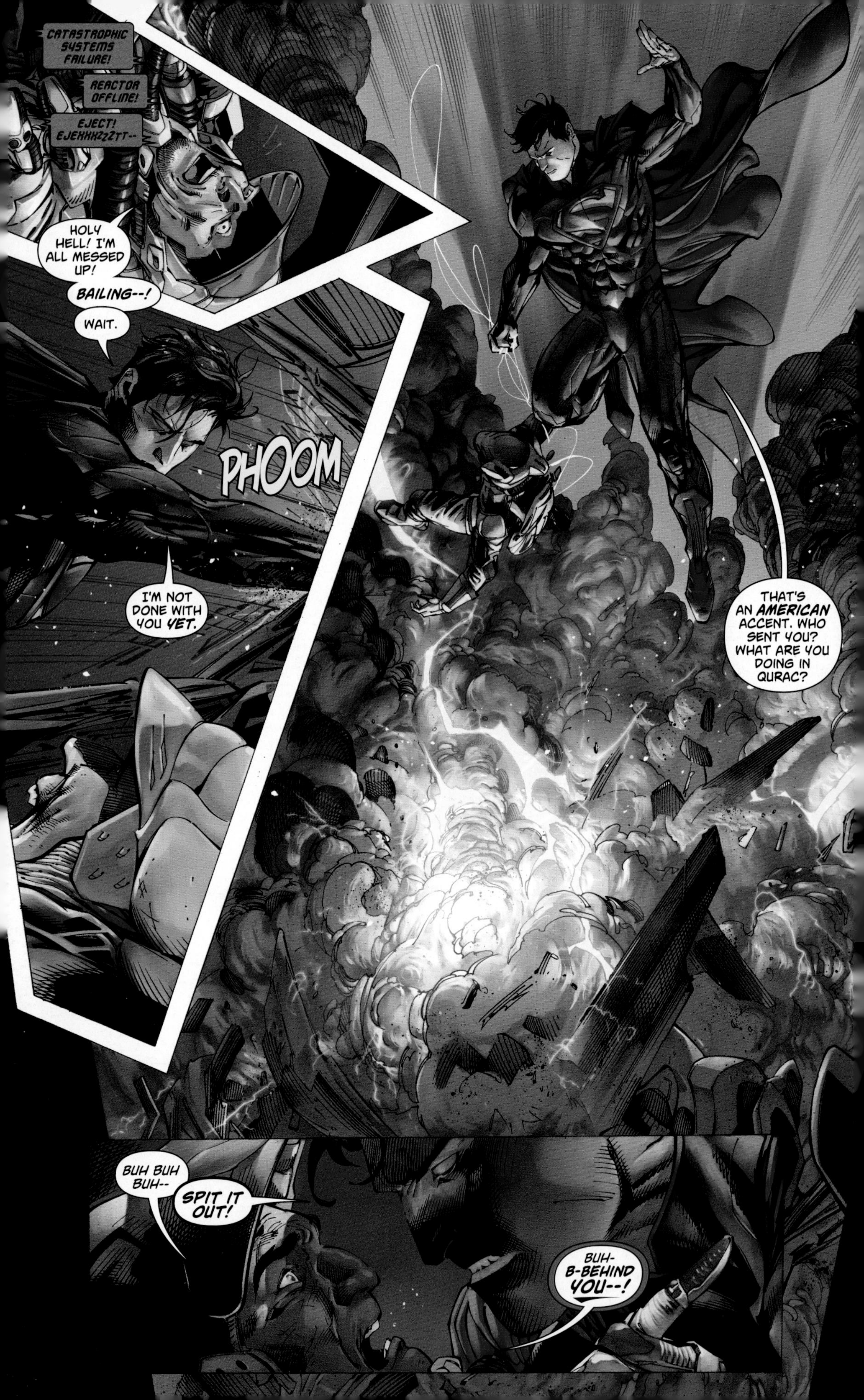
CATASTROPHIC SYSTEMS FAILURE!
REACTOR OFFLINE!
EJECT! EJEHHHZZZTT--
HOLY HELL! I'M ALL MESSED UP!
BAILING--!
WAIT.
PHOOM
I'M NOT DONE WITH YOU YET.
THAT'S AN AMERICAN ACCENT. WHO SENT YOU? WHAT ARE YOU DOING IN QURAC?
BUH BUH BUH--
SPIT IT OUT!
BUH-B-BEHIND YOU--!

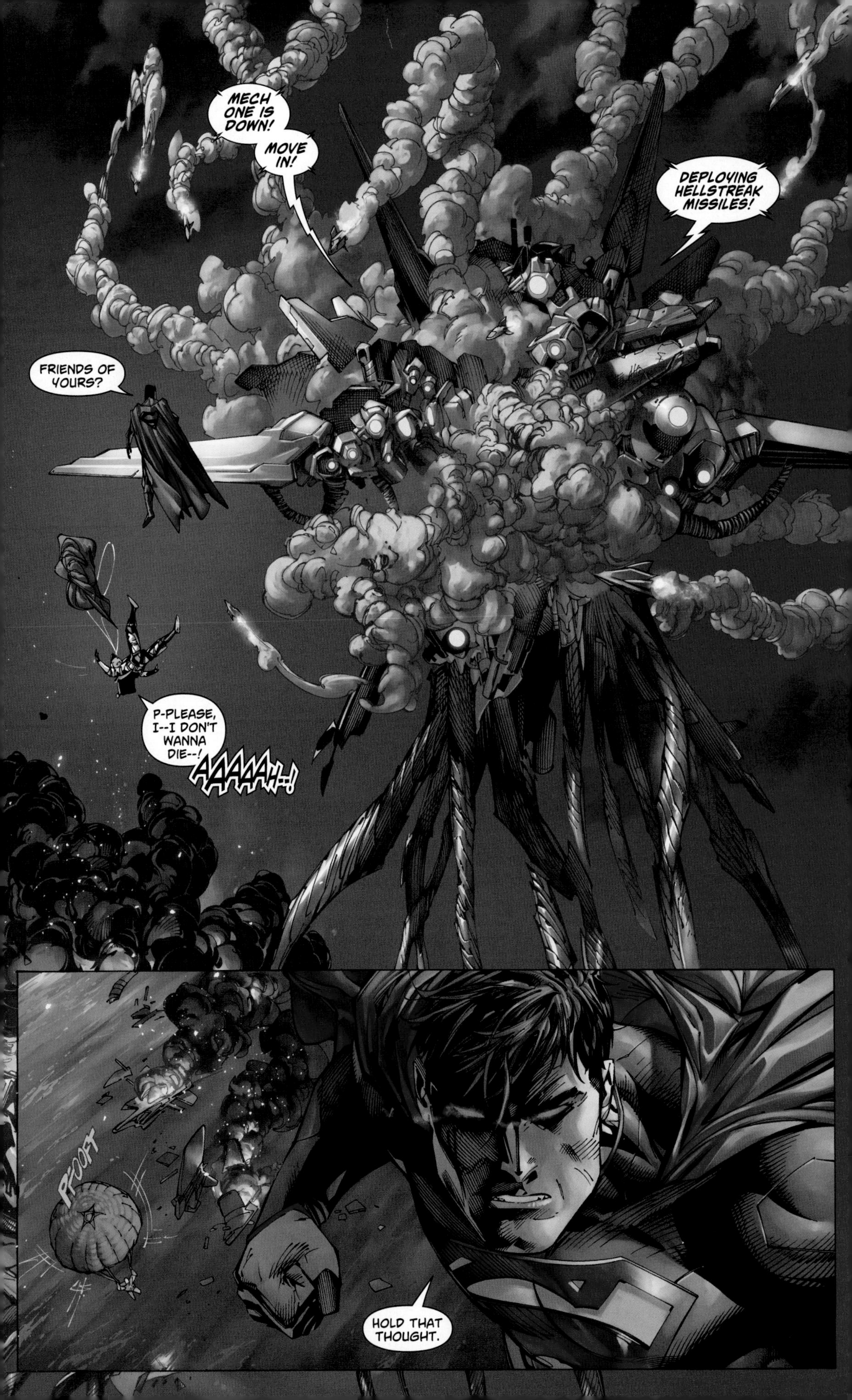
MECH ONE IS DOWN!
MOVE IN!
DEPLOYING HELLSTREAK MISSILES!
FRIENDS OF YOURS?
P-PLEASE, I--I DON'T WANNA DIE--!
AAAAAH--!
P'FOOFT
HOLD THAT THOUGHT.

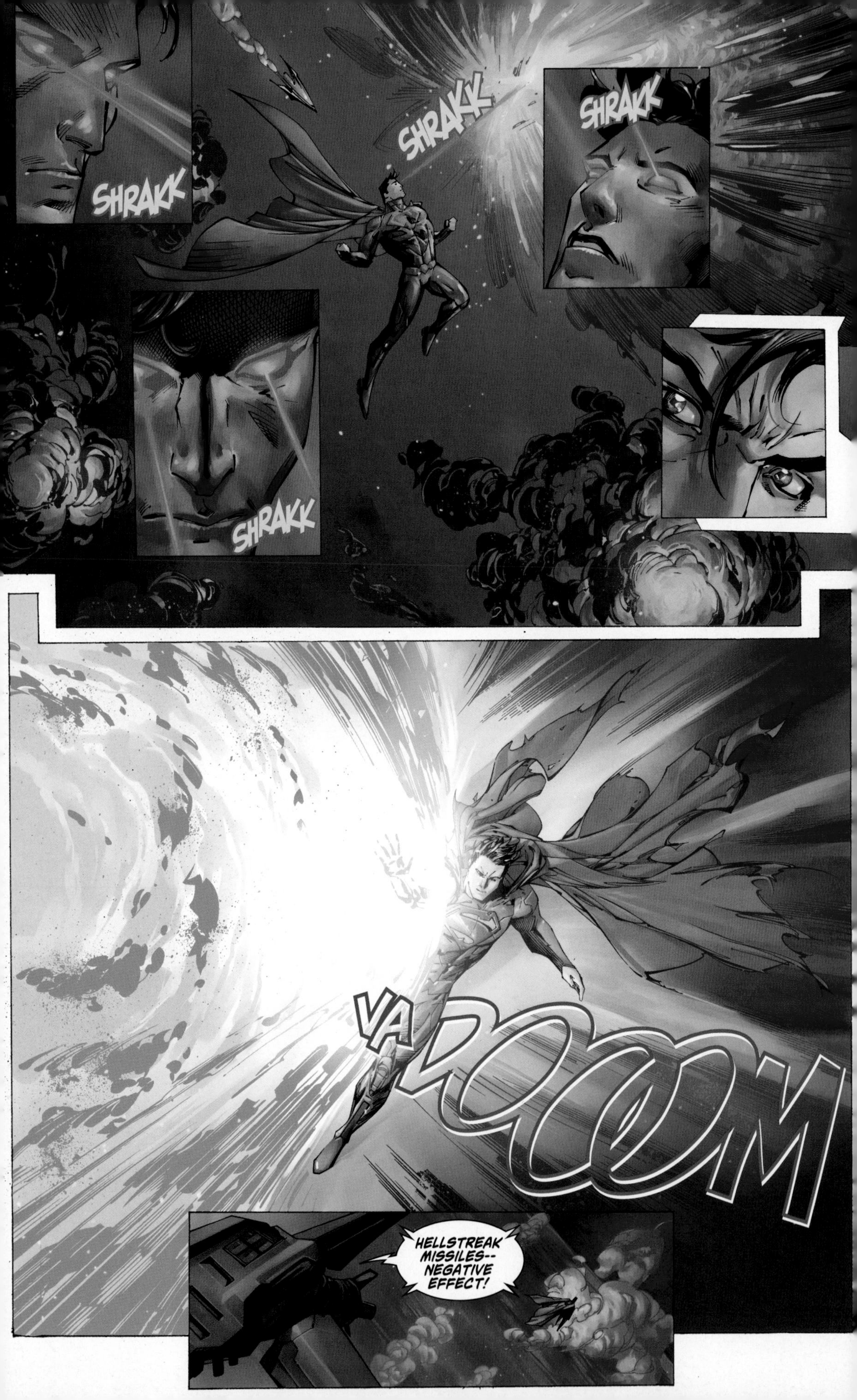
SHRAKK
SHRAKK
SHRAKK
SHRAKK
VADOOOM
HELLSTREAK MISSILES--NEGATIVE EFFECT!

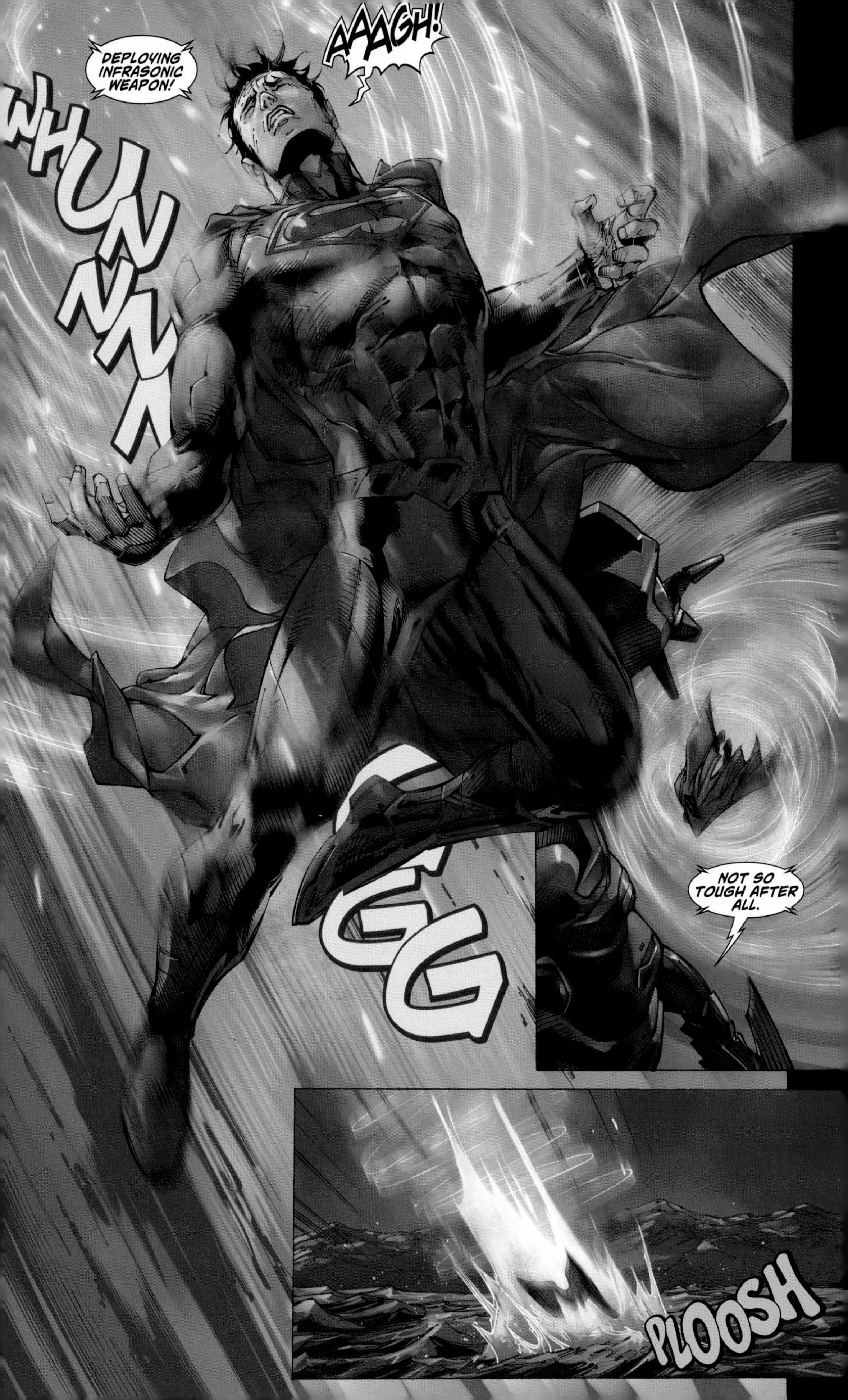
DEPLOYING INFRASONIC WEAPON!
AAAGH!
WHUNNNN
GGG
NOT SO TOUGH AFTER ALL.
PLOOSH

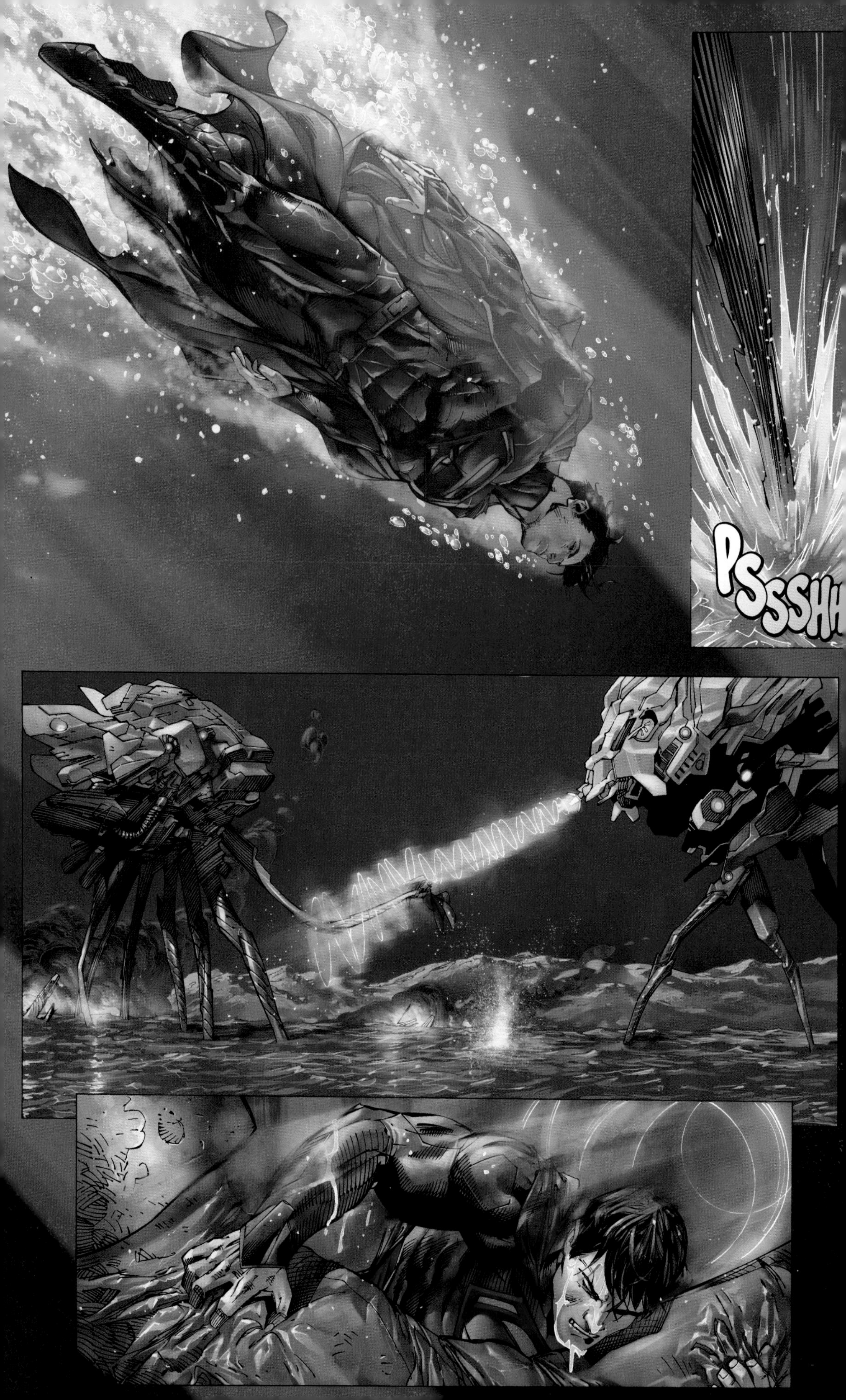
PSSSHH

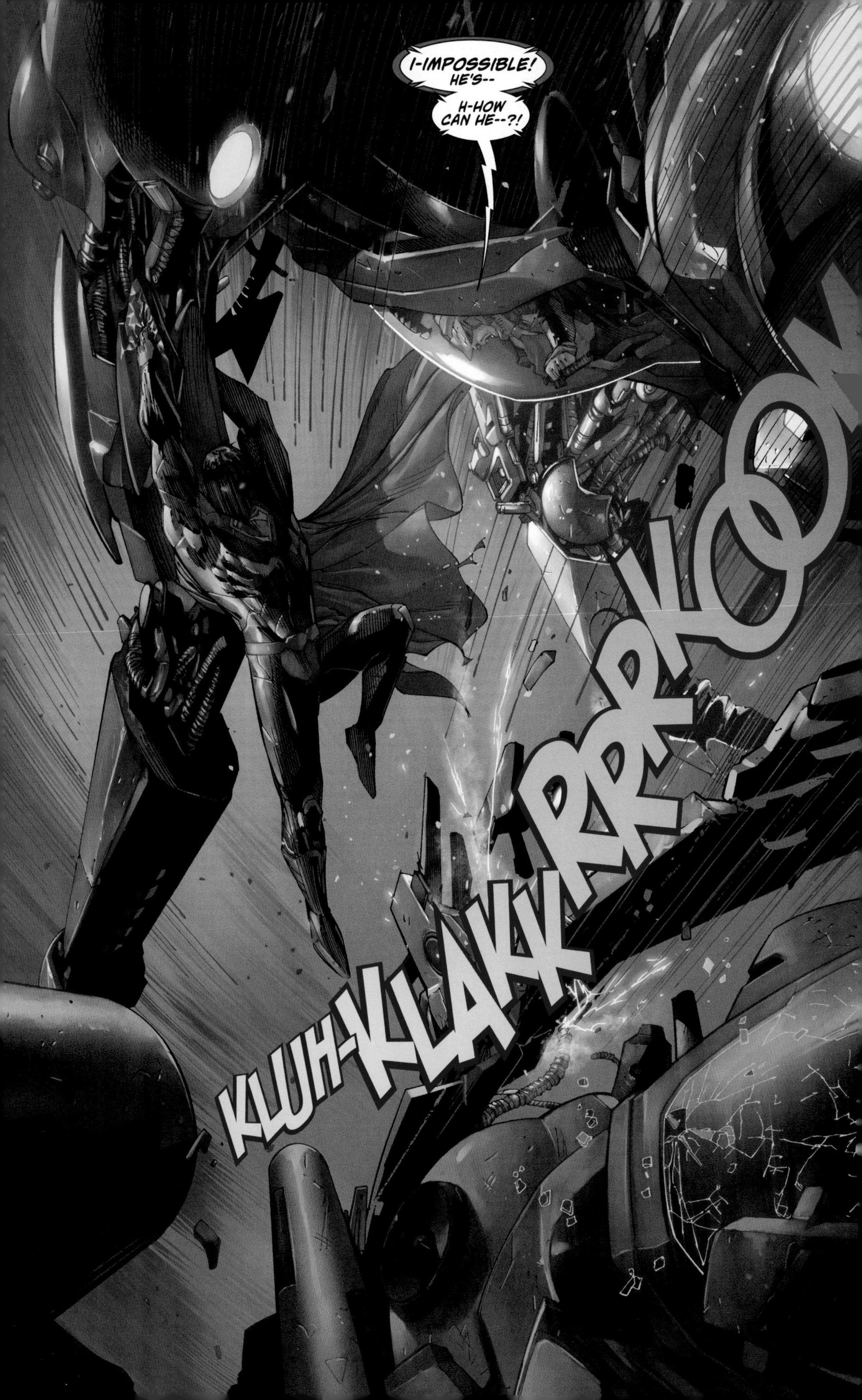
I-IMPOSSIBLE! HE'S--
H-HOW CAN HE--?!
KLUH-KLAKK
RRRKOOM

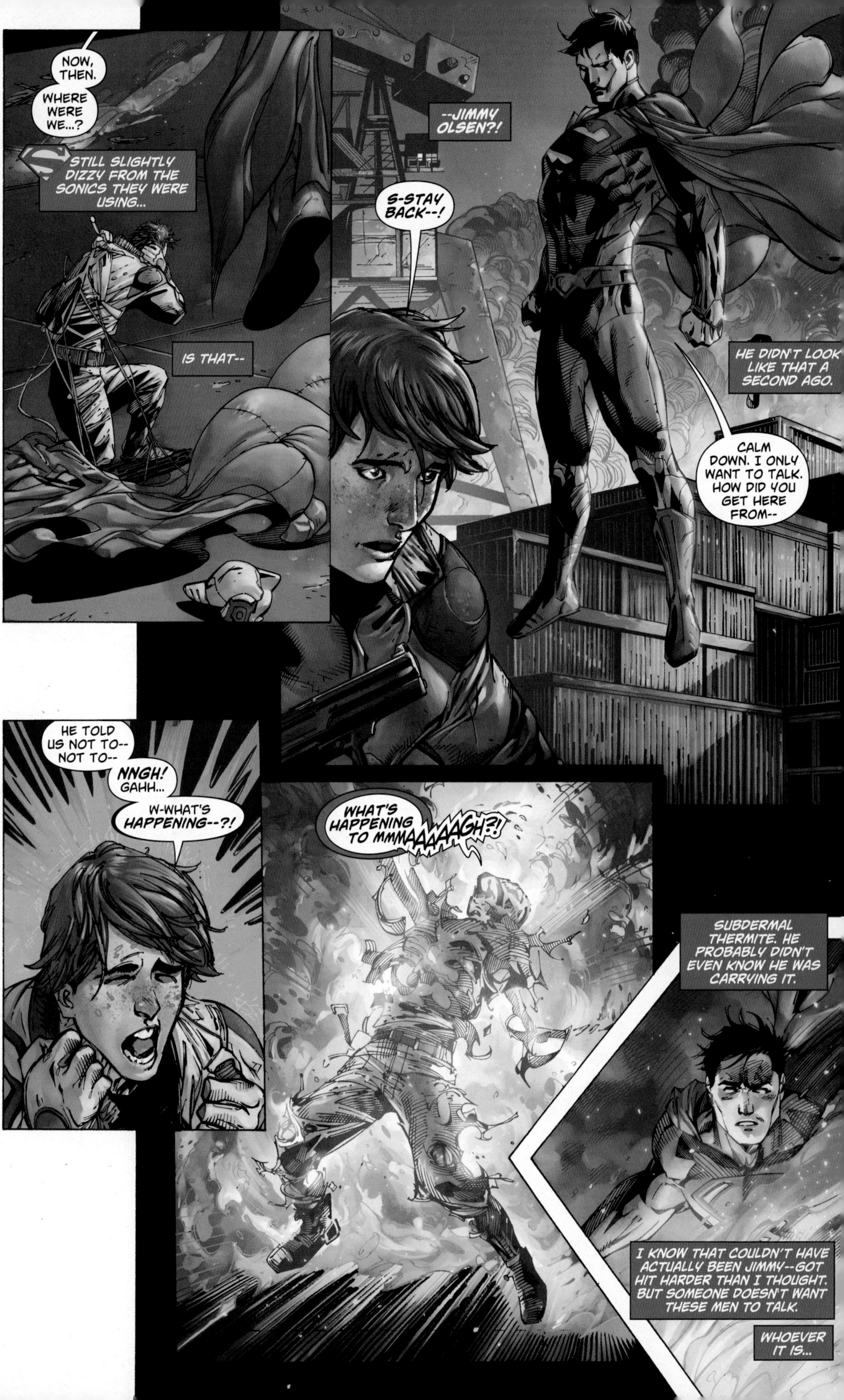
NOW, THEN.
WHERE WERE WE...?
STILL SLIGHTLY DIZZY FROM THE SONICS THEY WERE USING...
IS THAT--
--JIMMY OLSEN?!
S-STAY BACK--!
HE DIDN'T LOOK LIKE THAT A SECOND AGO.
CALM DOWN. I ONLY WANT TO TALK. HOW DID YOU GET HERE FROM--
HE TOLD US NOT TO-- NOT TO--
NNGH! GAHH...
W-WHAT'S HAPPENING--?!
WHAT'S HAPPENING TO MMMAAAAAGH?!
SUBDERMAL THERMITE. HE PROBABLY DIDN'T EVEN KNOW HE WAS CARRYING IT.
I KNOW THAT COULDN'T HAVE ACTUALLY BEEN JIMMY--GOT HIT HARDER THAN I THOUGHT. BUT SOMEONE DOESN'T WANT THESE MEN TO TALK.
WHOEVER IT IS...

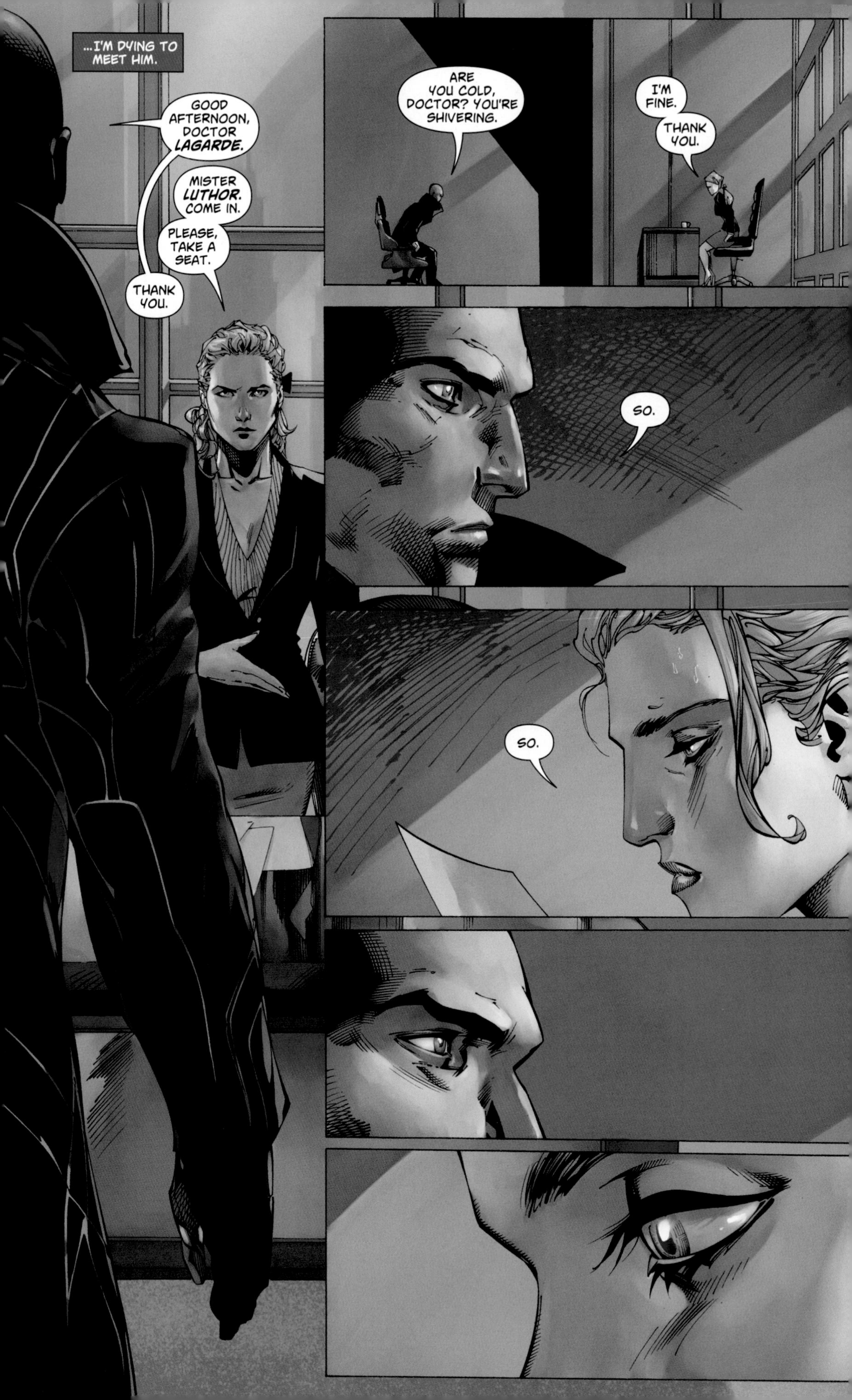
...I'M DYING TO MEET HIM.
GOOD AFTERNOON, DOCTOR LAGARDE.
MISTER LUTHOR. COME IN.
PLEASE, TAKE A SEAT.
THANK YOU.
ARE YOU COLD, DOCTOR? YOU'RE SHIVERING.
I'M FINE.
THANK YOU.
SO.
SO.

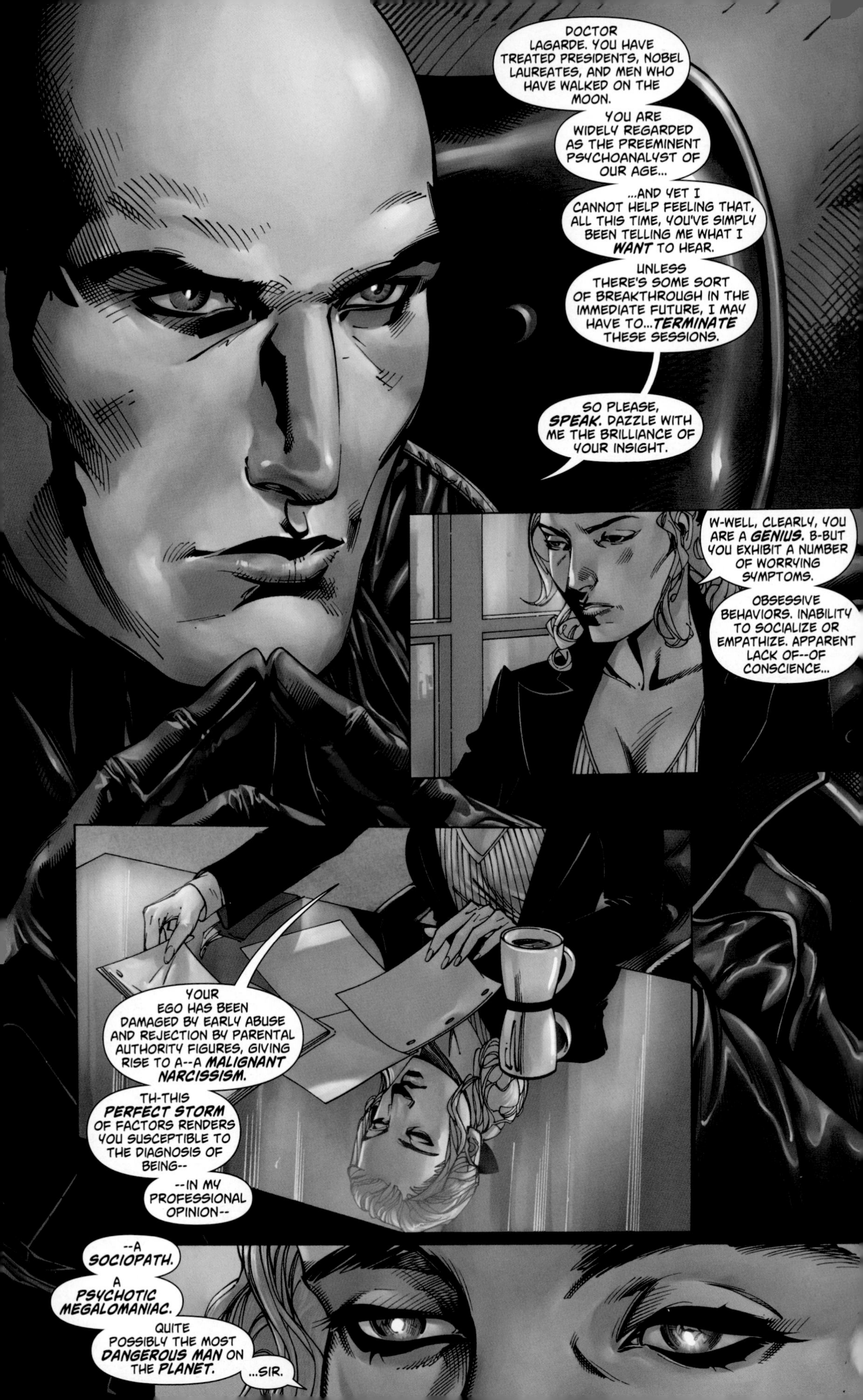
DOCTOR LAGARDE. YOU HAVE TREATED PRESIDENTS, NOBEL LAUREATES, AND MEN WHO HAVE WALKED ON THE MOON.
YOU ARE WIDELY REGARDED AS THE PREEMINENT PSYCHOANALYST OF OUR AGE...
...AND YET I CANNOT HELP FEELING THAT, ALL THIS TIME, YOU'VE SIMPLY BEEN TELLING ME WHAT I **WANT** TO HEAR.
UNLESS THERE'S SOME SORT OF BREAKTHROUGH IN THE IMMEDIATE FUTURE, I MAY HAVE TO...**TERMINATE** THESE SESSIONS.
SO PLEASE, **SPEAK.** DAZZLE WITH ME THE BRILLIANCE OF YOUR INSIGHT.
W-WELL, CLEARLY, YOU ARE A **GENIUS.** B-BUT YOU EXHIBIT A NUMBER OF WORRYING SYMPTOMS.
OBSESSIVE BEHAVIORS. INABILITY TO SOCIALIZE OR EMPATHIZE. APPARENT LACK OF--OF CONSCIENCE...
YOUR EGO HAS BEEN DAMAGED BY EARLY ABUSE AND REJECTION BY PARENTAL AUTHORITY FIGURES, GIVING RISE TO A--A **MALIGNANT NARCISSISM.**
TH-THIS **PERFECT STORM** OF FACTORS RENDERS YOU SUSCEPTIBLE TO THE DIAGNOSIS OF BEING--
--IN MY PROFESSIONAL OPINION--
--A **SOCIOPATH.**
A **PSYCHOTIC MEGALOMANIAC.**
QUITE POSSIBLY THE MOST **DANGEROUS MAN** ON THE **PLANET.**
...SIR.

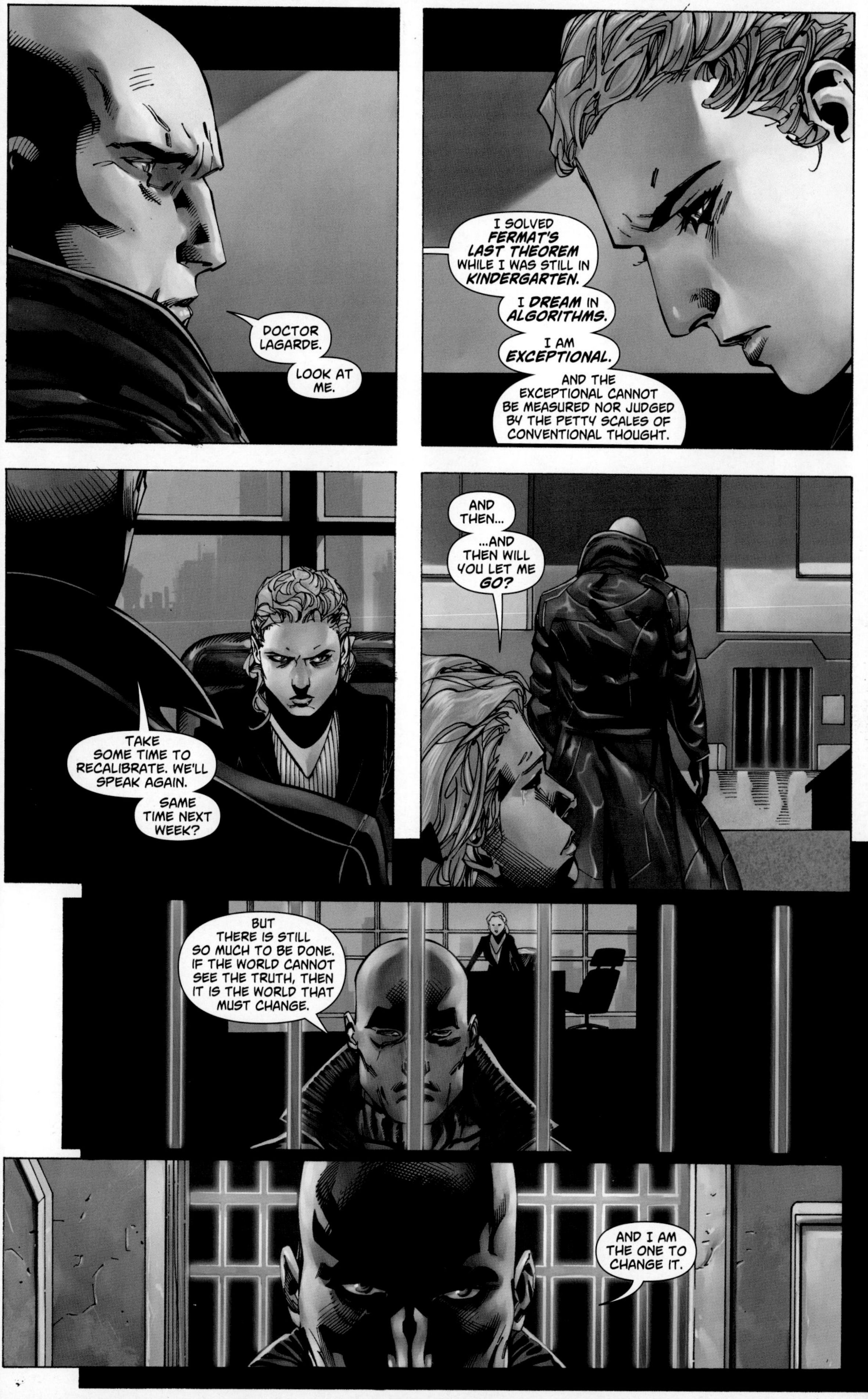
DOCTOR LAGARDE.
LOOK AT ME.
I SOLVED FERMAT'S LAST THEOREM WHILE I WAS STILL IN KINDERGARTEN.
I DREAM IN ALGORITHMS.
I AM EXCEPTIONAL.
AND THE EXCEPTIONAL CANNOT BE MEASURED NOR JUDGED BY THE PETTY SCALES OF CONVENTIONAL THOUGHT.
TAKE SOME TIME TO RECALIBRATE. WE'LL SPEAK AGAIN.
SAME TIME NEXT WEEK?
AND THEN...
...AND THEN WILL YOU LET ME GO?
BUT THERE IS STILL SO MUCH TO BE DONE. IF THE WORLD CANNOT SEE THE TRUTH, THEN IT IS THE WORLD THAT MUST CHANGE.
AND I AM THE ONE TO CHANGE IT.

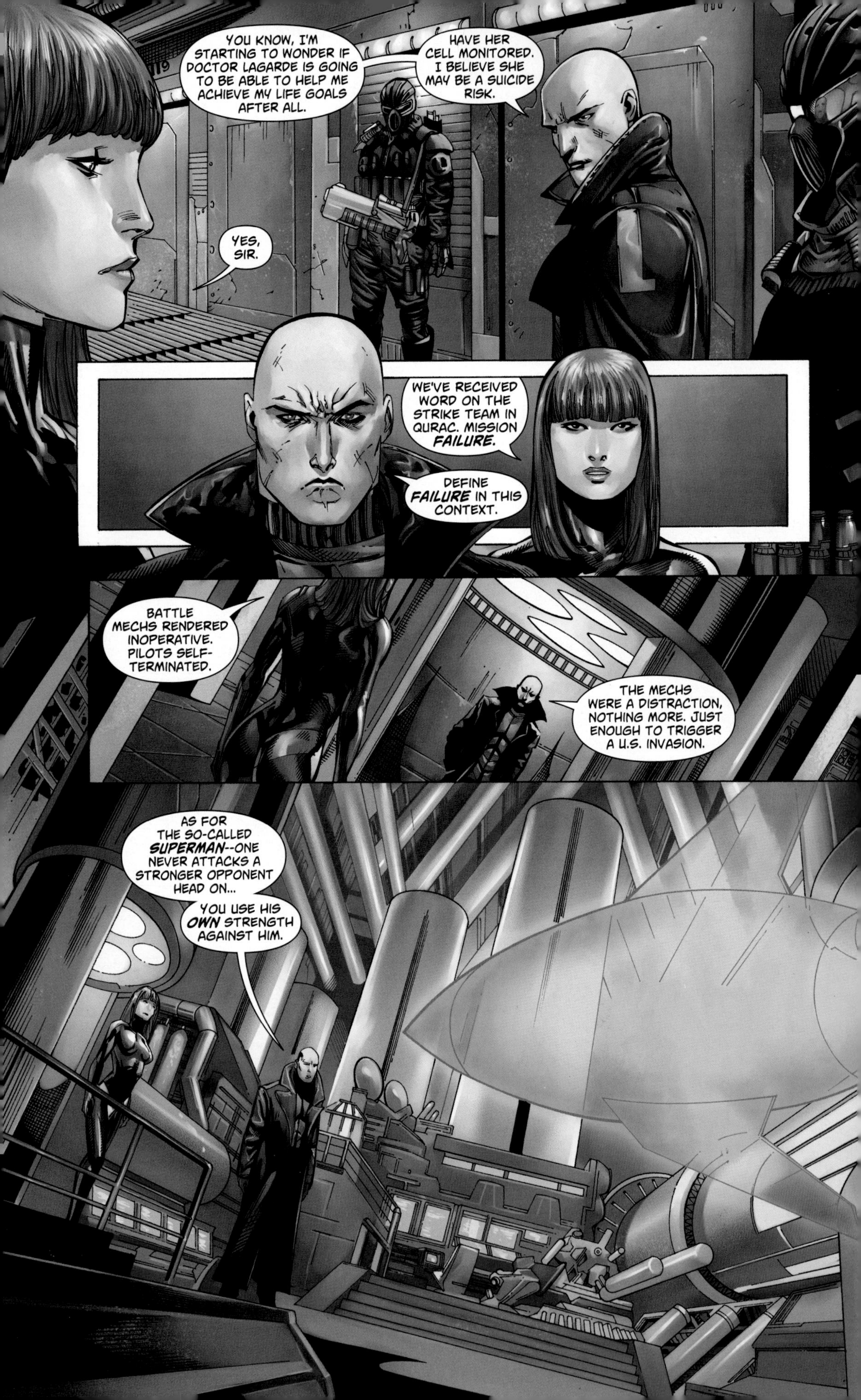
YOU KNOW, I'M STARTING TO WONDER IF DOCTOR LAGARDE IS GOING TO BE ABLE TO HELP ME ACHIEVE MY LIFE GOALS AFTER ALL.
HAVE HER CELL MONITORED. I BELIEVE SHE MAY BE A SUICIDE RISK.
YES, SIR.
WE'VE RECEIVED WORD ON THE STRIKE TEAM IN QURAC. MISSION **FAILURE**.
DEFINE **FAILURE** IN THIS CONTEXT.
BATTLE MECHS RENDERED INOPERATIVE. PILOTS SELF-TERMINATED.
THE MECHS WERE A DISTRACTION, NOTHING MORE. JUST ENOUGH TO TRIGGER A U.S. INVASION.
AS FOR THE SO-CALLED **SUPERMAN**--ONE NEVER ATTACKS A STRONGER OPPONENT HEAD ON...
YOU USE HIS **OWN** STRENGTH AGAINST HIM.

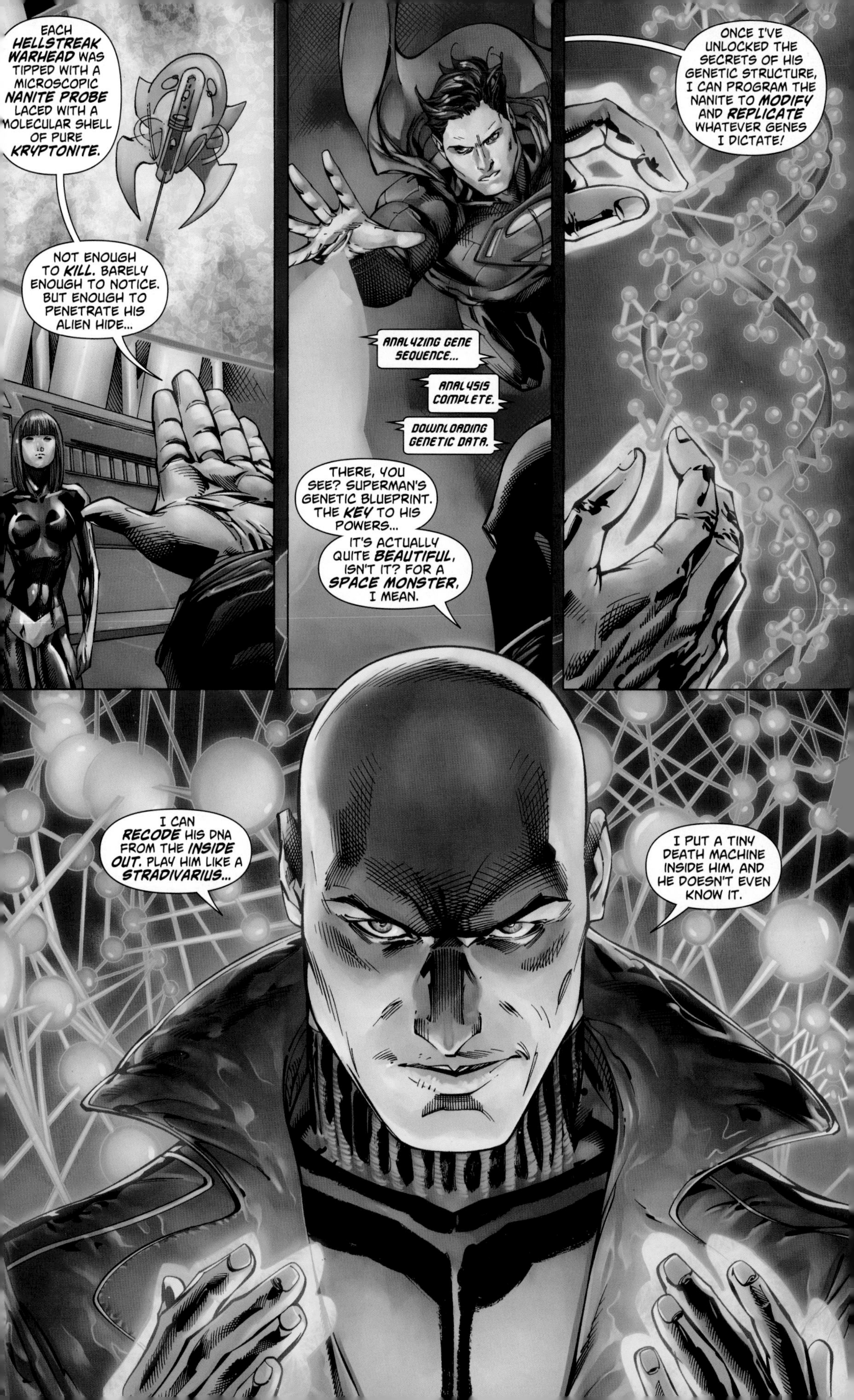
EACH HELLSTREAK WARHEAD WAS TIPPED WITH A MICROSCOPIC NANITE PROBE LACED WITH A MOLECULAR SHELL OF PURE KRYPTONITE.
NOT ENOUGH TO KILL. BARELY ENOUGH TO NOTICE. BUT ENOUGH TO PENETRATE HIS ALIEN HIDE...
ANALYZING GENE SEQUENCE...
ANALYSIS COMPLETE.
DOWNLOADING GENETIC DATA.
THERE, YOU SEE? SUPERMAN'S GENETIC BLUEPRINT. THE KEY TO HIS POWERS...
IT'S ACTUALLY QUITE BEAUTIFUL, ISN'T IT? FOR A SPACE MONSTER, I MEAN.
ONCE I'VE UNLOCKED THE SECRETS OF HIS GENETIC STRUCTURE, I CAN PROGRAM THE NANITE TO MODIFY AND REPLICATE WHATEVER GENES I DICTATE!
I CAN RECODE HIS DNA FROM THE INSIDE OUT. PLAY HIM LIKE A STRADIVARIUS...
I PUT A TINY DEATH MACHINE INSIDE HIM, AND HE DOESN'T EVEN KNOW IT.

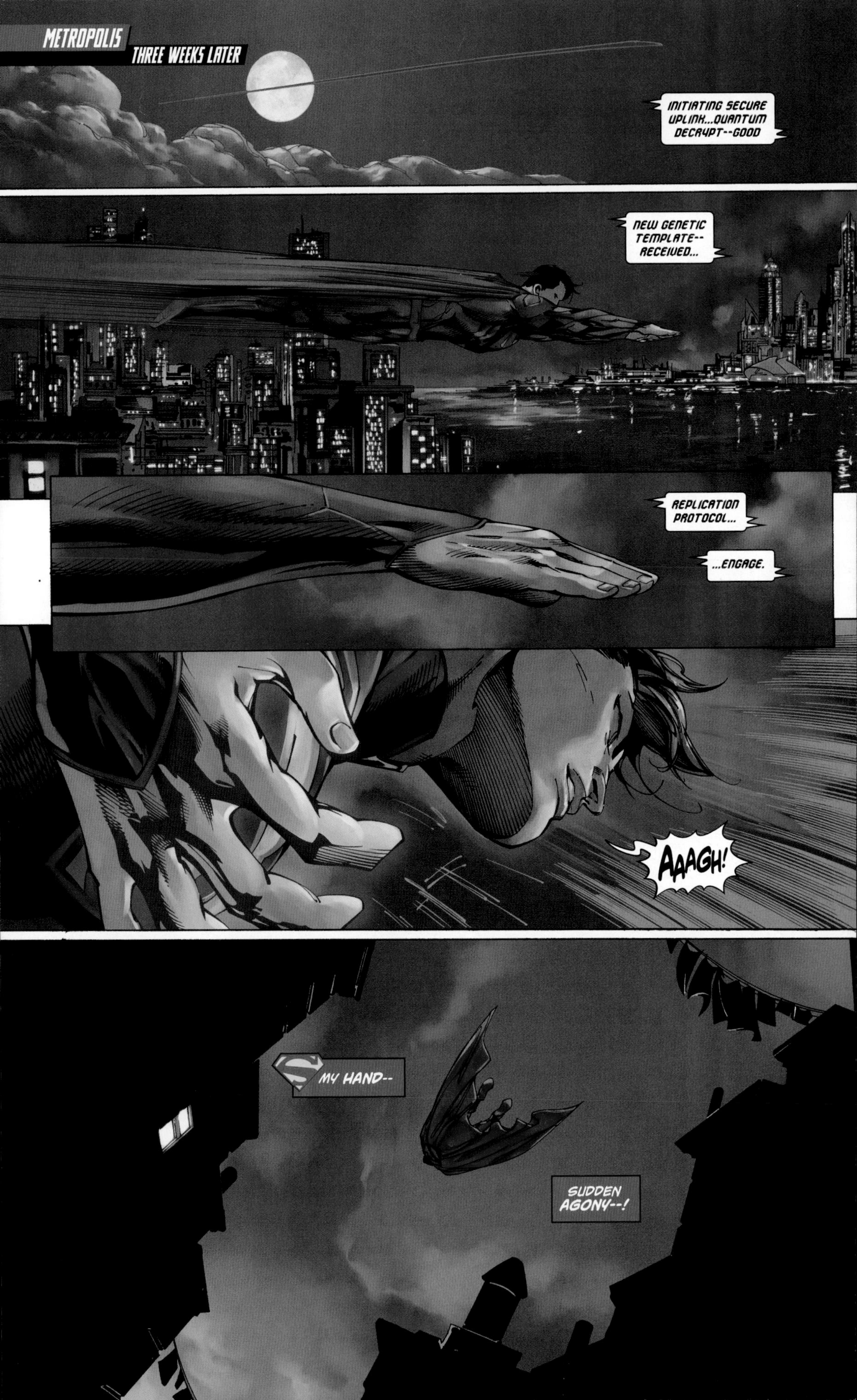
METROPOLIS
THREE WEEKS LATER
INITIATING SECURE UPLINK...QUANTUM DECRYPT--GOOD
NEW GENETIC TEMPLATE--RECEIVED...
REPLICATION PROTOCOL...
...ENGAGE.
AAAGH!
MY HAND--
SUDDEN AGONY--!

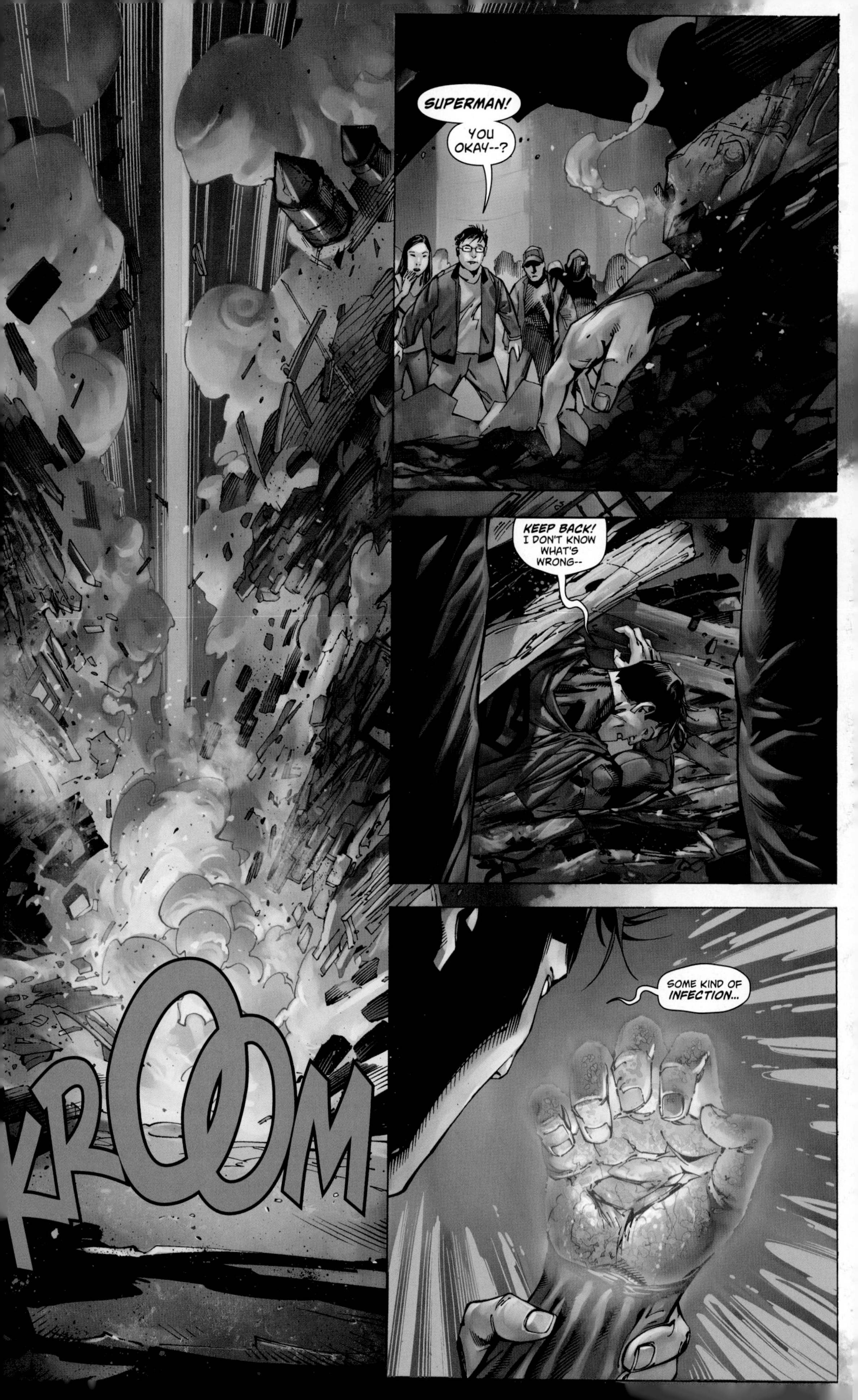
KRØØM
SUPERMAN!
YOU OKAY--?
KEEP BACK! I DON'T KNOW WHAT'S WRONG--
SOME KIND OF INFECTION...

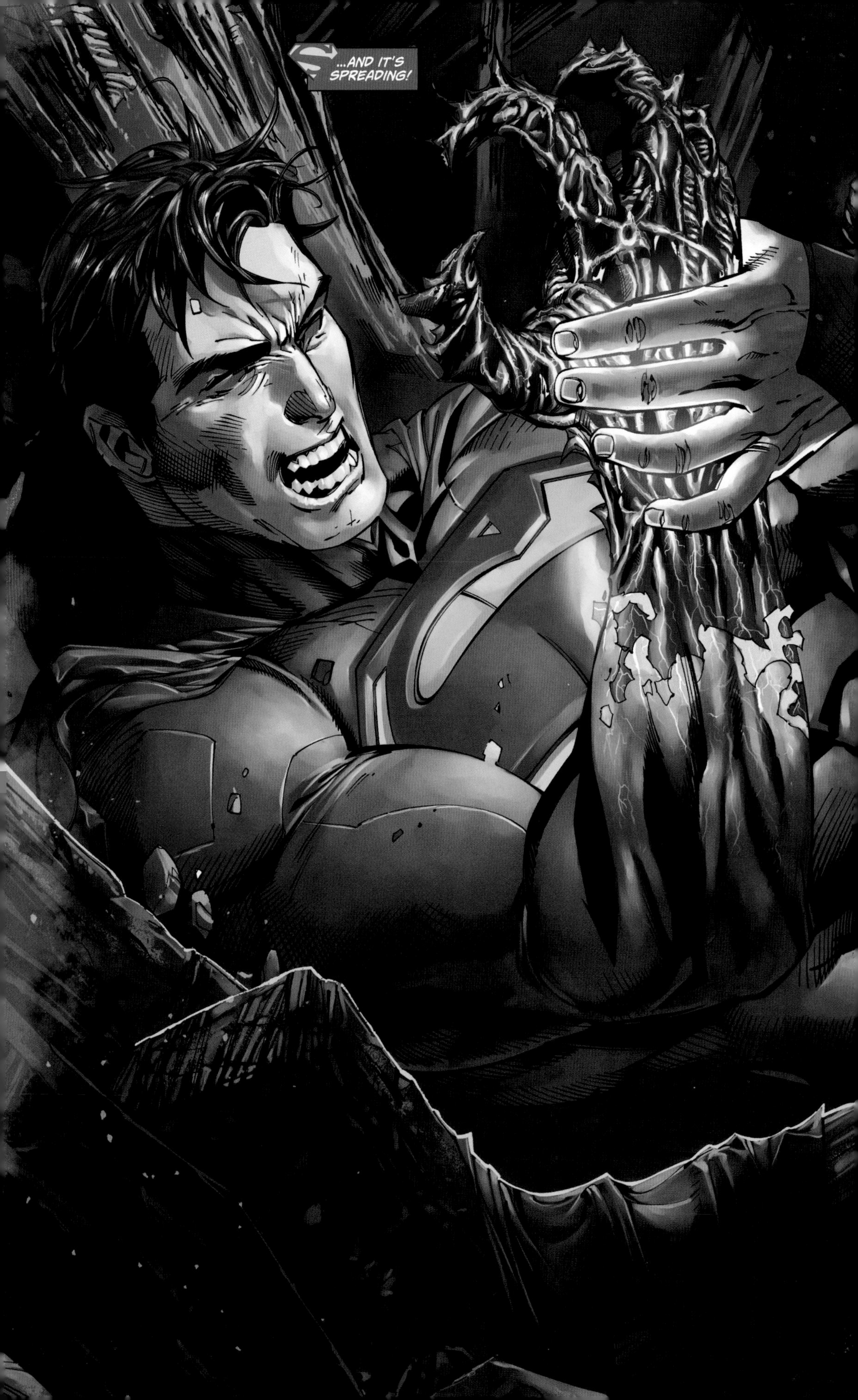
...AND IT'S SPREADING!

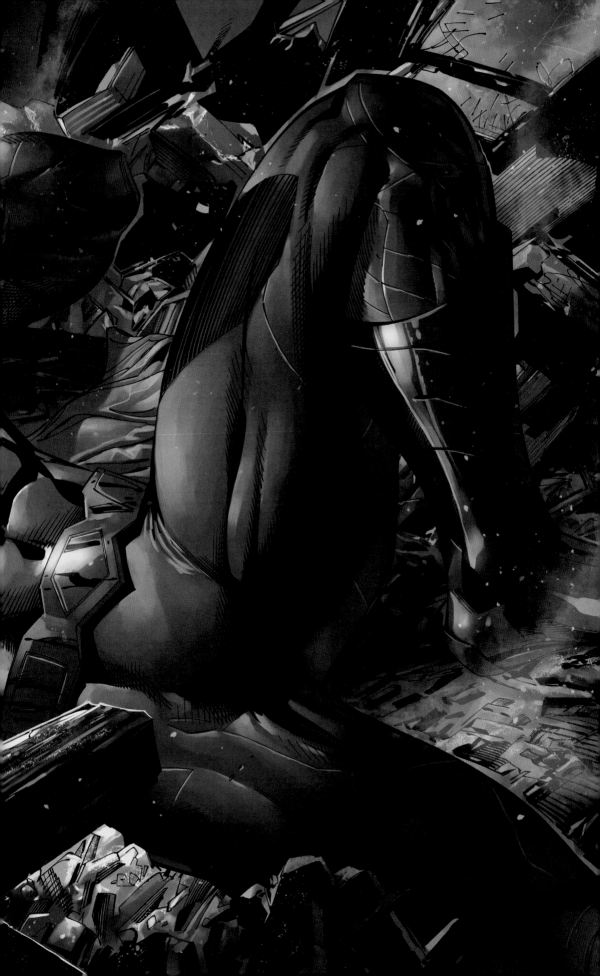

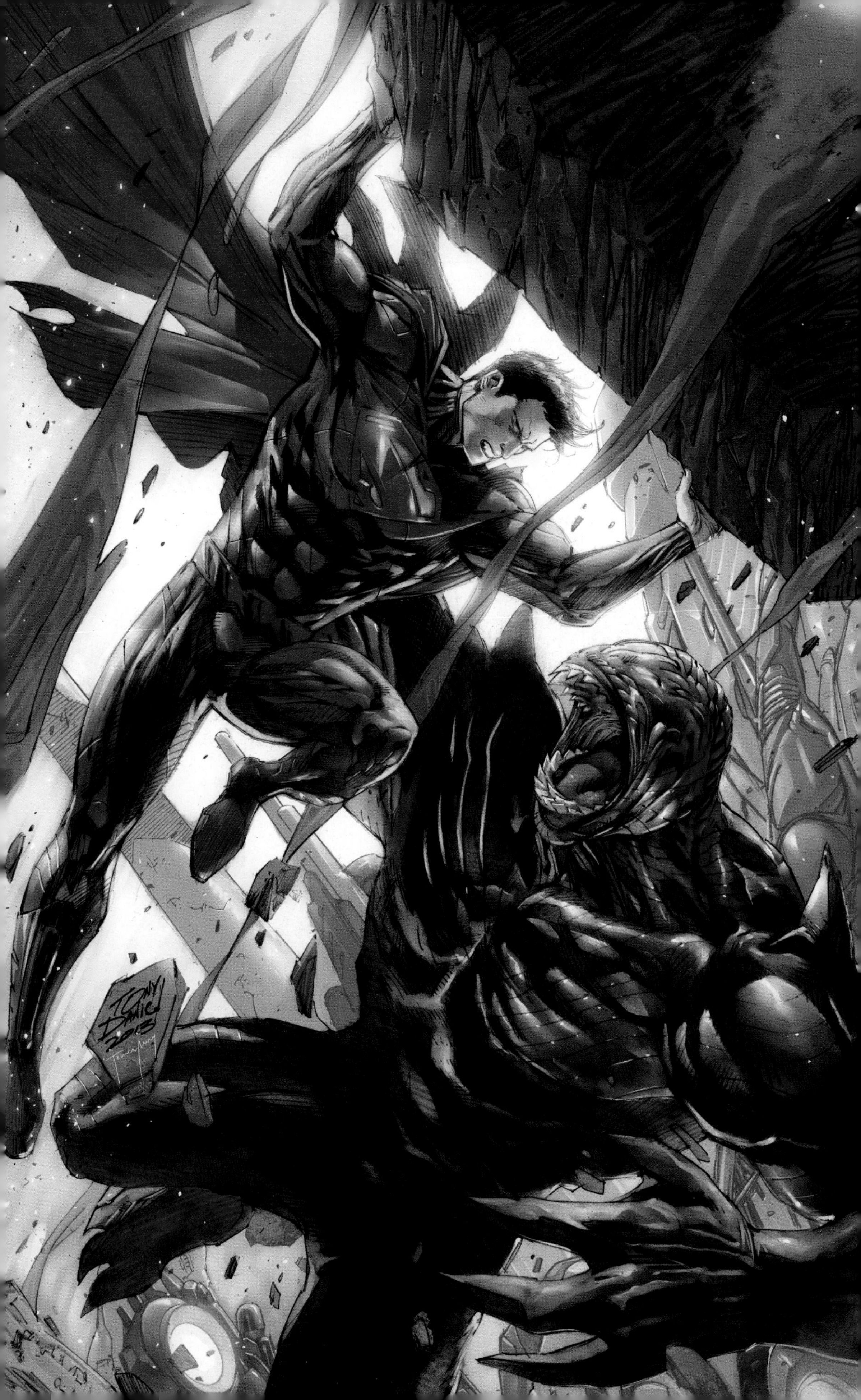

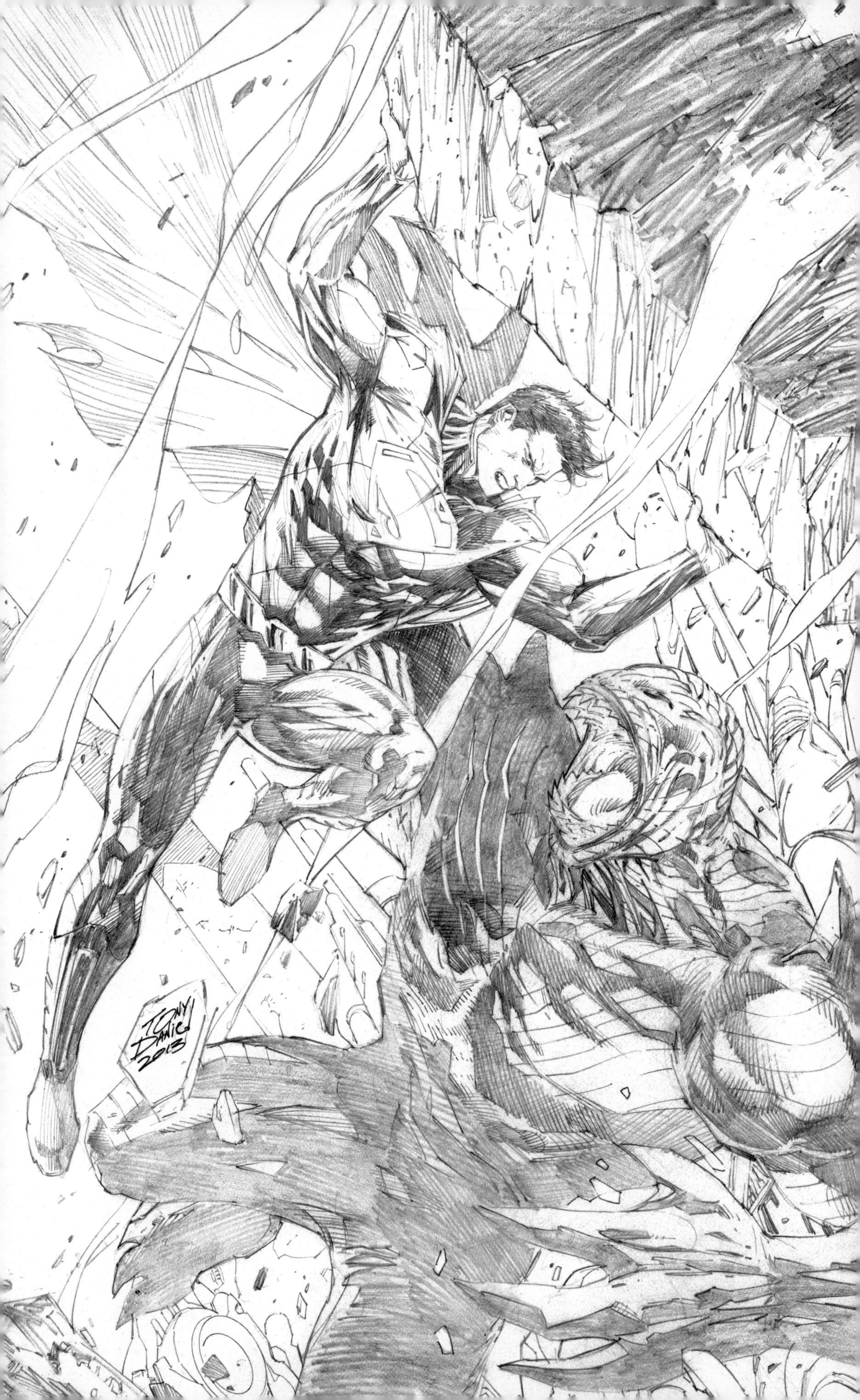

TONY
DANIEL
2013

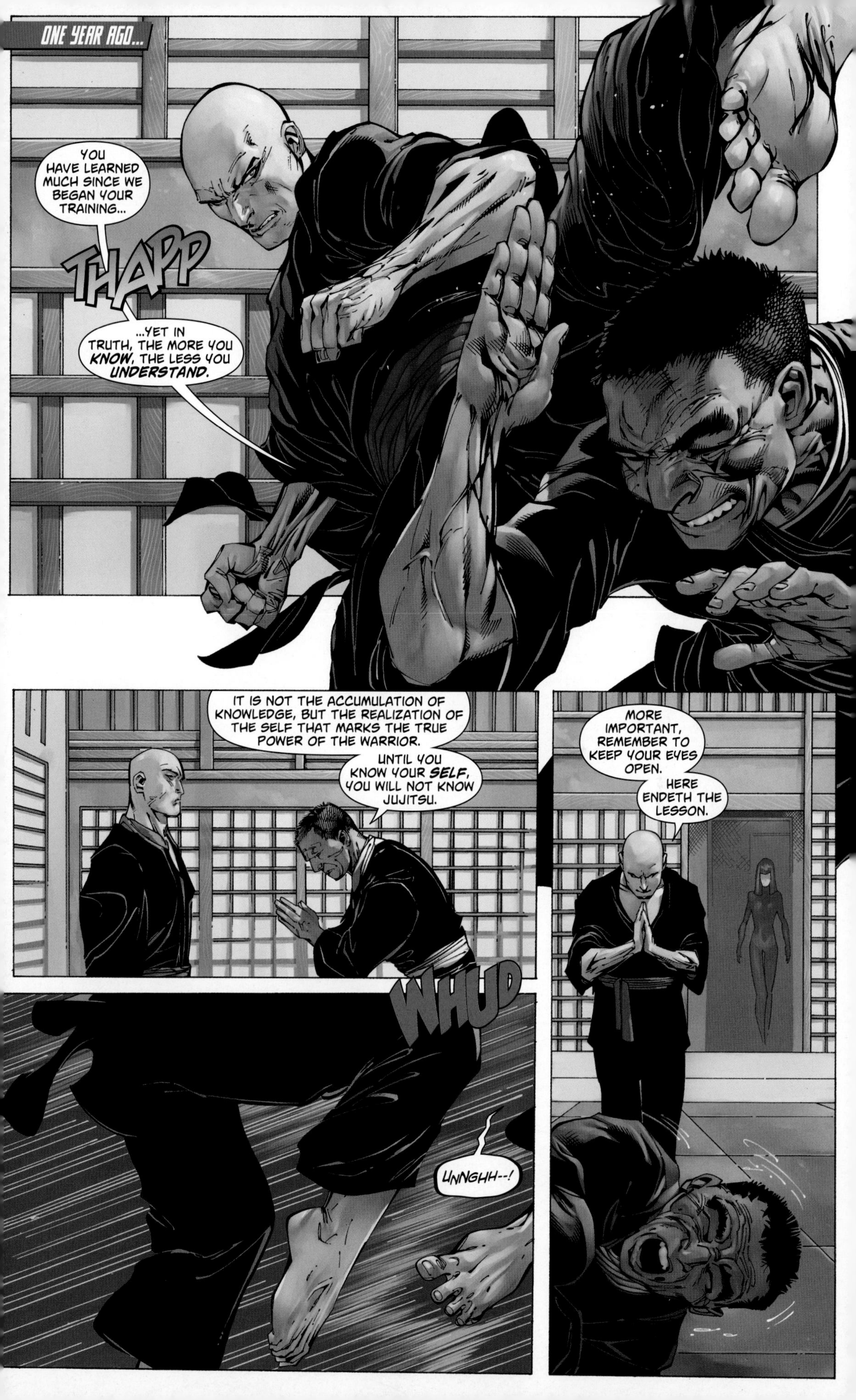
ONE YEAR AGO...
YOU HAVE LEARNED MUCH SINCE WE BEGAN YOUR TRAINING...
THAPP
...YET IN TRUTH, THE MORE YOU KNOW, THE LESS YOU UNDERSTAND.
IT IS NOT THE ACCUMULATION OF KNOWLEDGE, BUT THE REALIZATION OF THE SELF THAT MARKS THE TRUE POWER OF THE WARRIOR.
UNTIL YOU KNOW YOUR SELF, YOU WILL NOT KNOW JUJITSU.
WHUD
UNNGHH--!
MORE IMPORTANT, REMEMBER TO KEEP YOUR EYES OPEN.
HERE ENDETH THE LESSON.

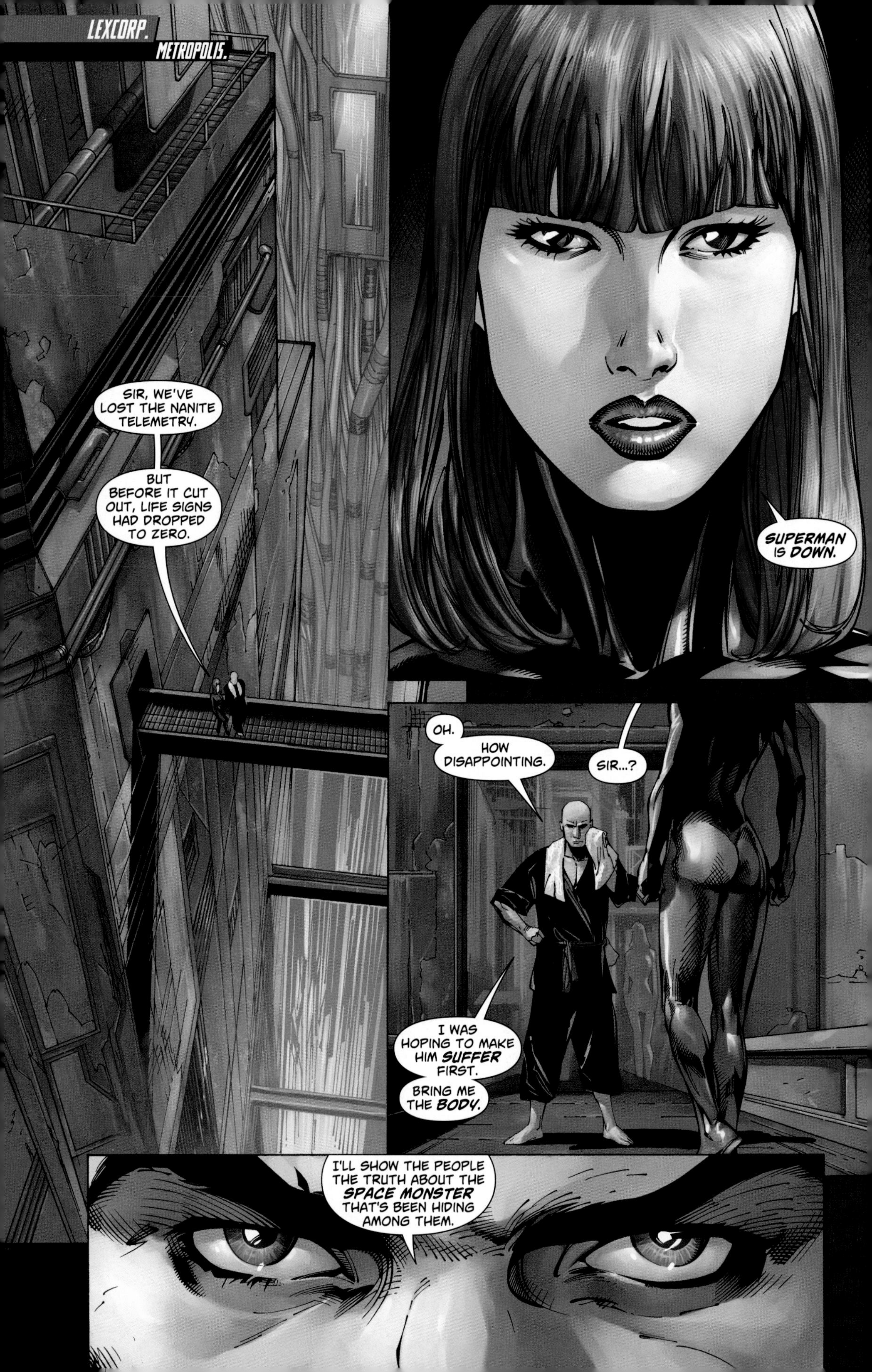
LEXCORP.
METROPOLIS.
SIR, WE'VE LOST THE NANITE TELEMETRY.
BUT BEFORE IT CUT OUT, LIFE SIGNS HAD DROPPED TO ZERO.
SUPERMAN IS DOWN.
OH.
HOW DISAPPOINTING.
SIR...?
I WAS HOPING TO MAKE HIM SUFFER FIRST.
BRING ME THE BODY.
I'LL SHOW THE PEOPLE THE TRUTH ABOUT THE SPACE MONSTER THAT'S BEEN HIDING AMONG THEM.

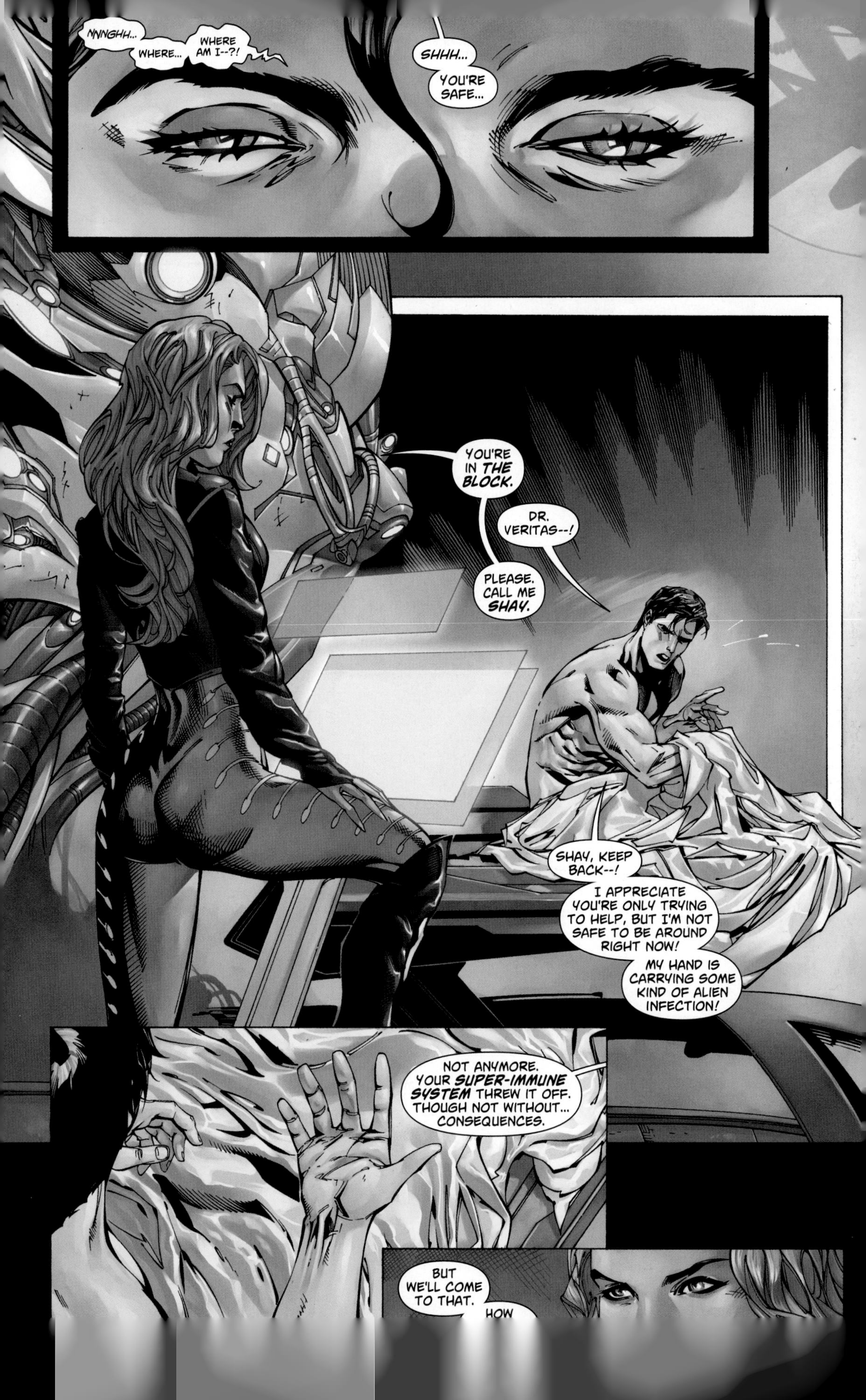
NNNGHH...
WHERE...
WHERE AM I--?!
SHHH...
YOU'RE SAFE...
YOU'RE IN THE BLOCK.
DR. VERITAS--!
PLEASE. CALL ME SHAY.
SHAY, KEEP BACK--!
I APPRECIATE YOU'RE ONLY TRYING TO HELP, BUT I'M NOT SAFE TO BE AROUND RIGHT NOW!
MY HAND IS CARRYING SOME KIND OF ALIEN INFECTION!
NOT ANYMORE. YOUR SUPER-IMMUNE SYSTEM THREW IT OFF. THOUGH NOT WITHOUT... CONSEQUENCES.
BUT WE'LL COME TO THAT.
HOW

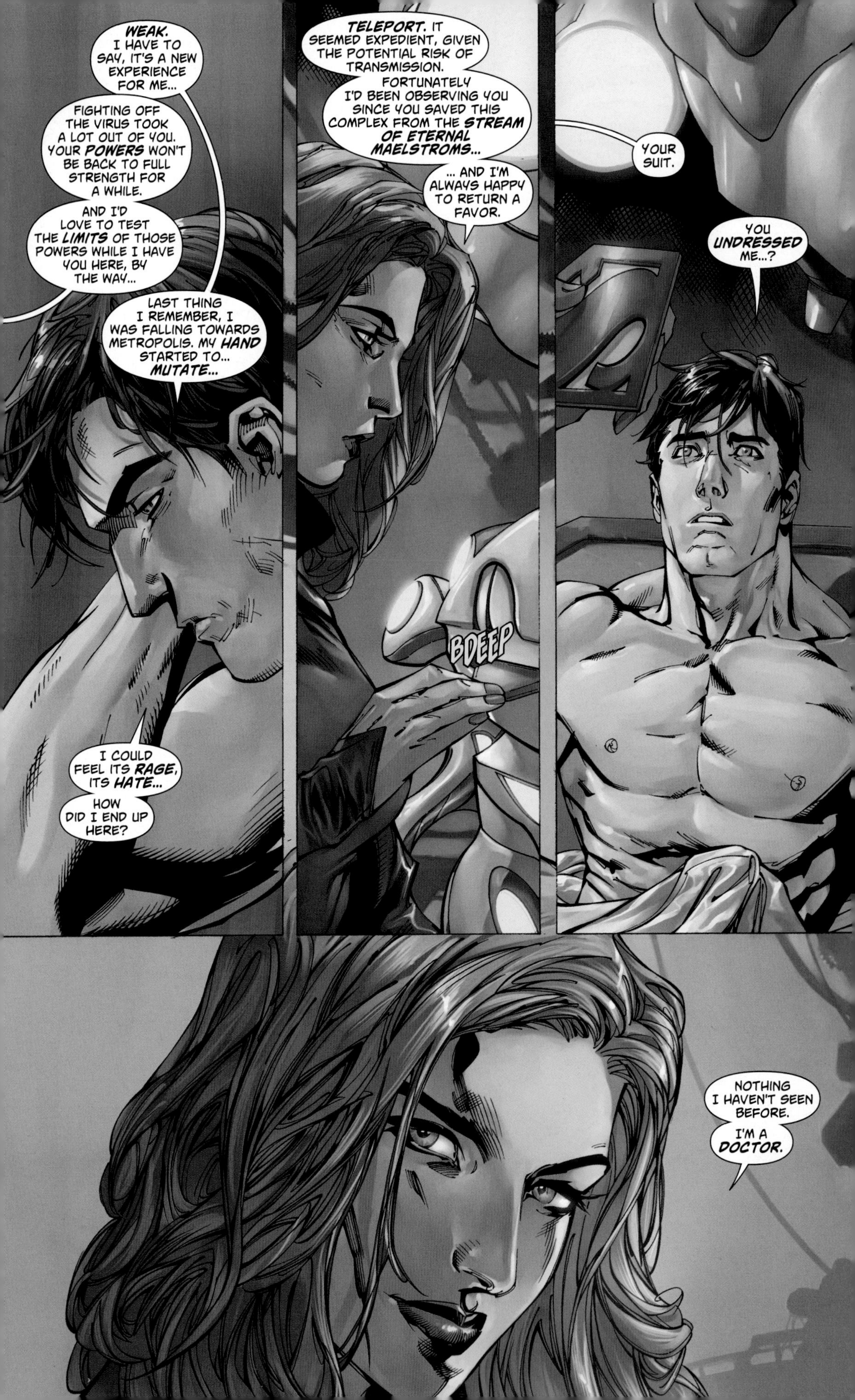

WEAK. I HAVE TO SAY, IT'S A NEW EXPERIENCE FOR ME...
FIGHTING OFF THE VIRUS TOOK A LOT OUT OF YOU. YOUR POWERS WON'T BE BACK TO FULL STRENGTH FOR A WHILE.
AND I'D LOVE TO TEST THE LIMITS OF THOSE POWERS WHILE I HAVE YOU HERE, BY THE WAY...
LAST THING I REMEMBER, I WAS FALLING TOWARDS METROPOLIS. MY HAND STARTED TO... MUTATE...
I COULD FEEL ITS RAGE, ITS HATE...
HOW DID I END UP HERE?
TELEPORT. IT SEEMED EXPEDIENT, GIVEN THE POTENTIAL RISK OF TRANSMISSION.
FORTUNATELY I'D BEEN OBSERVING YOU SINCE YOU SAVED THIS COMPLEX FROM THE STREAM OF ETERNAL MAELSTROMS...
... AND I'M ALWAYS HAPPY TO RETURN A FAVOR.
BDEEP
YOUR SUIT.
YOU UNDRESSED ME...?
NOTHING I HAVEN'T SEEN BEFORE.
I'M A DOCTOR.

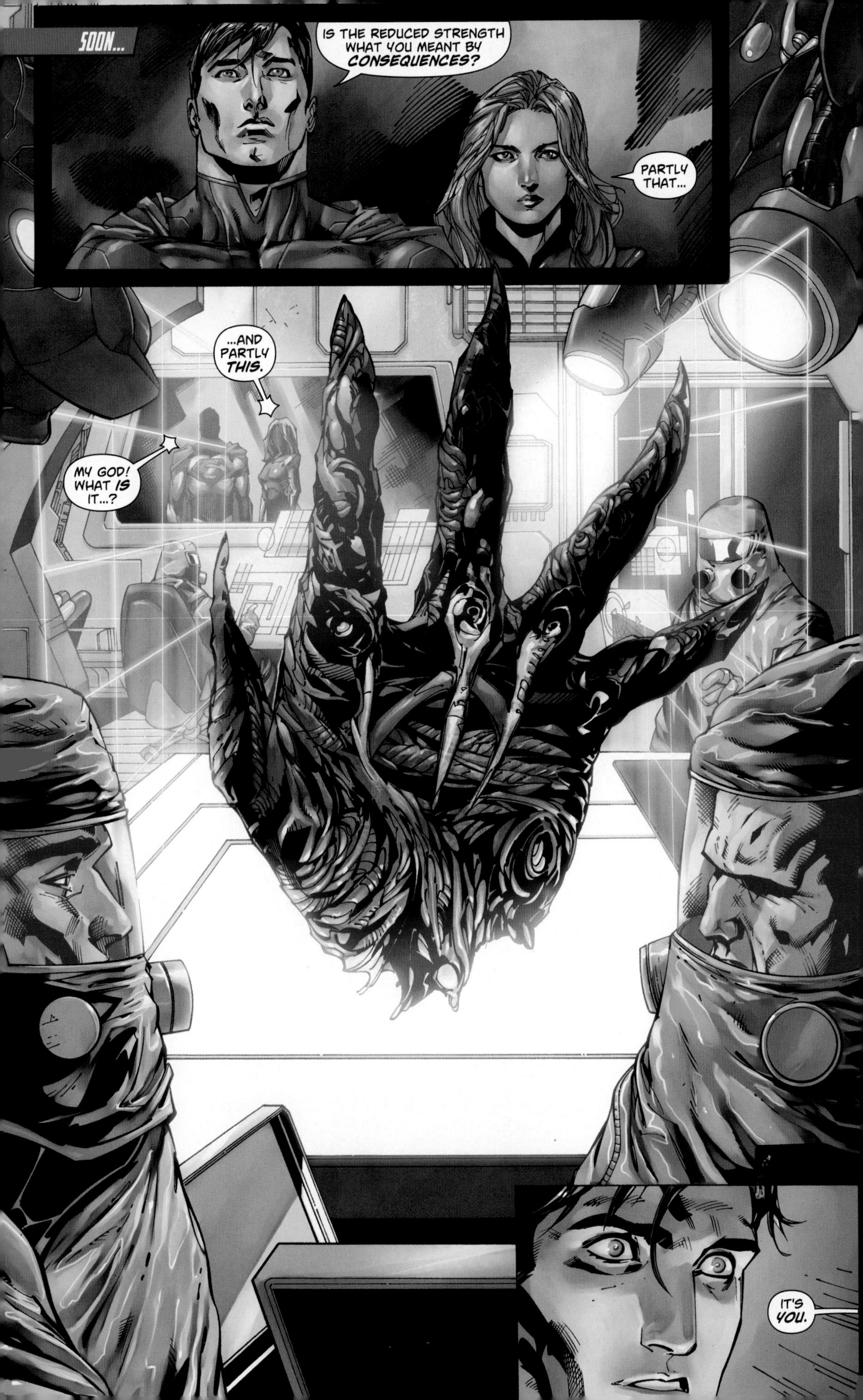
SOON...
IS THE REDUCED STRENGTH WHAT YOU MEANT BY CONSEQUENCES?
PARTLY THAT...
...AND PARTLY THIS.
MY GOD! WHAT IS IT...?
IT'S YOU.

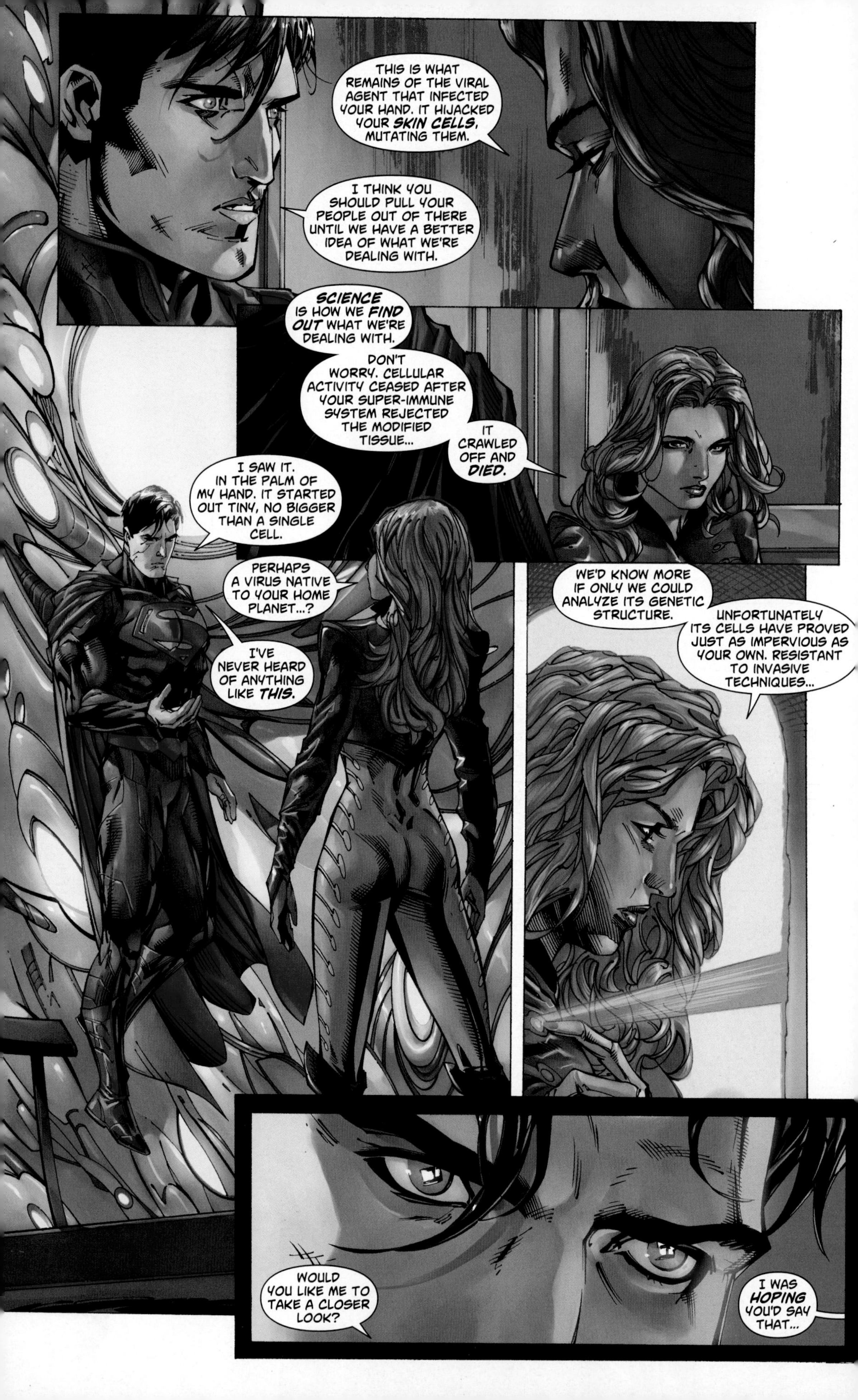
THIS IS WHAT REMAINS OF THE VIRAL AGENT THAT INFECTED YOUR HAND. IT HIJACKED YOUR SKIN CELLS, MUTATING THEM.
I THINK YOU SHOULD PULL YOUR PEOPLE OUT OF THERE UNTIL WE HAVE A BETTER IDEA OF WHAT WE'RE DEALING WITH.
SCIENCE IS HOW WE FIND OUT WHAT WE'RE DEALING WITH.
DON'T WORRY. CELLULAR ACTIVITY CEASED AFTER YOUR SUPER-IMMUNE SYSTEM REJECTED THE MODIFIED TISSUE...
IT CRAWLED OFF AND DIED.
I SAW IT. IN THE PALM OF MY HAND. IT STARTED OUT TINY, NO BIGGER THAN A SINGLE CELL.
PERHAPS A VIRUS NATIVE TO YOUR HOME PLANET...?
I'VE NEVER HEARD OF ANYTHING LIKE THIS.
WE'D KNOW MORE IF ONLY WE COULD ANALYZE ITS GENETIC STRUCTURE.
UNFORTUNATELY ITS CELLS HAVE PROVED JUST AS IMPERVIOUS AS YOUR OWN. RESISTANT TO INVASIVE TECHNIQUES...
WOULD YOU LIKE ME TO TAKE A CLOSER LOOK?
I WAS HOPING YOU'D SAY THAT...

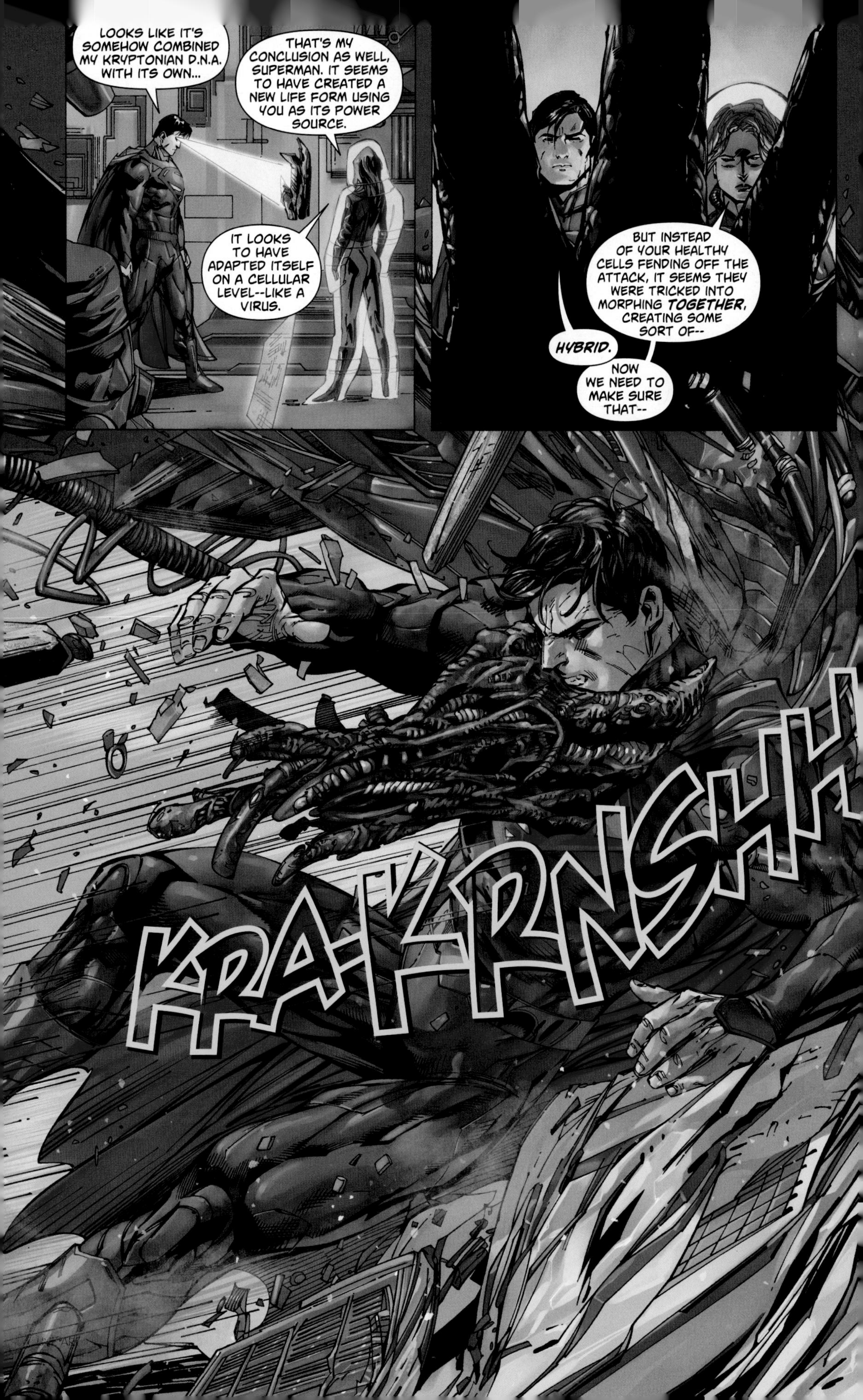

LOOKS LIKE IT'S SOMEHOW COMBINED MY KRYPTONIAN D.N.A. WITH ITS OWN...
THAT'S MY CONCLUSION AS WELL, SUPERMAN. IT SEEMS TO HAVE CREATED A NEW LIFE FORM USING YOU AS ITS POWER SOURCE.
IT LOOKS TO HAVE ADAPTED ITSELF ON A CELLULAR LEVEL--LIKE A VIRUS.
BUT INSTEAD OF YOUR HEALTHY CELLS FENDING OFF THE ATTACK, IT SEEMS THEY WERE TRICKED INTO MORPHING *TOGETHER*, CREATING SOME SORT OF--
HYBRID.
NOW WE NEED TO MAKE SURE THAT--
KRA-K'RNSHH

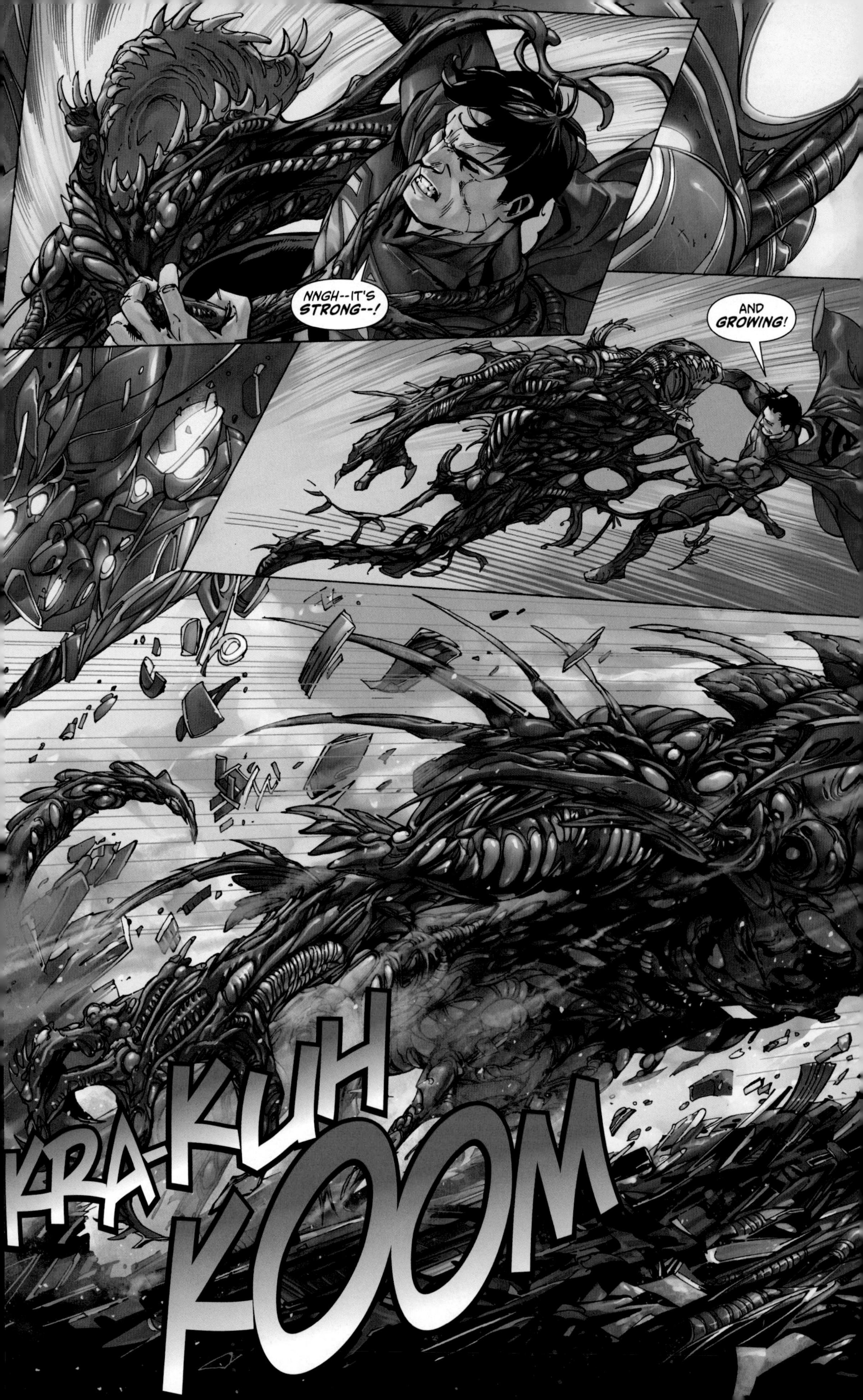
NNGH--IT'S STRONG--!
AND GROWING!
KRA-KUH KOOM

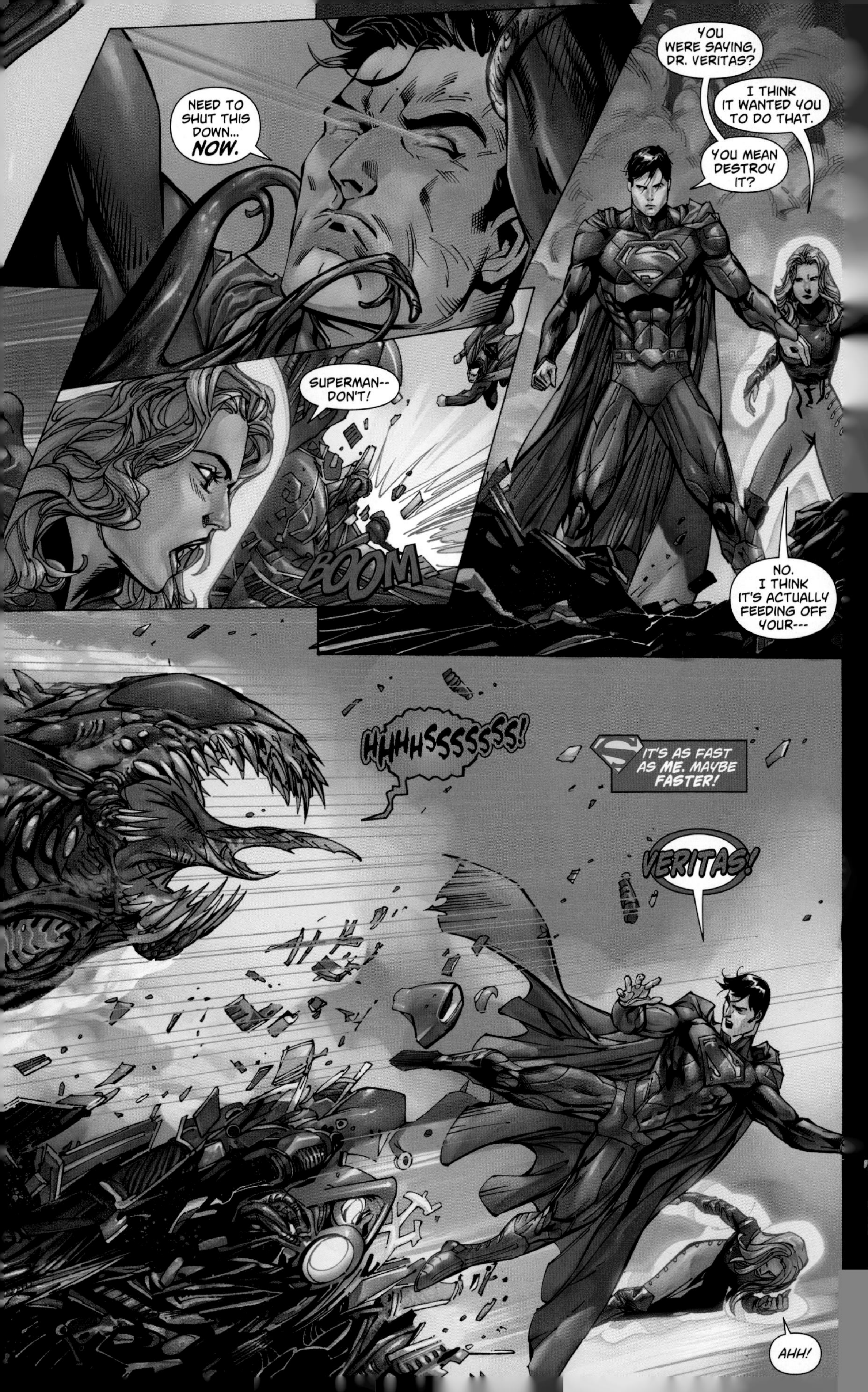
NEED TO SHUT THIS DOWN... NOW.
SUPERMAN-- DON'T!
BOOM
YOU WERE SAYING, DR. VERITAS?
I THINK IT WANTED YOU TO DO THAT.
YOU MEAN DESTROY IT?
NO. I THINK IT'S ACTUALLY FEEDING OFF YOUR---
HHHHSSSSSSS!
IT'S AS FAST AS ME. MAYBE FASTER!
VERITAS!
AHH!

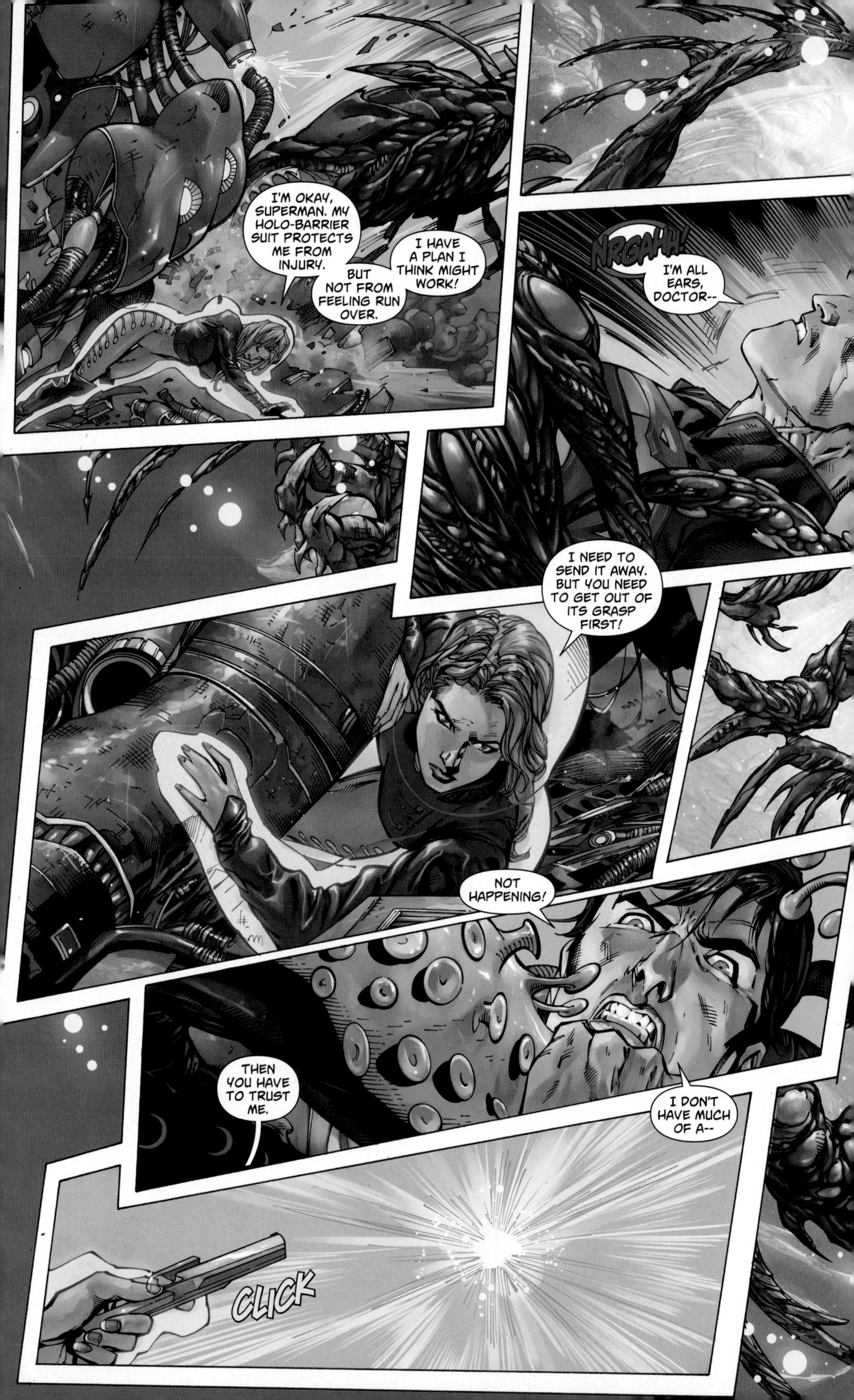
I'M OKAY, SUPERMAN. MY HOLO-BARRIER SUIT PROTECTS ME FROM INJURY.
BUT NOT FROM FEELING RUN OVER.
I HAVE A PLAN I THINK MIGHT WORK!
NRGAHH!
I'M ALL EARS, DOCTOR--
I NEED TO SEND IT AWAY. BUT YOU NEED TO GET OUT OF ITS GRASP FIRST!
NOT HAPPENING!
THEN YOU HAVE TO TRUST ME.
I DON'T HAVE MUCH OF A--
CLICK

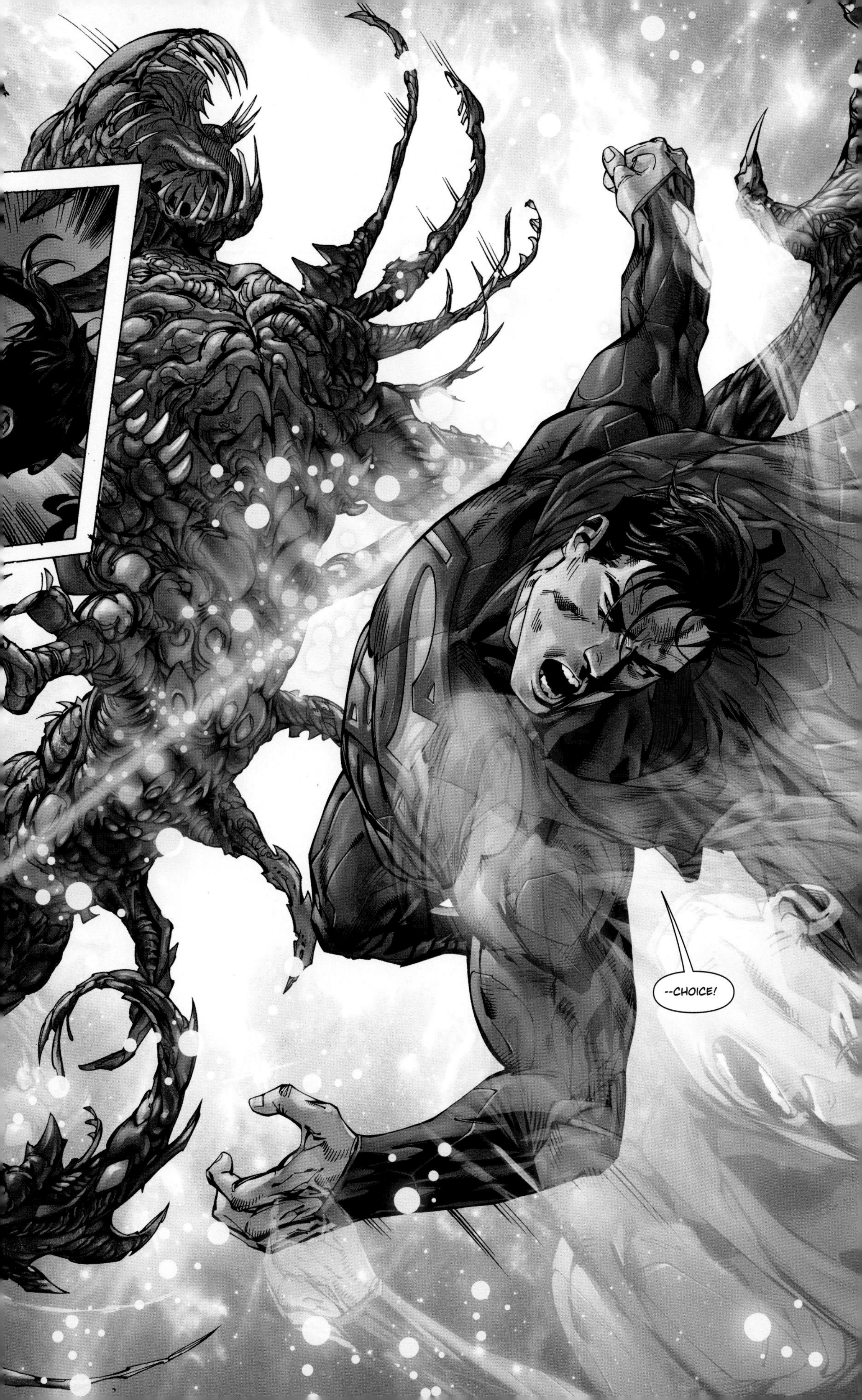
--CHOICE!

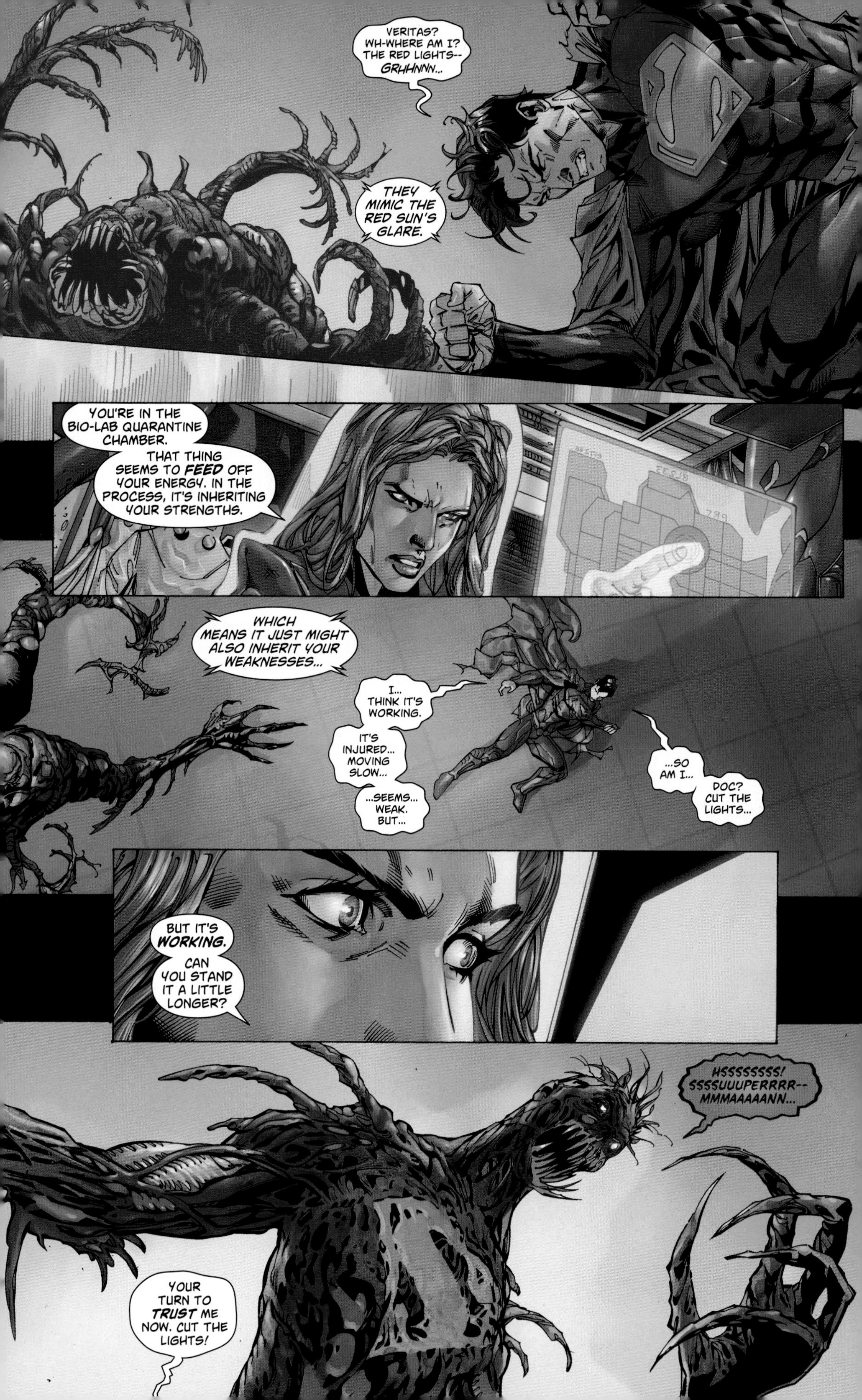
VERITAS? WH-WHERE AM I? THE RED LIGHTS-- GRHHNNN...
THEY MIMIC THE RED SUN'S GLARE.
YOU'RE IN THE BIO-LAB QUARANTINE CHAMBER.
THAT THING SEEMS TO FEED OFF YOUR ENERGY. IN THE PROCESS, IT'S INHERITING YOUR STRENGTHS.
WHICH MEANS IT JUST MIGHT ALSO INHERIT YOUR WEAKNESSES...
I... THINK IT'S WORKING.
IT'S INJURED... MOVING SLOW...
...SEEMS... WEAK. BUT...
...SO AM I...
DOC? CUT THE LIGHTS...
BUT IT'S WORKING.
CAN YOU STAND IT A LITTLE LONGER?
HSSSSSSSS! SSSSUUUPERRRR-- MMMAAAAANN...
YOUR TURN TO TRUST ME NOW. CUT THE LIGHTS!

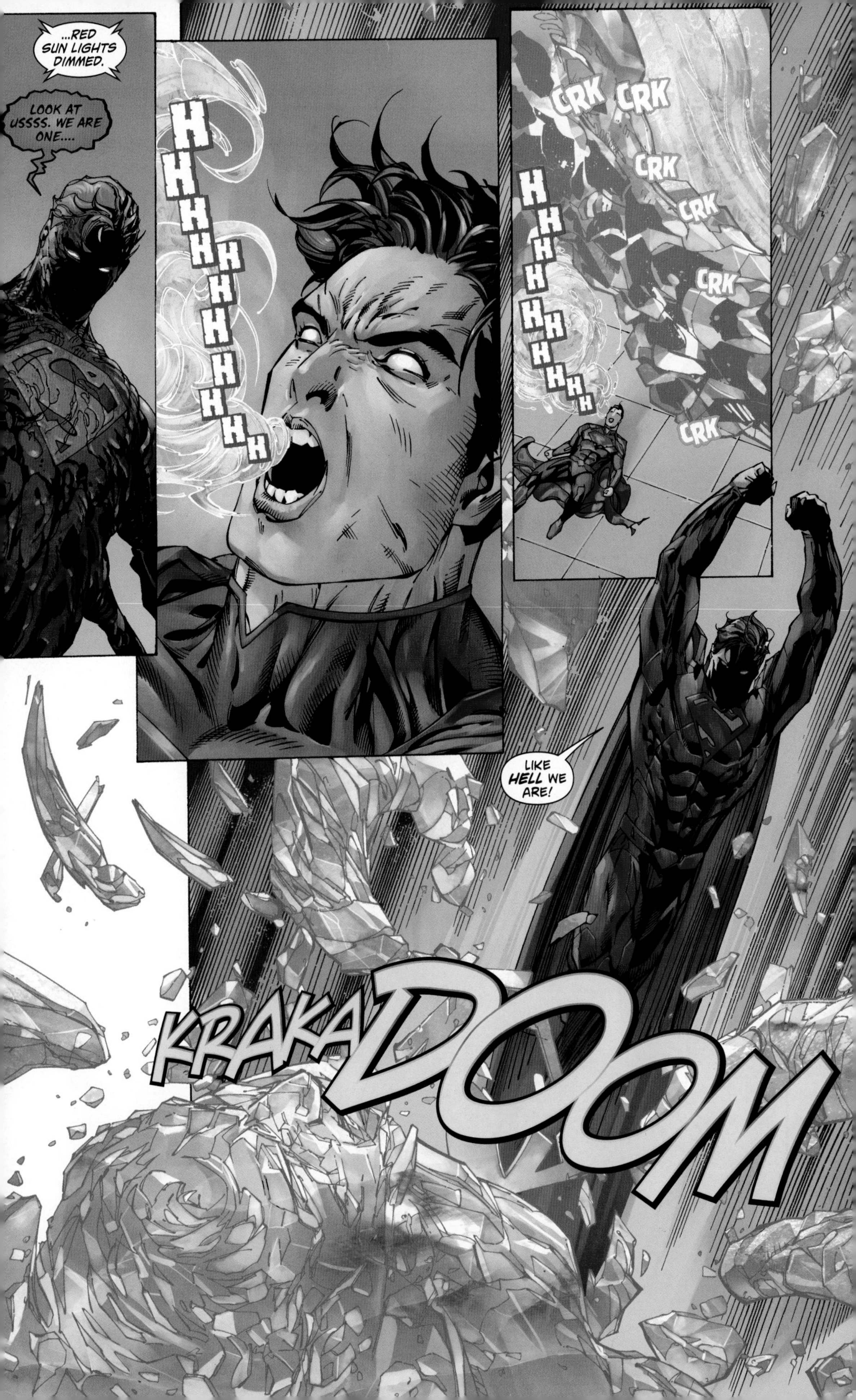

...RED SUN LIGHTS DIMMED.
LOOK AT USSSS. WE ARE ONE....
HHHHHHHHHHH
CRK CRK
CRK
CRK
CRK
CRK
HHHHHHHHHHHHH
LIKE HELL WE ARE!
KRAKADOOM

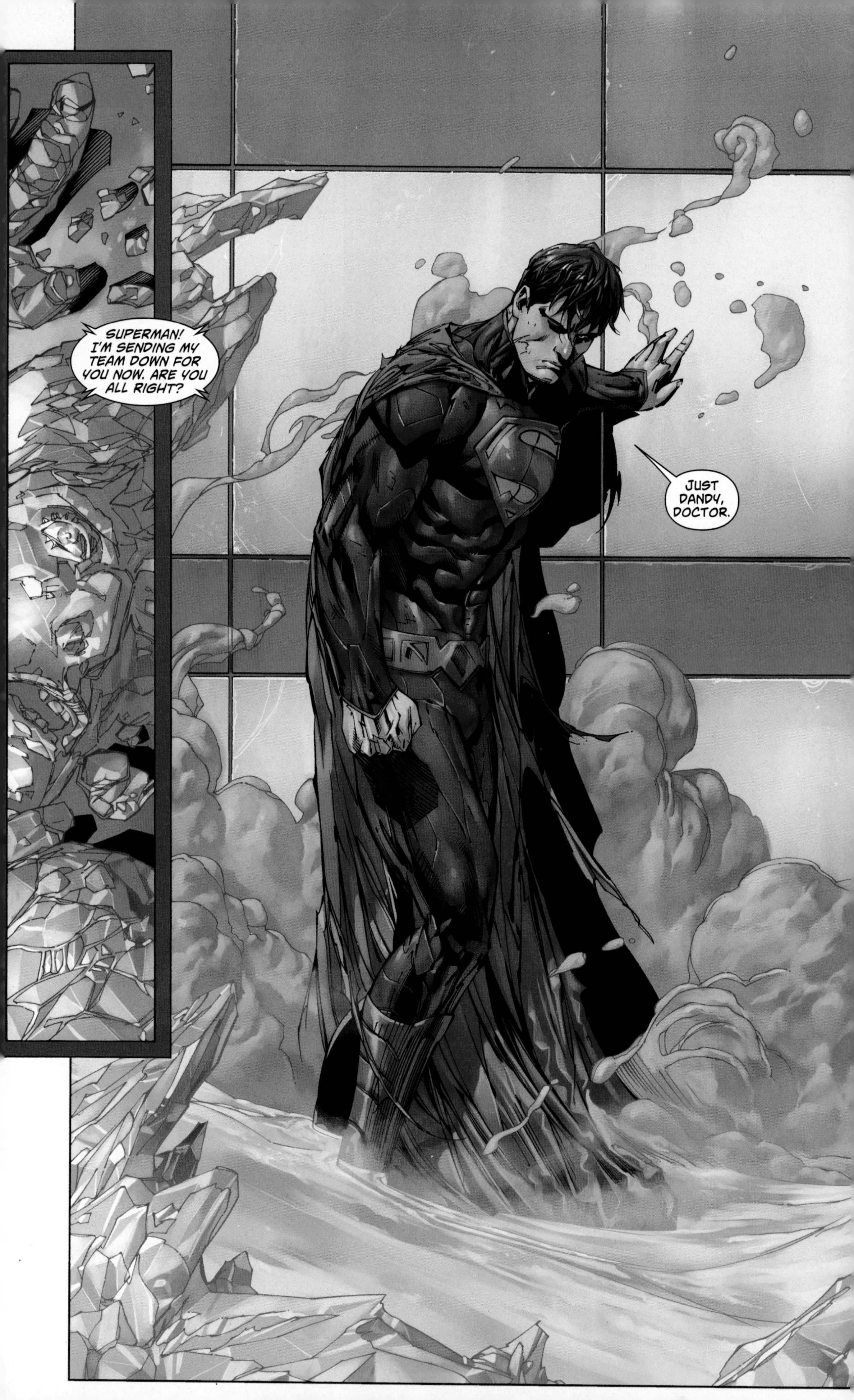
SUPERMAN! I'M SENDING MY TEAM DOWN FOR YOU NOW. ARE YOU ALL RIGHT?
JUST DANDY, DOCTOR.

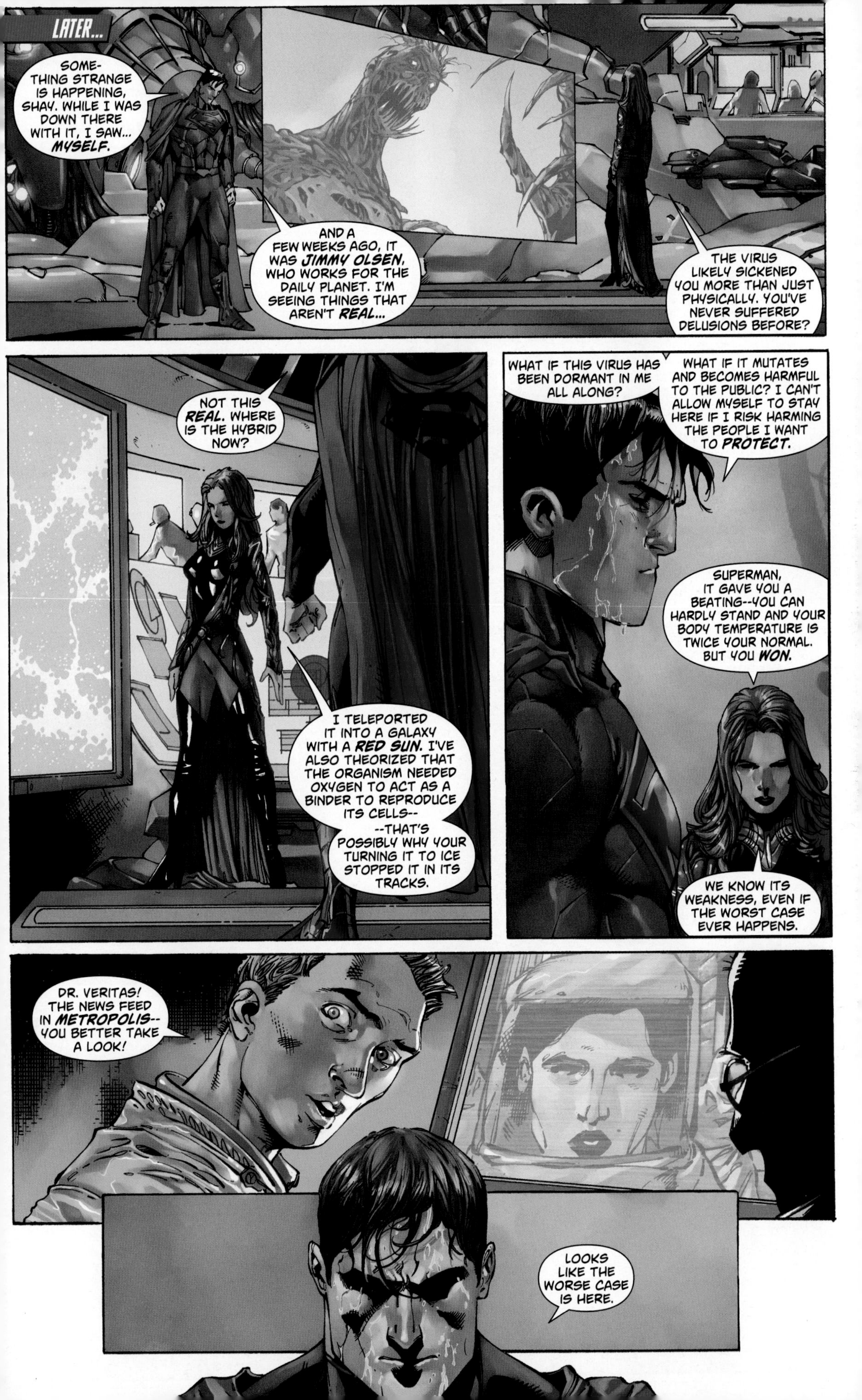
LATER...
SOMETHING STRANGE IS HAPPENING, SHAY. WHILE I WAS DOWN THERE WITH IT, I SAW... MYSELF.
AND A FEW WEEKS AGO, IT WAS JIMMY OLSEN, WHO WORKS FOR THE DAILY PLANET. I'M SEEING THINGS THAT AREN'T REAL...
THE VIRUS LIKELY SICKENED YOU MORE THAN JUST PHYSICALLY. YOU'VE NEVER SUFFERED DELUSIONS BEFORE?
NOT THIS REAL. WHERE IS THE HYBRID NOW?
I TELEPORTED IT INTO A GALAXY WITH A RED SUN. I'VE ALSO THEORIZED THAT THE ORGANISM NEEDED OXYGEN TO ACT AS A BINDER TO REPRODUCE ITS CELLS--
--THAT'S POSSIBLY WHY YOUR TURNING IT TO ICE STOPPED IT IN ITS TRACKS.
WHAT IF THIS VIRUS HAS BEEN DORMANT IN ME ALL ALONG?
WHAT IF IT MUTATES AND BECOMES HARMFUL TO THE PUBLIC? I CAN'T ALLOW MYSELF TO STAY HERE IF I RISK HARMING THE PEOPLE I WANT TO PROTECT.
SUPERMAN, IT GAVE YOU A BEATING--YOU CAN HARDLY STAND AND YOUR BODY TEMPERATURE IS TWICE YOUR NORMAL. BUT YOU WON.
WE KNOW ITS WEAKNESS, EVEN IF THE WORST CASE EVER HAPPENS.
DR. VERITAS! THE NEWS FEED IN METROPOLIS--YOU BETTER TAKE A LOOK!
LOOKS LIKE THE WORSE CASE IS HERE.

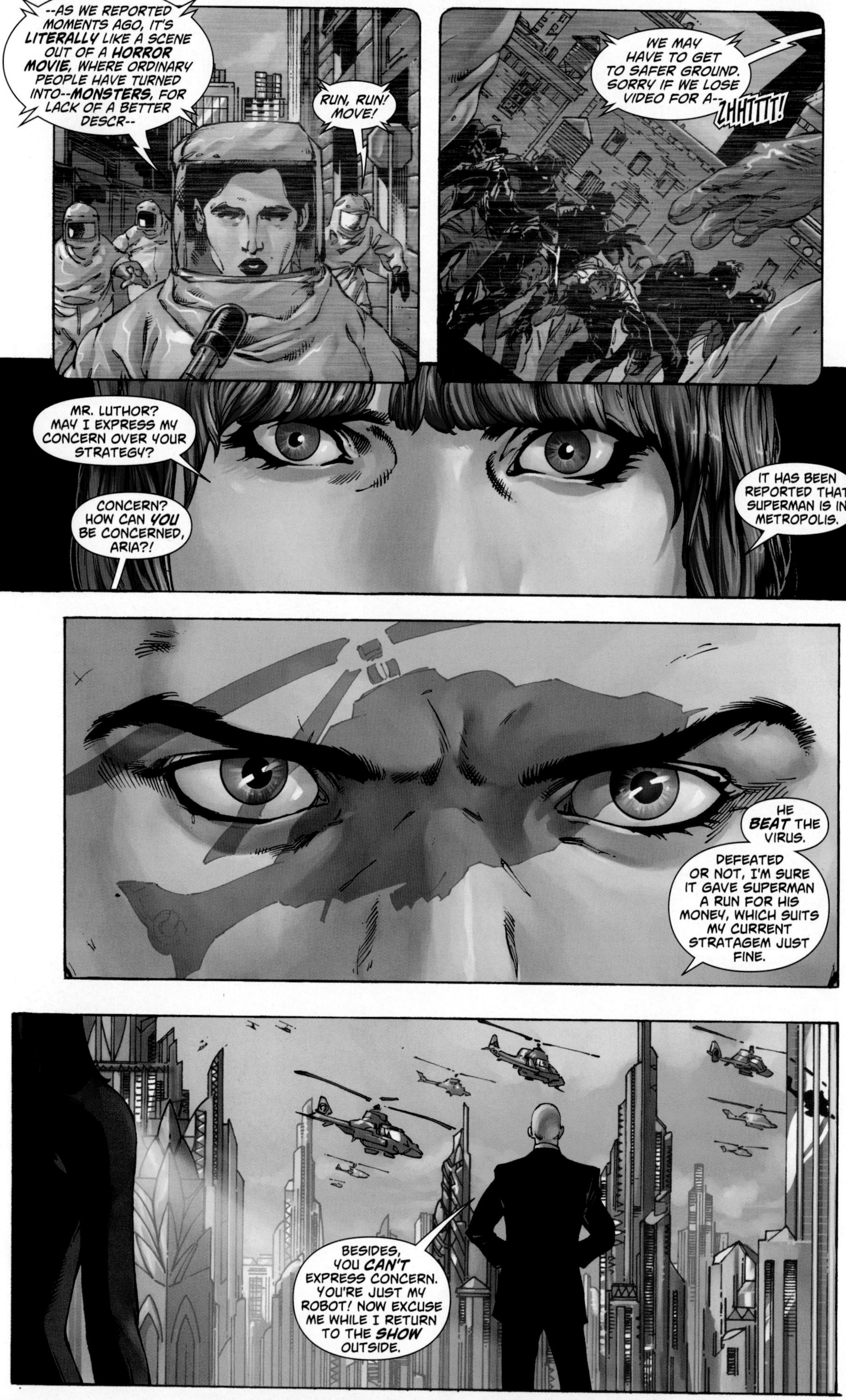
--AS WE REPORTED MOMENTS AGO, IT'S LITERALLY LIKE A SCENE OUT OF A HORROR MOVIE, WHERE ORDINARY PEOPLE HAVE TURNED INTO--MONSTERS, FOR LACK OF A BETTER DESCR--
RUN, RUN! MOVE!
WE MAY HAVE TO GET TO SAFER GROUND. SORRY IF WE LOSE VIDEO FOR A--
ZHHTTTT!
MR. LUTHOR? MAY I EXPRESS MY CONCERN OVER YOUR STRATEGY?
CONCERN? HOW CAN YOU BE CONCERNED, ARIA?!
IT HAS BEEN REPORTED THAT SUPERMAN IS IN METROPOLIS.
HE BEAT THE VIRUS.
DEFEATED OR NOT, I'M SURE IT GAVE SUPERMAN A RUN FOR HIS MONEY, WHICH SUITS MY CURRENT STRATAGEM JUST FINE.
BESIDES, YOU CAN'T EXPRESS CONCERN. YOU'RE JUST MY ROBOT! NOW EXCUSE ME WHILE I RETURN TO THE SHOW OUTSIDE.

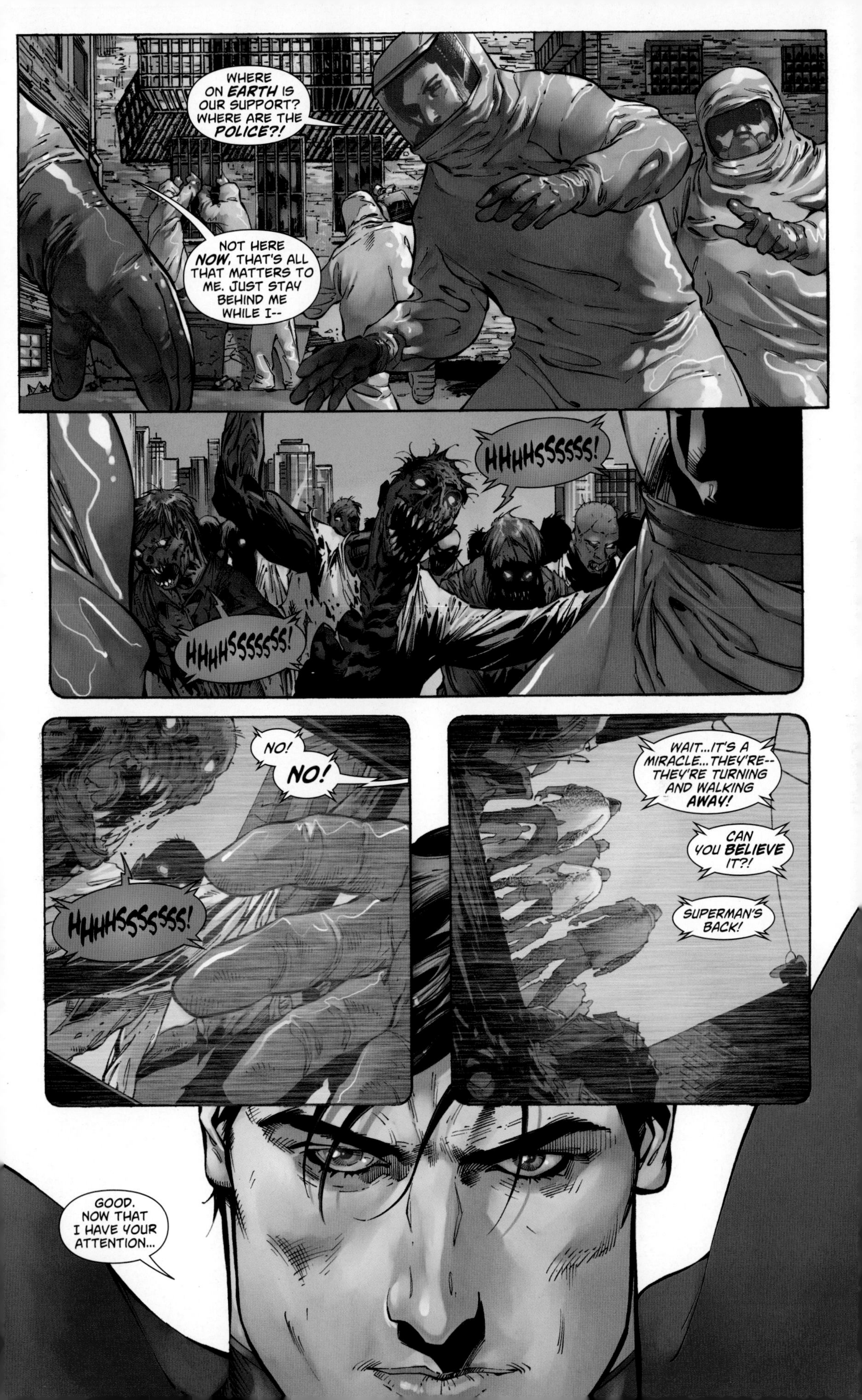
WHERE ON EARTH IS OUR SUPPORT? WHERE ARE THE POLICE?!
NOT HERE NOW, THAT'S ALL THAT MATTERS TO ME. JUST STAY BEHIND ME WHILE I--
HHHHSSSSSS!
HHHHSSSSSSS!
NO!
NO!
HHHHSSSSSSS!
WAIT...IT'S A MIRACLE...THEY'RE--THEY'RE TURNING AND WALKING AWAY!
CAN YOU BELIEVE IT?!
SUPERMAN'S BACK!
GOOD. NOW THAT I HAVE YOUR ATTENTION...

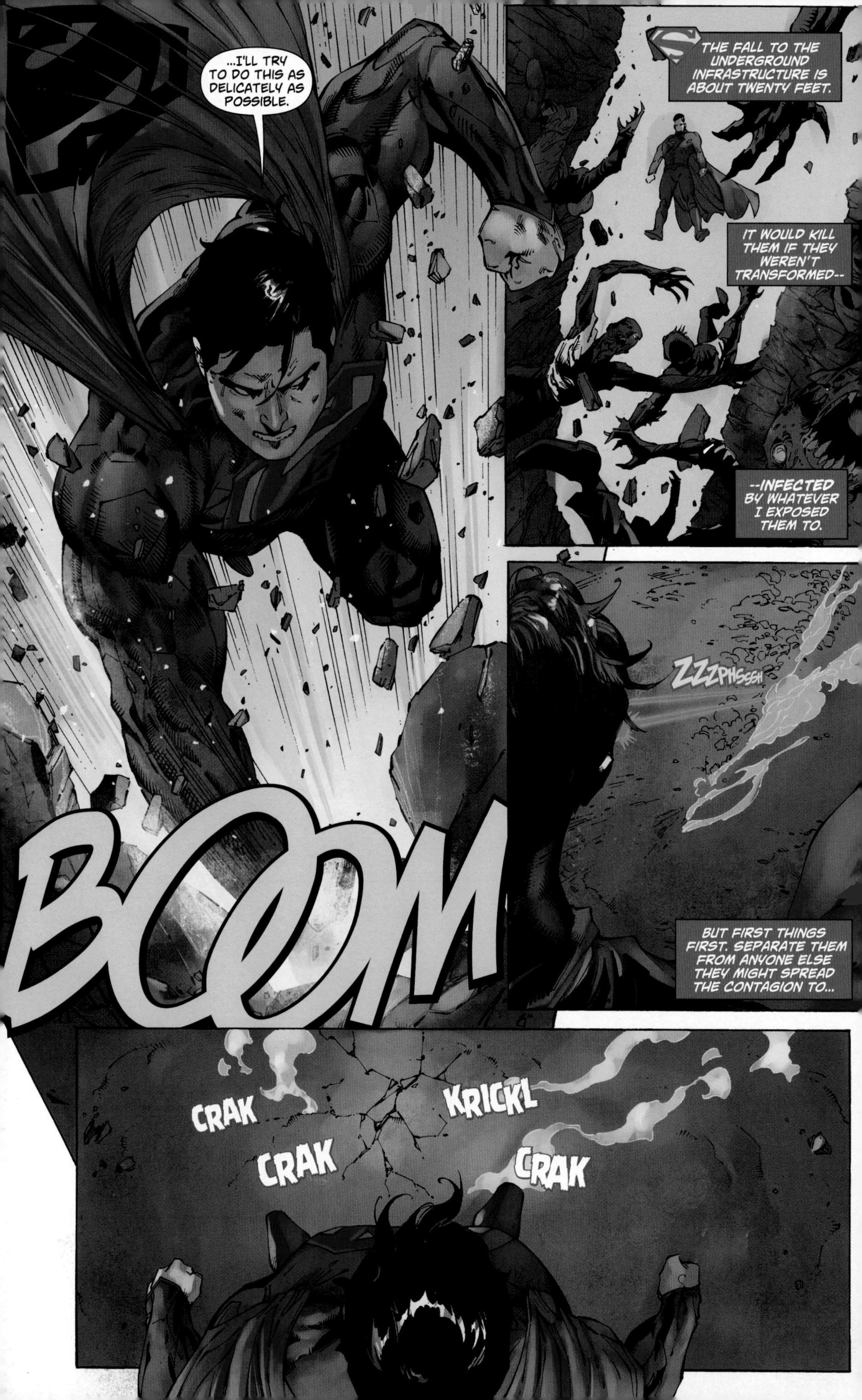
...I'LL TRY TO DO THIS AS DELICATELY AS POSSIBLE.
THE FALL TO THE UNDERGROUND INFRASTRUCTURE IS ABOUT TWENTY FEET.
IT WOULD KILL THEM IF THEY WEREN'T TRANSFORMED--
--INFECTED BY WHATEVER I EXPOSED THEM TO.
BOOM
ZZZPHSSSH
BUT FIRST THINGS FIRST. SEPARATE THEM FROM ANYONE ELSE THEY MIGHT SPREAD THE CONTAGION TO...
CRAK
KRICKL
CRAK
CRAK

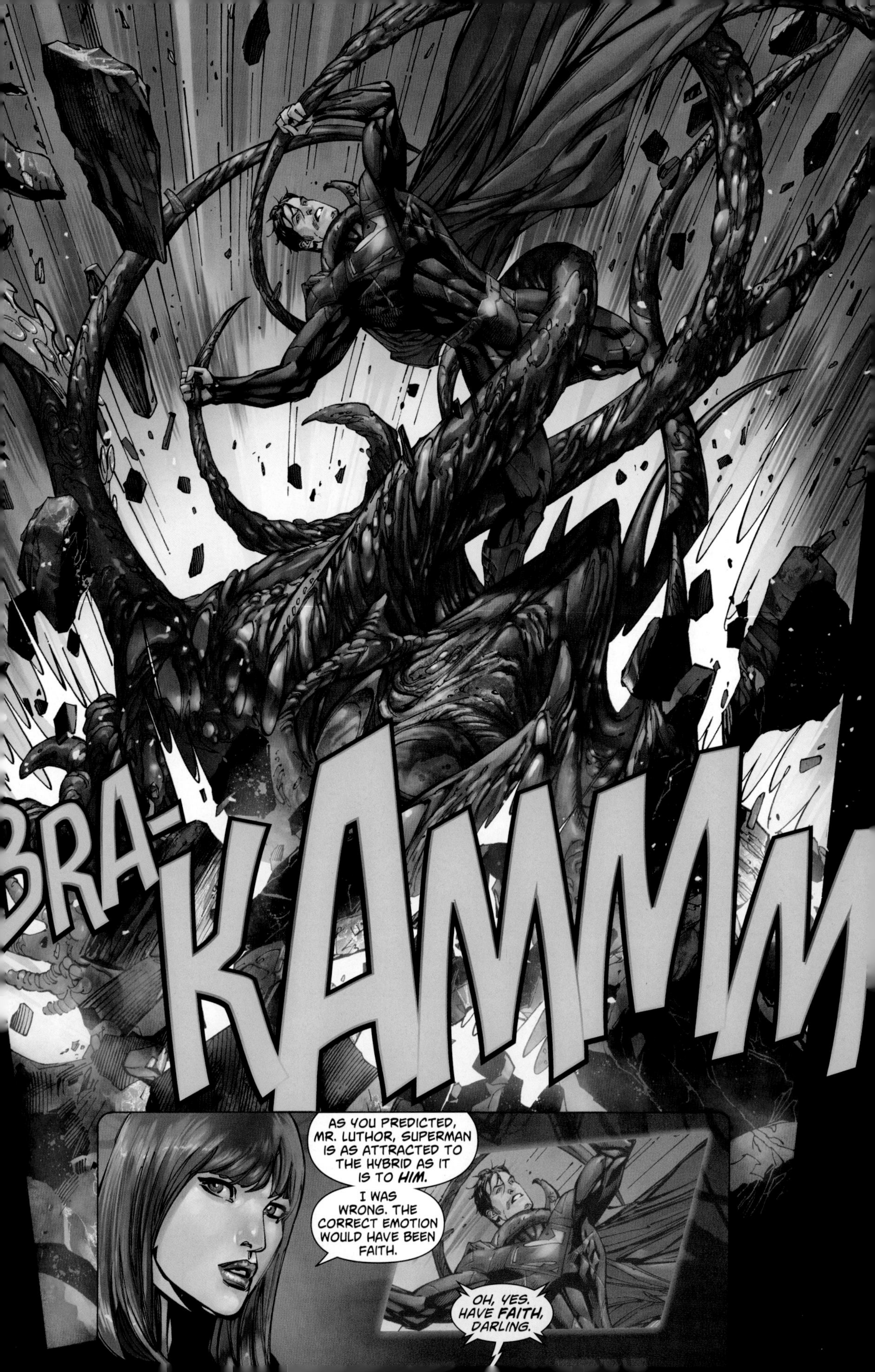
BRA-KAMMM
AS YOU PREDICTED, MR. LUTHOR, SUPERMAN IS AS ATTRACTED TO THE HYBRID AS IT IS TO *HIM*.
I WAS WRONG. THE CORRECT EMOTION WOULD HAVE BEEN FAITH.
OH, YES. HAVE *FAITH*, DARLING.

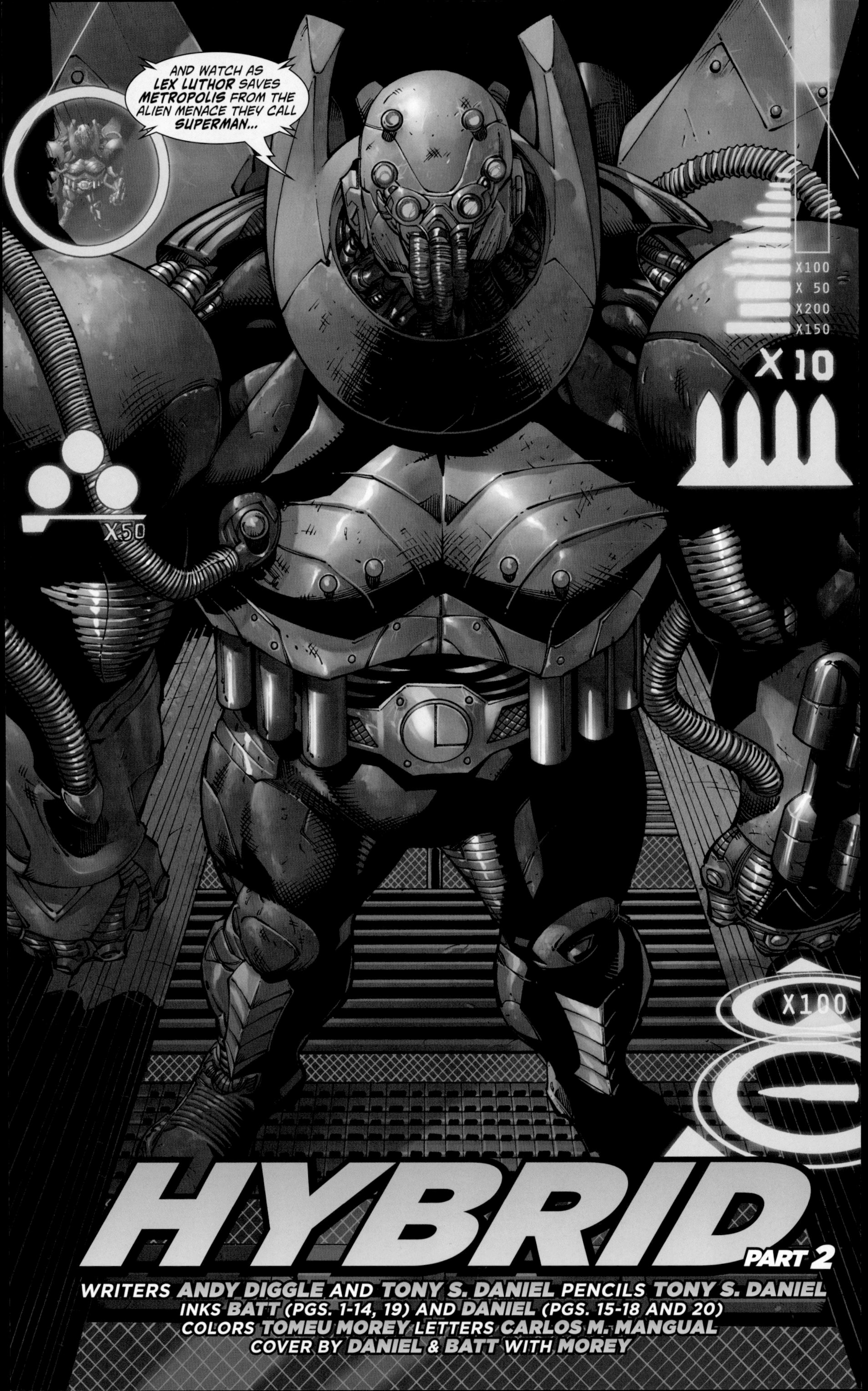
AND WATCH AS LEX LUTHOR SAVES METROPOLIS FROM THE ALIEN MENACE THEY CALL SUPERMAN...
X100
X 50
X200
X150
X10
X50
X100
HYBRID
PART 2
WRITERS ANDY DIGGLE AND TONY S. DANIEL PENCILS TONY S. DANIEL
INKS BATT (PGS. 1-14, 19) AND DANIEL (PGS. 15-18 AND 20)
COLORS TOMEU MOREY LETTERS CARLOS M. MANGUAL
COVER BY DANIEL & BATT WITH MOREY

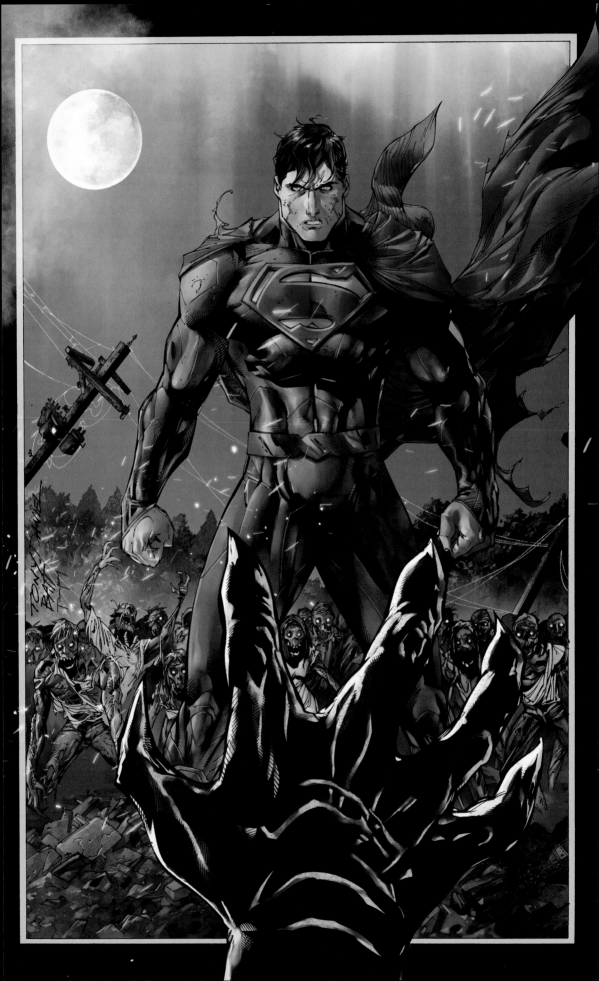

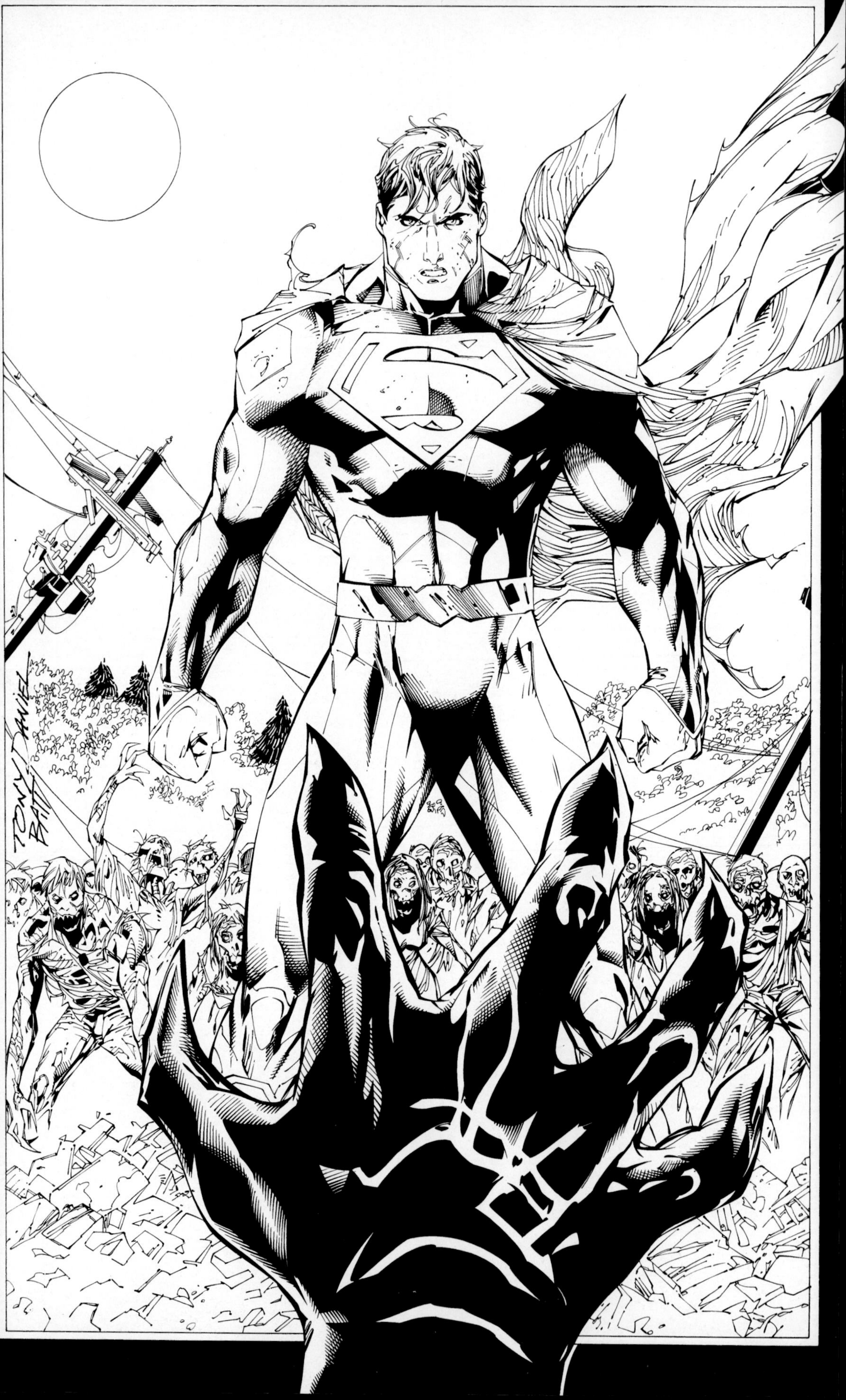
TONY DANIEL
BATT

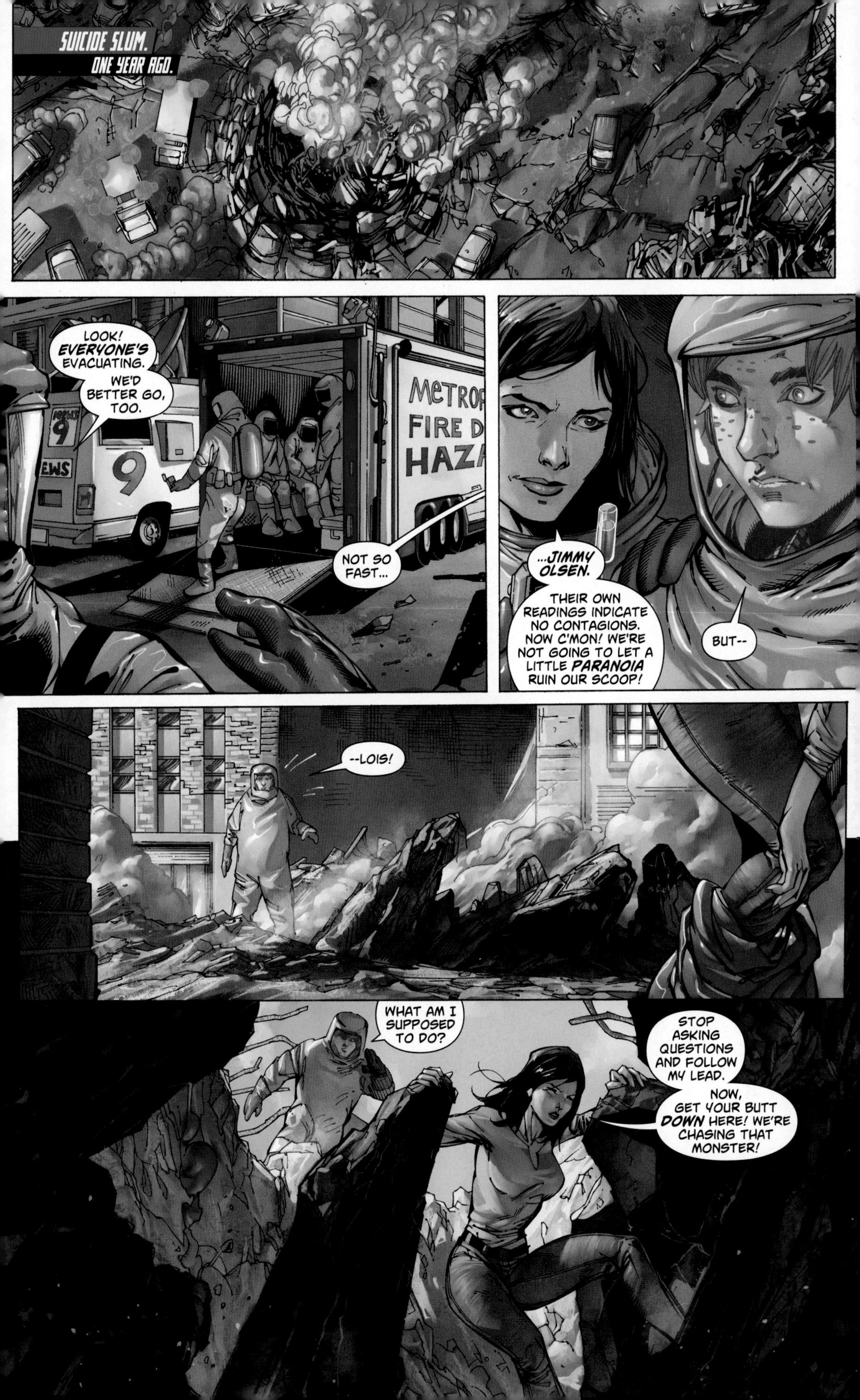
SUICIDE SLUM.
ONE YEAR AGO.
LOOK! EVERYONE'S EVACUATING. WE'D BETTER GO, TOO.
NOT SO FAST...
METROP FIRE D HAZA
...JIMMY OLSEN.
THEIR OWN READINGS INDICATE NO CONTAGIONS. NOW C'MON! WE'RE NOT GOING TO LET A LITTLE PARANOIA RUIN OUR SCOOP!
BUT--
--LOIS!
WHAT AM I SUPPOSED TO DO?
STOP ASKING QUESTIONS AND FOLLOW MY LEAD.
NOW, GET YOUR BUTT DOWN HERE! WE'RE CHASING THAT MONSTER!

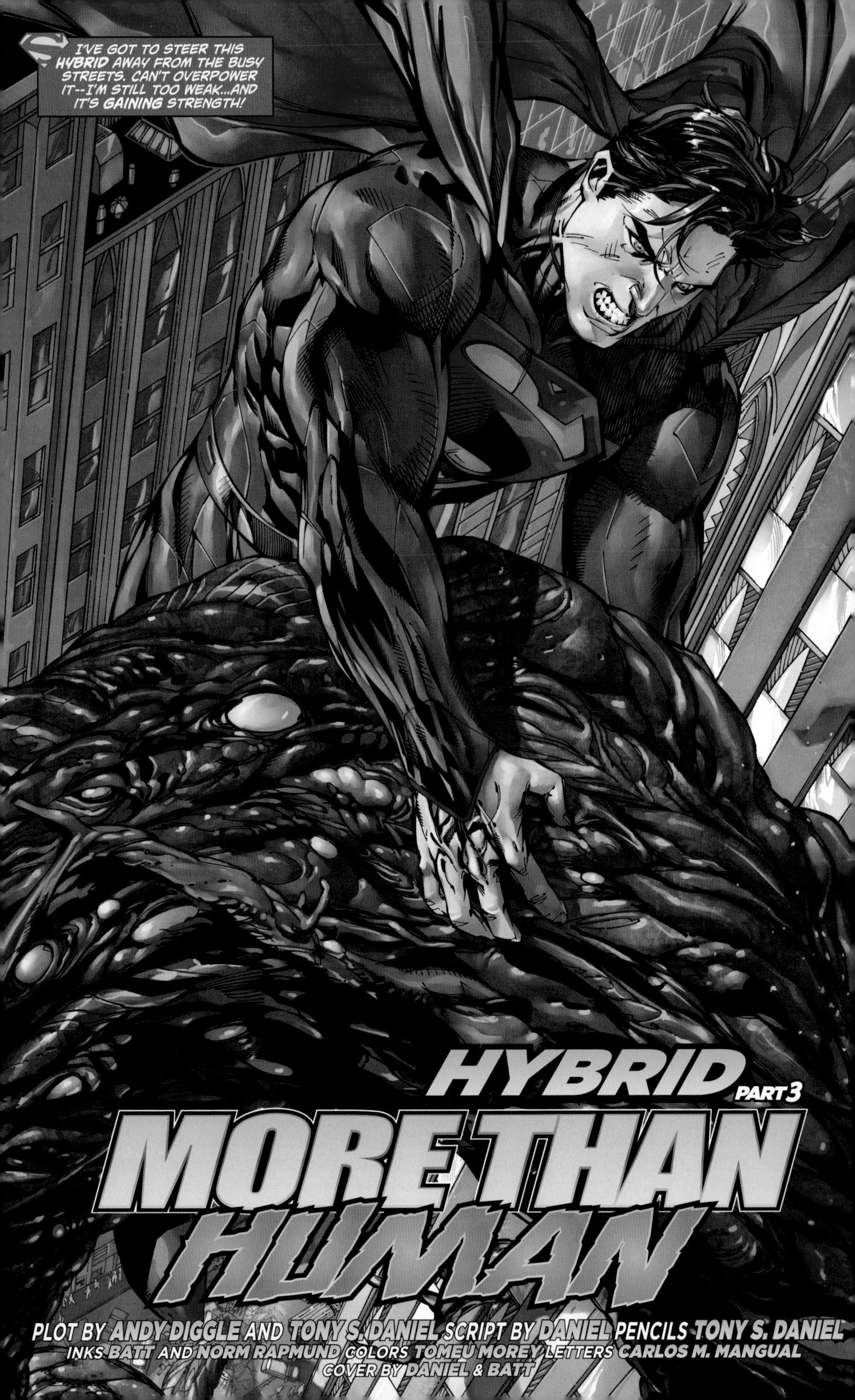
I'VE GOT TO STEER THIS HYBRID AWAY FROM THE BUSY STREETS. CAN'T OVERPOWER IT--I'M STILL TOO WEAK...AND IT'S GAINING STRENGTH!
HYBRID PART 3
MORE THAN HUMAN
PLOT BY ANDY DIGGLE AND TONY S. DANIEL SCRIPT BY DANIEL PENCILS TONY S. DANIEL
INKS BATT AND NORM RAPMUND COLORS TOMEU MOREY LETTERS CARLOS M. MANGUAL
COVER BY DANIEL & BATT

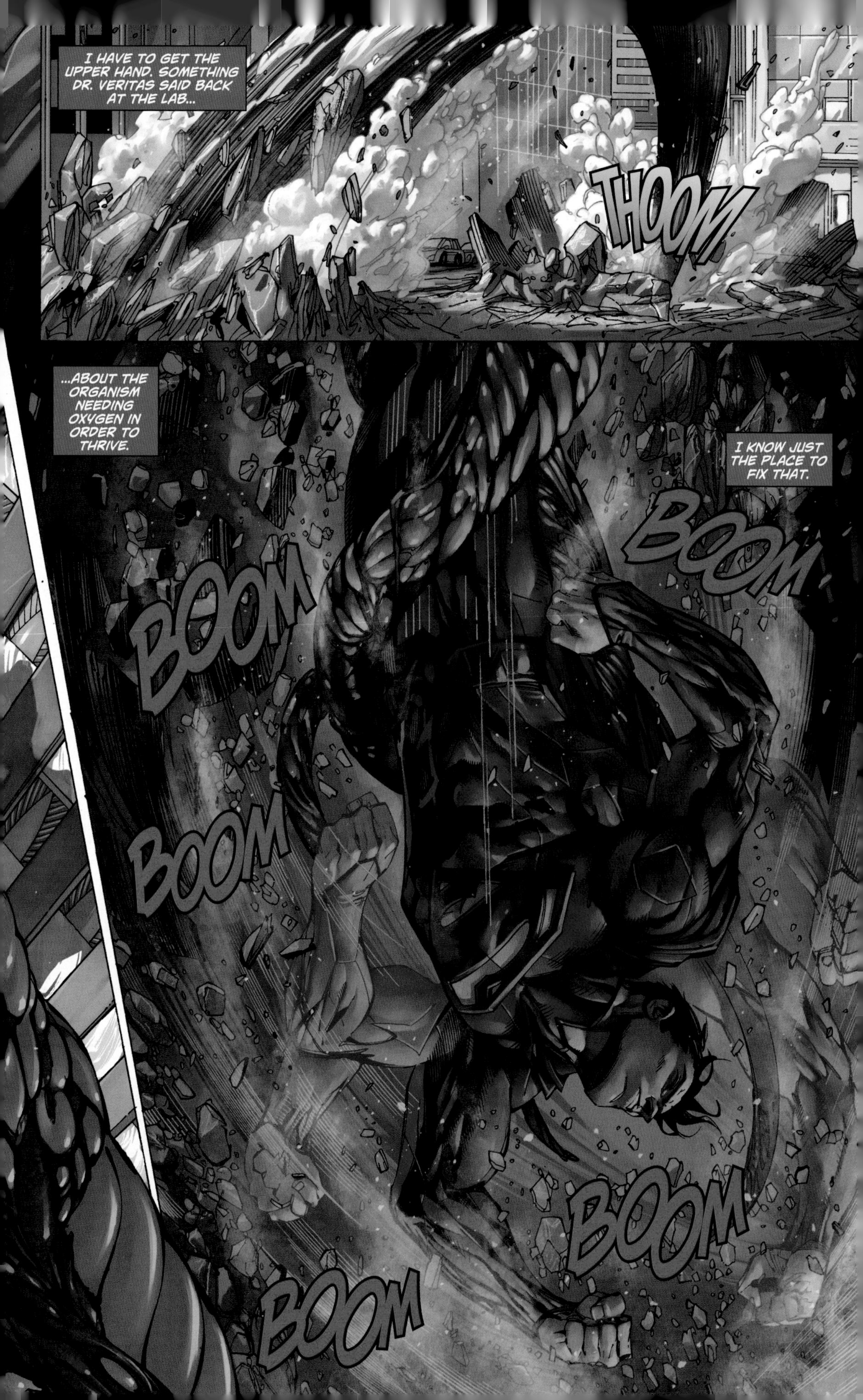
I HAVE TO GET THE UPPER HAND. SOMETHING DR. VERITAS SAID BACK AT THE LAB...
THOOM!
...ABOUT THE ORGANISM NEEDING OXYGEN IN ORDER TO THRIVE.
I KNOW JUST THE PLACE TO FIX THAT.
BOOM
BOOM
BOOM
BOOM
BOOM

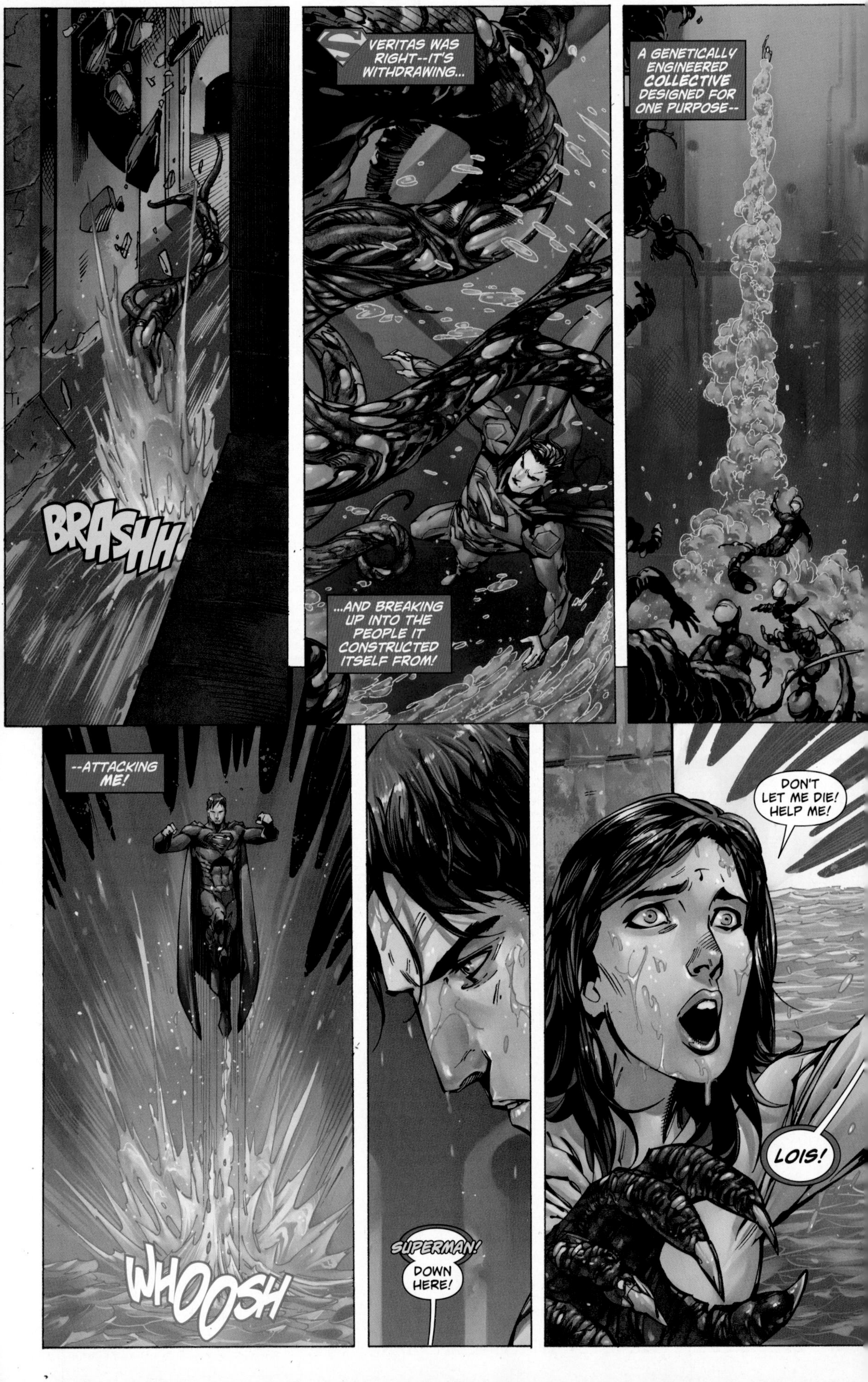
BRASHH
VERITAS WAS RIGHT--IT'S WITHDRAWING...
...AND BREAKING UP INTO THE PEOPLE IT CONSTRUCTED ITSELF FROM!
A GENETICALLY ENGINEERED COLLECTIVE DESIGNED FOR ONE PURPOSE--
--ATTACKING ME!
WHOOSH
SUPERMAN! DOWN HERE!
DON'T LET ME DIE! HELP ME!
LOIS!

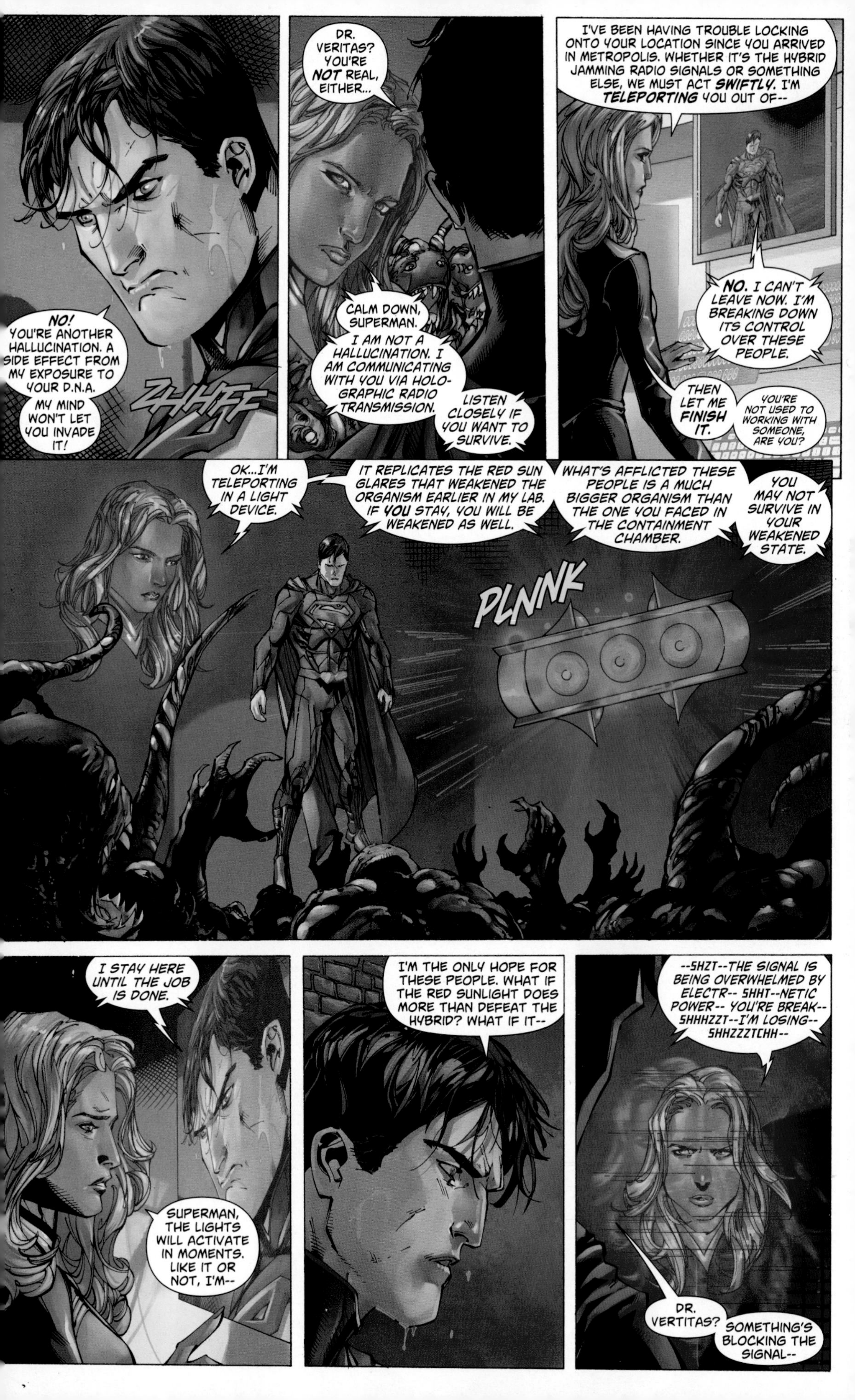
NO! YOU'RE ANOTHER HALLUCINATION. A SIDE EFFECT FROM MY EXPOSURE TO YOUR D.N.A.
MY MIND WON'T LET YOU INVADE IT!
ZHHFF
DR. VERITAS? YOU'RE NOT REAL, EITHER...
CALM DOWN, SUPERMAN.
I AM NOT A HALLUCINATION. I AM COMMUNICATING WITH YOU VIA HOLO-GRAPHIC RADIO TRANSMISSION.
LISTEN CLOSELY IF YOU WANT TO SURVIVE.
I'VE BEEN HAVING TROUBLE LOCKING ONTO YOUR LOCATION SINCE YOU ARRIVED IN METROPOLIS. WHETHER IT'S THE HYBRID JAMMING RADIO SIGNALS OR SOMETHING ELSE, WE MUST ACT SWIFTLY. I'M TELEPORTING YOU OUT OF--
NO. I CAN'T LEAVE NOW. I'M BREAKING DOWN ITS CONTROL OVER THESE PEOPLE.
THEN LET ME FINISH IT.
YOU'RE NOT USED TO WORKING WITH SOMEONE, ARE YOU?
OK...I'M TELEPORTING IN A LIGHT DEVICE.
IT REPLICATES THE RED SUN GLARES THAT WEAKENED THE ORGANISM EARLIER IN MY LAB. IF YOU STAY, YOU WILL BE WEAKENED AS WELL.
WHAT'S AFFLICTED THESE PEOPLE IS A MUCH BIGGER ORGANISM THAN THE ONE YOU FACED IN THE CONTAINMENT CHAMBER.
YOU MAY NOT SURVIVE IN YOUR WEAKENED STATE.
PLNNK
I STAY HERE UNTIL THE JOB IS DONE.
SUPERMAN, THE LIGHTS WILL ACTIVATE IN MOMENTS. LIKE IT OR NOT, I'M--
I'M THE ONLY HOPE FOR THESE PEOPLE. WHAT IF THE RED SUNLIGHT DOES MORE THAN DEFEAT THE HYBRID? WHAT IF IT--
--SHZT--THE SIGNAL IS BEING OVERWHELMED BY ELECTR-- SHHT--NETIC POWER-- YOU'RE BREAK-- SHHHZZT--I'M LOSING-- SHHZZZTCHH--
DR. VERTITAS?
SOMETHING'S BLOCKING THE SIGNAL--

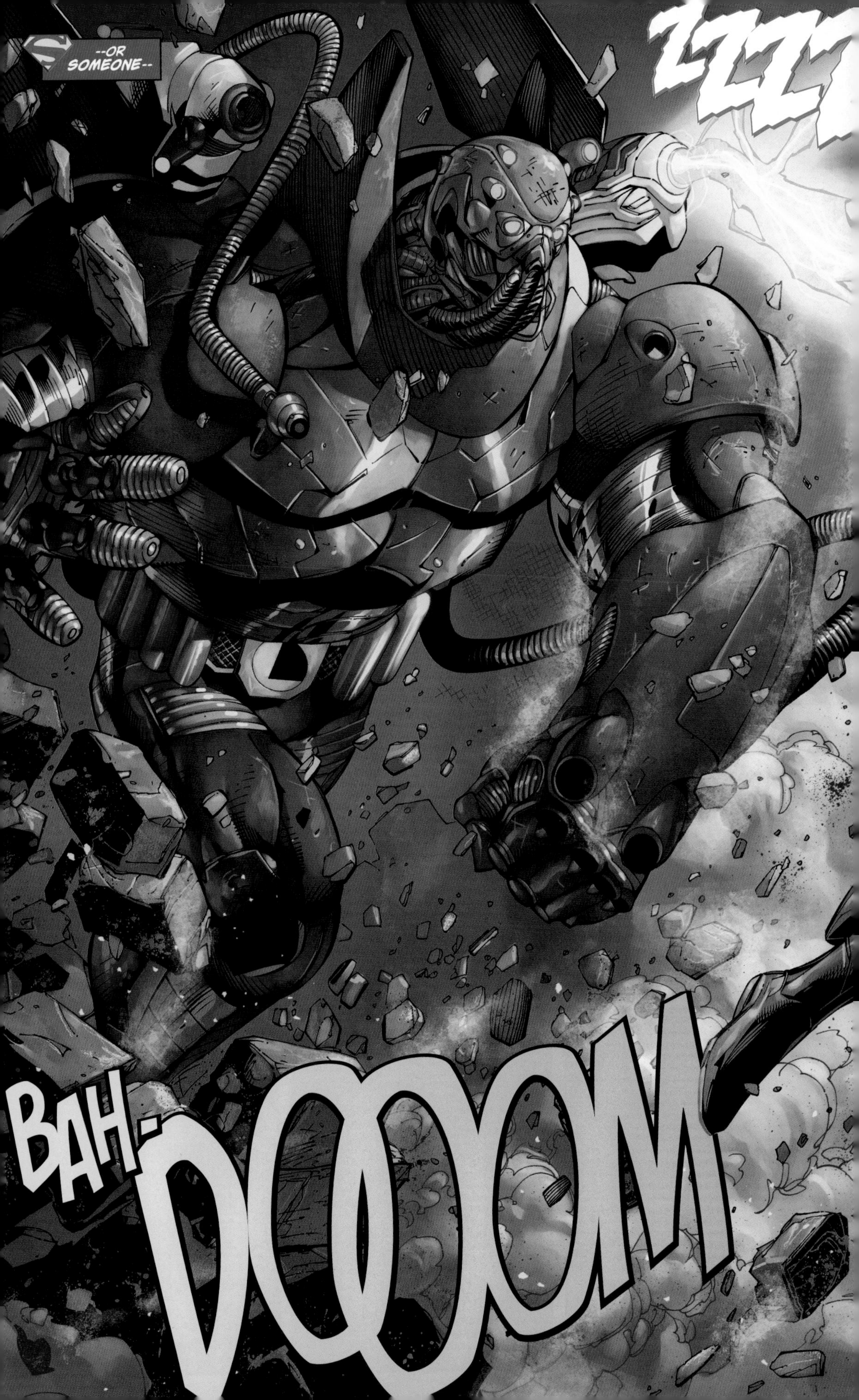
--OR SOMEONE--
ZZZZ
BAH-DOOOM

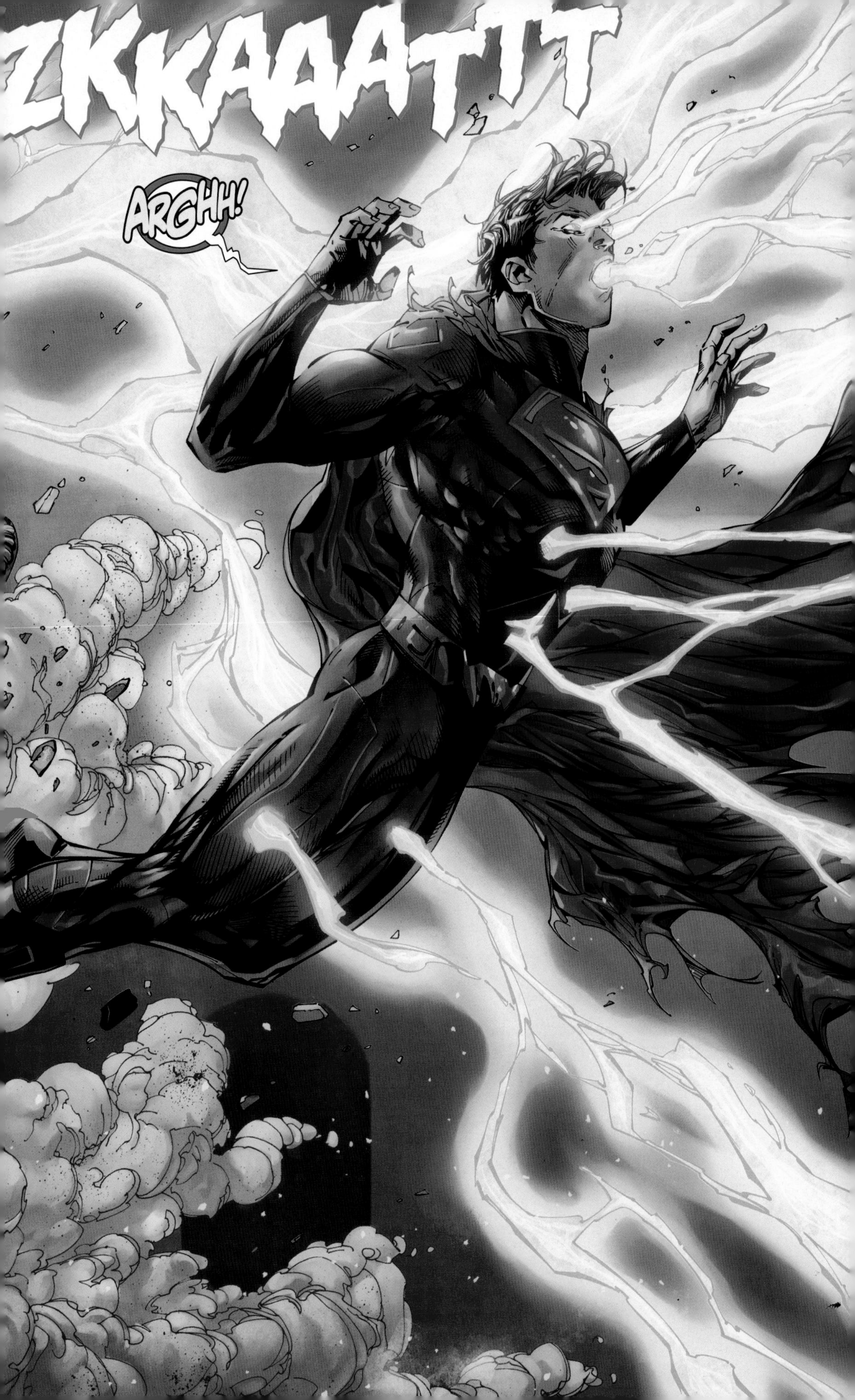
ZKKAAATTT
ARGHH!

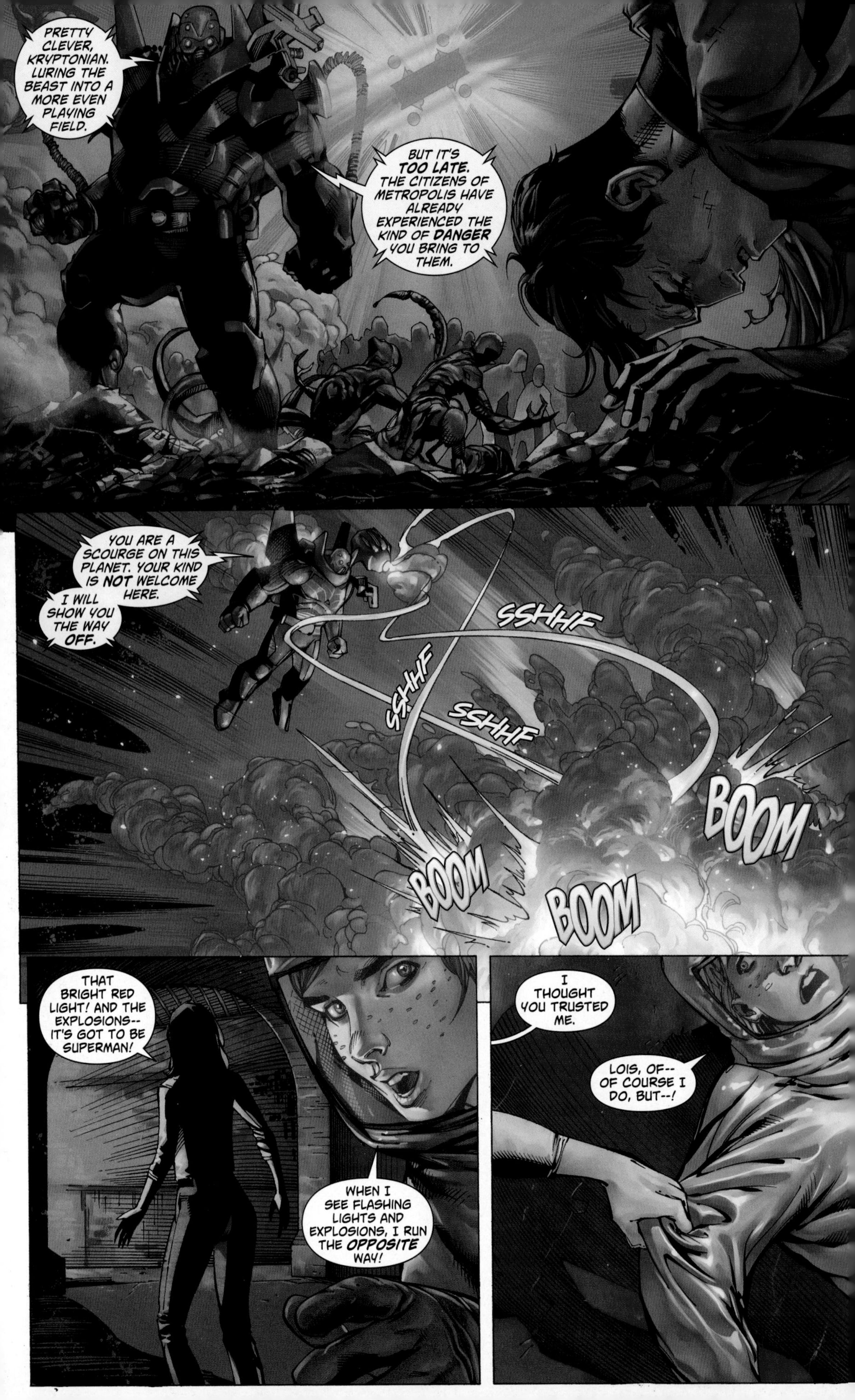
PRETTY CLEVER, KRYPTONIAN. LURING THE BEAST INTO A MORE EVEN PLAYING FIELD.
BUT IT'S TOO LATE. THE CITIZENS OF METROPOLIS HAVE ALREADY EXPERIENCED THE KIND OF DANGER YOU BRING TO THEM.
YOU ARE A SCOURGE ON THIS PLANET. YOUR KIND IS NOT WELCOME HERE.
I WILL SHOW YOU THE WAY OFF.
SSHHF
SSHHF
SSHHF
BOOM
BOOM
BOOM
THAT BRIGHT RED LIGHT! AND THE EXPLOSIONS-- IT'S GOT TO BE SUPERMAN!
WHEN I SEE FLASHING LIGHTS AND EXPLOSIONS, I RUN THE OPPOSITE WAY!
I THOUGHT YOU TRUSTED ME.
LOIS, OF-- OF COURSE I DO, BUT--!

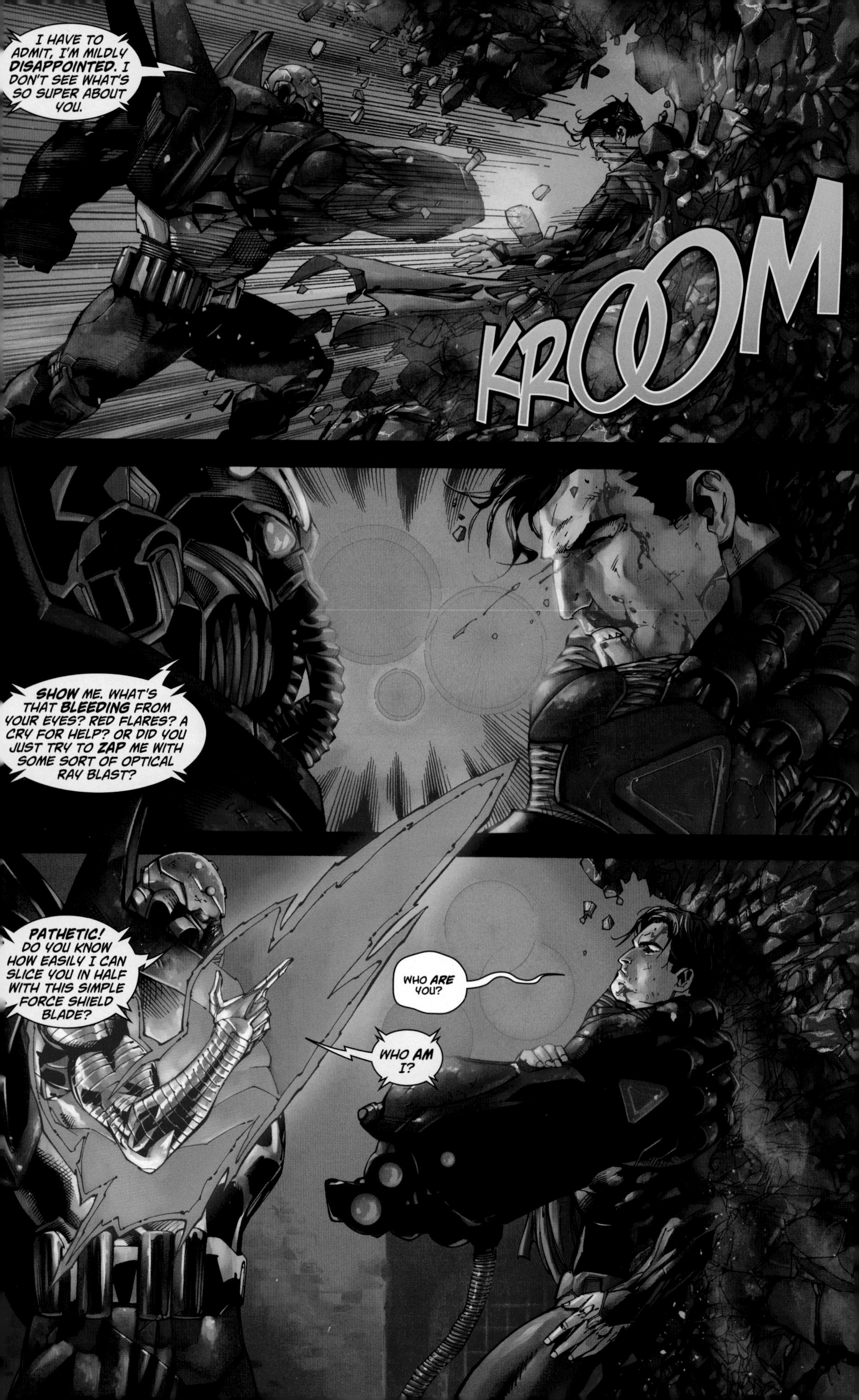
I HAVE TO ADMIT, I'M MILDLY **DISAPPOINTED**. I DON'T SEE WHAT'S SO SUPER ABOUT YOU.
KROOOM
SHOW ME. WHAT'S THAT **BLEEDING** FROM YOUR EYES? RED FLARES? A CRY FOR HELP? OR DID YOU JUST TRY TO **ZAP** ME WITH SOME SORT OF OPTICAL RAY BLAST?
PATHETIC! DO YOU KNOW HOW EASILY I CAN SLICE YOU IN HALF WITH THIS SIMPLE FORCE SHIELD BLADE?
WHO **ARE** YOU?
WHO **AM** I?

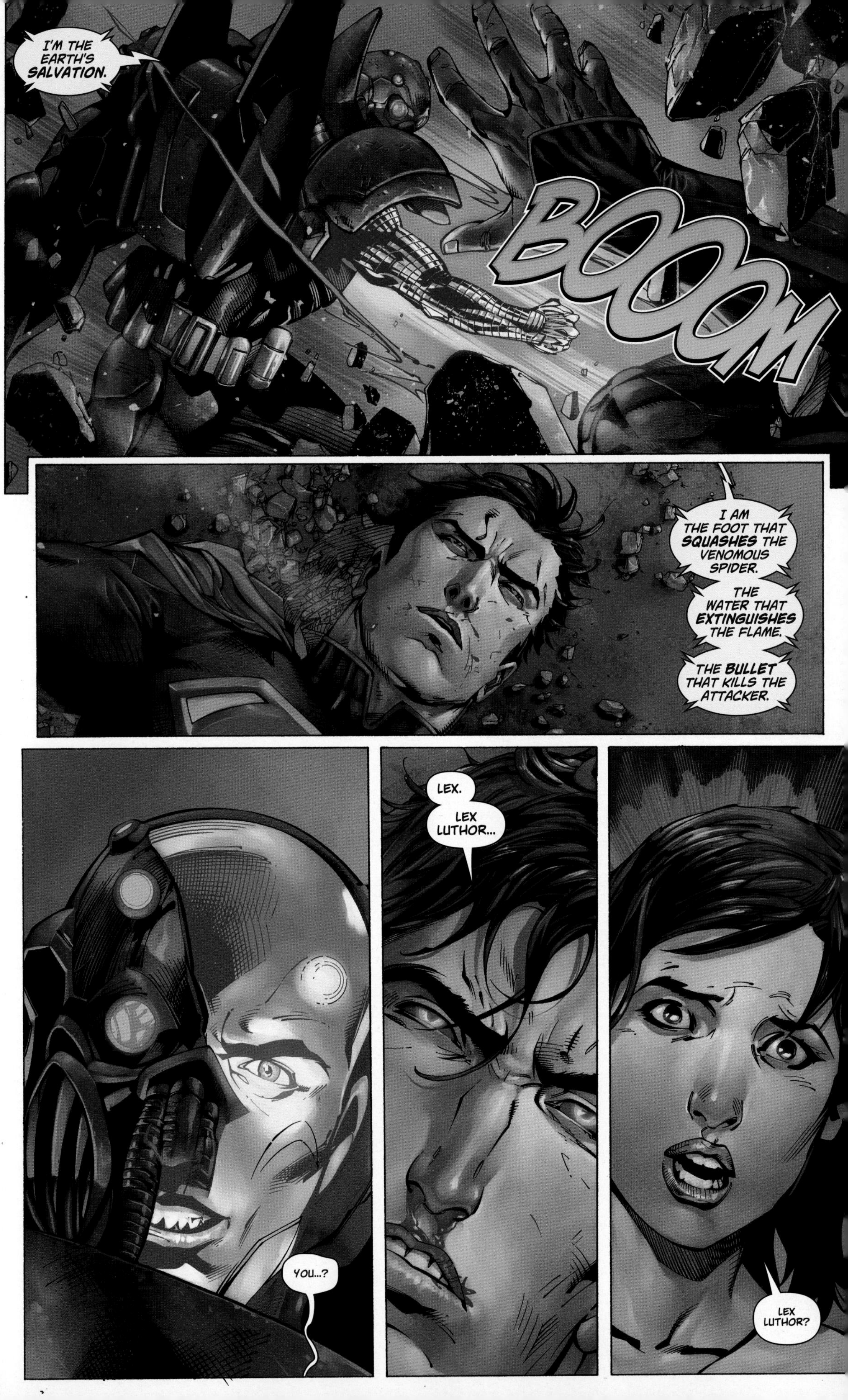
I'M THE EARTH'S SALVATION.
BOOOM
I AM THE FOOT THAT SQUASHES THE VENOMOUS SPIDER.
THE WATER THAT EXTINGUISHES THE FLAME.
THE BULLET THAT KILLS THE ATTACKER.
YOU...?
LEX.
LEX LUTHOR...
LEX LUTHOR?

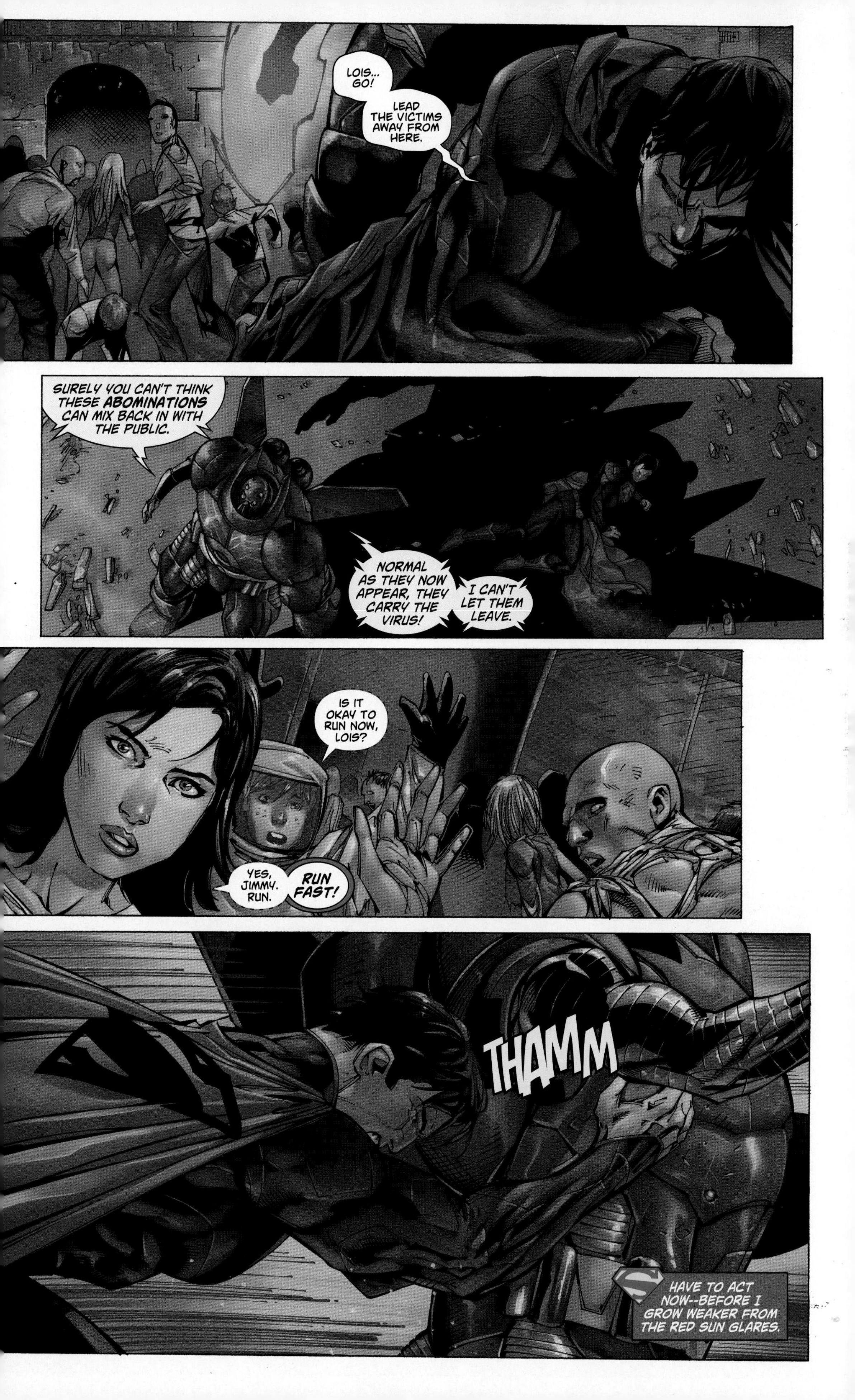
LOIS... GO!
LEAD THE VICTIMS AWAY FROM HERE.
SURELY YOU CAN'T THINK THESE ABOMINATIONS CAN MIX BACK IN WITH THE PUBLIC.
NORMAL AS THEY NOW APPEAR, THEY CARRY THE VIRUS!
I CAN'T LET THEM LEAVE.
IS IT OKAY TO RUN NOW, LOIS?
YES, JIMMY. RUN.
RUN FAST!
THAMM
HAVE TO ACT NOW--BEFORE I GROW WEAKER FROM THE RED SUN GLARES.

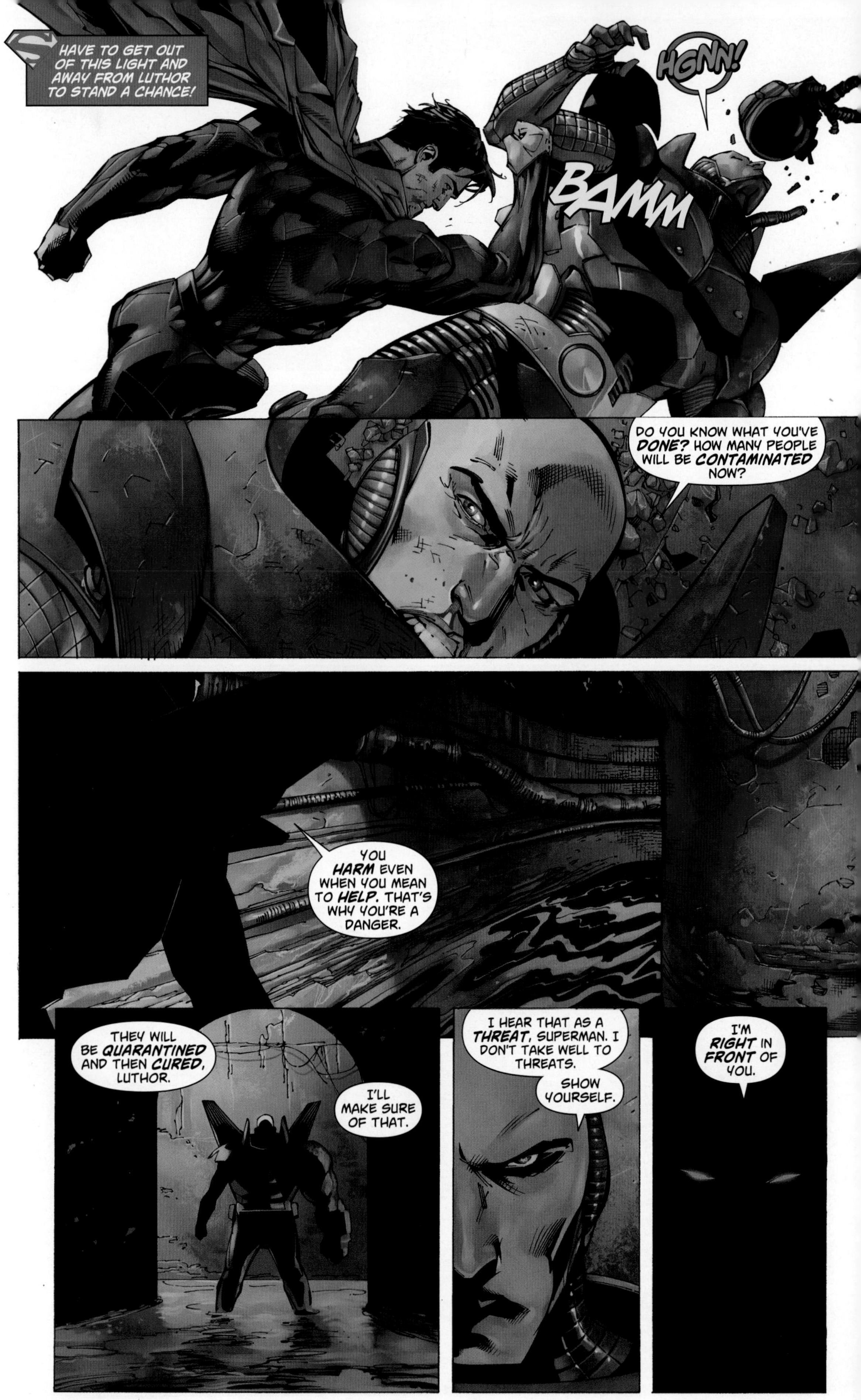
HAVE TO GET OUT OF THIS LIGHT AND AWAY FROM LUTHOR TO STAND A CHANCE!
HGNN!
BAMM
DO YOU KNOW WHAT YOU'VE DONE? HOW MANY PEOPLE WILL BE CONTAMINATED NOW?
YOU HARM EVEN WHEN YOU MEAN TO HELP. THAT'S WHY YOU'RE A DANGER.
THEY WILL BE QUARANTINED AND THEN CURED, LUTHOR.
I'LL MAKE SURE OF THAT.
I HEAR THAT AS A THREAT, SUPERMAN. I DON'T TAKE WELL TO THREATS.
SHOW YOURSELF.
I'M RIGHT IN FRONT OF YOU.

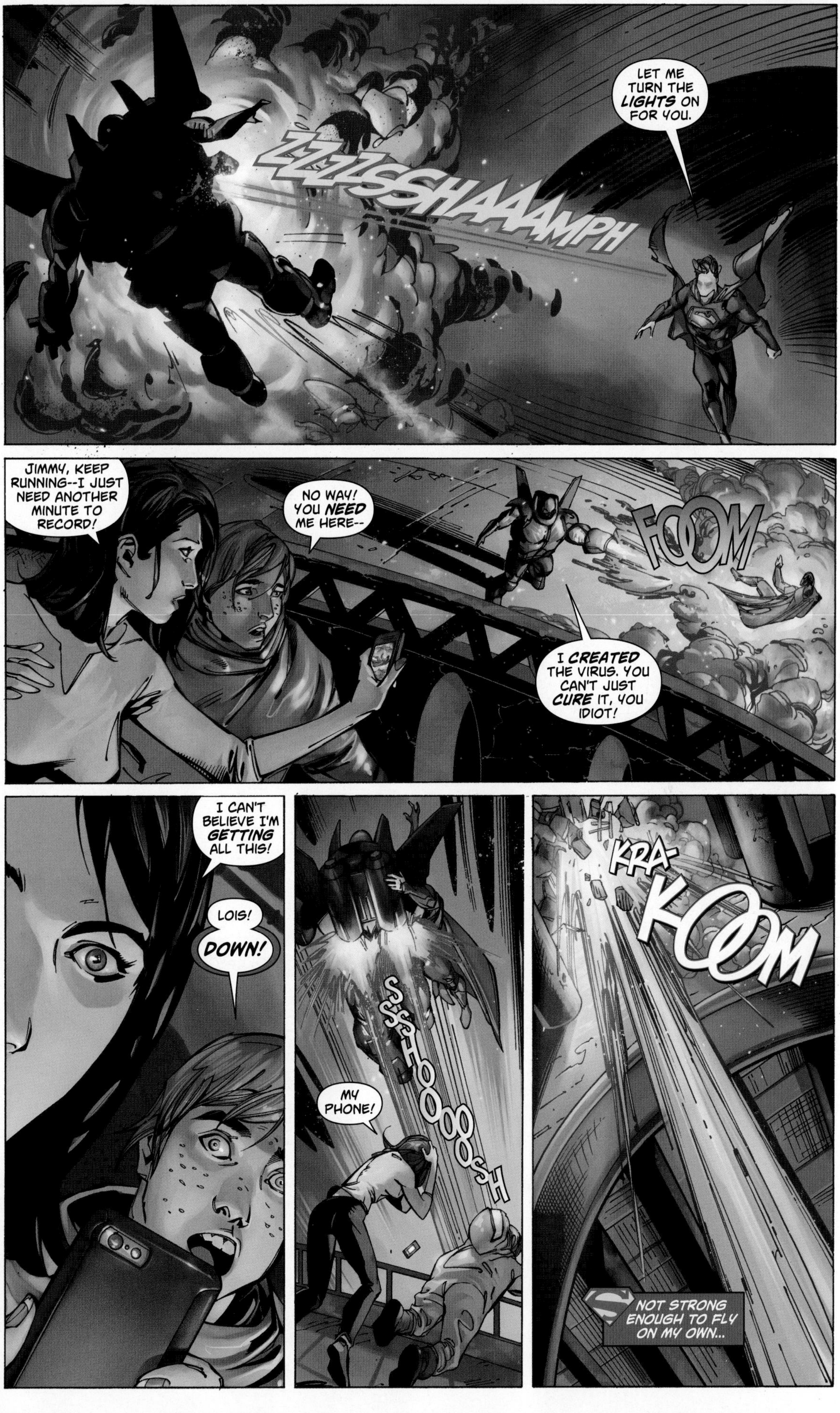
LET ME TURN THE LIGHTS ON FOR YOU.
ZZZSSHAAAMPH
JIMMY, KEEP RUNNING--I JUST NEED ANOTHER MINUTE TO RECORD!
NO WAY! YOU NEED ME HERE--
FOOM
I CREATED THE VIRUS. YOU CAN'T JUST CURE IT, YOU IDIOT!
I CAN'T BELIEVE I'M GETTING ALL THIS!
LOIS!
DOWN!
SSSHOOOOOSH
MY PHONE!
KRA-KOOM
NOT STRONG ENOUGH TO FLY ON MY OWN...

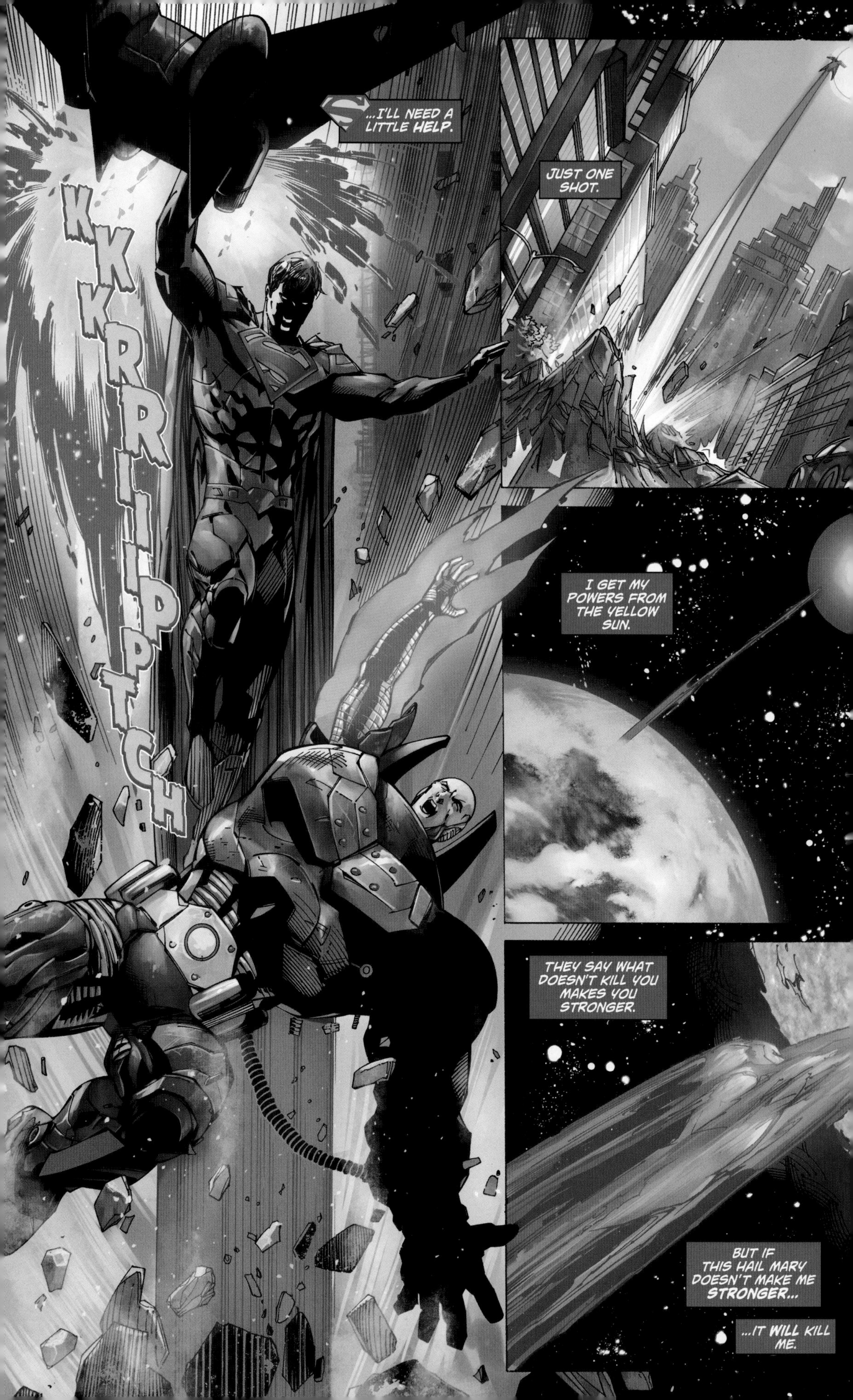
...I'LL NEED A LITTLE HELP.
KKKRRRIIIPPTCH
JUST ONE SHOT.
I GET MY POWERS FROM THE YELLOW SUN.
THEY SAY WHAT DOESN'T KILL YOU MAKES YOU STRONGER.
BUT IF THIS HAIL MARY DOESN'T MAKE ME STRONGER...
...IT WILL KILL ME.

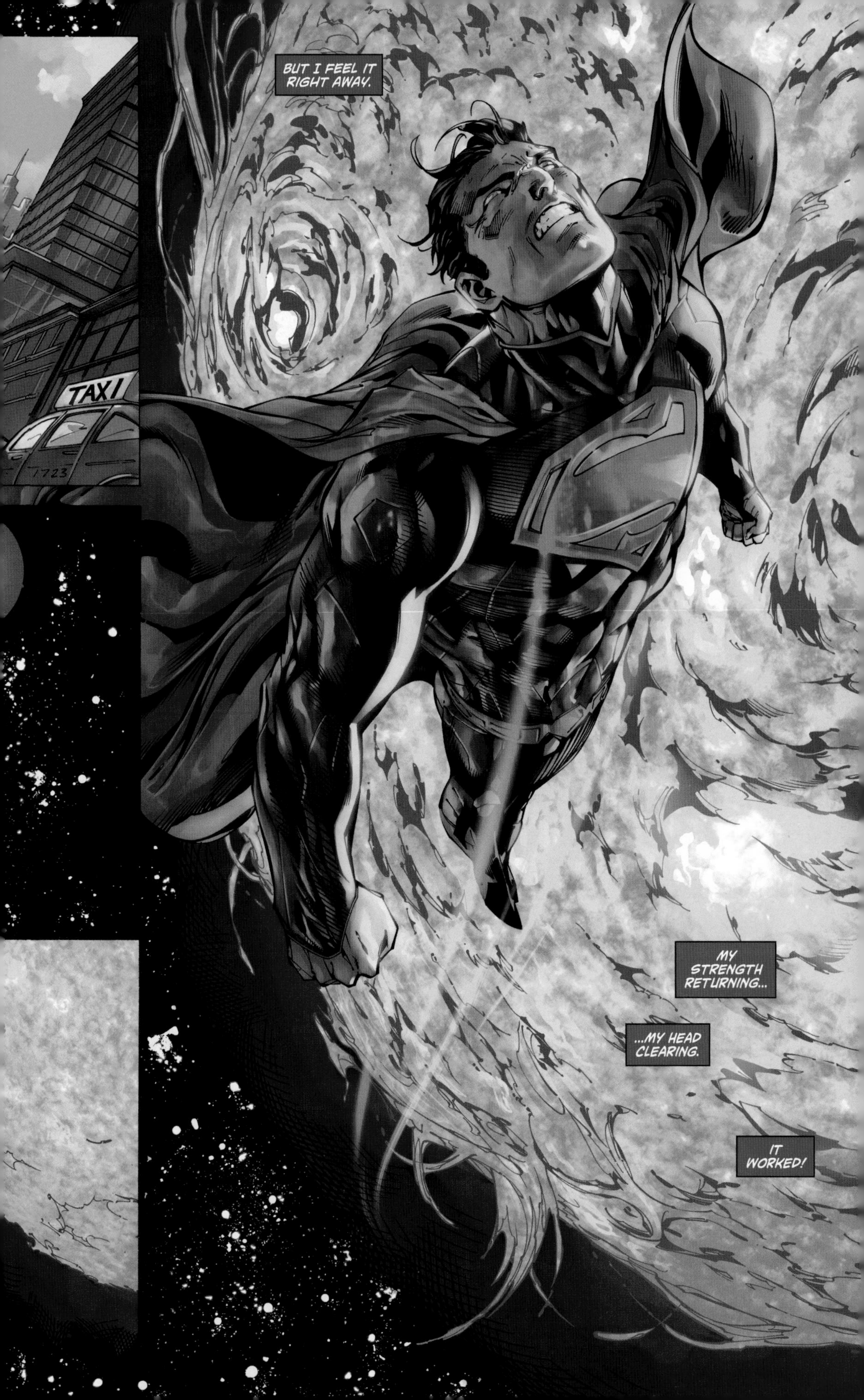
BUT I FEEL IT RIGHT AWAY.
TAXI
1723
MY STRENGTH RETURNING...
...MY HEAD CLEARING.
IT WORKED!

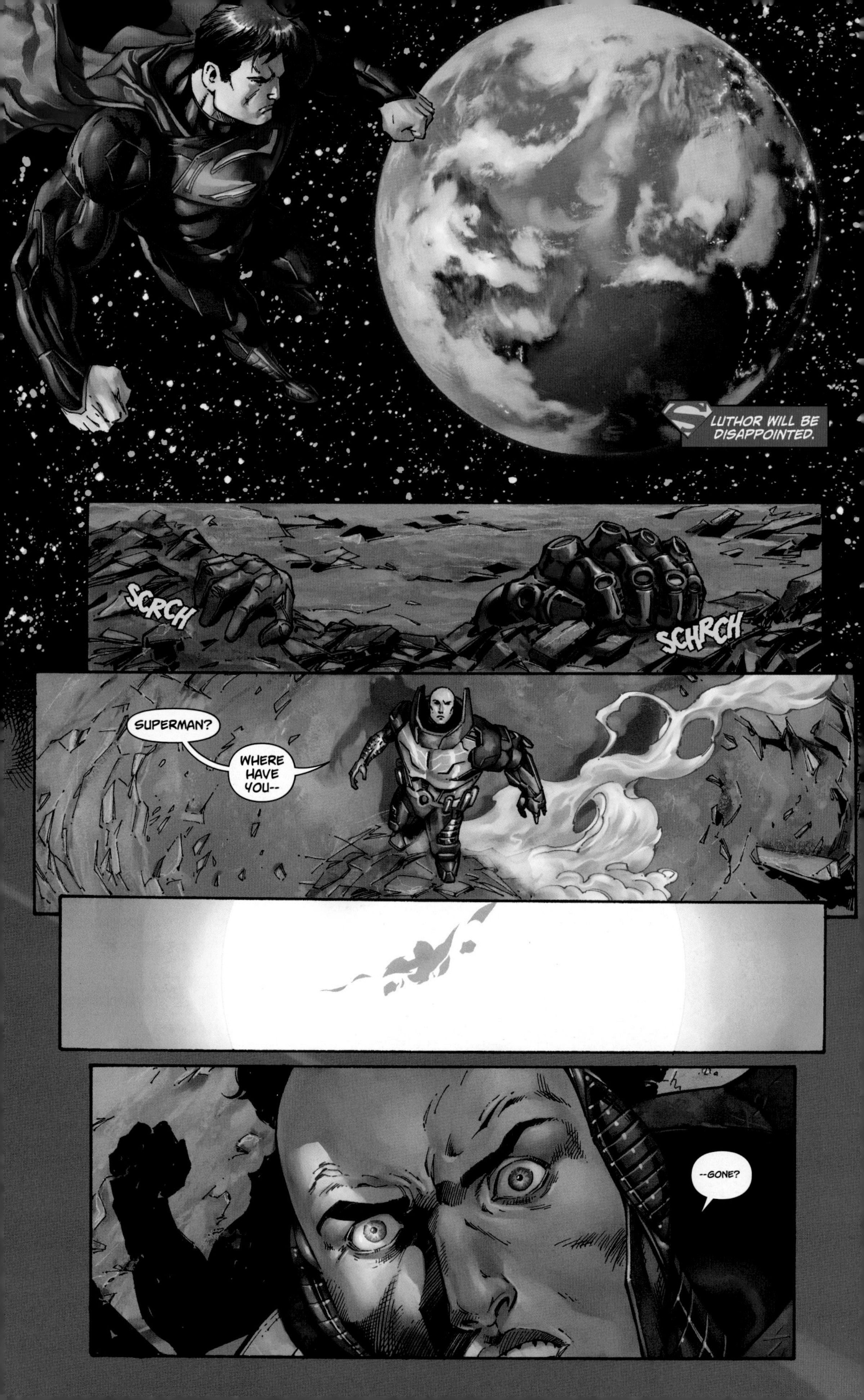
LUTHOR WILL BE DISAPPOINTED.
SCRCH
SCHRCH
SUPERMAN?
WHERE HAVE YOU--
--GONE?

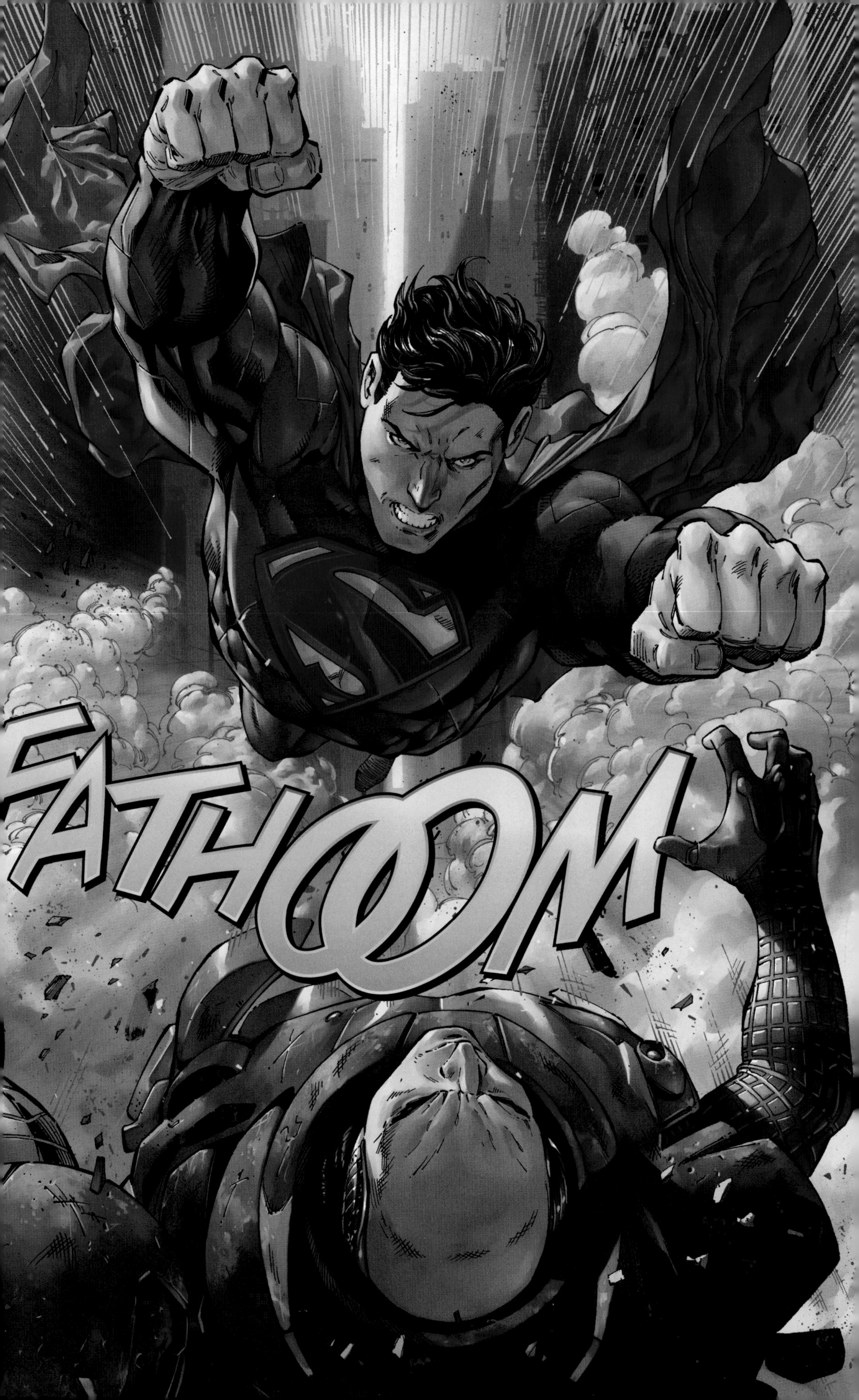
FATHOOM

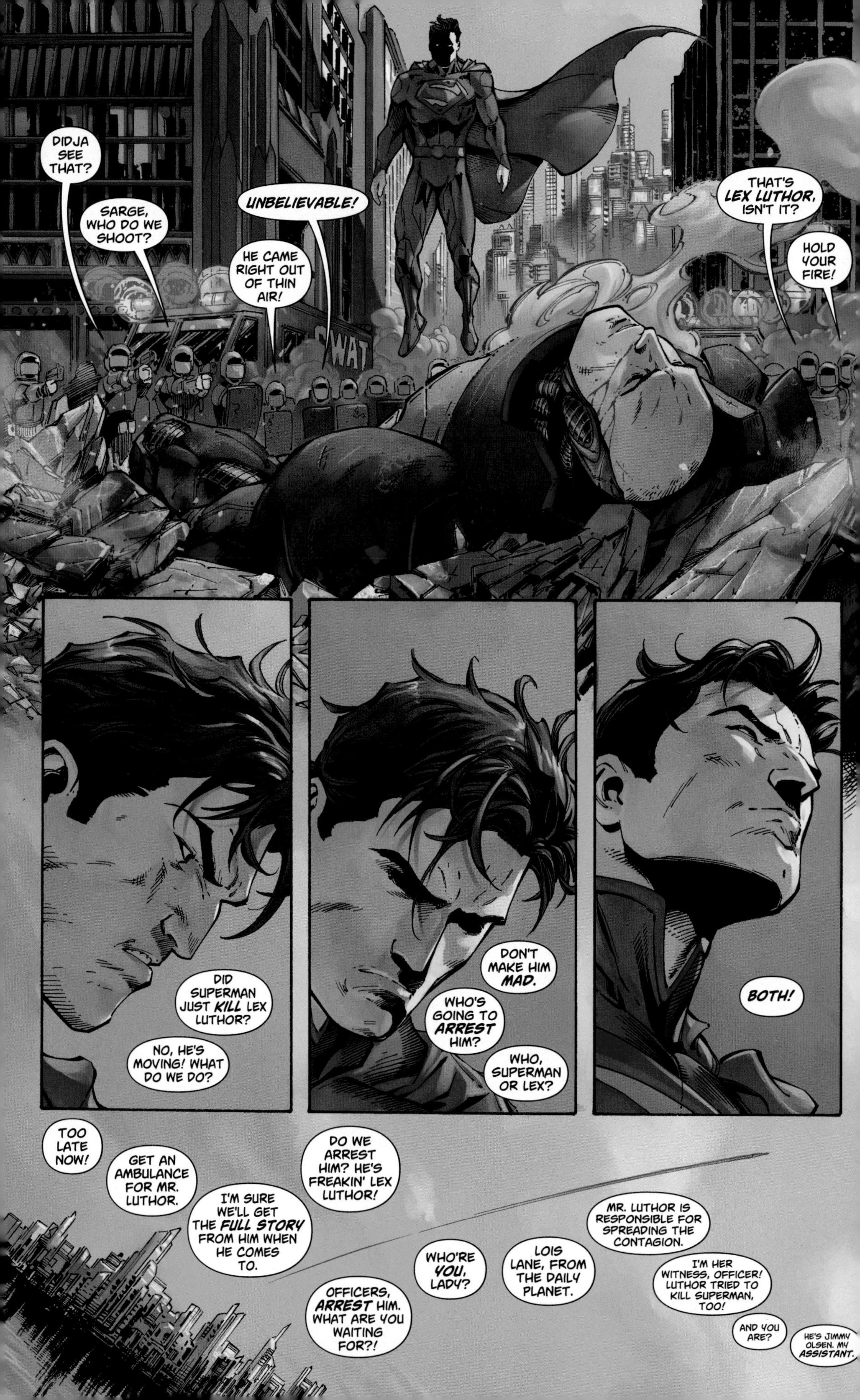
DIDJA SEE THAT?
SARGE, WHO DO WE SHOOT?
UNBELIEVABLE!
HE CAME RIGHT OUT OF THIN AIR!
THAT'S LEX LUTHOR, ISN'T IT?
HOLD YOUR FIRE!
DID SUPERMAN JUST KILL LEX LUTHOR?
NO, HE'S MOVING! WHAT DO WE DO?
DON'T MAKE HIM MAD.
WHO'S GOING TO ARREST HIM?
WHO, SUPERMAN OR LEX?
BOTH!
TOO LATE NOW!
GET AN AMBULANCE FOR MR. LUTHOR.
I'M SURE WE'LL GET THE FULL STORY FROM HIM WHEN HE COMES TO.
DO WE ARREST HIM? HE'S FREAKIN' LEX LUTHOR!
OFFICERS, ARREST HIM. WHAT ARE YOU WAITING FOR?!
WHO'RE YOU, LADY?
LOIS LANE, FROM THE DAILY PLANET.
MR. LUTHOR IS RESPONSIBLE FOR SPREADING THE CONTAGION.
I'M HER WITNESS, OFFICER! LUTHOR TRIED TO KILL SUPERMAN, TOO!
AND YOU ARE?
HE'S JIMMY OLSEN. MY ASSISTANT.

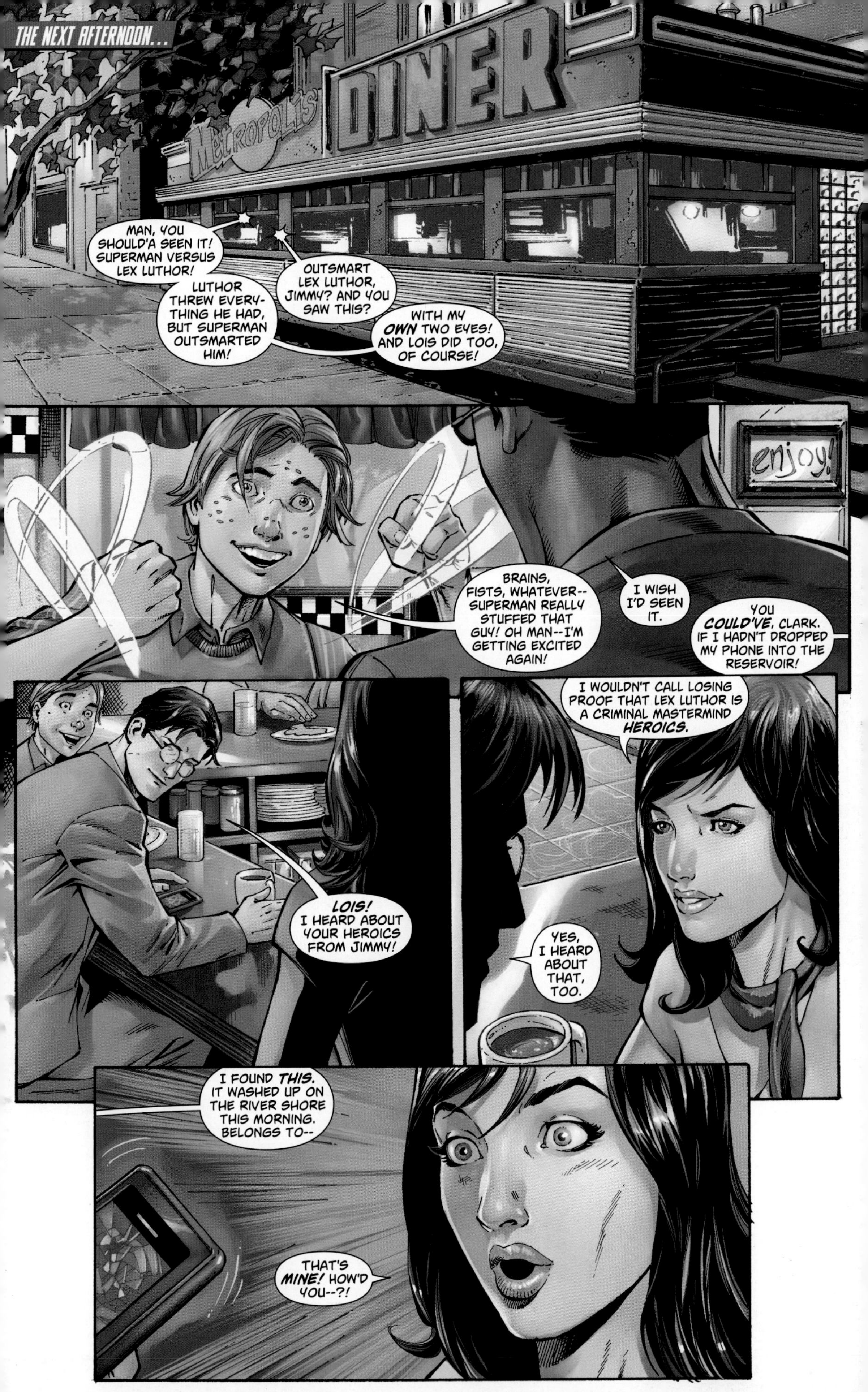
THE NEXT AFTERNOON...
METROPOLIS DINER
MAN, YOU SHOULD'A SEEN IT! SUPERMAN VERSUS LEX LUTHOR!
LUTHOR THREW EVERY-THING HE HAD, BUT SUPERMAN OUTSMARTED HIM!
OUTSMART LEX LUTHOR, JIMMY? AND YOU SAW THIS?
WITH MY OWN TWO EYES! AND LOIS DID TOO, OF COURSE!
enjoy!
BRAINS, FISTS, WHATEVER-- SUPERMAN REALLY STUFFED THAT GUY! OH MAN--I'M GETTING EXCITED AGAIN!
I WISH I'D SEEN IT.
YOU COULD'VE, CLARK. IF I HADN'T DROPPED MY PHONE INTO THE RESERVOIR!
LOIS! I HEARD ABOUT YOUR HEROICS FROM JIMMY!
I WOULDN'T CALL LOSING PROOF THAT LEX LUTHOR IS A CRIMINAL MASTERMIND HEROICS.
YES, I HEARD ABOUT THAT, TOO.
I FOUND THIS. IT WASHED UP ON THE RIVER SHORE THIS MORNING. BELONGS TO--
THAT'S MINE! HOW'D YOU--?!

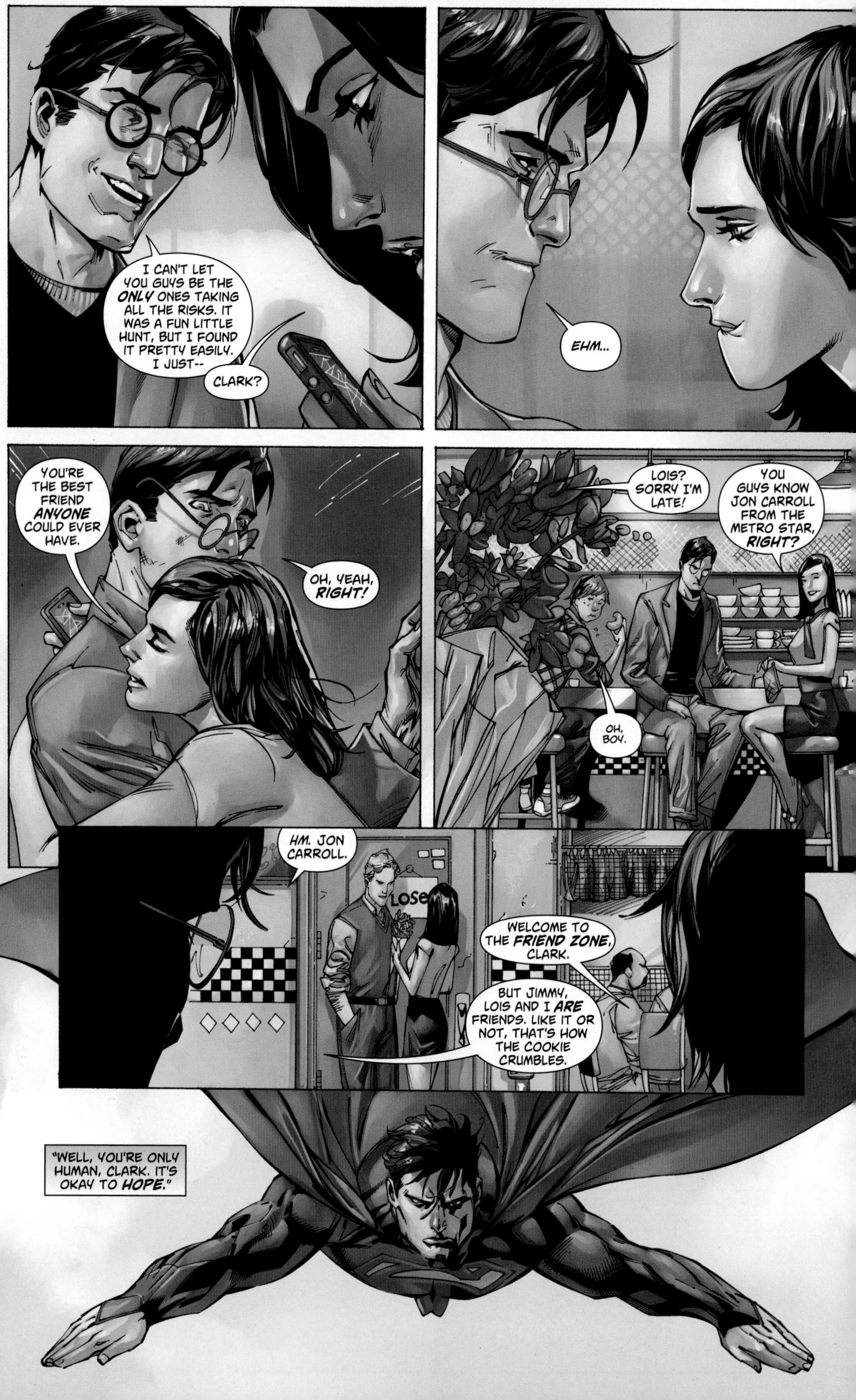
I CAN'T LET YOU GUYS BE THE ONLY ONES TAKING ALL THE RISKS. IT WAS A FUN LITTLE HUNT, BUT I FOUND IT PRETTY EASILY. I JUST--
CLARK?
EHM...
YOU'RE THE BEST FRIEND ANYONE COULD EVER HAVE.
OH, YEAH, RIGHT!
LOIS? SORRY I'M LATE!
YOU GUYS KNOW JON CARROLL FROM THE METRO STAR, RIGHT?
OH, BOY.
HM. JON CARROLL.
LOSE
WELCOME TO THE FRIEND ZONE, CLARK.
BUT JIMMY, LOIS AND I ARE FRIENDS. LIKE IT OR NOT, THAT'S HOW THE COOKIE CRUMBLES.
"WELL, YOU'RE ONLY HUMAN, CLARK. IT'S OKAY TO HOPE."

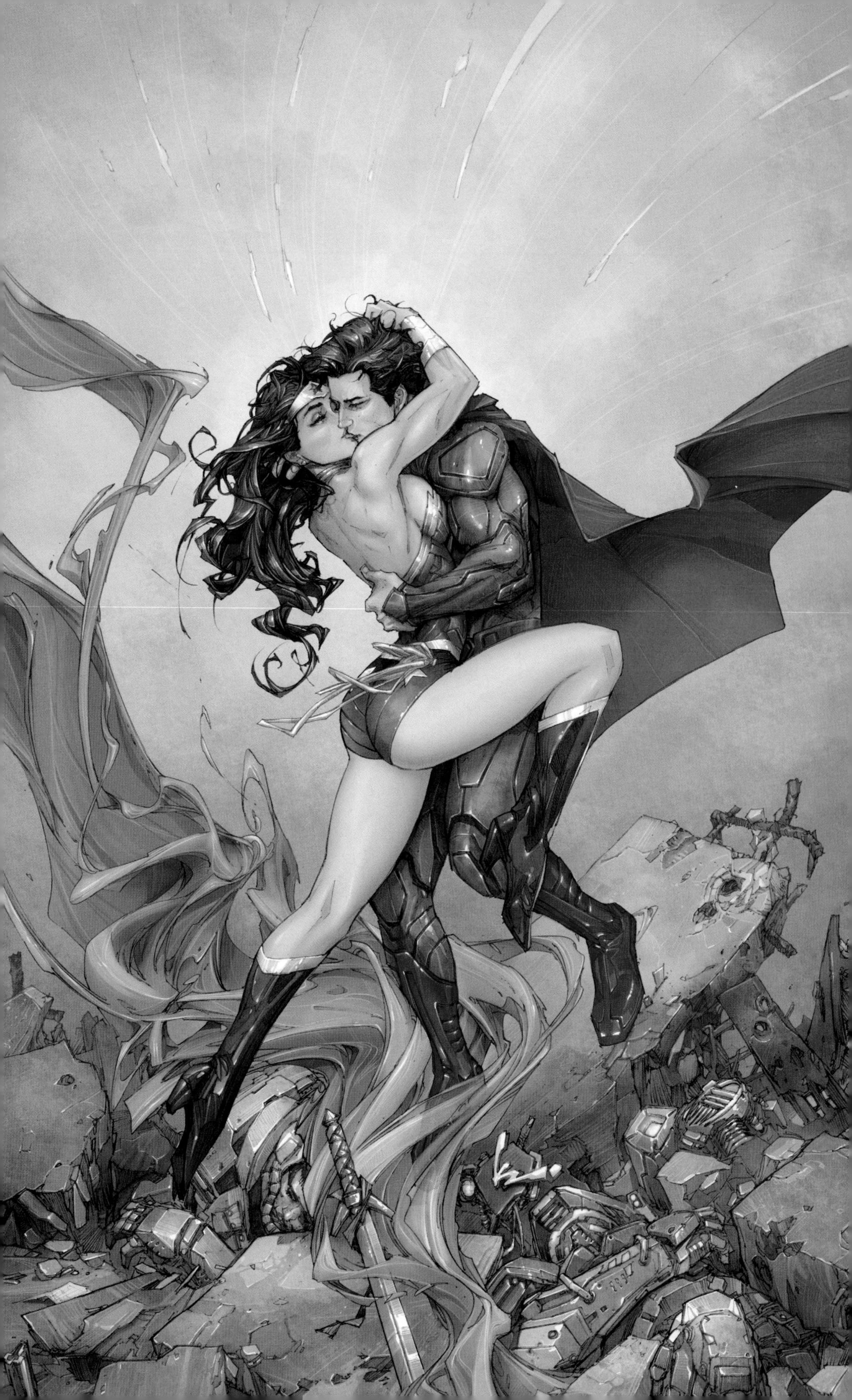

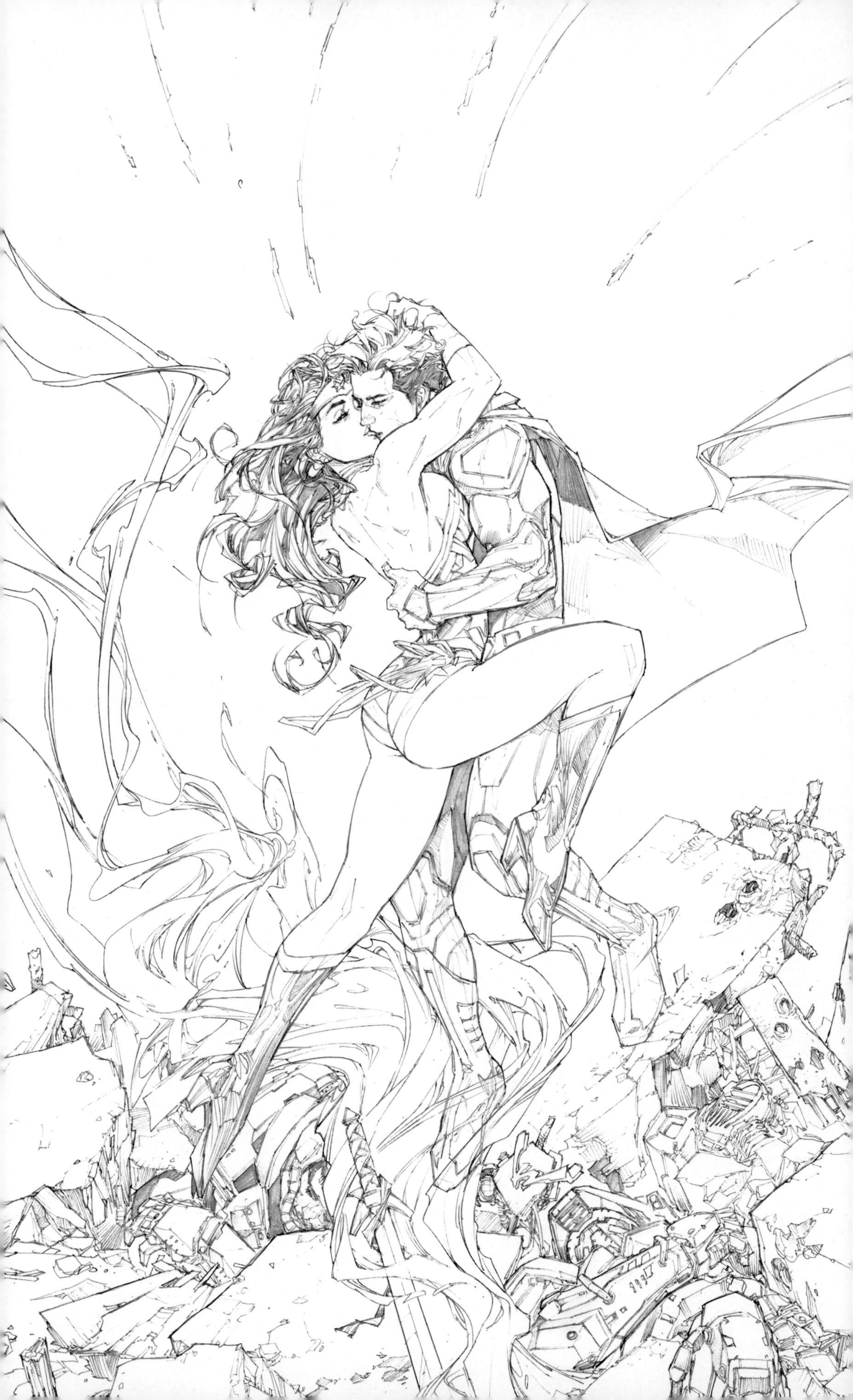

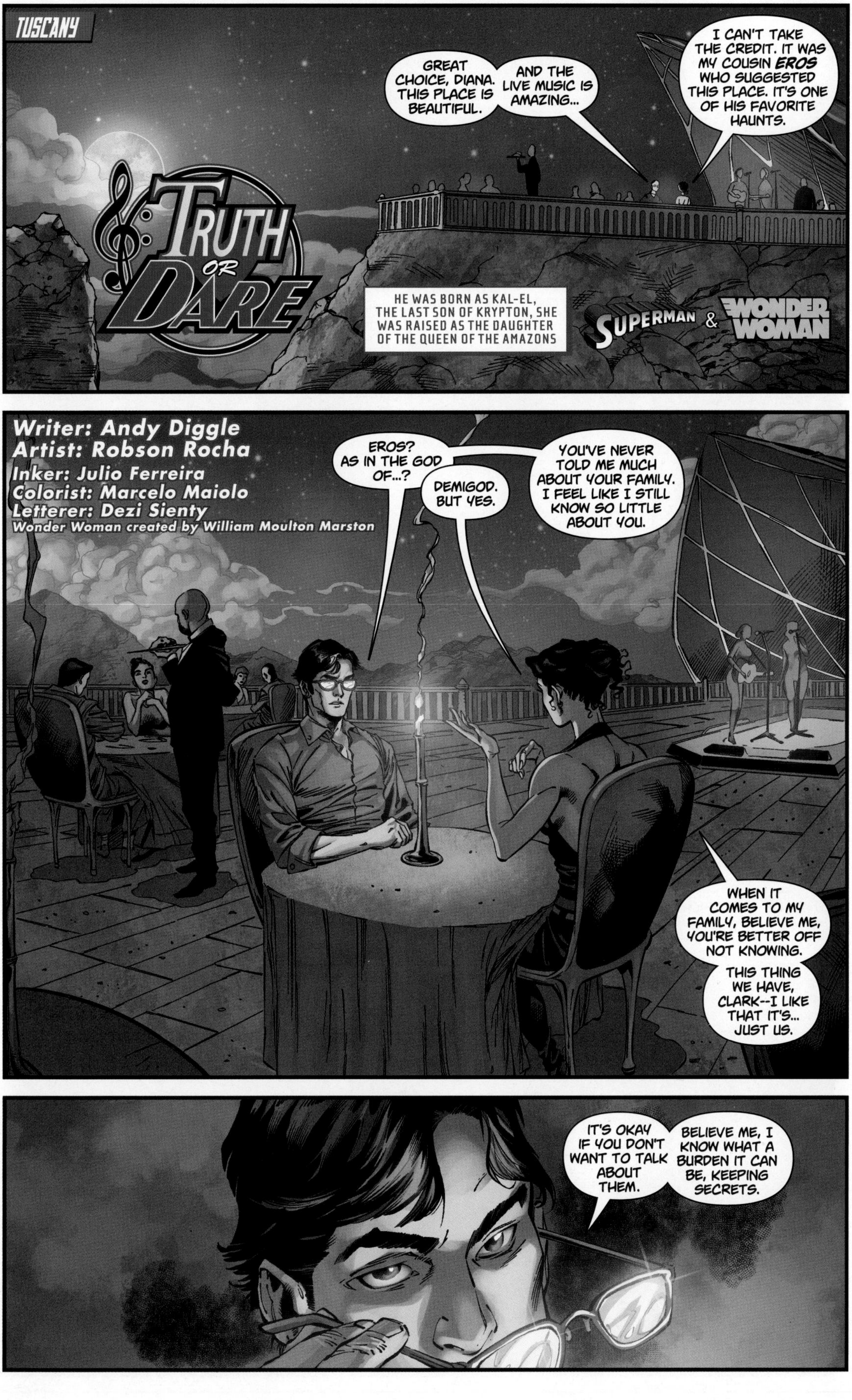

TUSCANY
GREAT CHOICE, DIANA. THIS PLACE IS BEAUTIFUL.
AND THE LIVE MUSIC IS AMAZING...
I CAN'T TAKE THE CREDIT. IT WAS MY COUSIN EROS WHO SUGGESTED THIS PLACE. IT'S ONE OF HIS FAVORITE HAUNTS.
TRUTH OR DARE
HE WAS BORN AS KAL-EL, THE LAST SON OF KRYPTON, SHE WAS RAISED AS THE DAUGHTER OF THE QUEEN OF THE AMAZONS
SUPERMAN & WONDER WOMAN
Writer: Andy Diggle
Artist: Robson Rocha
Inker: Julio Ferreira
Colorist: Marcelo Maiolo
Letterer: Dezi Sienty
Wonder Woman created by William Moulton Marston
EROS? AS IN THE GOD OF...?
DEMIGOD. BUT YES.
YOU'VE NEVER TOLD ME MUCH ABOUT YOUR FAMILY. I FEEL LIKE I STILL KNOW SO LITTLE ABOUT YOU.
WHEN IT COMES TO MY FAMILY, BELIEVE ME, YOU'RE BETTER OFF NOT KNOWING.
THIS THING WE HAVE, CLARK--I LIKE THAT IT'S... JUST US.
IT'S OKAY IF YOU DON'T WANT TO TALK ABOUT THEM.
BELIEVE ME, I KNOW WHAT A BURDEN IT CAN BE, KEEPING SECRETS.

IS THAT SO? ARE YOU SAYING YOU HAVEN'T BEEN COMPLETELY HONEST WITH ME?! BECAUSE I HAVE A *LASSO* THAT CAN CURE YOU OF THAT...

NO, IT'S JUST... ALL MY LIFE, I'VE PRETENDED TO BE SOMEBODY ELSE. FIGHTING FOR TRUTH-- WHILE HIDING THE TRUTH ABOUT MYSELF FROM EVERYONE I'M *CLOSEST* TO...

FOR THEIR OWN PROTECTION! THAT'S NOT HYPOCRISY. THAT'S HEROISM.

I DON'T KNOW. ALL I KNOW IS THAT WHEN I'M WITH YOU, I DON'T HAVE TO WORRY ABOUT ANY OF THAT.

I CAN JUST BE...*ME*.

YOU SEEM SO SURE OF YOUR PLACE IN THE WORLD, WHILE I'M STILL TRYING TO FIND MY OWN.

MY MOTHER GAVE ME A WEAPON OF *TRUTH*. THINGS COULD HAVE BEEN SO DIFFERENT, IF ONLY...

MY WHOLE *LIFE* PROVED TO BE A LIE.

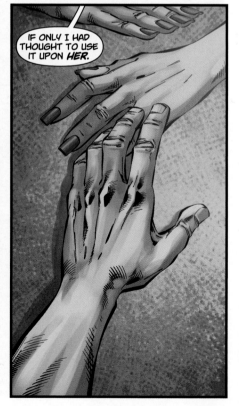

IF ONLY I HAD THOUGHT TO USE IT UPON *HER*.

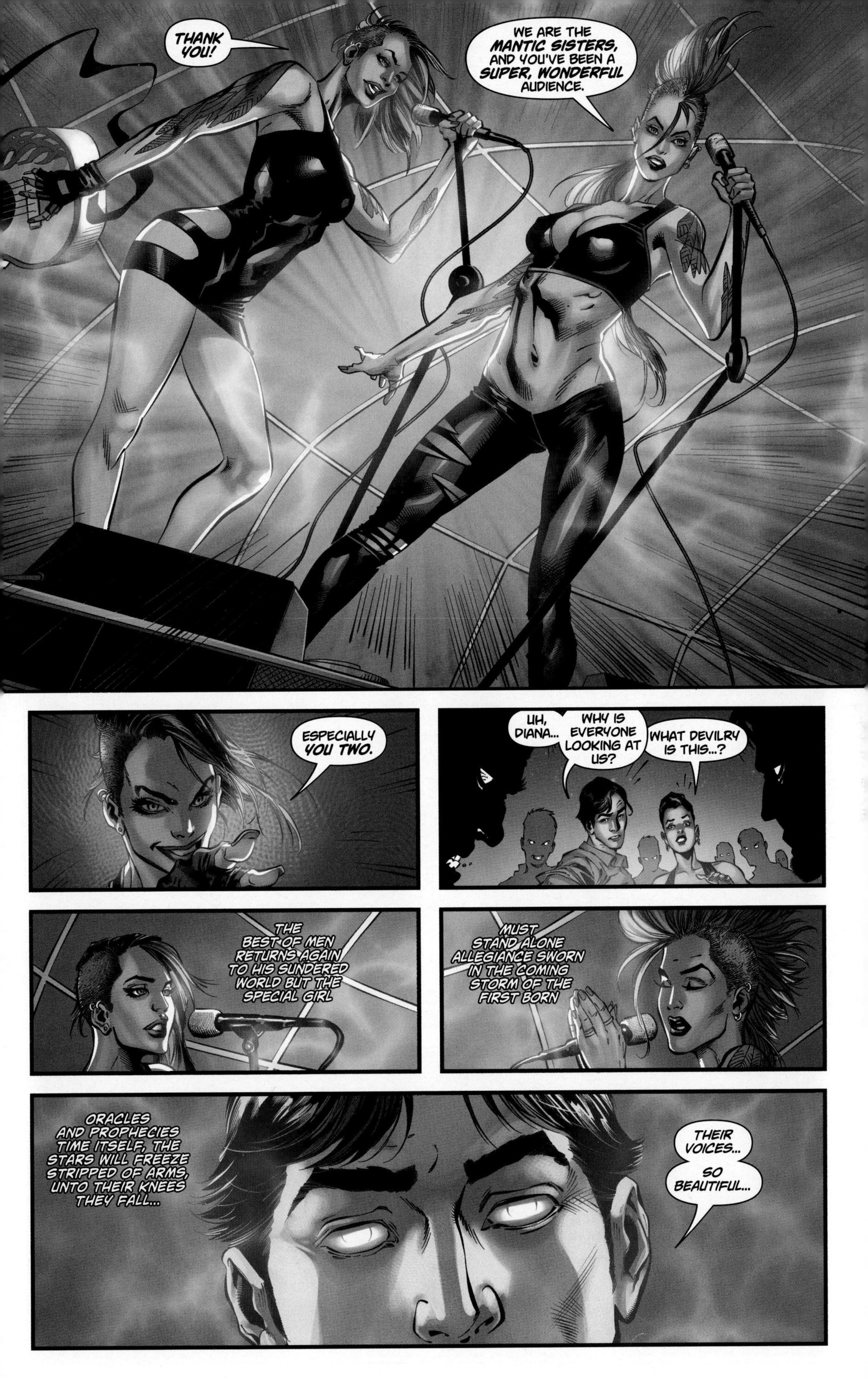
THANK YOU!
WE ARE THE MANTIC SISTERS, AND YOU'VE BEEN A SUPER, WONDERFUL AUDIENCE.
ESPECIALLY YOU TWO.
UH, DIANA...
WHY IS EVERYONE LOOKING AT US?
WHAT DEVILRY IS THIS...?
THE BEST OF MEN RETURNS AGAIN TO HIS SUNDERED WORLD BUT THE SPECIAL GIRL
MUST STAND ALONE ALLEGIANCE SWORN IN THE COMING STORM OF THE FIRST BORN
ORACLES AND PROPHECIES TIME ITSELF, THE STARS WILL FREEZE STRIPPED OF ARMS, UNTO THEIR KNEES THEY FALL...
THEIR VOICES...
SO BEAUTIFUL...

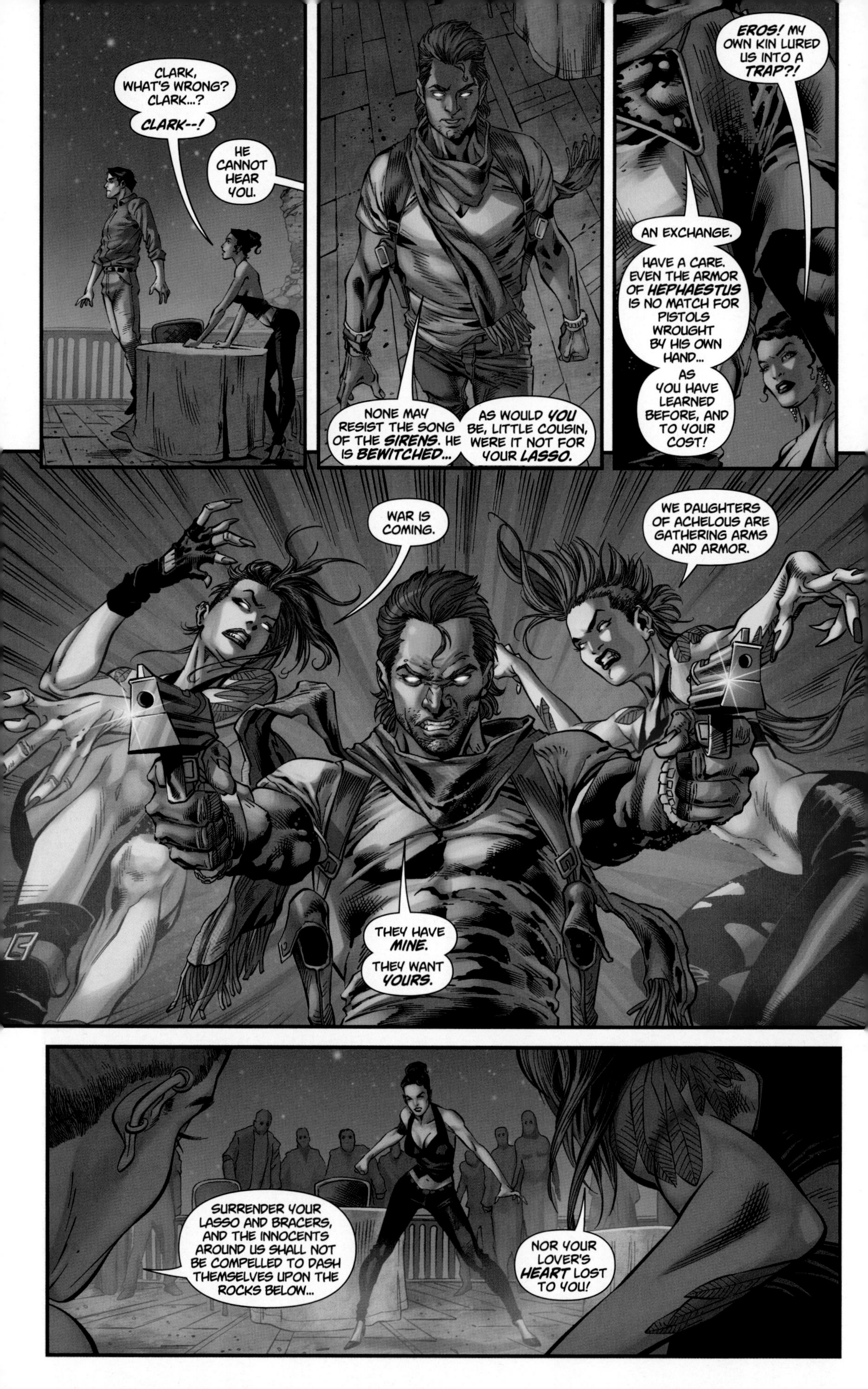
CLARK, WHAT'S WRONG? CLARK...? CLARK--!
HE CANNOT HEAR YOU.
NONE MAY RESIST THE SONG OF THE SIRENS. HE IS BEWITCHED...
AS WOULD YOU BE, LITTLE COUSIN, WERE IT NOT FOR YOUR LASSO.
EROS! MY OWN KIN LURED US INTO A TRAP?!
AN EXCHANGE.
HAVE A CARE. EVEN THE ARMOR OF HEPHAESTUS IS NO MATCH FOR PISTOLS WROUGHT BY HIS OWN HAND...
AS YOU HAVE LEARNED BEFORE, AND TO YOUR COST!
WAR IS COMING.
WE DAUGHTERS OF ACHELOUS ARE GATHERING ARMS AND ARMOR.
THEY HAVE MINE.
THEY WANT YOURS.
SURRENDER YOUR LASSO AND BRACERS, AND THE INNOCENTS AROUND US SHALL NOT BE COMPELLED TO DASH THEMSELVES UPON THE ROCKS BELOW...
NOR YOUR LOVER'S HEART LOST TO YOU!

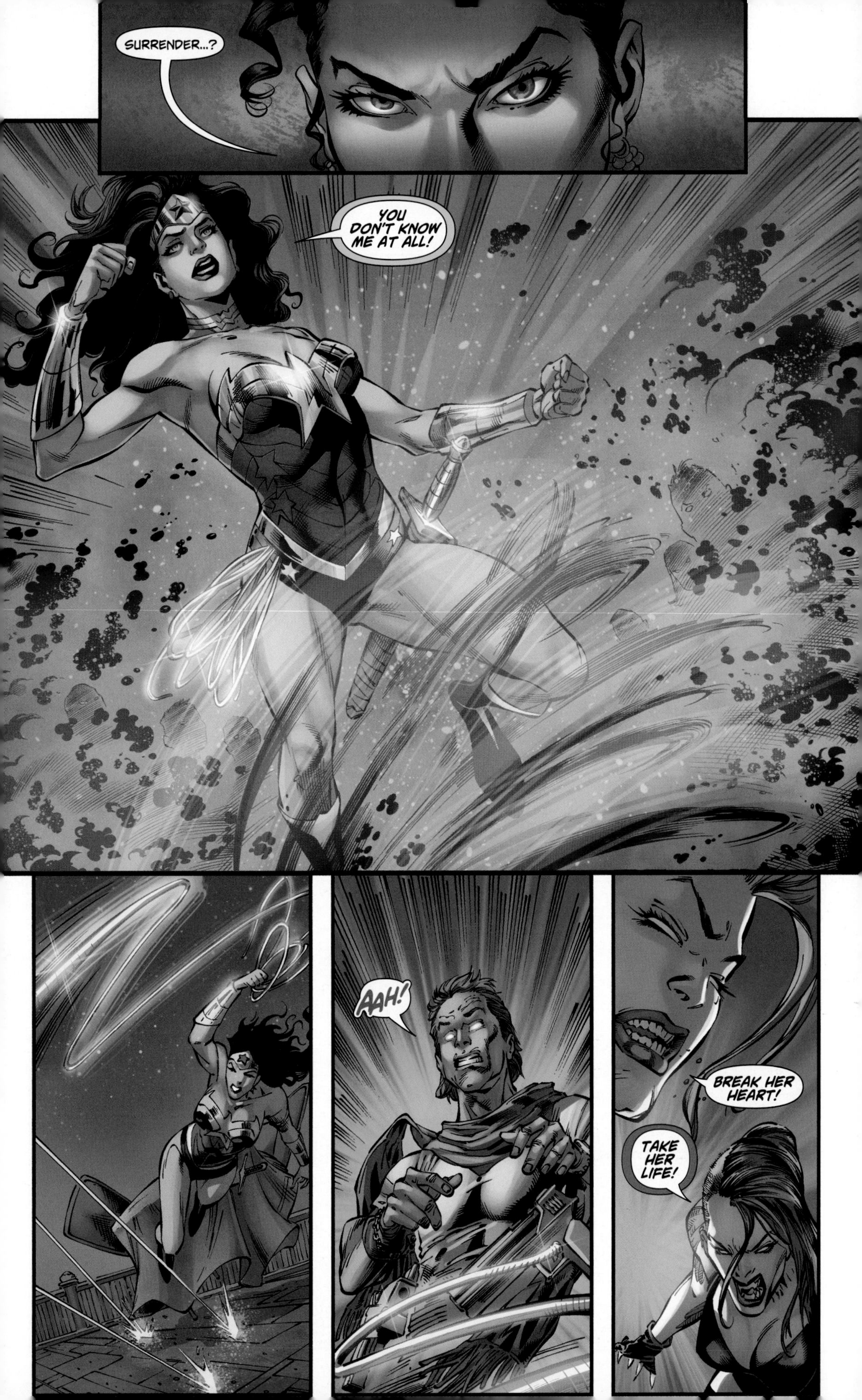
SURRENDER...?
YOU DON'T KNOW ME AT ALL!
AAH!
BREAK HER HEART!
TAKE HER LIFE!

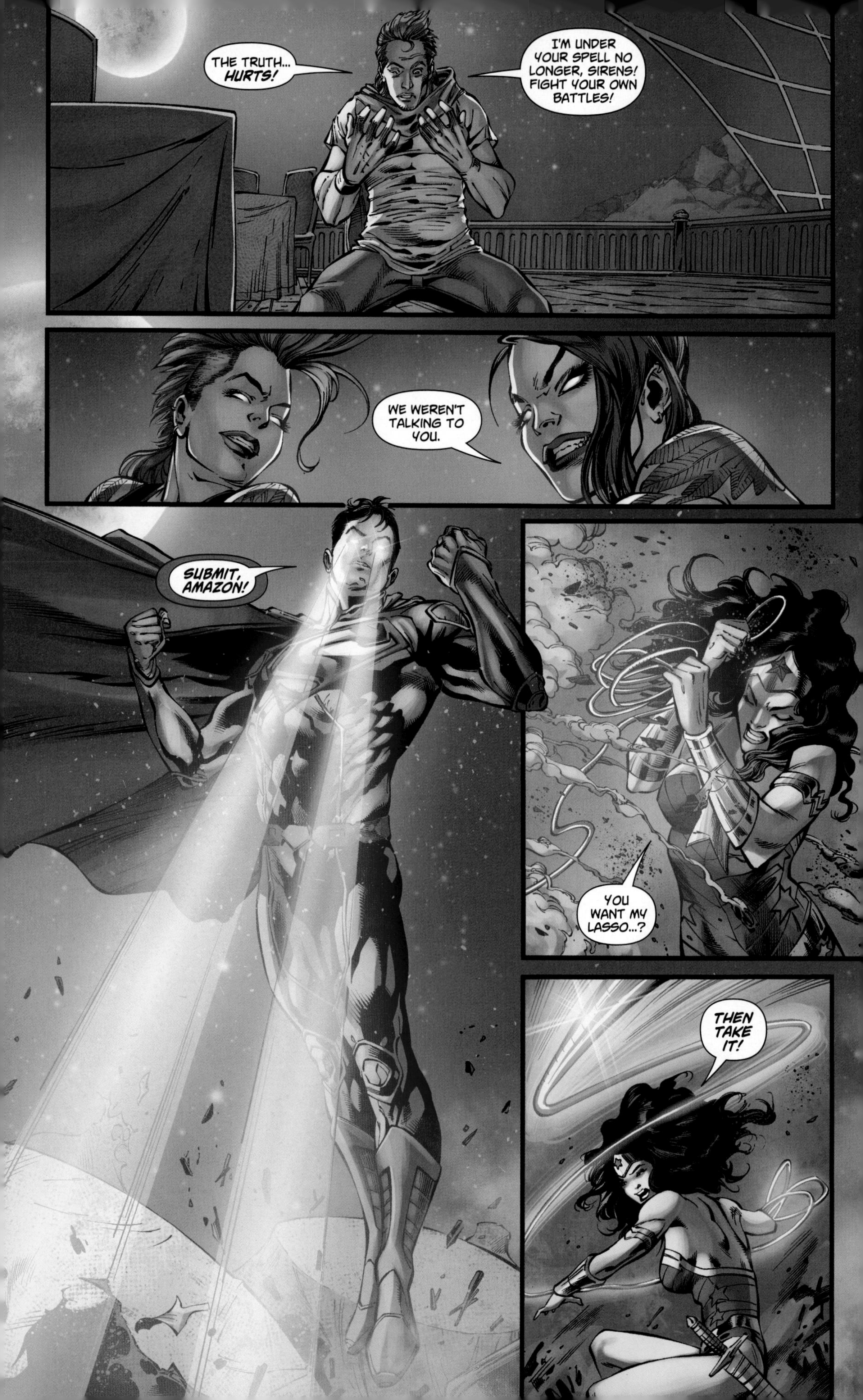
THE TRUTH... HURTS!
I'M UNDER YOUR SPELL NO LONGER, SIRENS! FIGHT YOUR OWN BATTLES!
WE WEREN'T TALKING TO YOU.
SUBMIT, AMAZON!
YOU WANT MY LASSO...?
THEN TAKE IT!

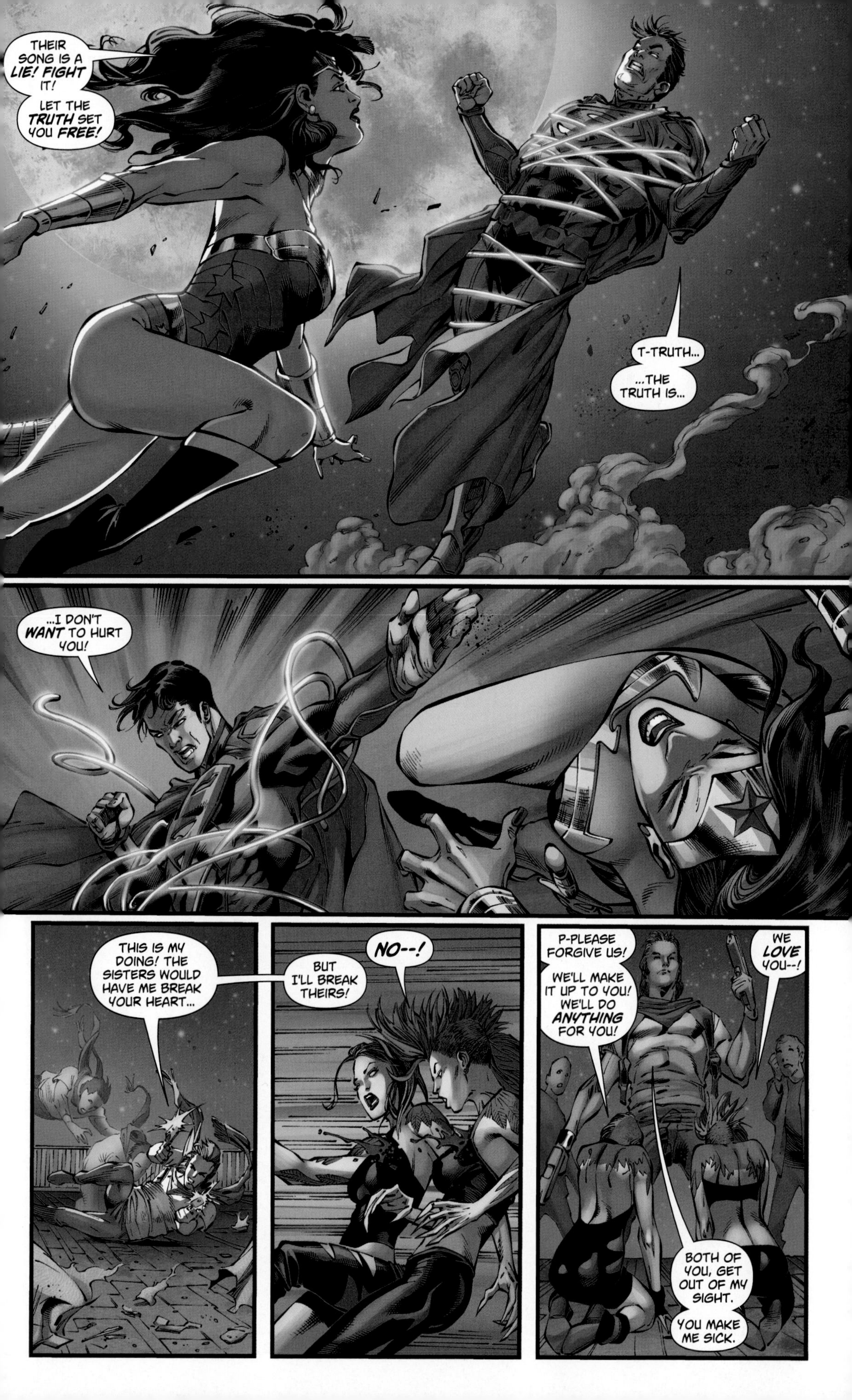
THEIR SONG IS A LIE! FIGHT IT!
LET THE TRUTH SET YOU FREE!
T-TRUTH...
...THE TRUTH IS...
...I DON'T WANT TO HURT YOU!
THIS IS MY DOING! THE SISTERS WOULD HAVE ME BREAK YOUR HEART...
BUT I'LL BREAK THEIRS!
NO--!
P-PLEASE FORGIVE US!
WE'LL MAKE IT UP TO YOU! WE'LL DO ANYTHING FOR YOU!
WE LOVE YOU--!
BOTH OF YOU, GET OUT OF MY SIGHT.
YOU MAKE ME SICK.

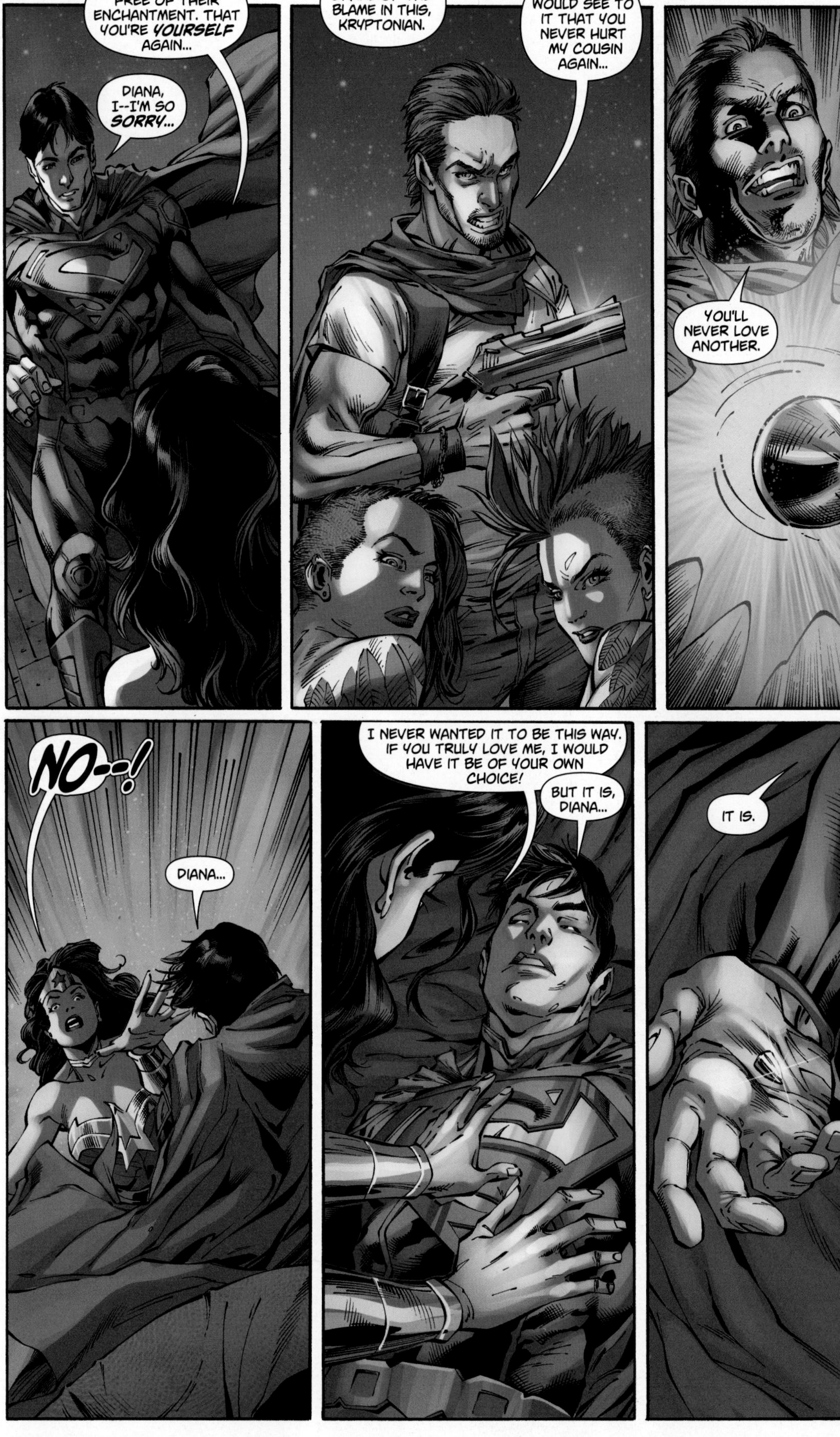
TELL ME YOU'RE FREE OF THEIR ENCHANTMENT. THAT YOU'RE YOURSELF AGAIN...
DIANA, I--I'M SO SORRY...
I ACCEPT MY SHARE OF THE BLAME IN THIS, KRYPTONIAN.
BUT I WOULD SEE TO IT THAT YOU NEVER HURT MY COUSIN AGAIN...
YOU'LL NEVER LOVE ANOTHER.
NO--!
DIANA...
I NEVER WANTED IT TO BE THIS WAY. IF YOU TRULY LOVE ME, I WOULD HAVE IT BE OF YOUR OWN CHOICE!
BUT IT IS, DIANA...
IT IS.

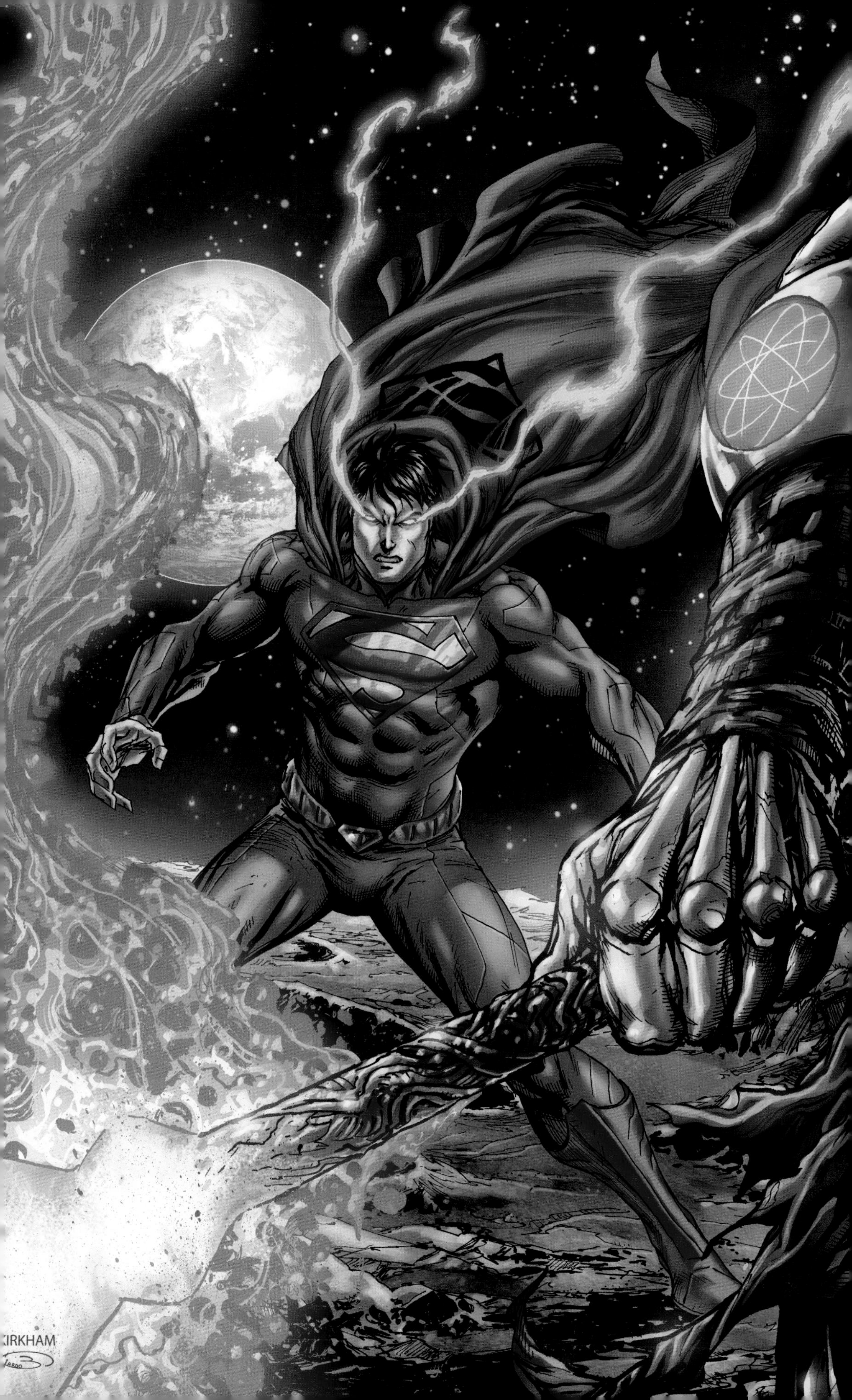

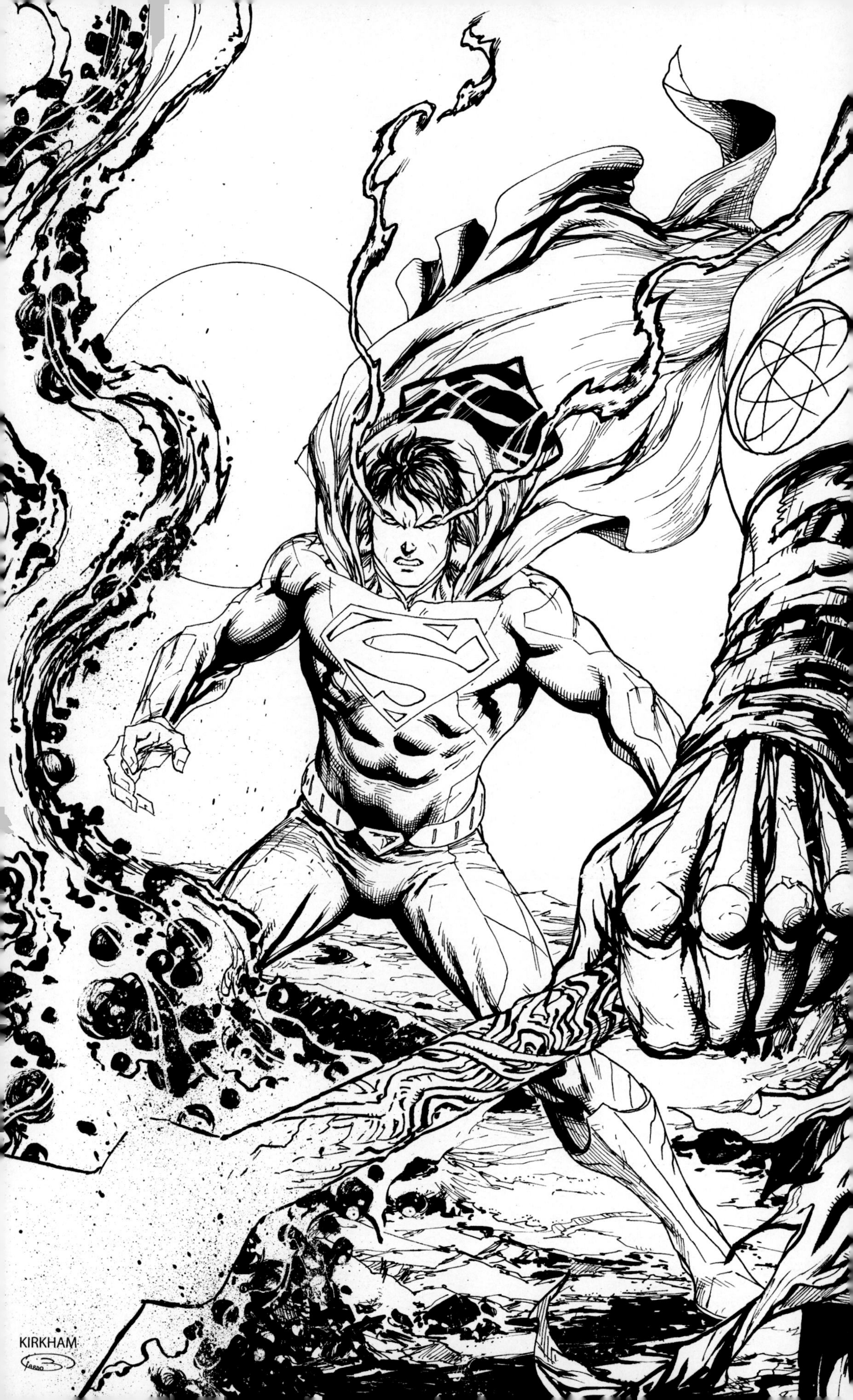
KIRKHAM

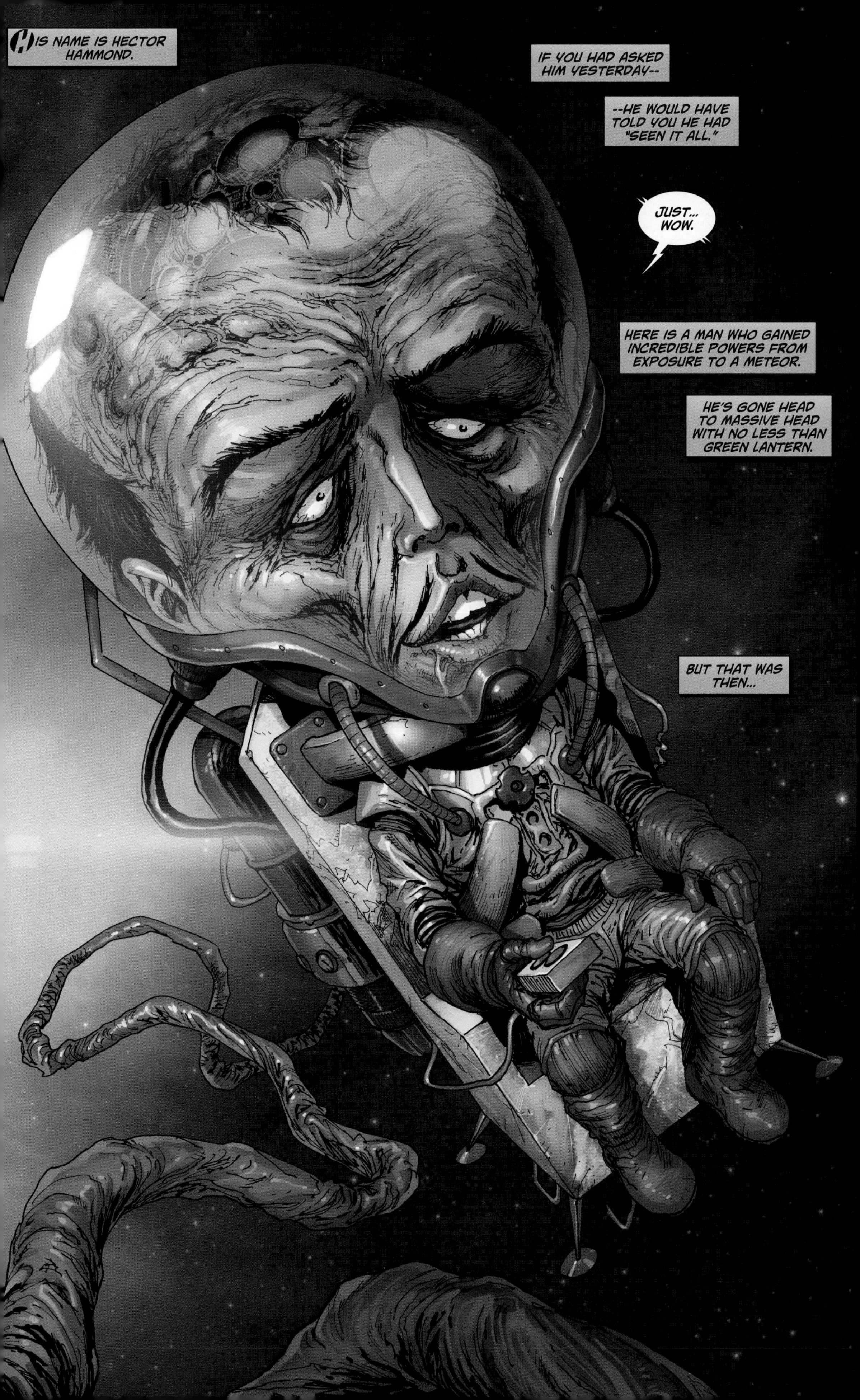
HIS NAME IS HECTOR HAMMOND.
IF YOU HAD ASKED HIM YESTERDAY--
--HE WOULD HAVE TOLD YOU HE HAD "SEEN IT ALL."
JUST... WOW.
HERE IS A MAN WHO GAINED INCREDIBLE POWERS FROM EXPOSURE TO A METEOR.
HE'S GONE HEAD TO MASSIVE HEAD WITH NO LESS THAN GREEN LANTERN.
BUT THAT WAS THEN...

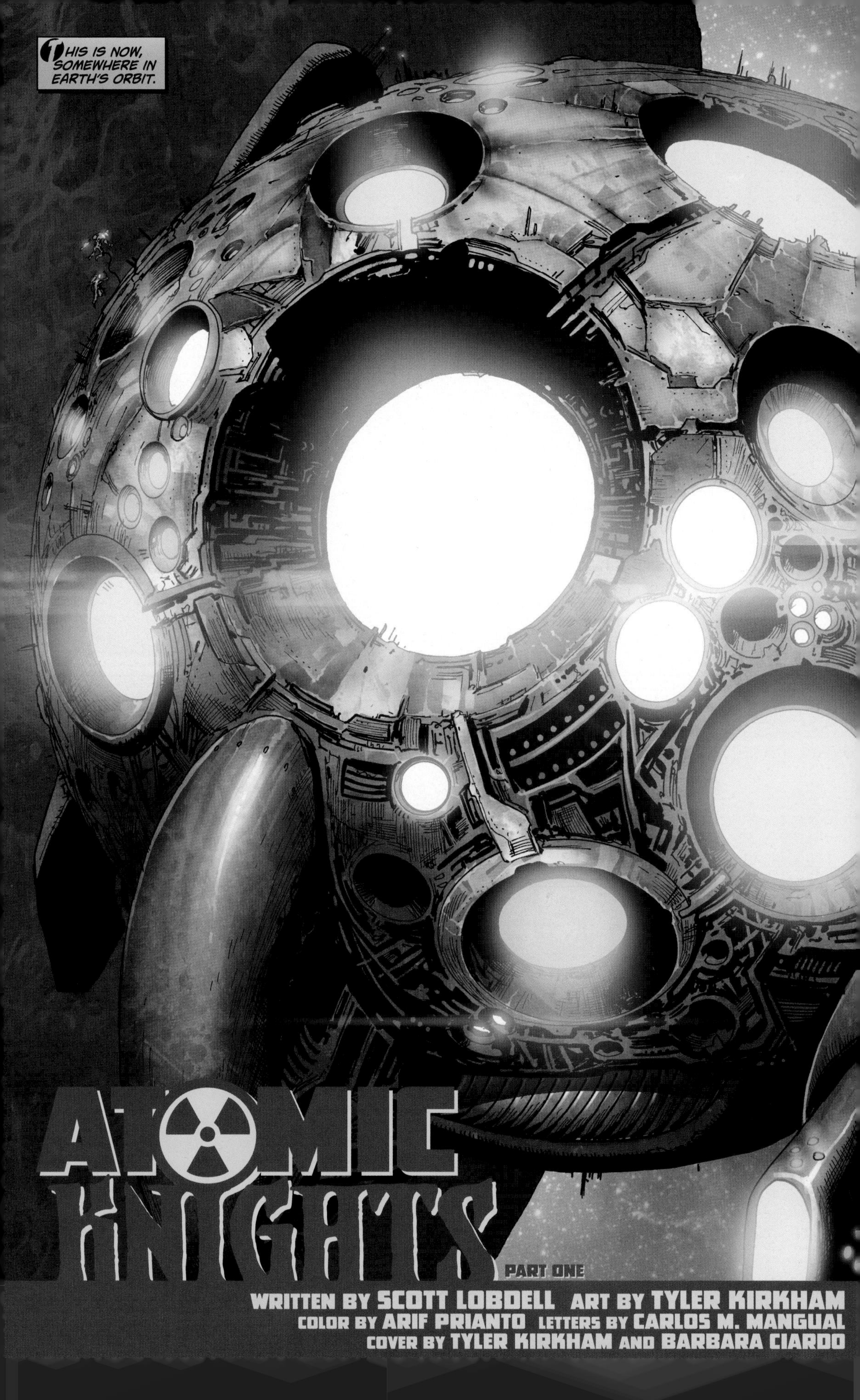
THIS IS NOW, SOMEWHERE IN EARTH'S ORBIT.
ATOMIC KNIGHTS
PART ONE
WRITTEN BY SCOTT LOBDELL ART BY TYLER KIRKHAM
COLOR BY ARIF PRIANTO LETTERS BY CARLOS M. MANGUAL
COVER BY TYLER KIRKHAM AND BARBARA CIARDO

IT'S NOT LIKE I HAVEN'T BEEN OFF-PLANET BEFORE.
I'VE BATTLED LANTERNS IN THE FARTHEST REACHES OF SPACE.
BUT THIS?
BUILT BY THE SHEER WILL AND INTELLECT OF THE H.I.V.E.?*
THOUGH IT WAS DESIGNED TO WIPE OUT ENTIRE NATIONS IN THE BLINK OF AN EYE...?
IT'S JUST SO... BEAUTIFUL.
AHIGH!
TZZZT
EH?
A TELEPORTATION EFFECT?
SO HELP ME, IF THIS IS ONE OF THE JUSTICE LEAGUE...
*HOLISTIC INTEGRATION FOR VIRAL EQUALITY--ED

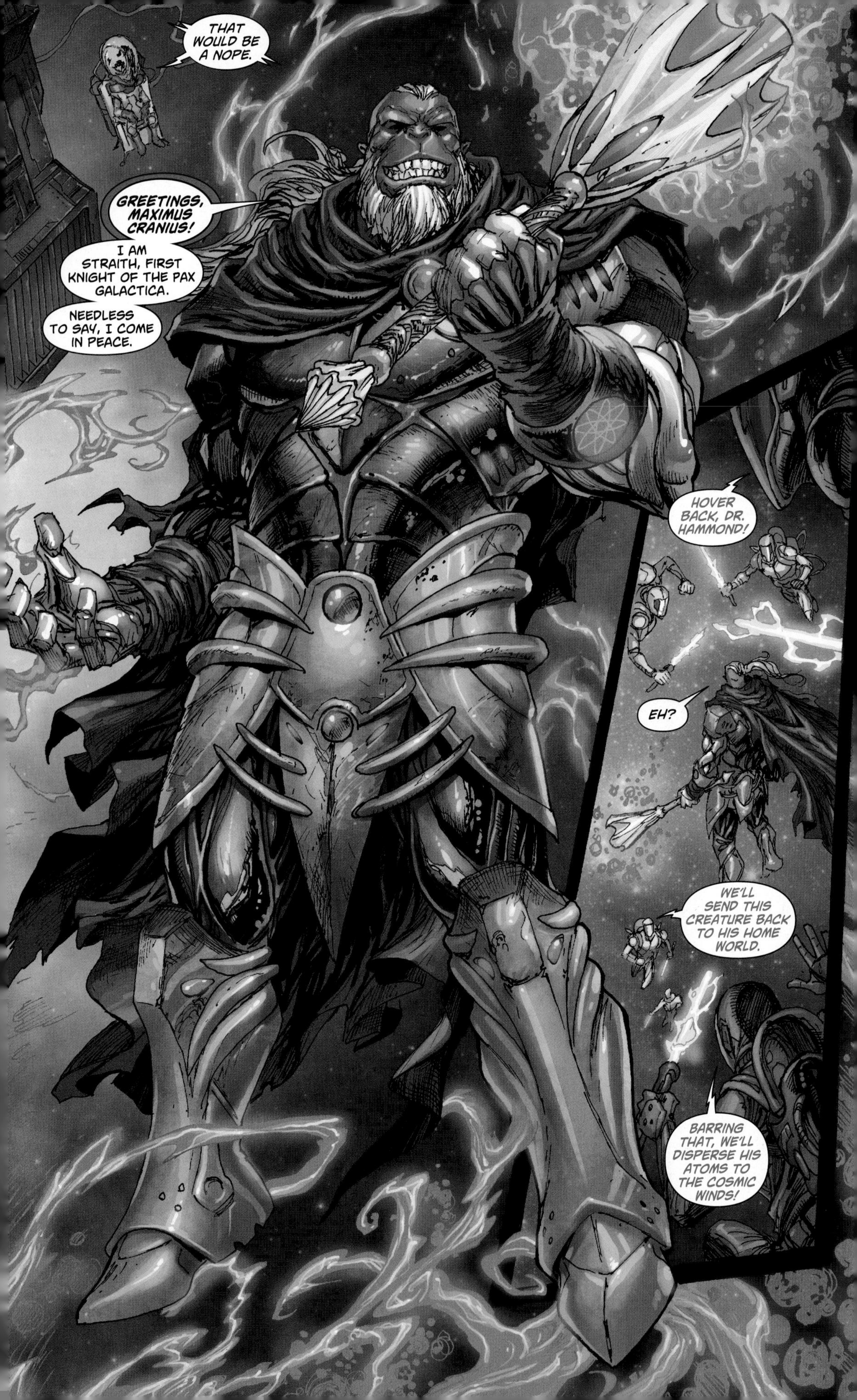
THAT WOULD BE A NOPE.
GREETINGS, MAXIMUS CRANIUS!
I AM STRAITH, FIRST KNIGHT OF THE PAX GALACTICA.
NEEDLESS TO SAY, I COME IN PEACE.
HOVER BACK, DR. HAMMOND!
EH?
WE'LL SEND THIS CREATURE BACK TO HIS HOME WORLD.
BARRING THAT, WE'LL DISPERSE HIS ATOMS TO THE COSMIC WINDS!

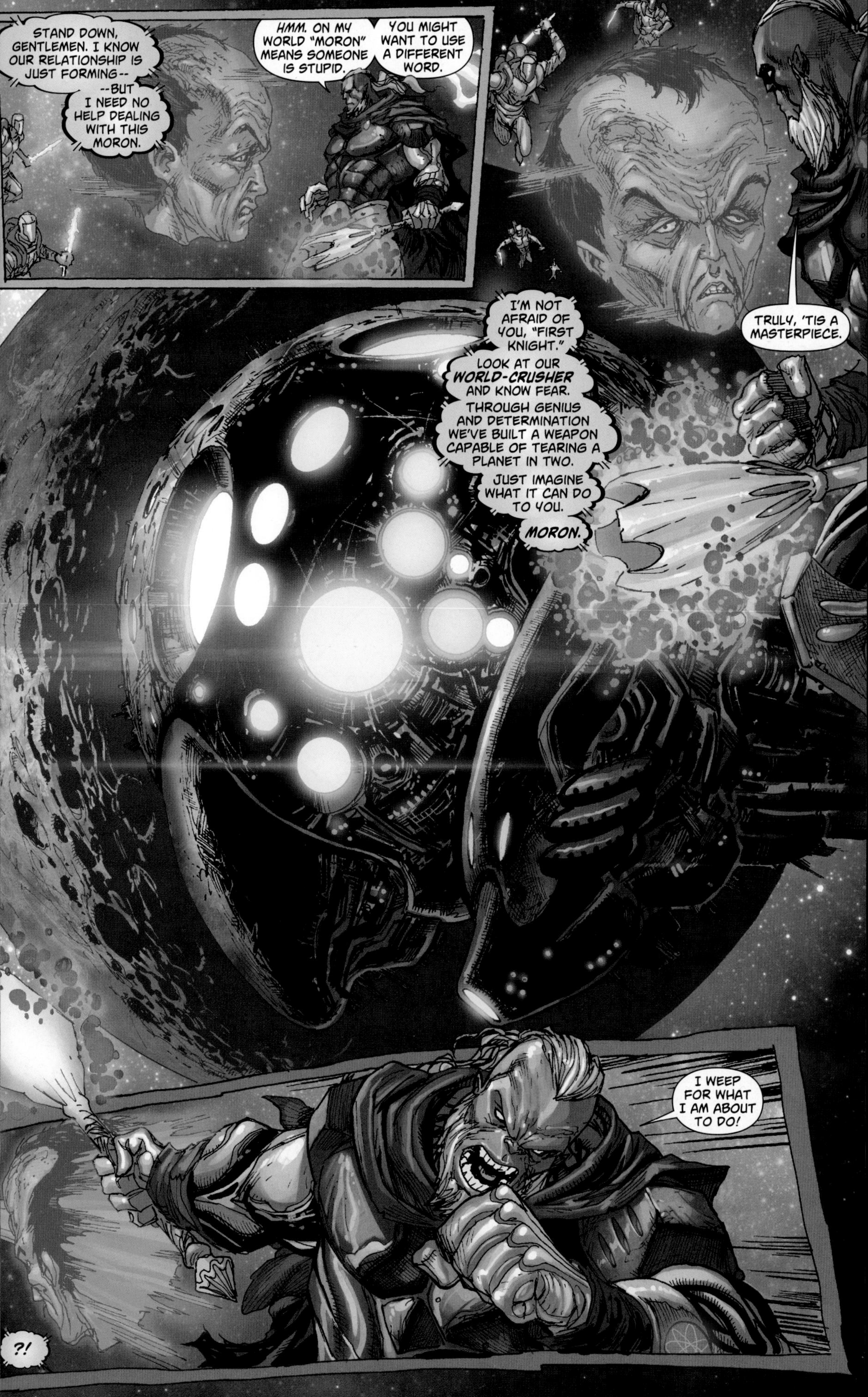
STAND DOWN, GENTLEMEN. I KNOW OUR RELATIONSHIP IS JUST FORMING--
--BUT I NEED NO HELP DEALING WITH THIS MORON.
HMM. ON MY WORLD "MORON" MEANS SOMEONE IS STUPID.
YOU MIGHT WANT TO USE A DIFFERENT WORD.
I'M NOT AFRAID OF YOU, "FIRST KNIGHT."
LOOK AT OUR WORLD-CRUSHER AND KNOW FEAR.
THROUGH GENIUS AND DETERMINATION WE'VE BUILT A WEAPON CAPABLE OF TEARING A PLANET IN TWO.
JUST IMAGINE WHAT IT CAN DO TO YOU.
MORON.
TRULY, 'TIS A MASTERPIECE.
I WEEP FOR WHAT I AM ABOUT TO DO!
?!

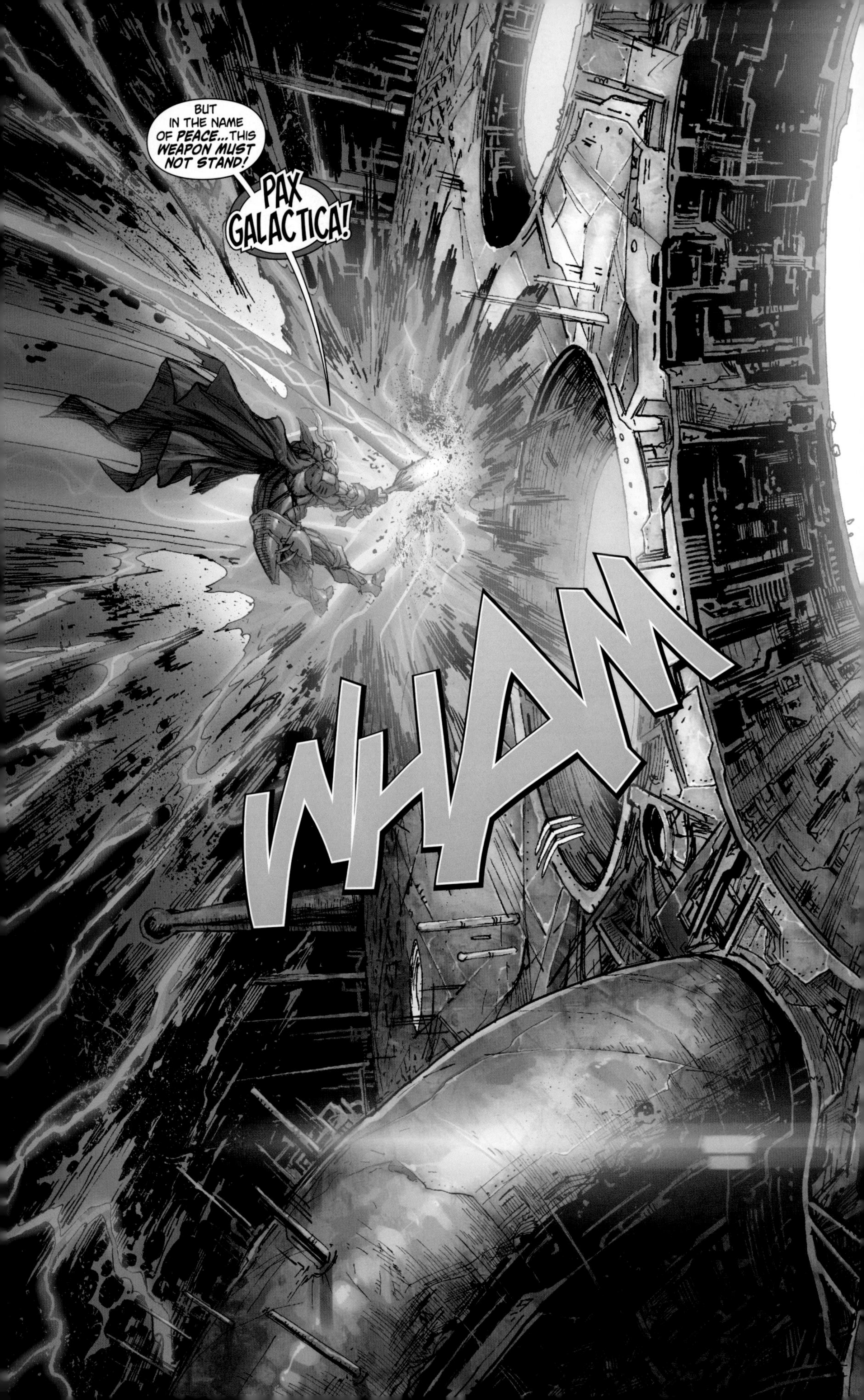
BUT IN THE NAME OF PEACE...THIS WEAPON MUST NOT STAND!
PAX GALACTICA!
WHAM

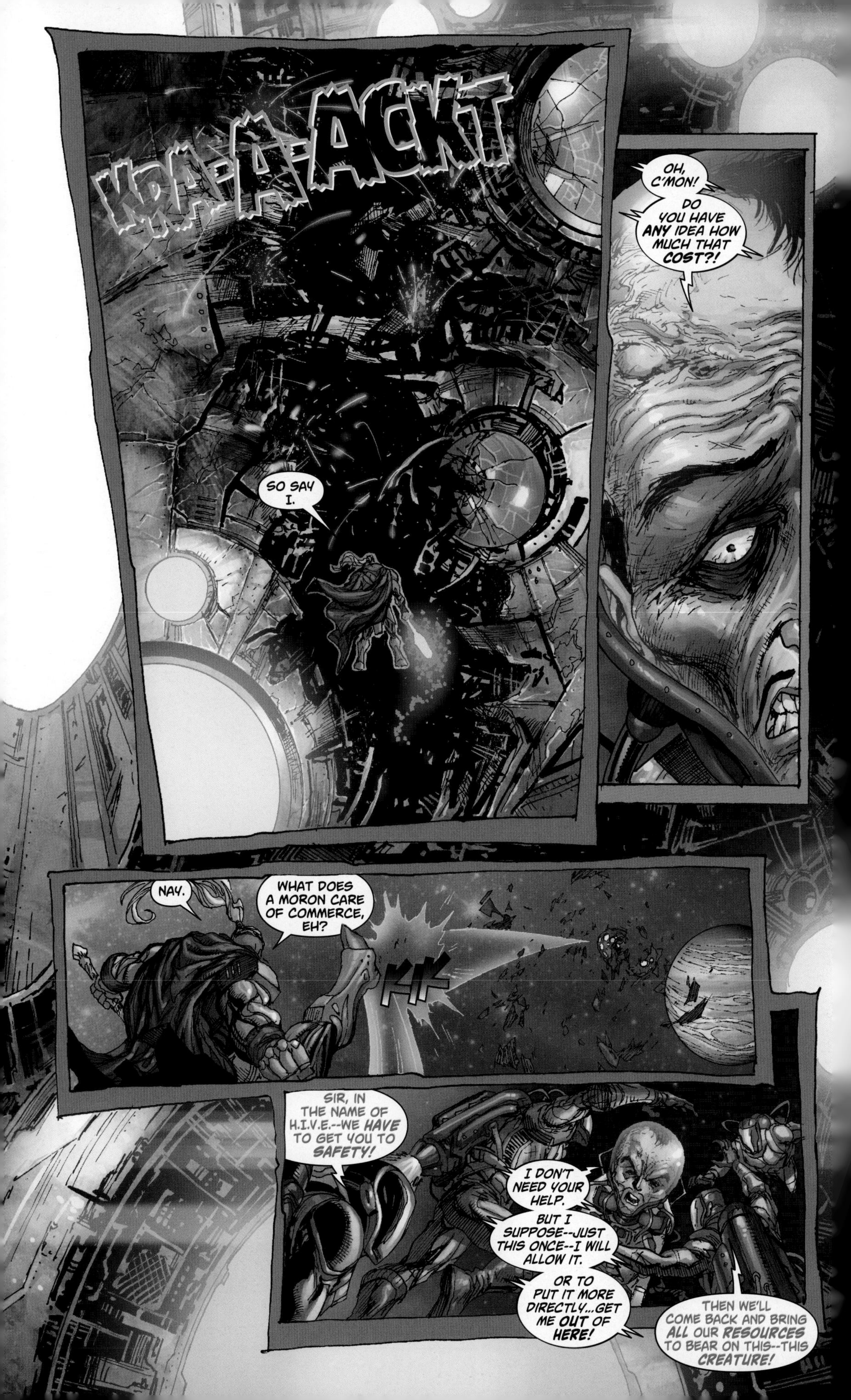
KRA-A-A-ACK!
SO SAY I.
OH, C'MON!
DO YOU HAVE ANY IDEA HOW MUCH THAT COST?!
NAY.
WHAT DOES A MORON CARE OF COMMERCE, EH?
KIK
SIR, IN THE NAME OF H.I.V.E.--WE HAVE TO GET YOU TO SAFETY!
I DON'T NEED YOUR HELP.
BUT I SUPPOSE--JUST THIS ONCE--I WILL ALLOW IT.
OR TO PUT IT MORE DIRECTLY...GET ME OUT OF HERE!
THEN WE'LL COME BACK AND BRING ALL OUR RESOURCES TO BEAR ON THIS--THIS CREATURE!

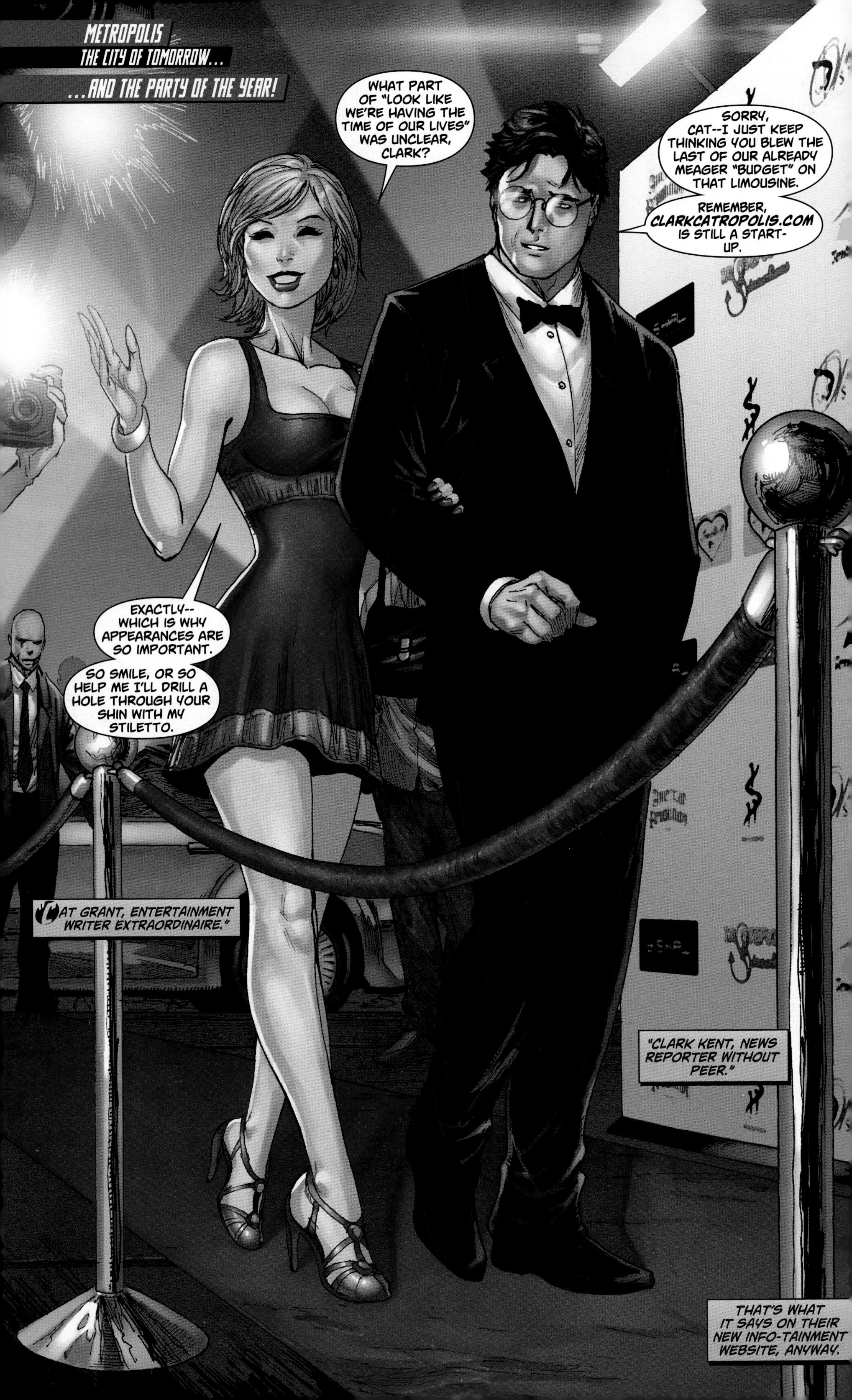
METROPOLIS
THE CITY OF TOMORROW...
...AND THE PARTY OF THE YEAR!
WHAT PART OF "LOOK LIKE WE'RE HAVING THE TIME OF OUR LIVES" WAS UNCLEAR, CLARK?
SORRY, CAT--I JUST KEEP THINKING YOU BLEW THE LAST OF OUR ALREADY MEAGER "BUDGET" ON THAT LIMOUSINE.
REMEMBER, CLARKCATROPOLIS.COM IS STILL A START-UP.
EXACTLY--WHICH IS WHY APPEARANCES ARE SO IMPORTANT.
SO SMILE, OR SO HELP ME I'LL DRILL A HOLE THROUGH YOUR SHIN WITH MY STILETTO.
"CAT GRANT, ENTERTAINMENT WRITER EXTRAORDINAIRE."
"CLARK KENT, NEWS REPORTER WITHOUT PEER."
THAT'S WHAT IT SAYS ON THEIR NEW INFO-TAINMENT WEBSITE, ANYWAY.

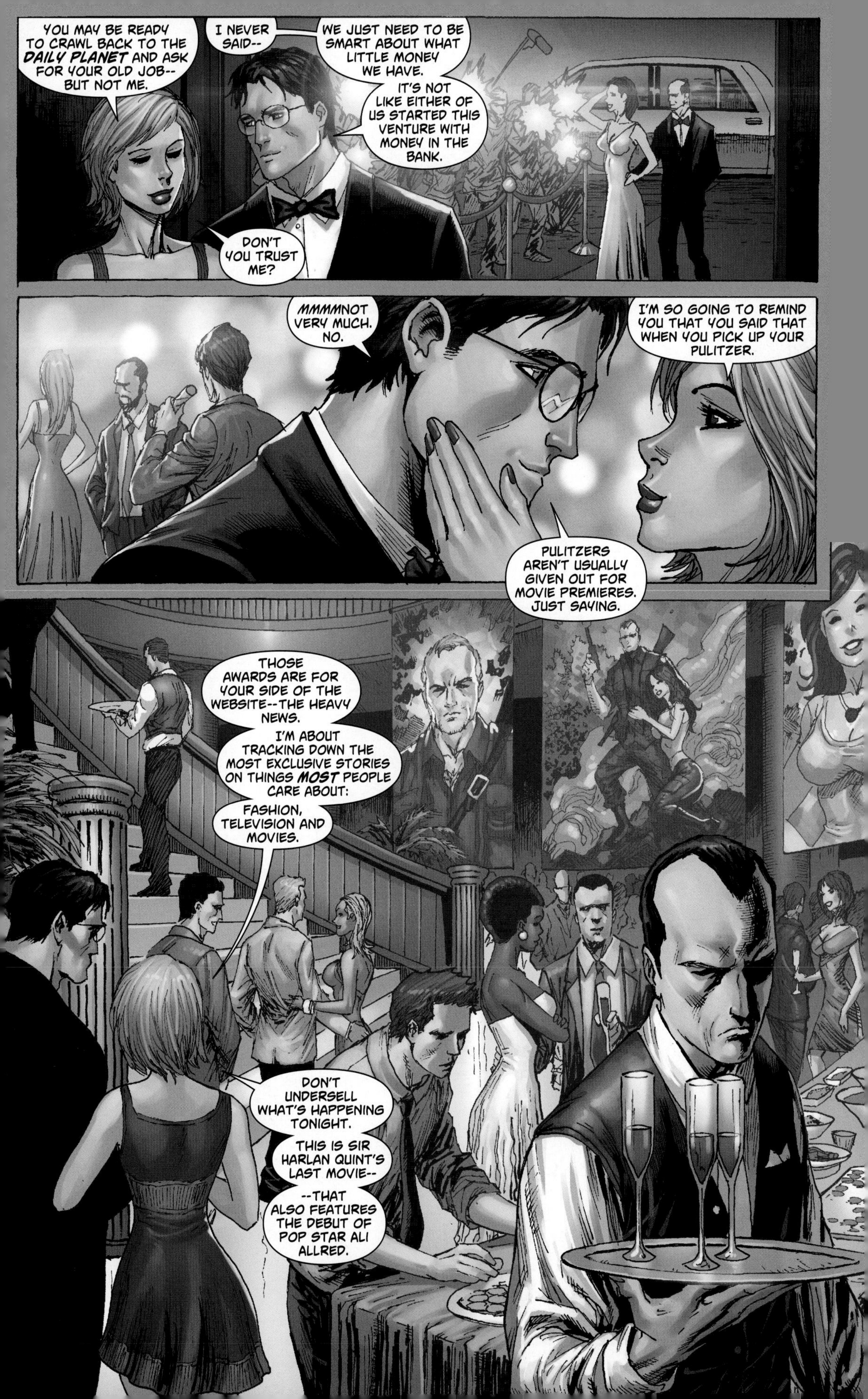
YOU MAY BE READY TO CRAWL BACK TO THE *DAILY PLANET* AND ASK FOR YOUR OLD JOB-- BUT NOT ME.
I NEVER SAID--
WE JUST NEED TO BE SMART ABOUT WHAT LITTLE MONEY WE HAVE.
IT'S NOT LIKE EITHER OF US STARTED THIS VENTURE WITH MONEY IN THE BANK.
DON'T YOU TRUST ME?
MMMMNOT VERY MUCH. NO.
I'M SO GOING TO REMIND YOU THAT YOU SAID THAT WHEN YOU PICK UP YOUR PULITZER.
PULITZERS AREN'T USUALLY GIVEN OUT FOR MOVIE PREMIERES. JUST SAYING.
THOSE AWARDS ARE FOR YOUR SIDE OF THE WEBSITE--THE HEAVY NEWS.
I'M ABOUT TRACKING DOWN THE MOST EXCLUSIVE STORIES ON THINGS *MOST* PEOPLE CARE ABOUT:
FASHION, TELEVISION AND MOVIES.
DON'T UNDERSELL WHAT'S HAPPENING TONIGHT.
THIS IS SIR HARLAN QUINT'S LAST MOVIE--
--THAT ALSO FEATURES THE DEBUT OF POP STAR ALI ALLRED.

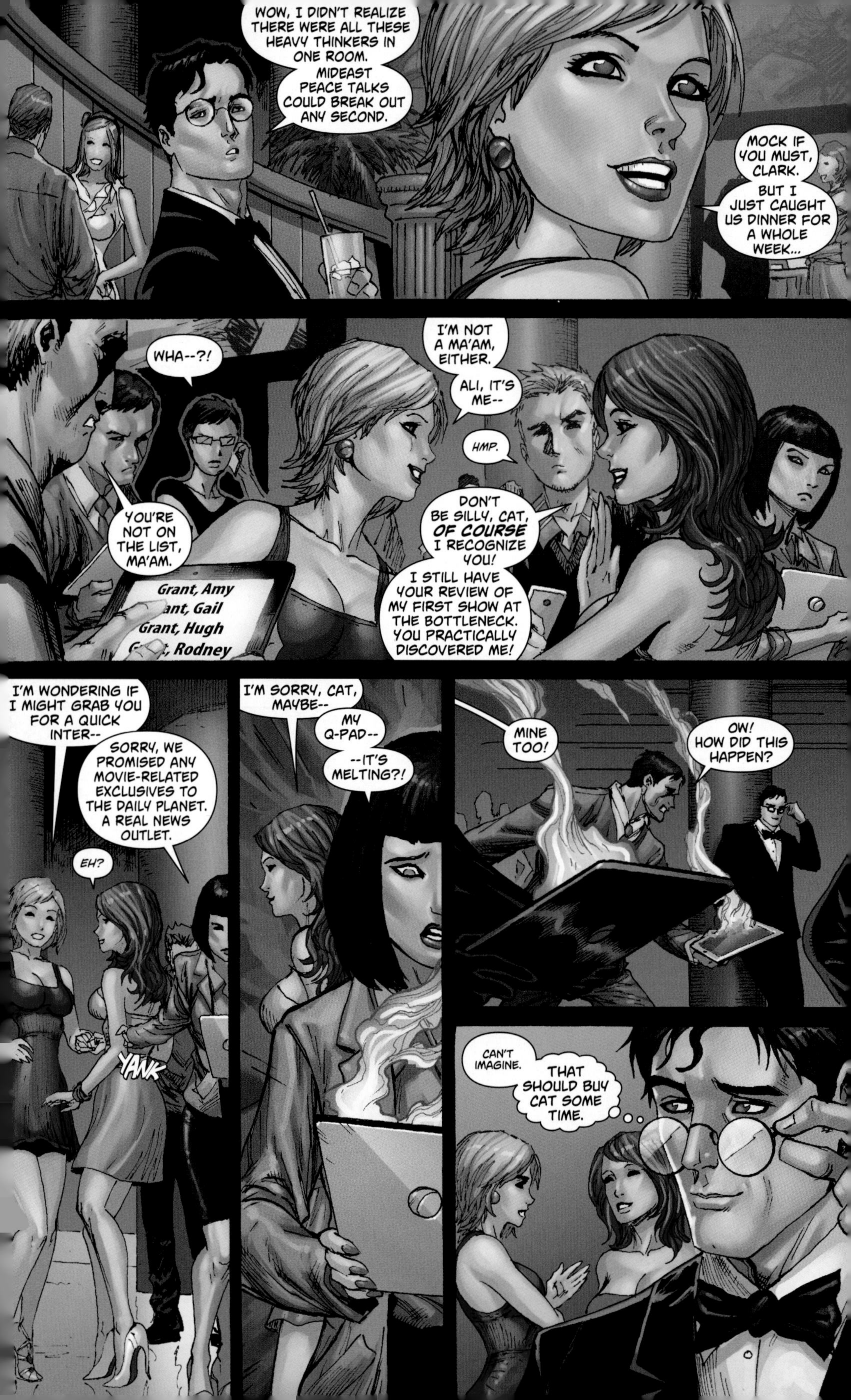
WOW, I DIDN'T REALIZE THERE WERE ALL THESE HEAVY THINKERS IN ONE ROOM.
MIDEAST PEACE TALKS COULD BREAK OUT ANY SECOND.
MOCK IF YOU MUST, CLARK.
BUT I JUST CAUGHT US DINNER FOR A WHOLE WEEK...
WHA--?!
YOU'RE NOT ON THE LIST, MA'AM.
Grant, Amy
ant, Gail
Grant, Hugh
t, Rodney
I'M NOT A MA'AM, EITHER.
ALI, IT'S ME--
HMP.
DON'T BE SILLY, CAT, OF COURSE I RECOGNIZE YOU!
I STILL HAVE YOUR REVIEW OF MY FIRST SHOW AT THE BOTTLENECK. YOU PRACTICALLY DISCOVERED ME!
I'M WONDERING IF I MIGHT GRAB YOU FOR A QUICK INTER--
SORRY, WE PROMISED ANY MOVIE-RELATED EXCLUSIVES TO THE DAILY PLANET. A REAL NEWS OUTLET.
EH?
YANK
I'M SORRY, CAT, MAYBE--
MY Q-PAD--
--IT'S MELTING?!
MINE TOO!
OW! HOW DID THIS HAPPEN?
CAN'T IMAGINE.
THAT SHOULD BUY CAT SOME TIME.

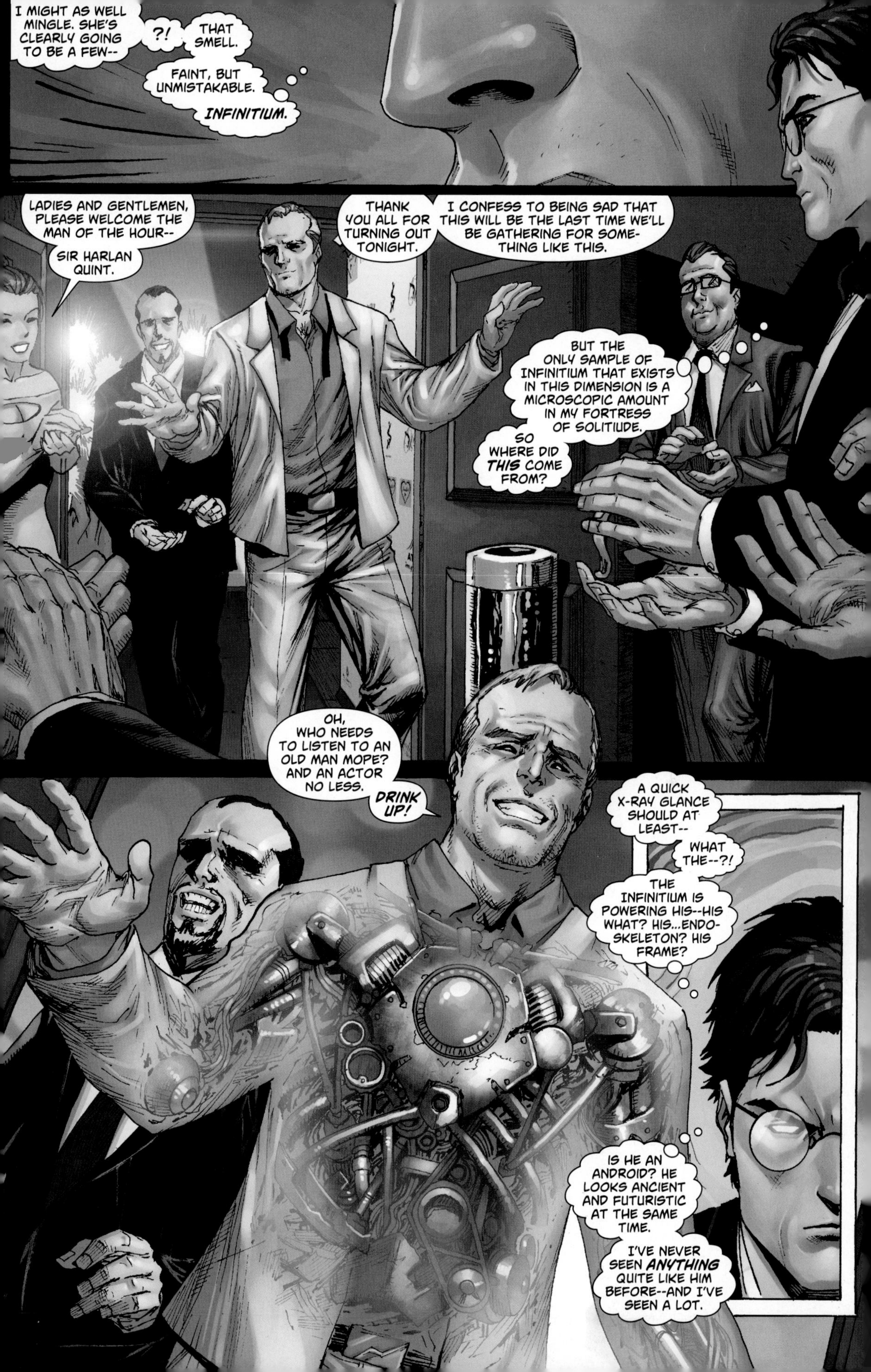
I MIGHT AS WELL MINGLE. SHE'S CLEARLY GOING TO BE A FEW--
?!
THAT SMELL.
FAINT, BUT UNMISTAKABLE.
INFINITIUM.
LADIES AND GENTLEMEN, PLEASE WELCOME THE MAN OF THE HOUR--
SIR HARLAN QUINT.
THANK YOU ALL FOR TURNING OUT TONIGHT.
I CONFESS TO BEING SAD THAT THIS WILL BE THE LAST TIME WE'LL BE GATHERING FOR SOMETHING LIKE THIS.
BUT THE ONLY SAMPLE OF INFINITIUM THAT EXISTS IN THIS DIMENSION IS A MICROSCOPIC AMOUNT IN MY FORTRESS OF SOLITIUDE.
SO WHERE DID THIS COME FROM?
OH, WHO NEEDS TO LISTEN TO AN OLD MAN MOPE? AND AN ACTOR NO LESS.
DRINK UP!
A QUICK X-RAY GLANCE SHOULD AT LEAST--
WHAT THE--?!
THE INFINITIUM IS POWERING HIS--HIS WHAT? HIS...ENDO-SKELETON? HIS FRAME?
IS HE AN ANDROID? HE LOOKS ANCIENT AND FUTURISTIC AT THE SAME TIME.
I'VE NEVER SEEN ANYTHING QUITE LIKE HIM BEFORE--AND I'VE SEEN A LOT.

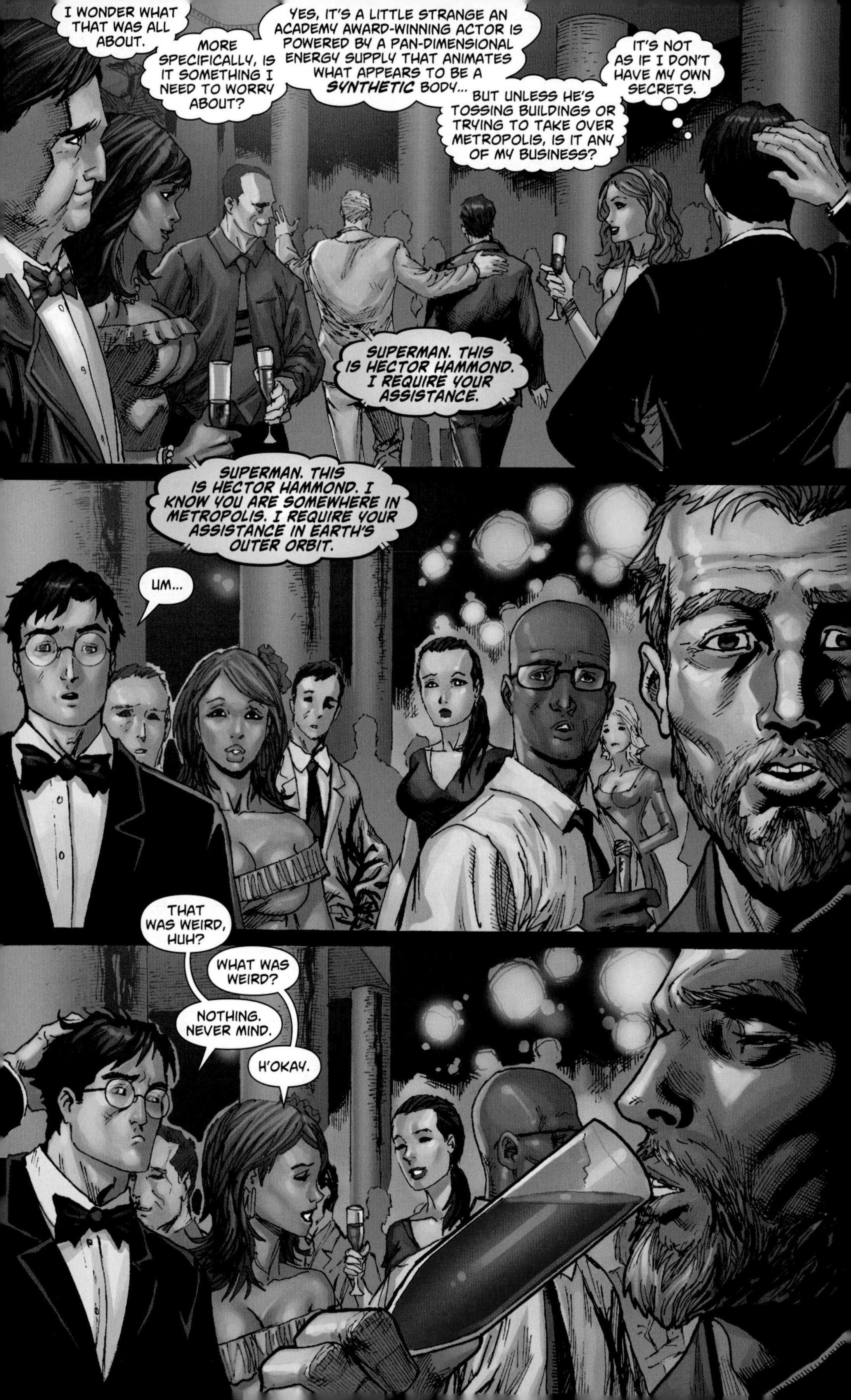
I WONDER WHAT THAT WAS ALL ABOUT.
MORE SPECIFICALLY, IS IT SOMETHING I NEED TO WORRY ABOUT?
YES, IT'S A LITTLE STRANGE AN ACADEMY AWARD-WINNING ACTOR IS POWERED BY A PAN-DIMENSIONAL ENERGY SUPPLY THAT ANIMATES WHAT APPEARS TO BE A SYNTHETIC BODY...
BUT UNLESS HE'S TOSSING BUILDINGS OR TRYING TO TAKE OVER METROPOLIS, IS IT ANY OF MY BUSINESS?
IT'S NOT AS IF I DON'T HAVE MY OWN SECRETS.
SUPERMAN. THIS IS HECTOR HAMMOND. I REQUIRE YOUR ASSISTANCE.
SUPERMAN. THIS IS HECTOR HAMMOND. I KNOW YOU ARE SOMEWHERE IN METROPOLIS. I REQUIRE YOUR ASSISTANCE IN EARTH'S OUTER ORBIT.
UM...
THAT WAS WEIRD, HUH?
WHAT WAS WEIRD?
NOTHING. NEVER MIND.
H'OKAY.

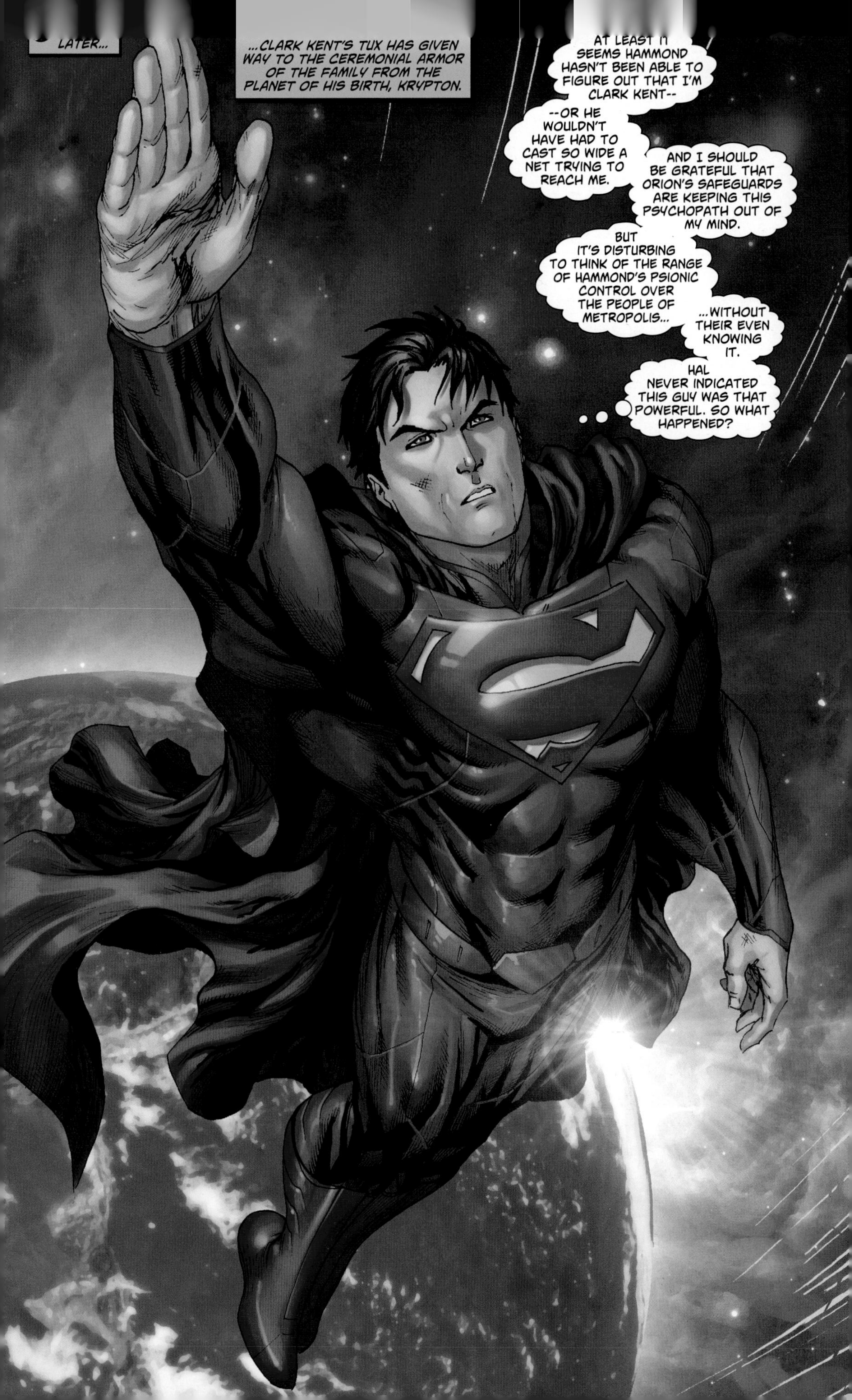

LATER...
...CLARK KENT'S TUX HAS GIVEN WAY TO THE CEREMONIAL ARMOR OF THE FAMILY FROM THE PLANET OF HIS BIRTH, KRYPTON.
AT LEAST IT SEEMS HAMMOND HASN'T BEEN ABLE TO FIGURE OUT THAT I'M CLARK KENT--
--OR HE WOULDN'T HAVE HAD TO CAST SO WIDE A NET TRYING TO REACH ME.
AND I SHOULD BE GRATEFUL THAT ORION'S SAFEGUARDS ARE KEEPING THIS PSYCHOPATH OUT OF MY MIND.
BUT IT'S DISTURBING TO THINK OF THE RANGE OF HAMMOND'S PSIONIC CONTROL OVER THE PEOPLE OF METROPOLIS...
...WITHOUT THEIR EVEN KNOWING IT.
HAL NEVER INDICATED THIS GUY WAS THAT POWERFUL. SO WHAT HAPPENED?

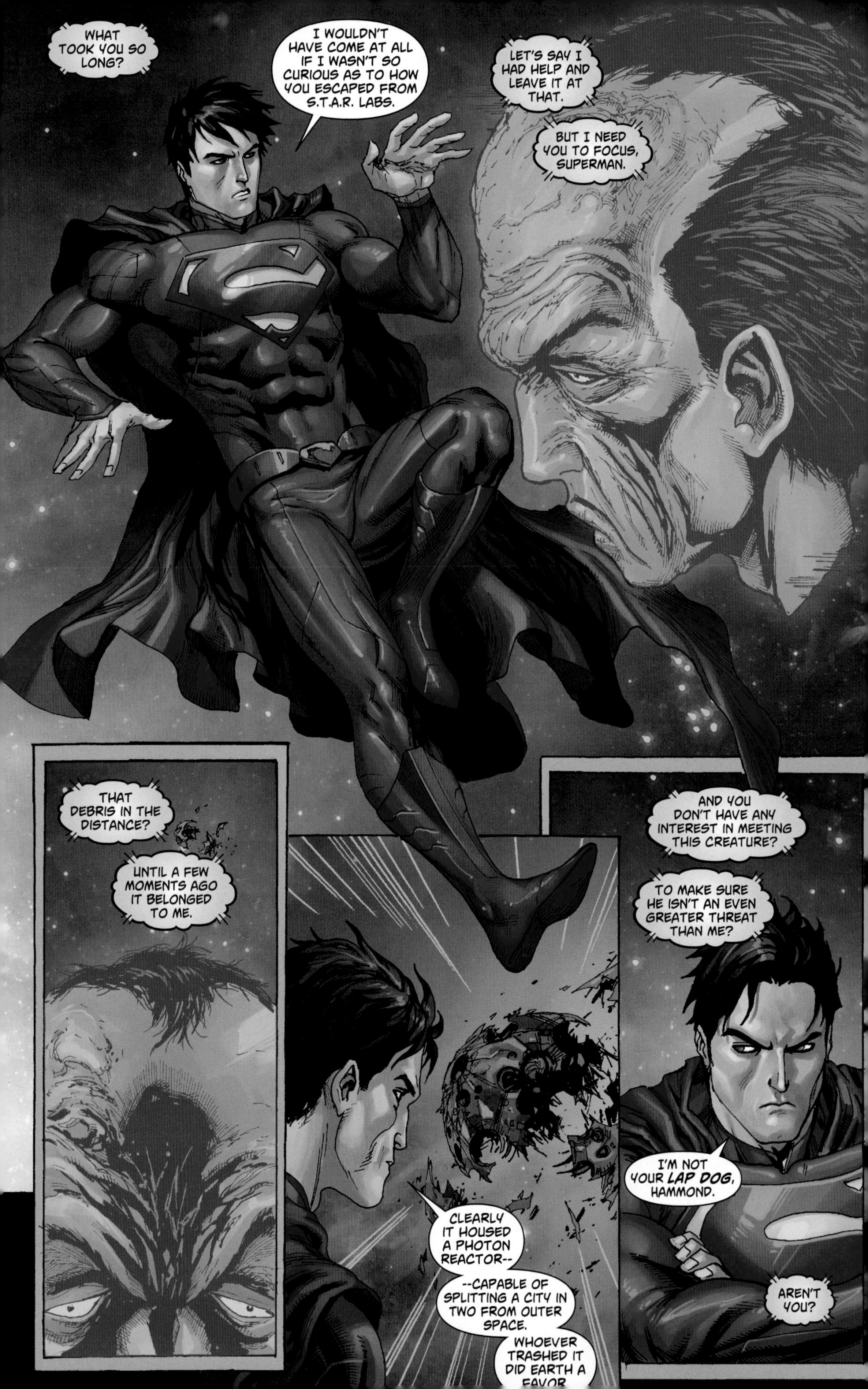

WHAT TOOK YOU SO LONG?
I WOULDN'T HAVE COME AT ALL IF I WASN'T SO CURIOUS AS TO HOW YOU ESCAPED FROM S.T.A.R. LABS.
LET'S SAY I HAD HELP AND LEAVE IT AT THAT.
BUT I NEED YOU TO FOCUS, SUPERMAN.
THAT DEBRIS IN THE DISTANCE?
UNTIL A FEW MOMENTS AGO IT BELONGED TO ME.
CLEARLY IT HOUSED A PHOTON REACTOR--
--CAPABLE OF SPLITTING A CITY IN TWO FROM OUTER SPACE.
WHOEVER TRASHED IT DID EARTH A FAVOR
AND YOU DON'T HAVE ANY INTEREST IN MEETING THIS CREATURE?
TO MAKE SURE HE ISN'T AN EVEN GREATER THREAT THAN ME?
I'M NOT YOUR LAP DOG, HAMMOND.
AREN'T YOU?

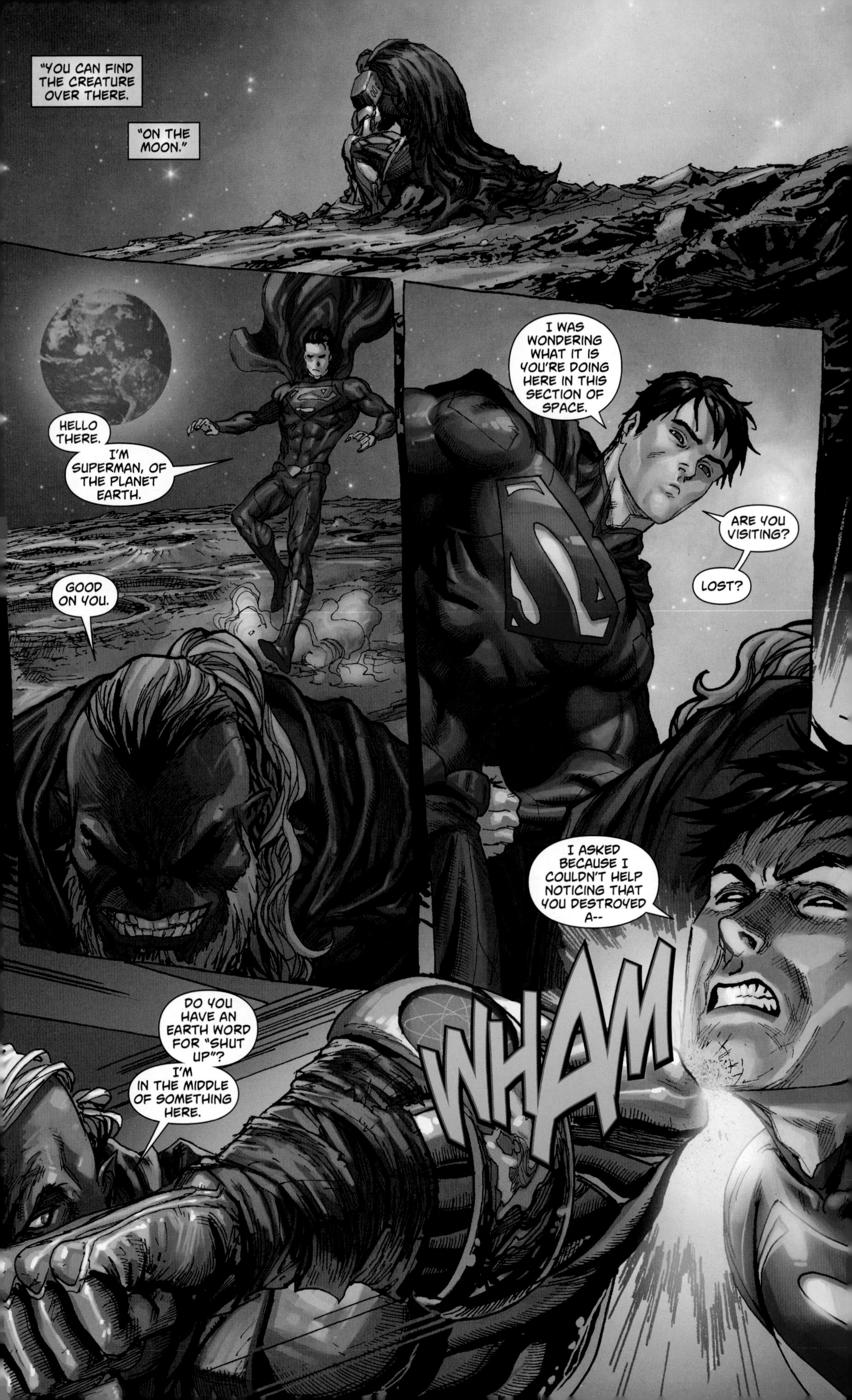
"YOU CAN FIND THE CREATURE OVER THERE.
"ON THE MOON."
HELLO THERE.
I'M SUPERMAN, OF THE PLANET EARTH.
GOOD ON YOU.
I WAS WONDERING WHAT IT IS YOU'RE DOING HERE IN THIS SECTION OF SPACE.
ARE YOU VISITING?
LOST?
I ASKED BECAUSE I COULDN'T HELP NOTICING THAT YOU DESTROYED A--
DO YOU HAVE AN EARTH WORD FOR "SHUT UP"?
I'M IN THE MIDDLE OF SOMETHING HERE.
WHAM

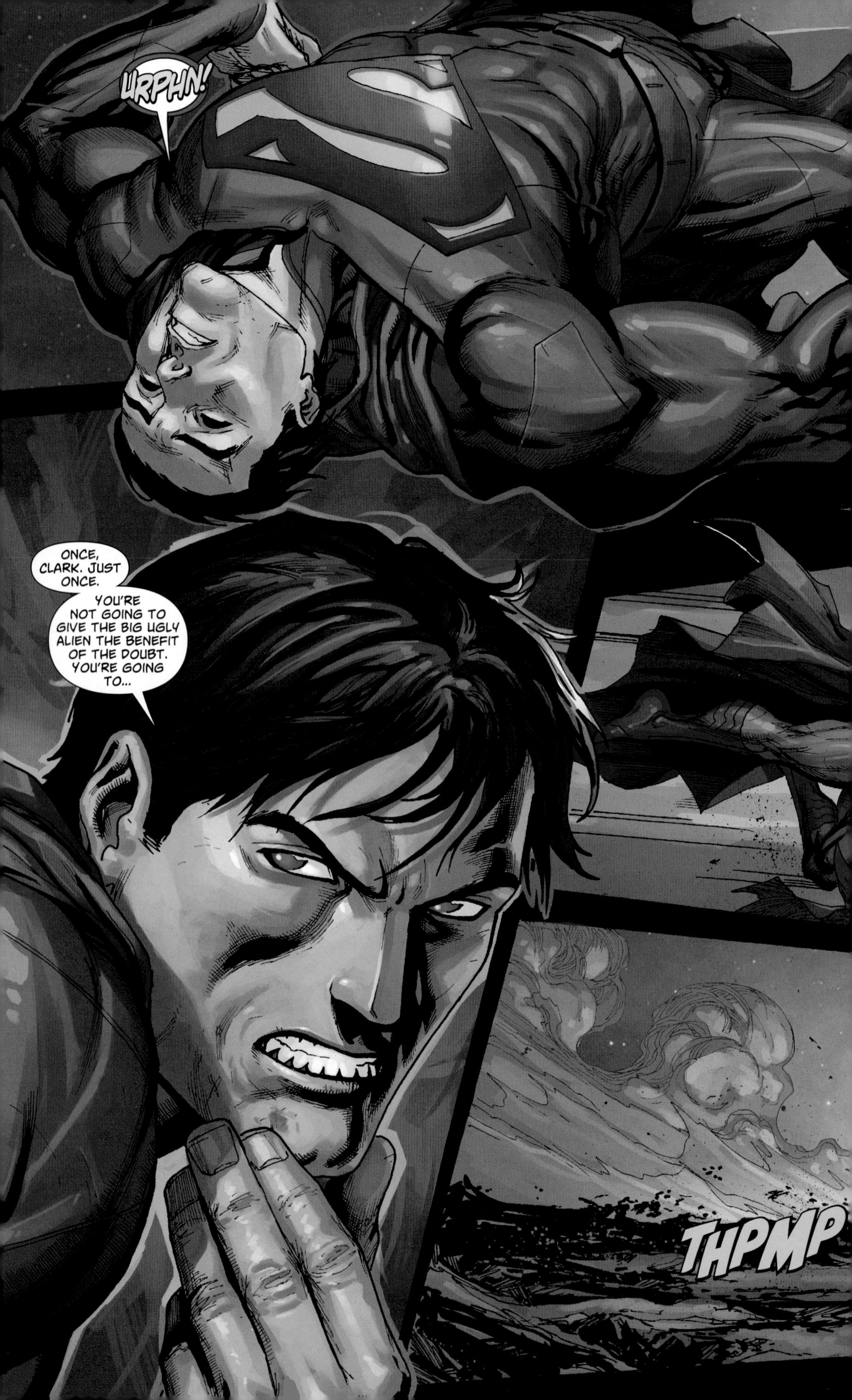
URPHN!
ONCE, CLARK. JUST ONCE.
YOU'RE NOT GOING TO GIVE THE BIG UGLY ALIEN THE BENEFIT OF THE DOUBT. YOU'RE GOING TO...
THPMP

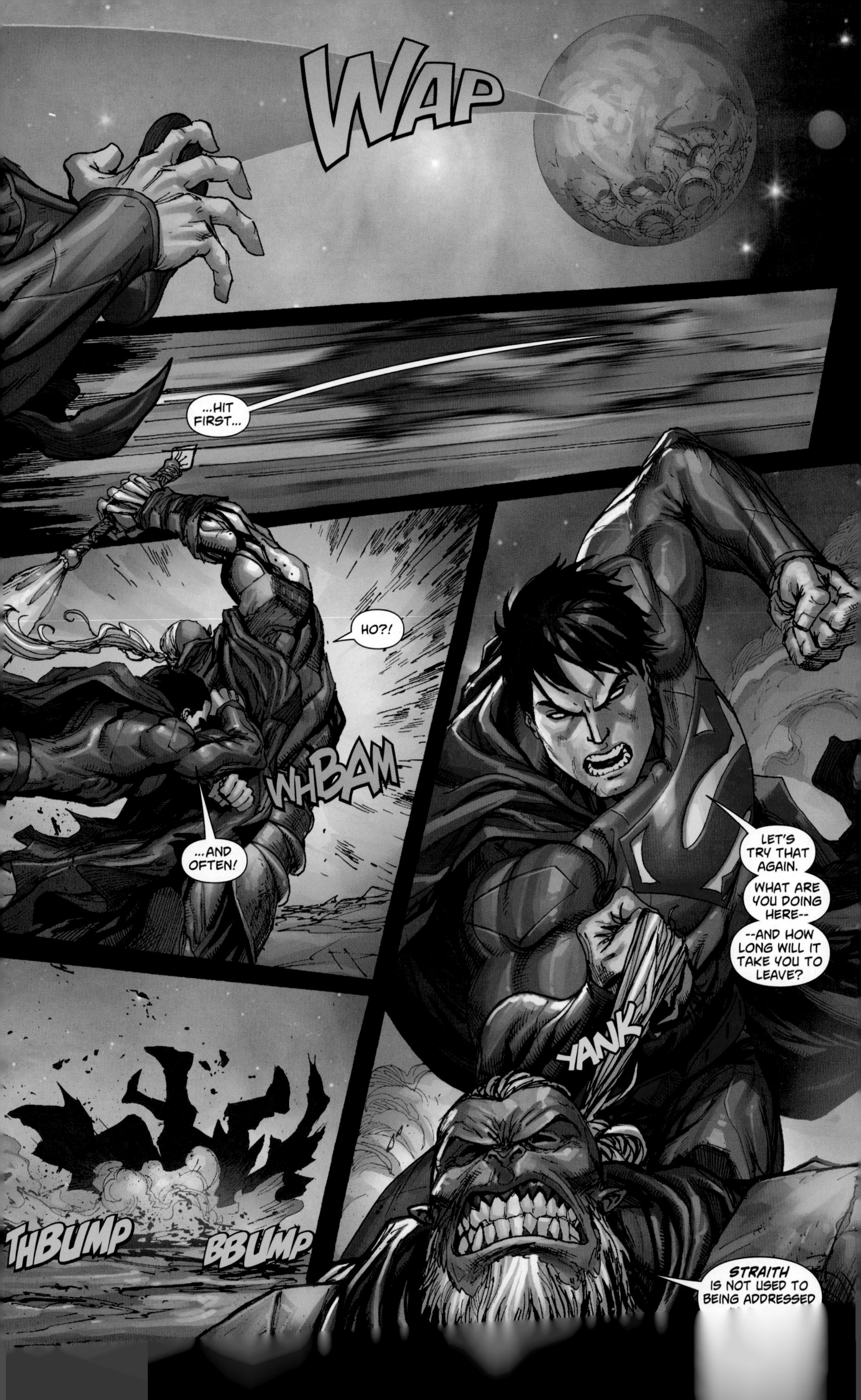
WAP
...HIT FIRST...
HO?!
WHBAM
...AND OFTEN!
LET'S TRY THAT AGAIN.
WHAT ARE YOU DOING HERE--
--AND HOW LONG WILL IT TAKE YOU TO LEAVE?
YANK
THBUMP
BBUMP
STRAITH IS NOT USED TO BEING ADDRESSED

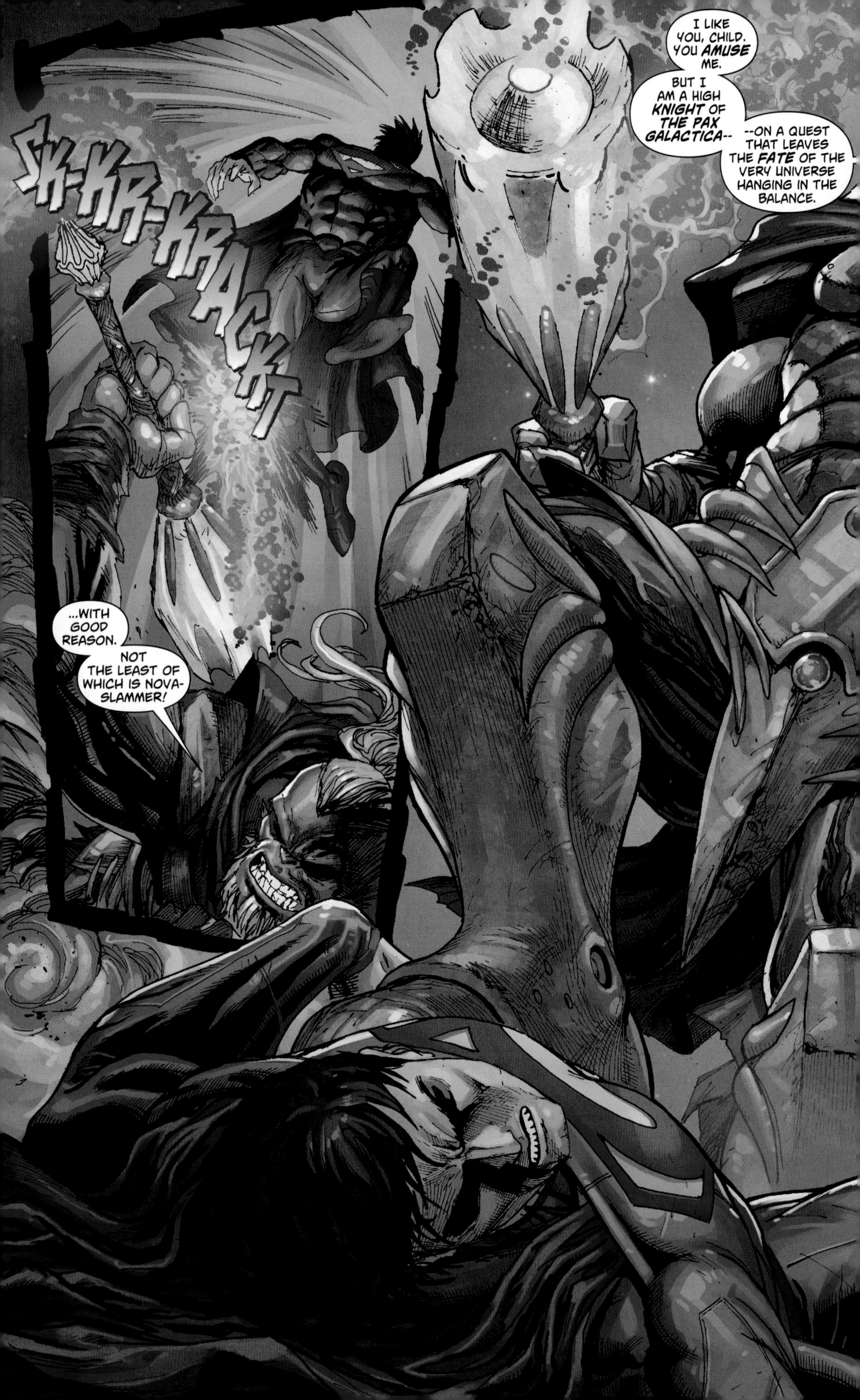
SK-KR-KRACKT
I LIKE YOU, CHILD. YOU AMUSE ME.
BUT I AM A HIGH KNIGHT OF THE PAX GALACTICA--
--ON A QUEST THAT LEAVES THE FATE OF THE VERY UNIVERSE HANGING IN THE BALANCE.
...WITH GOOD REASON.
NOT THE LEAST OF WHICH IS NOVA-SLAMMER!

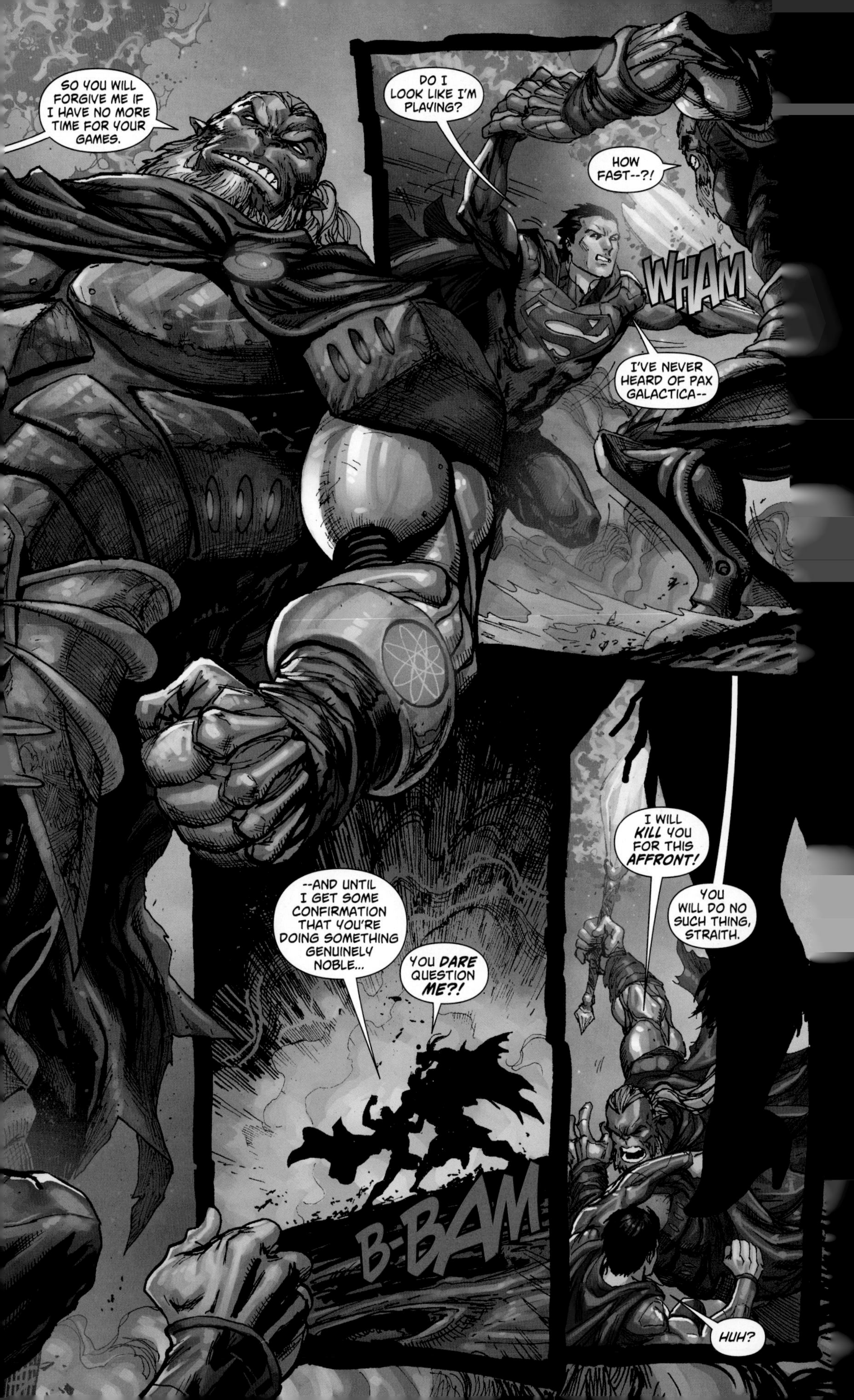
SO YOU WILL FORGIVE ME IF I HAVE NO MORE TIME FOR YOUR GAMES.
DO I LOOK LIKE I'M PLAYING?
HOW FAST--?!
WHAM
I'VE NEVER HEARD OF PAX GALACTICA--
--AND UNTIL I GET SOME CONFIRMATION THAT YOU'RE DOING SOMETHING GENUINELY NOBLE...
YOU DARE QUESTION ME?!
B-BAM
I WILL KILL YOU FOR THIS AFFRONT!
YOU WILL DO NO SUCH THING, STRAITH.
HUH?

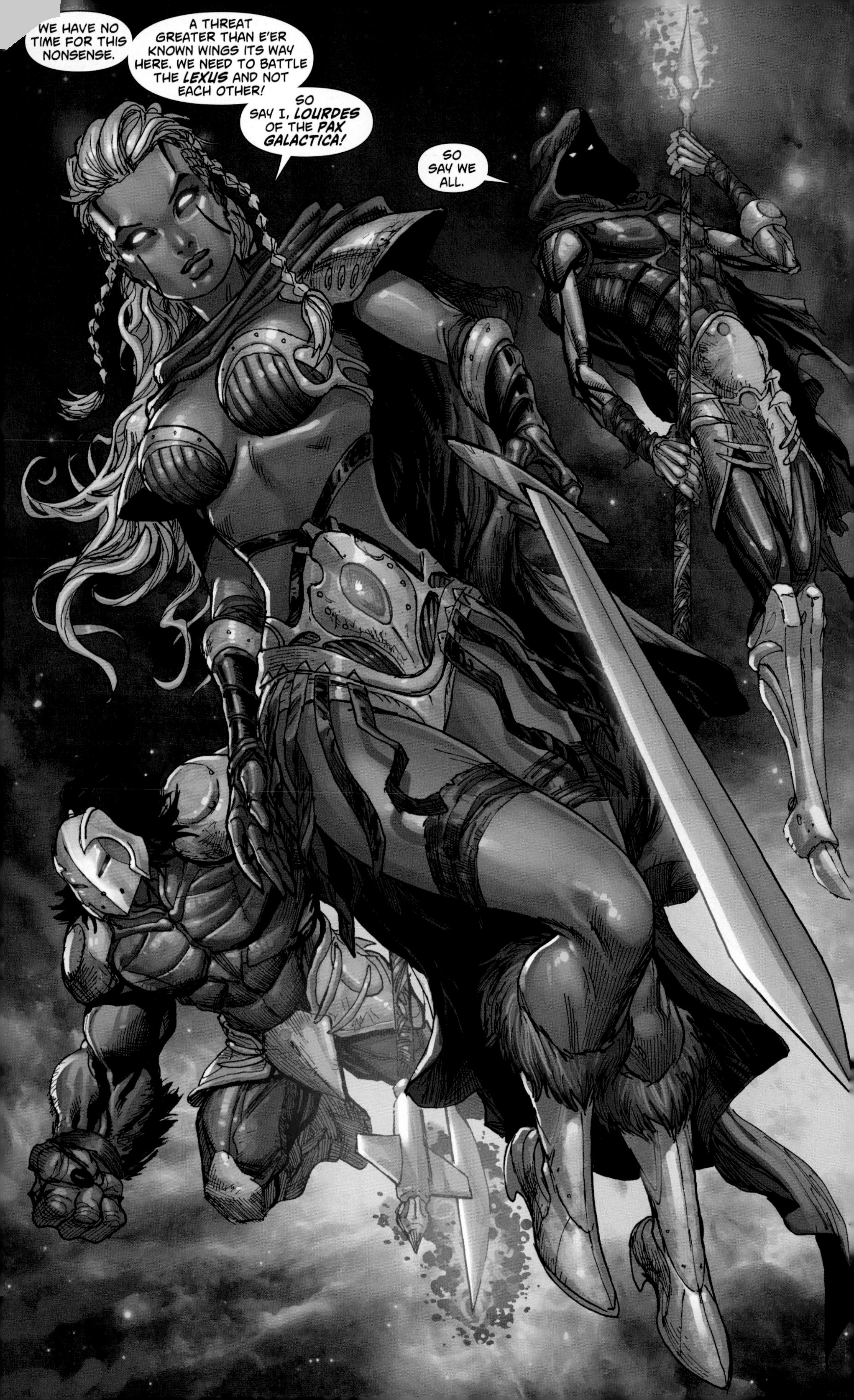
WE HAVE NO TIME FOR THIS NONSENSE.
A THREAT GREATER THAN E'ER KNOWN WINGS ITS WAY HERE. WE NEED TO BATTLE THE LEXUS AND NOT EACH OTHER!
SO SAY I, LOURDES OF THE PAX GALACTICA!
SO SAY WE ALL.

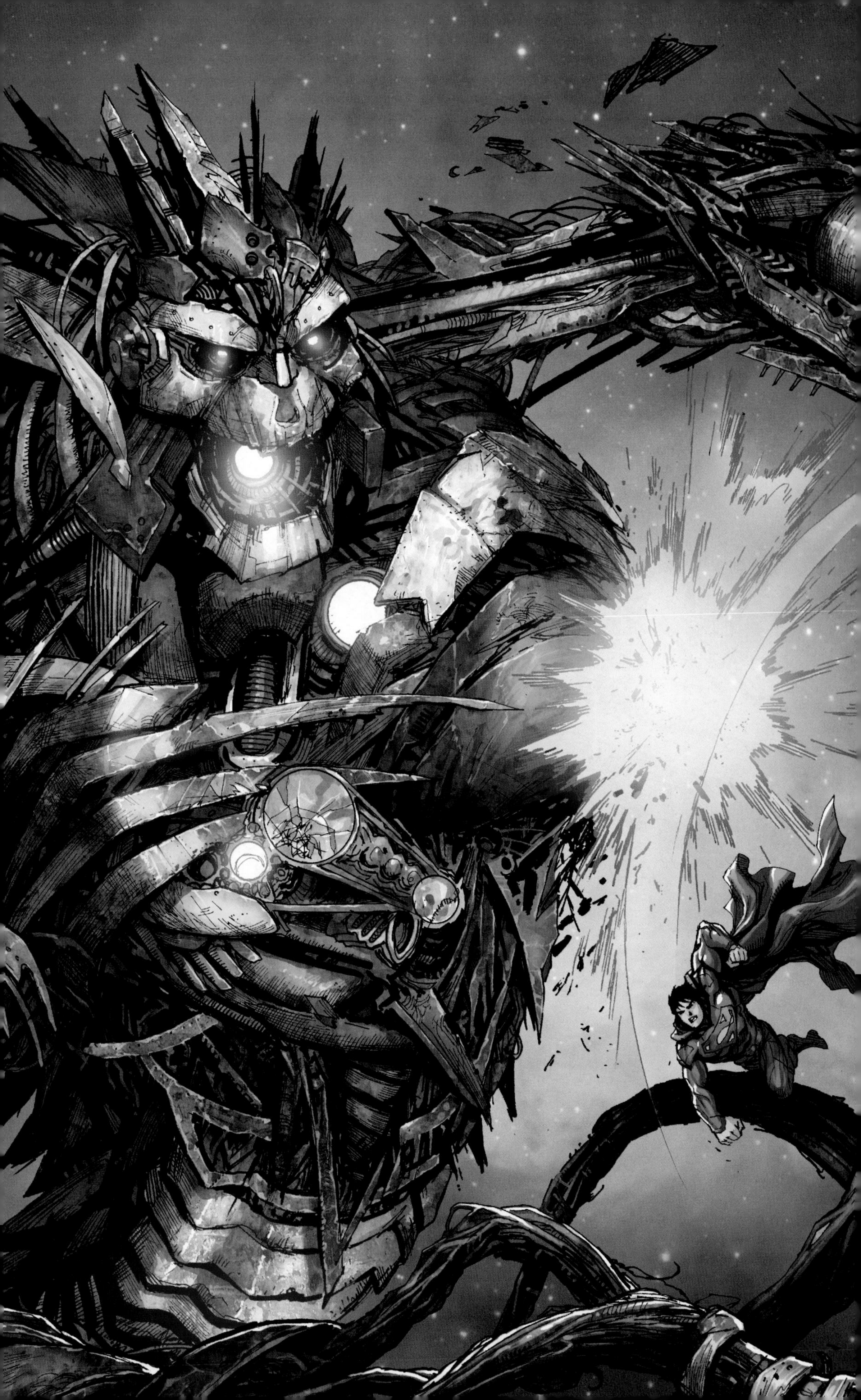

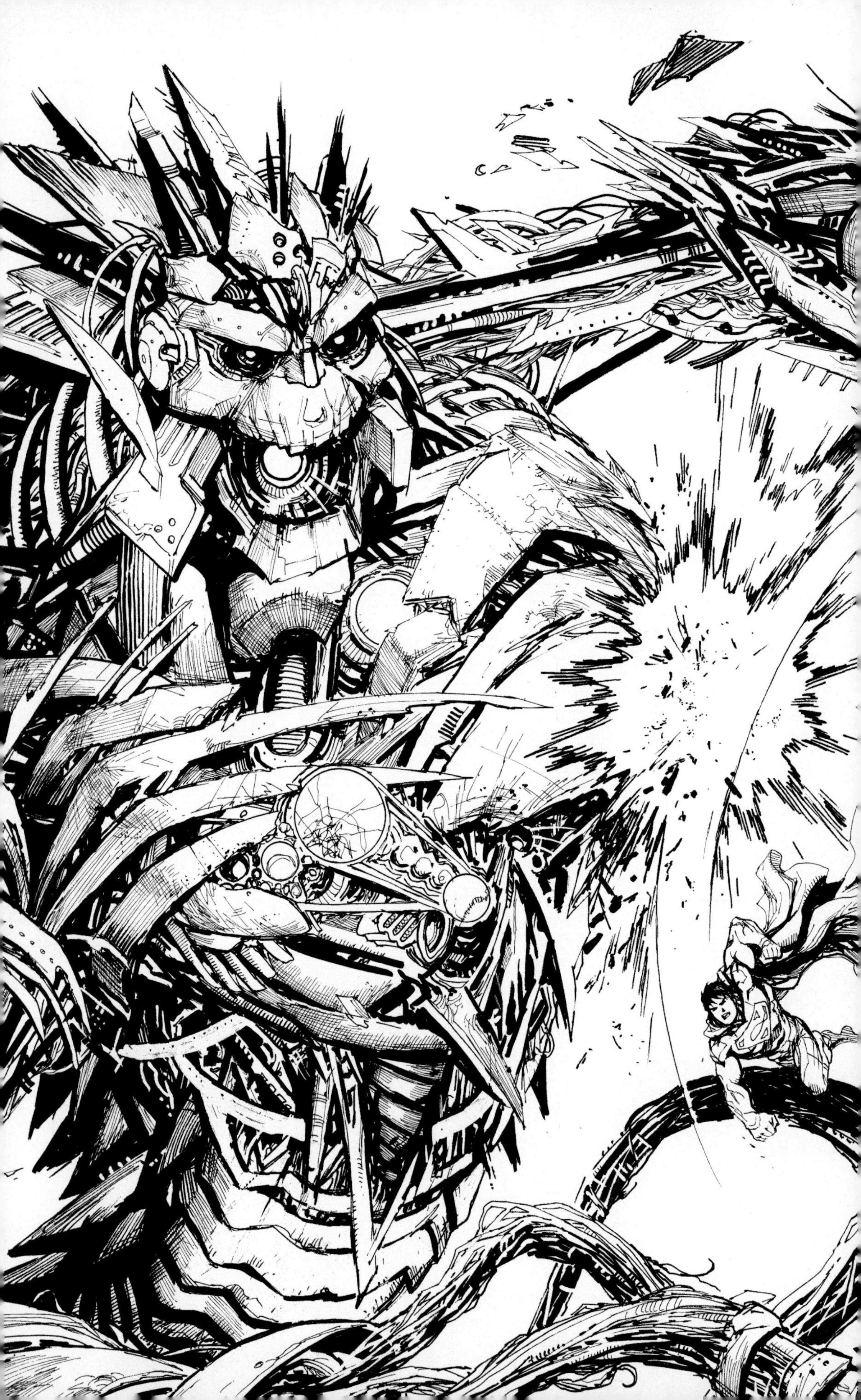

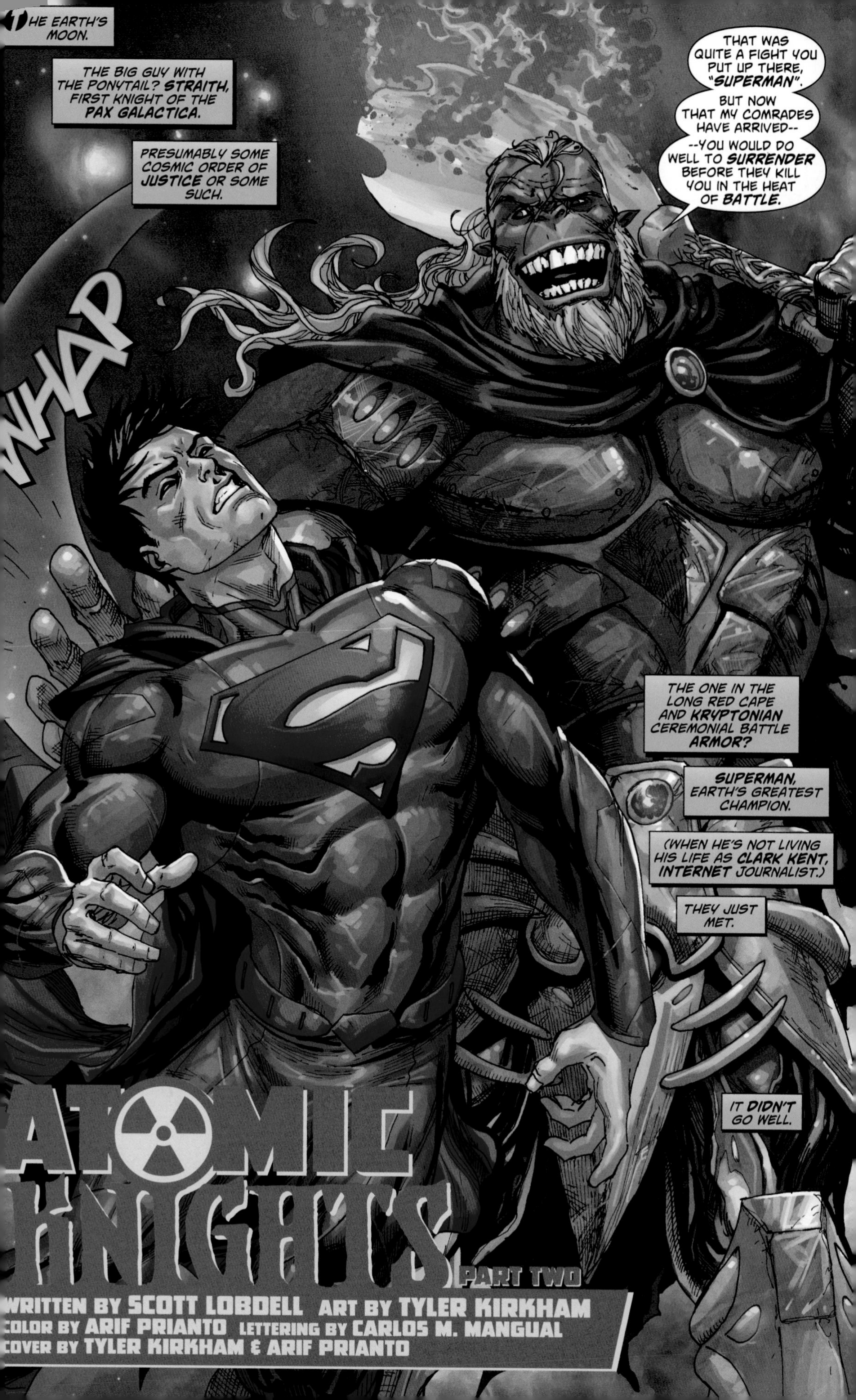
THE EARTH'S MOON.
THE BIG GUY WITH THE PONYTAIL? STRAITH, FIRST KNIGHT OF THE PAX GALACTICA.
PRESUMABLY SOME COSMIC ORDER OF JUSTICE OR SOME SUCH.
THAT WAS QUITE A FIGHT YOU PUT UP THERE, "SUPERMAN". BUT NOW THAT MY COMRADES HAVE ARRIVED--
--YOU WOULD DO WELL TO SURRENDER BEFORE THEY KILL YOU IN THE HEAT OF BATTLE.
WHAP
THE ONE IN THE LONG RED CAPE AND KRYPTONIAN CEREMONIAL BATTLE ARMOR?
SUPERMAN, EARTH'S GREATEST CHAMPION.
(WHEN HE'S NOT LIVING HIS LIFE AS CLARK KENT, INTERNET JOURNALIST.)
THEY JUST MET.
IT DIDN'T GO WELL.
ATOMIC KNIGHTS PART TWO
WRITTEN BY SCOTT LOBDELL ART BY TYLER KIRKHAM
COLOR BY ARIF PRIANTO LETTERING BY CARLOS M. MANGUAL
COVER BY TYLER KIRKHAM & ARIF PRIANTO

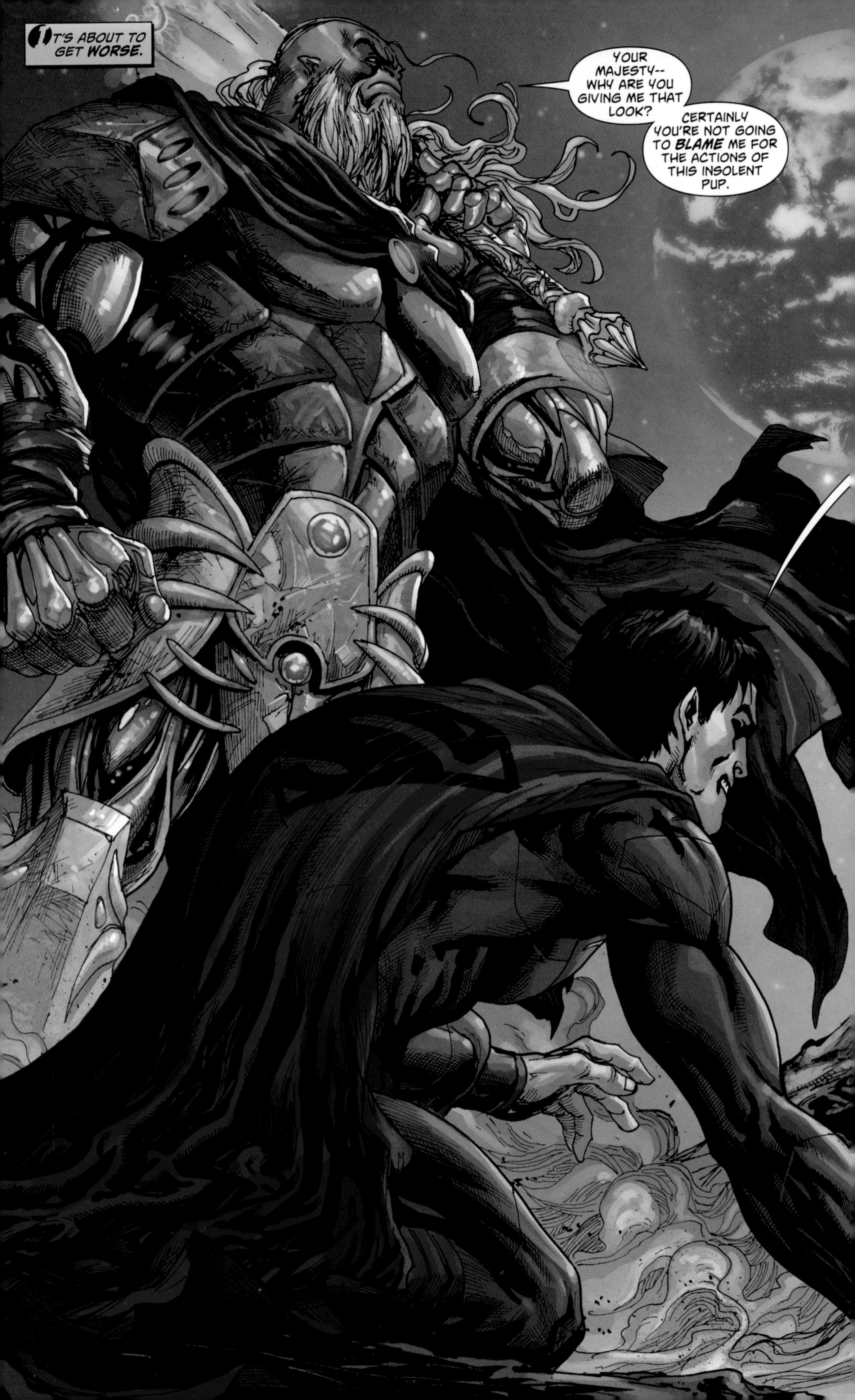
IT'S ABOUT TO GET WORSE.
YOUR MAJESTY-- WHY ARE YOU GIVING ME THAT LOOK?
CERTAINLY YOU'RE NOT GOING TO BLAME ME FOR THE ACTIONS OF THIS INSOLENT PUP.

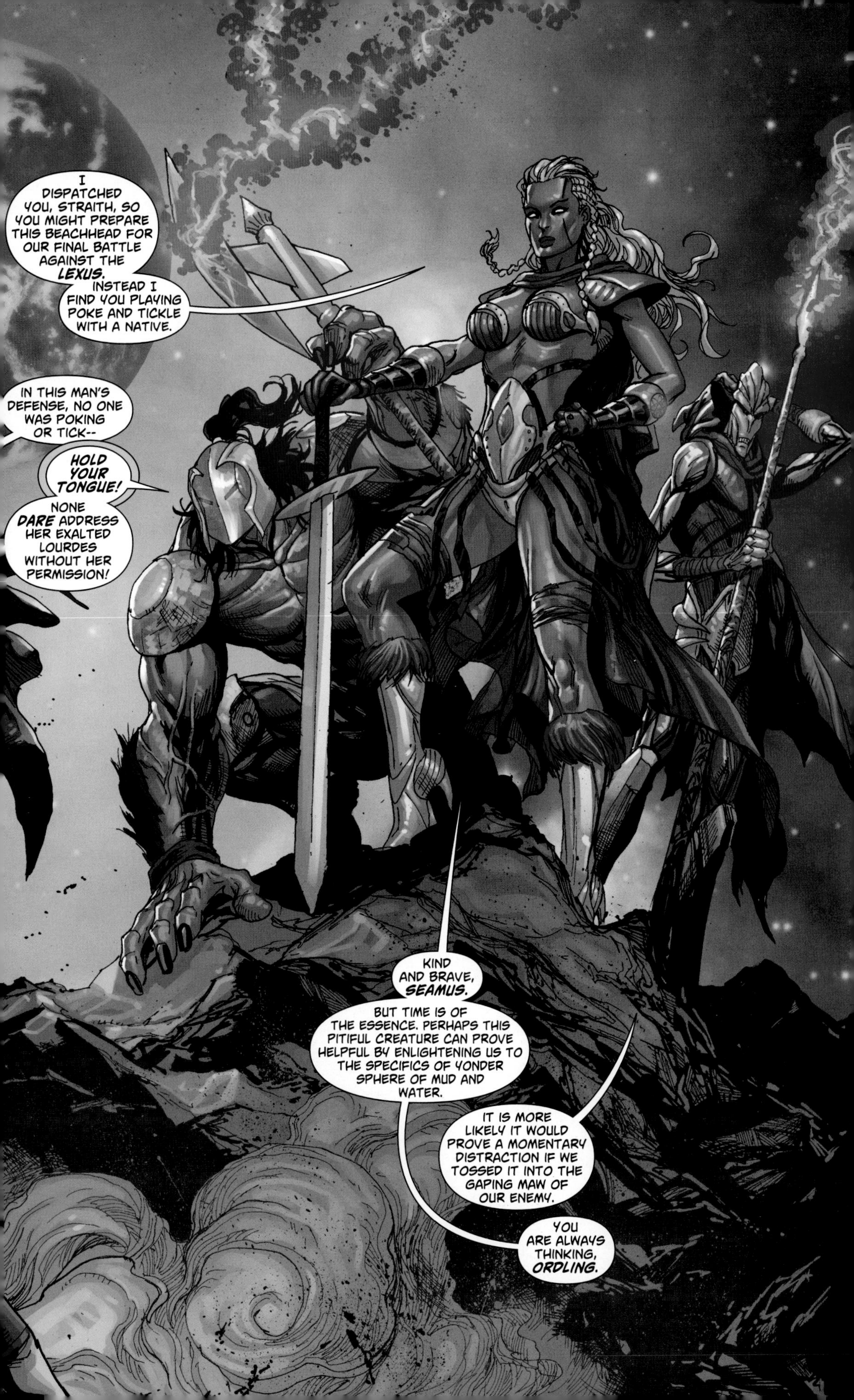
I DISPATCHED YOU, STRAITH, SO YOU MIGHT PREPARE THIS BEACHHEAD FOR OUR FINAL BATTLE AGAINST THE **LEXUS.**
INSTEAD I FIND YOU PLAYING POKE AND TICKLE WITH A NATIVE.
IN THIS MAN'S DEFENSE, NO ONE WAS POKING OR TICK--
HOLD YOUR TONGUE!
NONE **DARE** ADDRESS HER EXALTED LOURDES WITHOUT HER PERMISSION!
KIND AND BRAVE, **SEAMUS.**
BUT TIME IS OF THE ESSENCE. PERHAPS THIS PITIFUL CREATURE CAN PROVE HELPFUL BY ENLIGHTENING US TO THE SPECIFICS OF YONDER SPHERE OF MUD AND WATER.
IT IS MORE LIKELY IT WOULD PROVE A MOMENTARY DISTRACTION IF WE TOSSED IT INTO THE GAPING MAW OF OUR ENEMY.
YOU ARE ALWAYS THINKING, **ORDLING.**

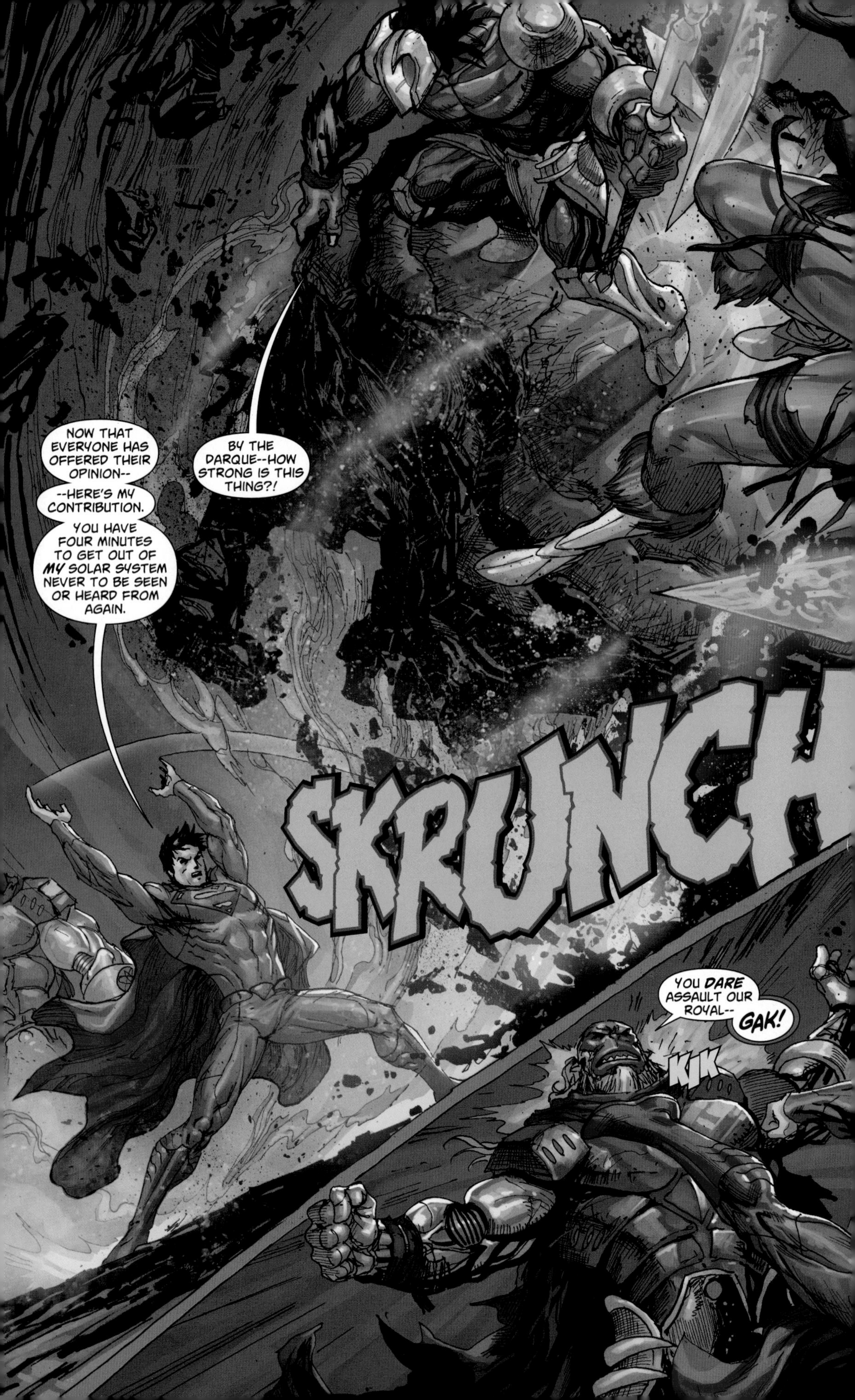
BY THE DARQUE--HOW STRONG IS THIS THING?!
NOW THAT EVERYONE HAS OFFERED THEIR OPINION--
--HERE'S MY CONTRIBUTION.
YOU HAVE FOUR MINUTES TO GET OUT OF MY SOLAR SYSTEM NEVER TO BE SEEN OR HEARD FROM AGAIN.
SKRUNCH
YOU DARE ASSAULT OUR ROYAL-- GAK!
KIK

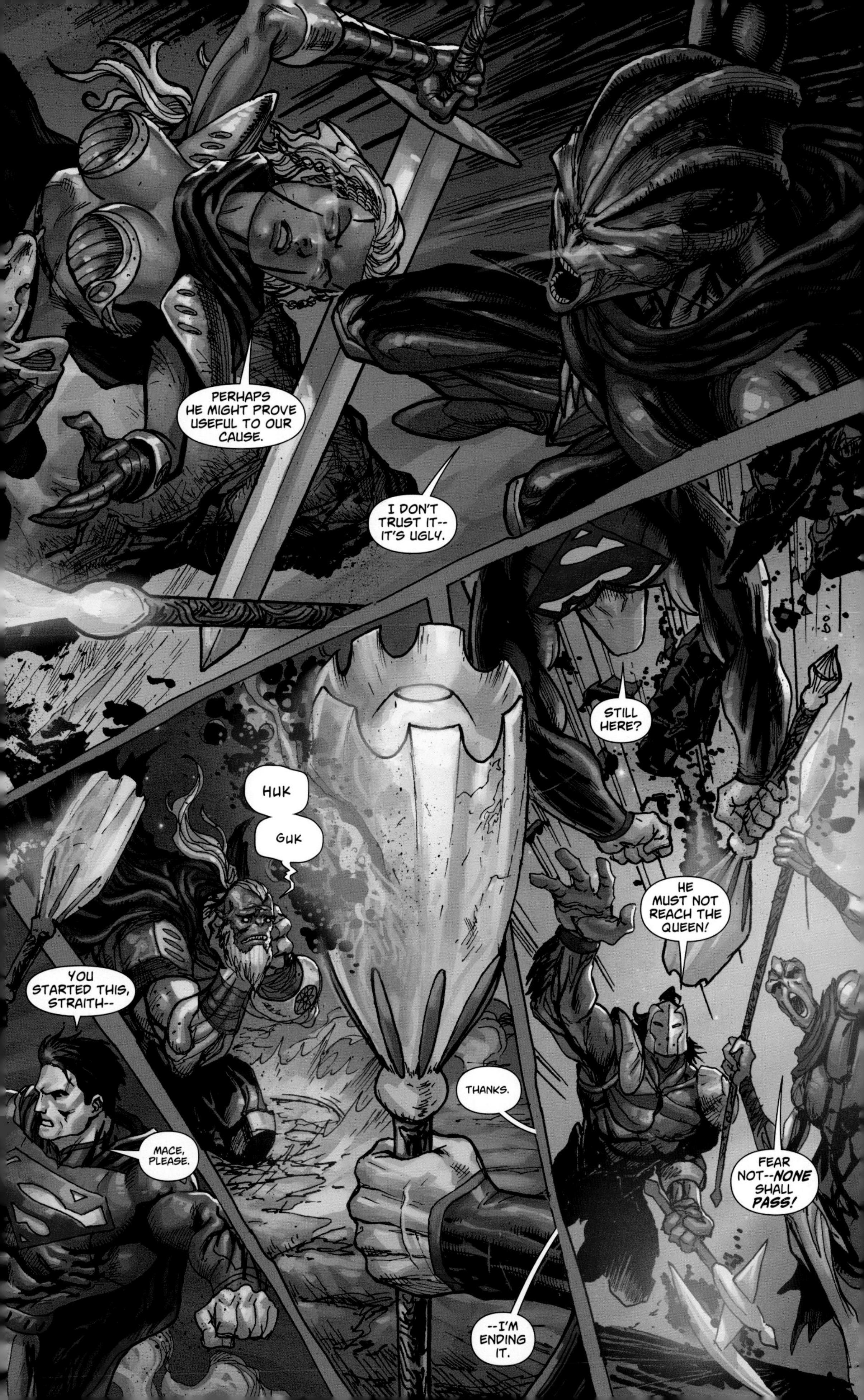
PERHAPS HE MIGHT PROVE USEFUL TO OUR CAUSE.
I DON'T TRUST IT-- IT'S UGLY.
STILL HERE?
HUK
GUK
HE MUST NOT REACH THE QUEEN!
YOU STARTED THIS, STRAITH--
THANKS.
MACE, PLEASE.
FEAR NOT--**NONE** SHALL **PASS!**
--I'M ENDING IT.

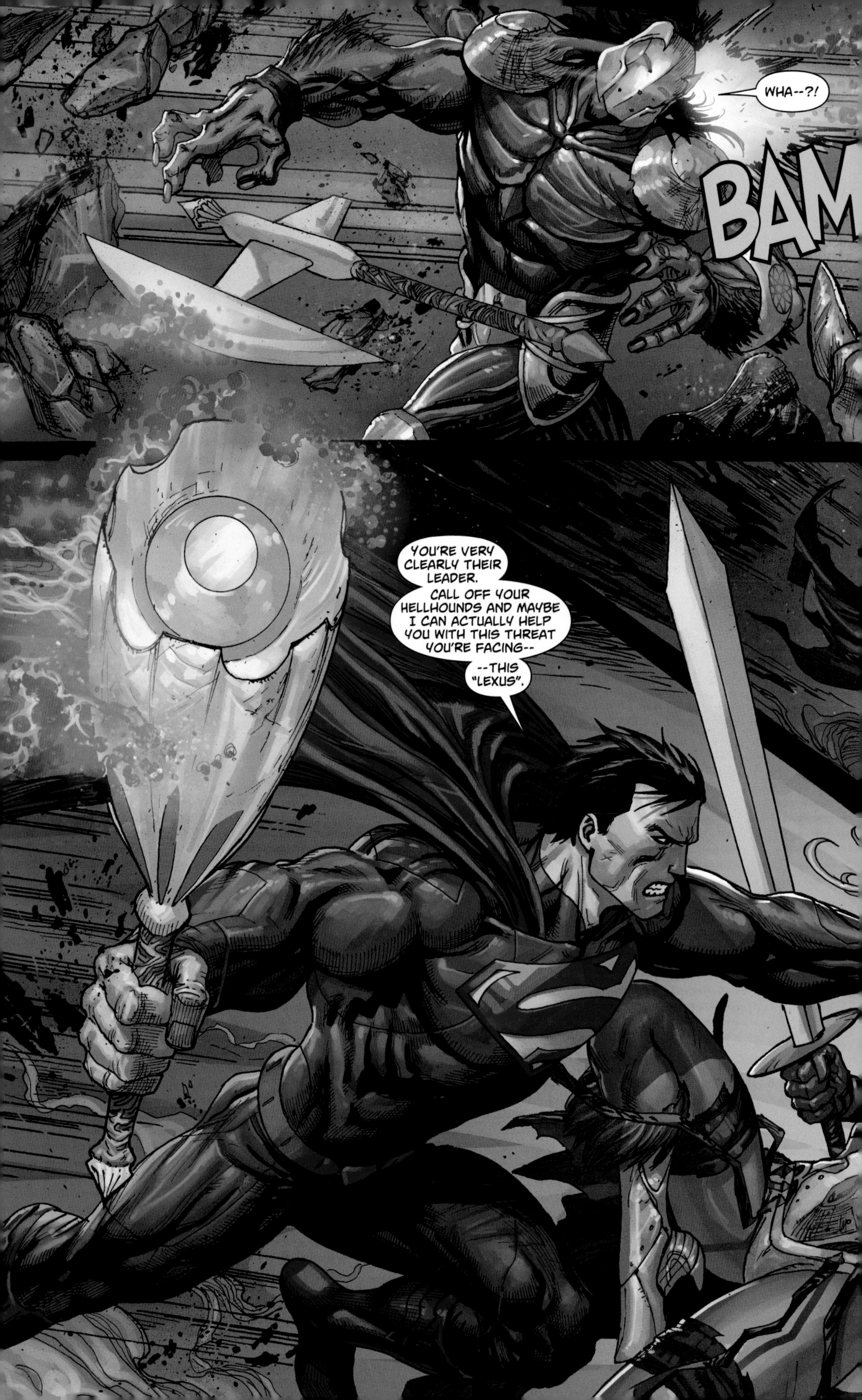
WHA--?!
BAM
YOU'RE VERY CLEARLY THEIR LEADER.
CALL OFF YOUR HELLHOUNDS AND MAYBE I CAN ACTUALLY HELP YOU WITH THIS THREAT YOU'RE FACING--
--THIS "LEXUS".

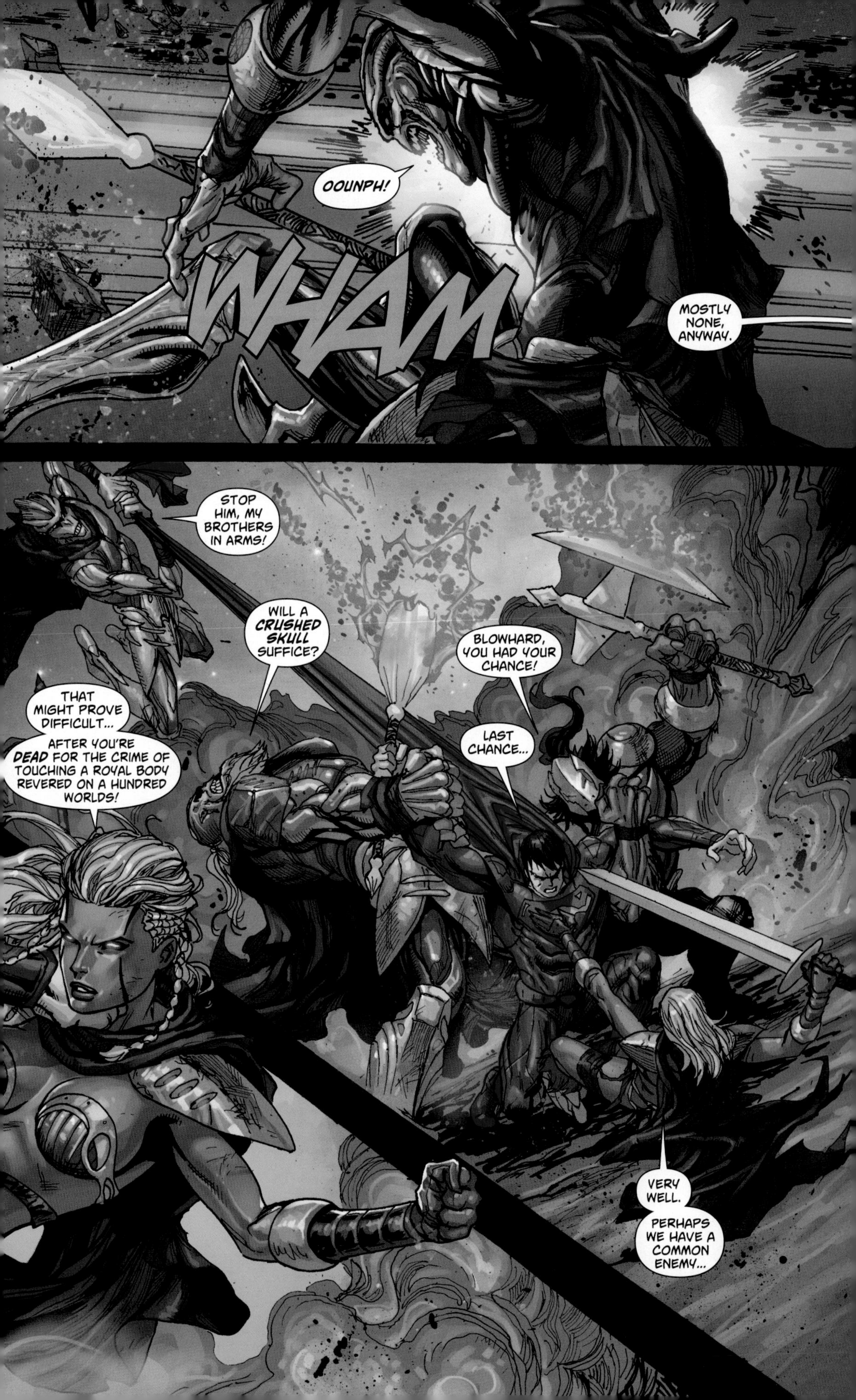
OOUNPH!
WHAM
MOSTLY NONE, ANYWAY.
STOP HIM, MY BROTHERS IN ARMS!
WILL A CRUSHED SKULL SUFFICE?
THAT MIGHT PROVE DIFFICULT...
AFTER YOU'RE DEAD FOR THE CRIME OF TOUCHING A ROYAL BODY REVERED ON A HUNDRED WORLDS!
BLOWHARD, YOU HAD YOUR CHANCE!
LAST CHANCE...
VERY WELL.
PERHAPS WE HAVE A COMMON ENEMY...

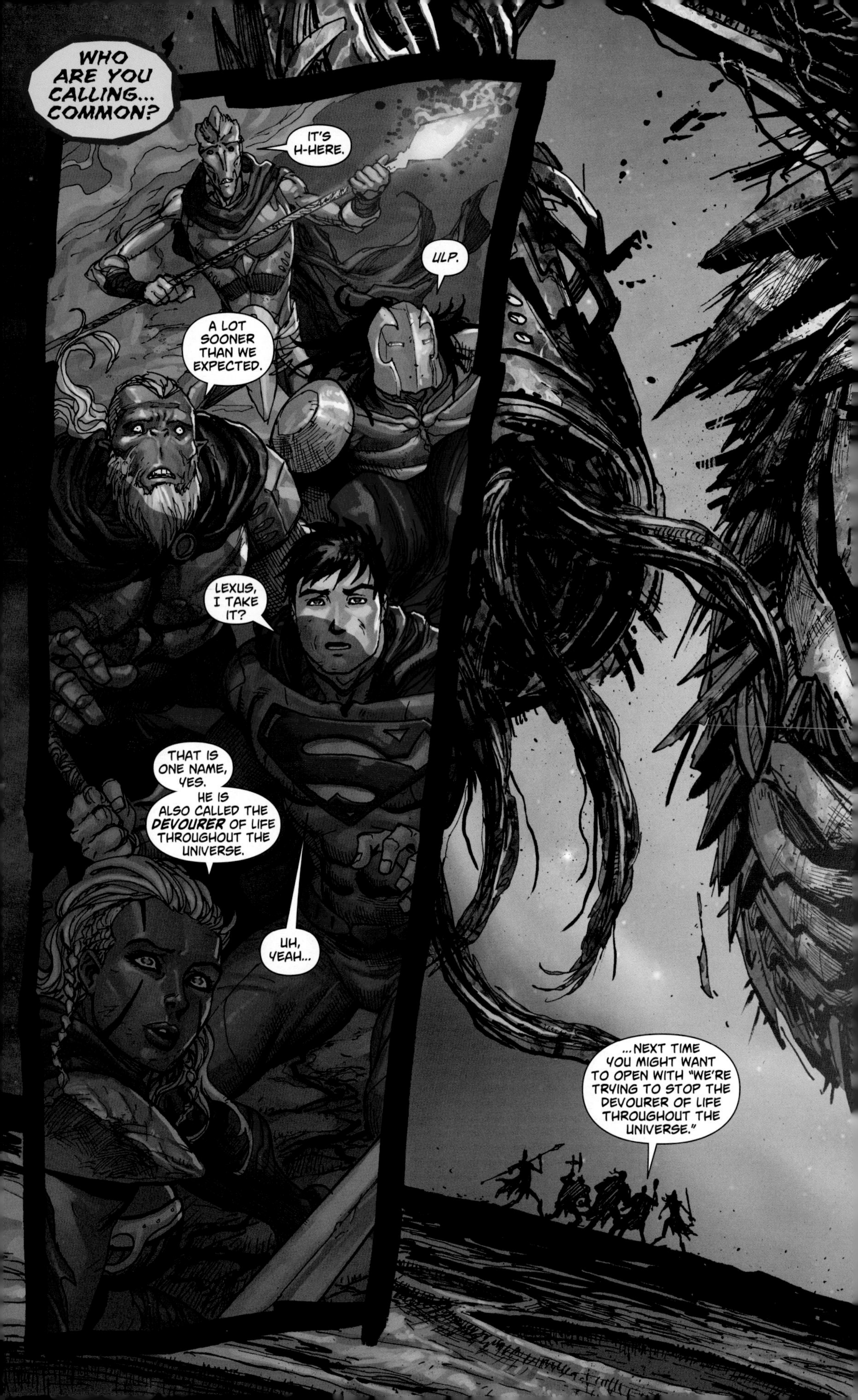
WHO ARE YOU CALLING... COMMON?
IT'S H-HERE.
ULP.
A LOT SOONER THAN WE EXPECTED.
LEXUS, I TAKE IT?
THAT IS ONE NAME, YES.
HE IS ALSO CALLED THE DEVOURER OF LIFE THROUGHOUT THE UNIVERSE.
UH, YEAH...
...NEXT TIME YOU MIGHT WANT TO OPEN WITH "WE'RE TRYING TO STOP THE DEVOURER OF LIFE THROUGHOUT THE UNIVERSE."

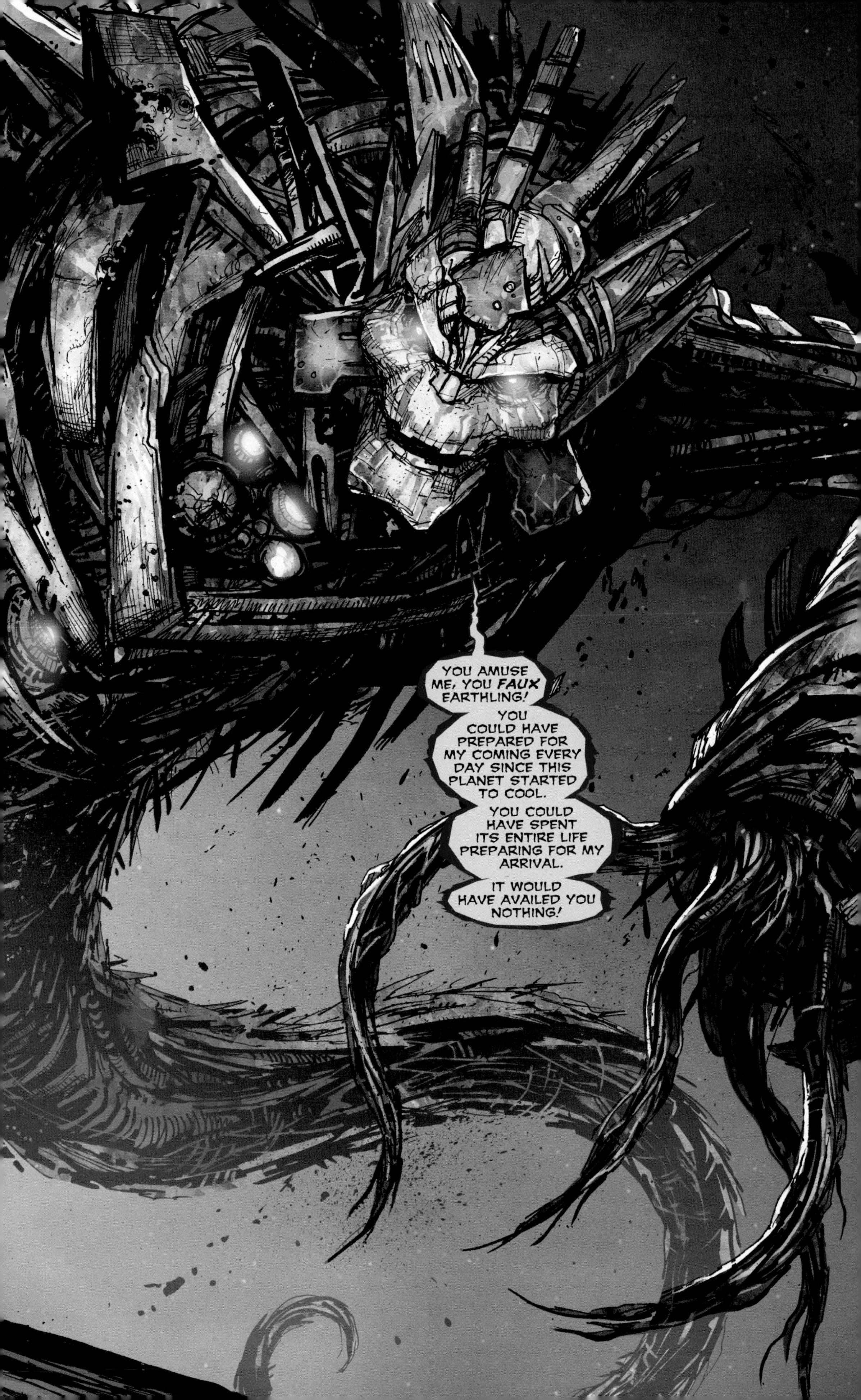
YOU AMUSE ME, YOU *FAUX* EARTHLING!
YOU COULD HAVE PREPARED FOR MY COMING EVERY DAY SINCE THIS PLANET STARTED TO COOL.
YOU COULD HAVE SPENT ITS ENTIRE LIFE PREPARING FOR MY ARRIVAL.
IT WOULD HAVE AVAILED YOU NOTHING!

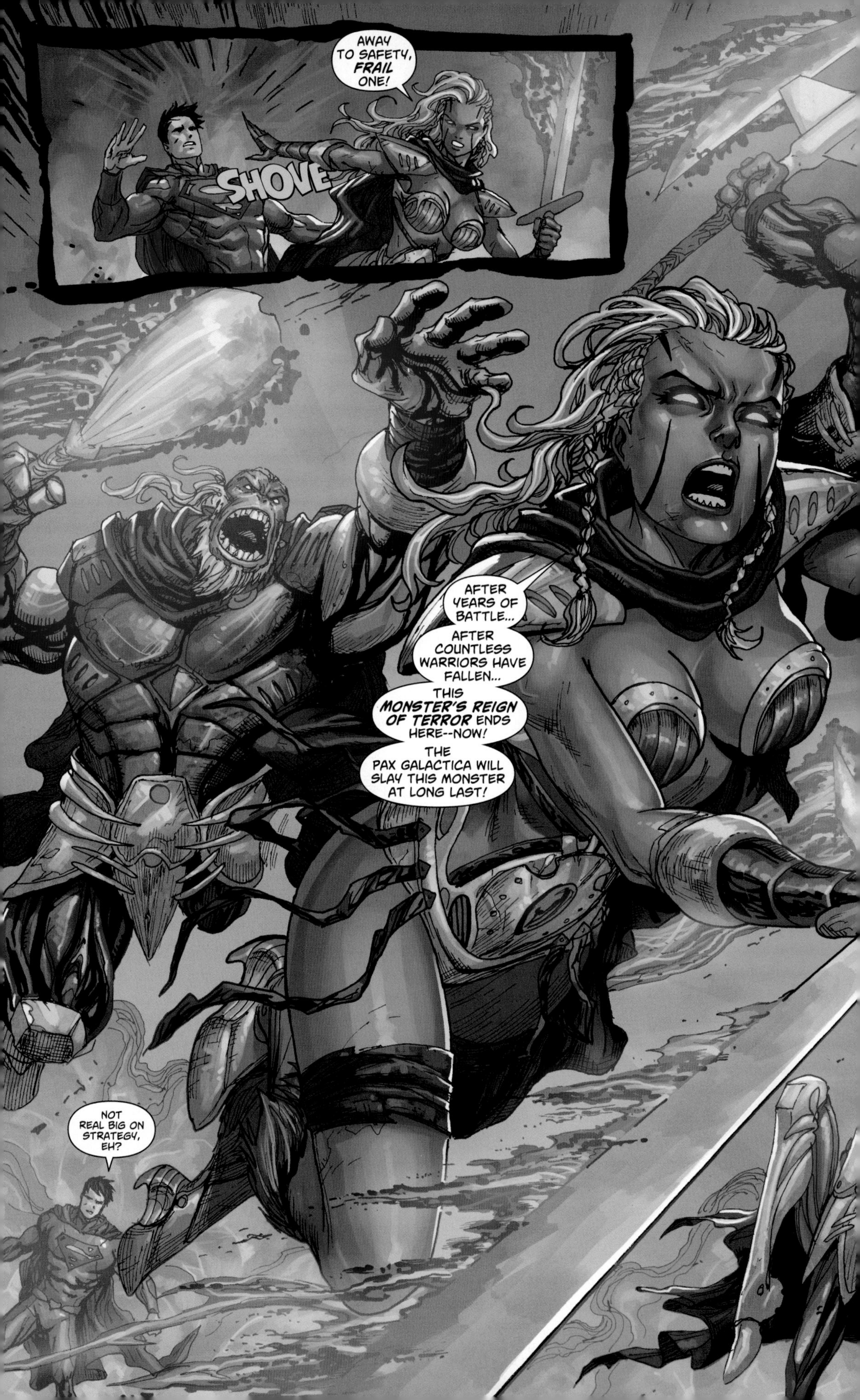
AWAY TO SAFETY, FRAIL ONE!
SHOVE
AFTER YEARS OF BATTLE...
AFTER COUNTLESS WARRIORS HAVE FALLEN...
THIS MONSTER'S REIGN OF TERROR ENDS HERE--NOW!
THE PAX GALACTICA WILL SLAY THIS MONSTER AT LONG LAST!
NOT REAL BIG ON STRATEGY, EH?

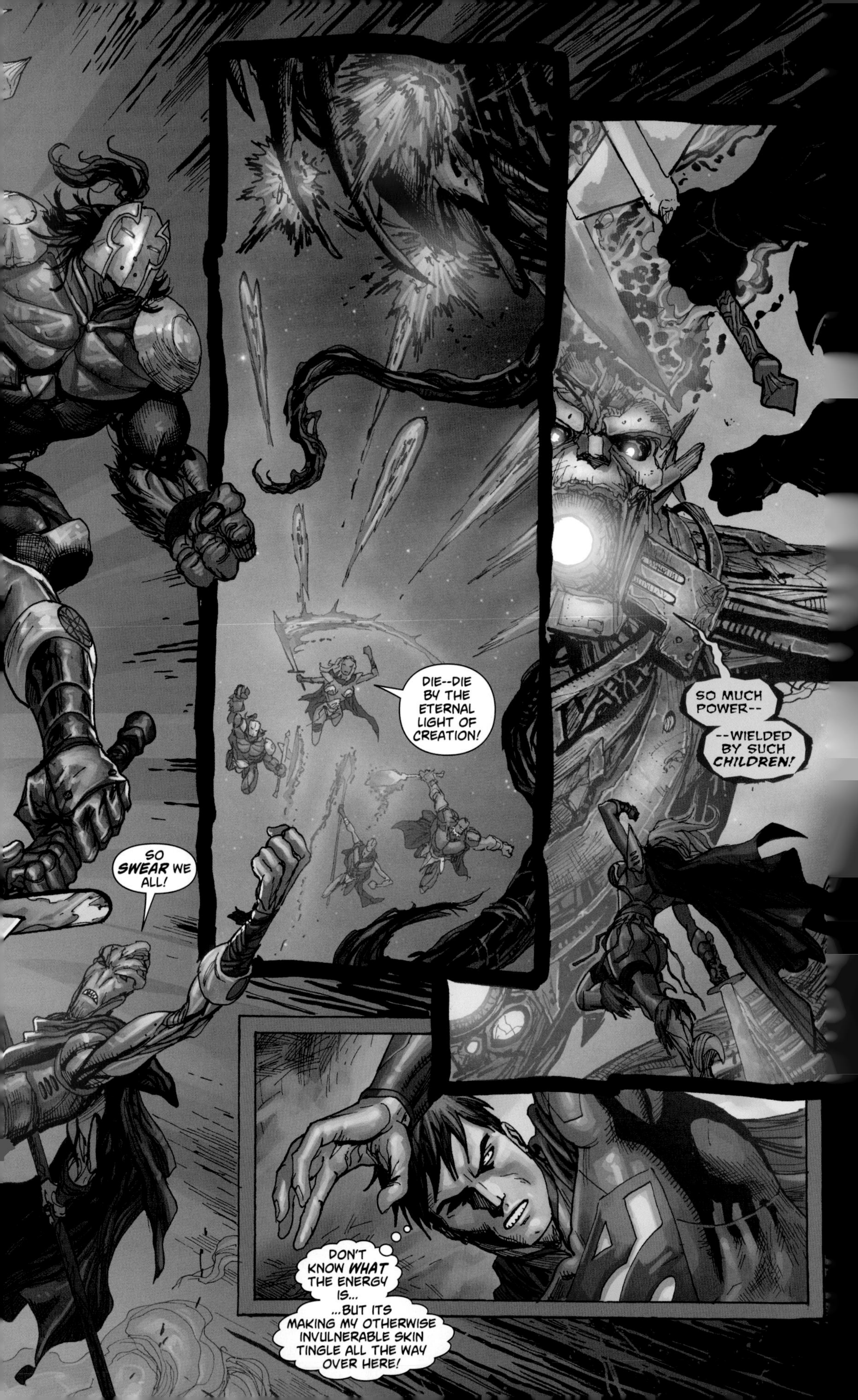
DIE--DIE BY THE ETERNAL LIGHT OF CREATION!
SO MUCH POWER--
--WIELDED BY SUCH CHILDREN!
SO SWEAR WE ALL!
DON'T KNOW WHAT THE ENERGY IS...
...BUT ITS MAKING MY OTHERWISE INVULNERABLE SKIN TINGLE ALL THE WAY OVER HERE!

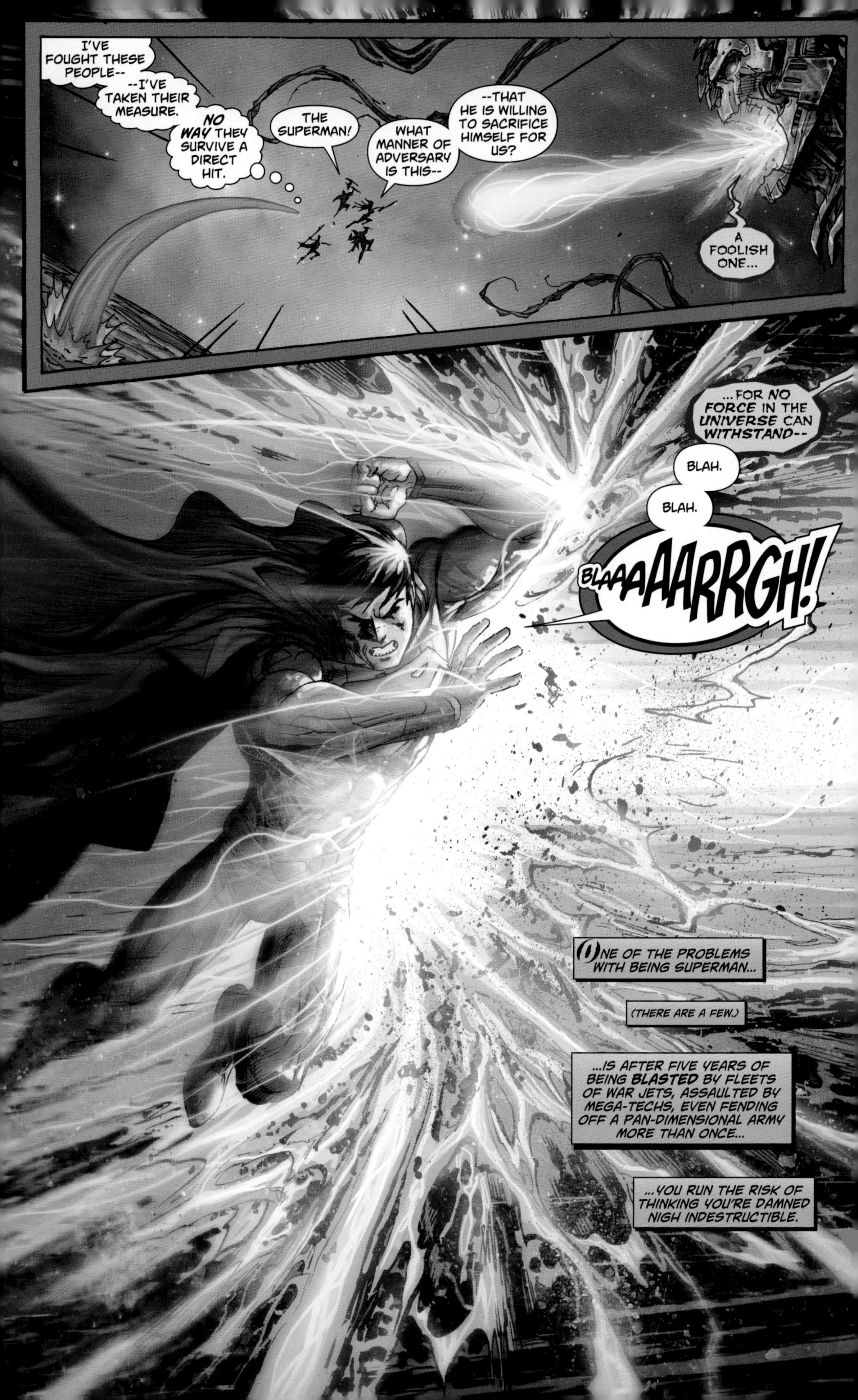
I'VE FOUGHT THESE PEOPLE--
--I'VE TAKEN THEIR MEASURE.
NO WAY THEY SURVIVE A DIRECT HIT.
THE SUPERMAN!
WHAT MANNER OF ADVERSARY IS THIS--
--THAT HE IS WILLING TO SACRIFICE HIMSELF FOR US?
A FOOLISH ONE...
...FOR NO FORCE IN THE UNIVERSE CAN WITHSTAND--
BLAH.
BLAH.
BLAAAAARRRGH!
ONE OF THE PROBLEMS WITH BEING SUPERMAN...
(THERE ARE A FEW.)
...IS AFTER FIVE YEARS OF BEING BLASTED BY FLEETS OF WAR JETS, ASSAULTED BY MEGA-TECHS, EVEN FENDING OFF A PAN-DIMENSIONAL ARMY MORE THAN ONCE...
...YOU RUN THE RISK OF THINKING YOU'RE DAMNED NIGH INDESTRUCTIBLE.

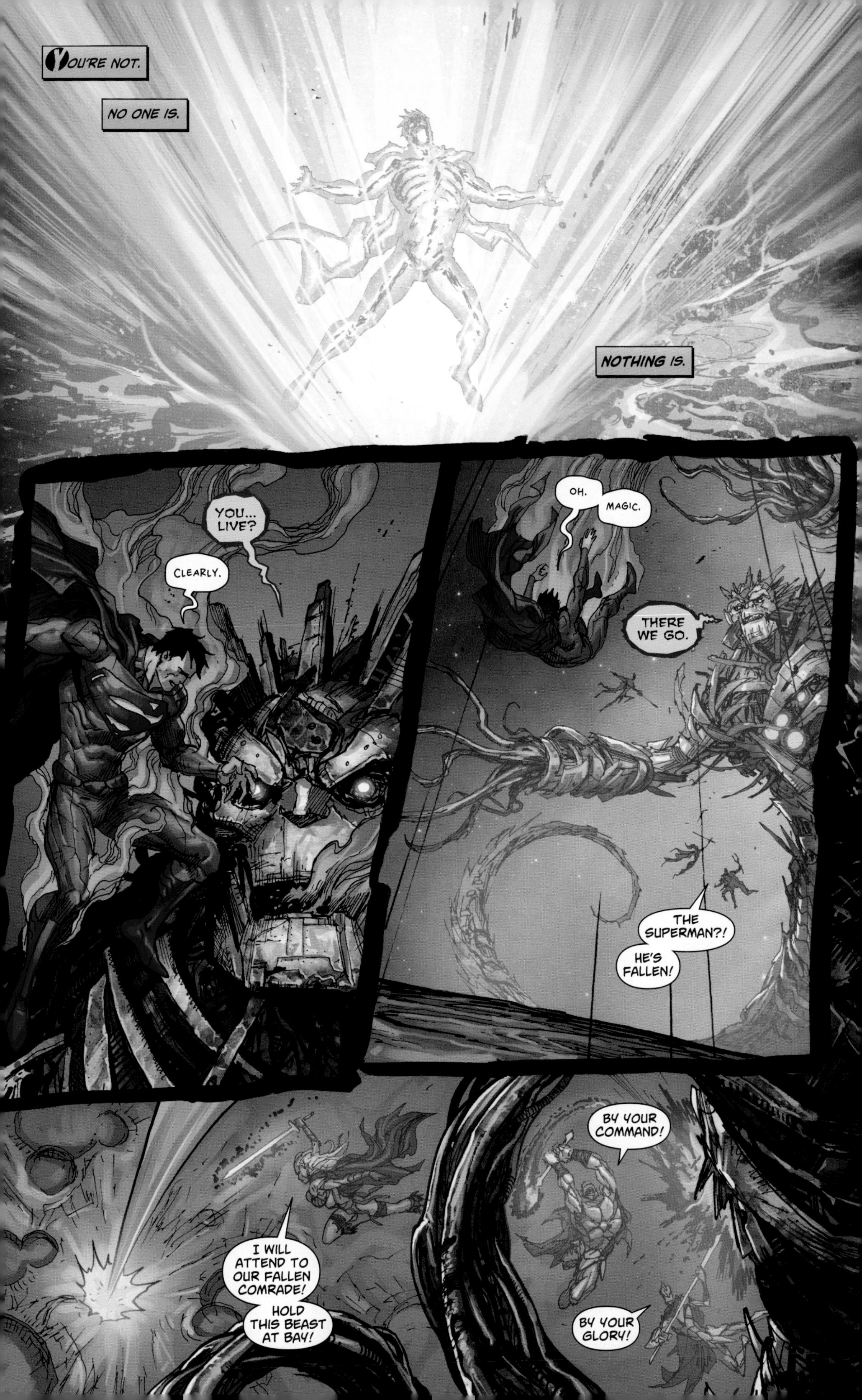

YOU'RE NOT.
NO ONE IS.
NOTHING IS.
YOU... LIVE?
CLEARLY.
OH.
MAGIC.
THERE WE GO.
THE SUPERMAN?!
HE'S FALLEN!
I WILL ATTEND TO OUR FALLEN COMRADE!
HOLD THIS BEAST AT BAY!
BY YOUR COMMAND!
BY YOUR GLORY!

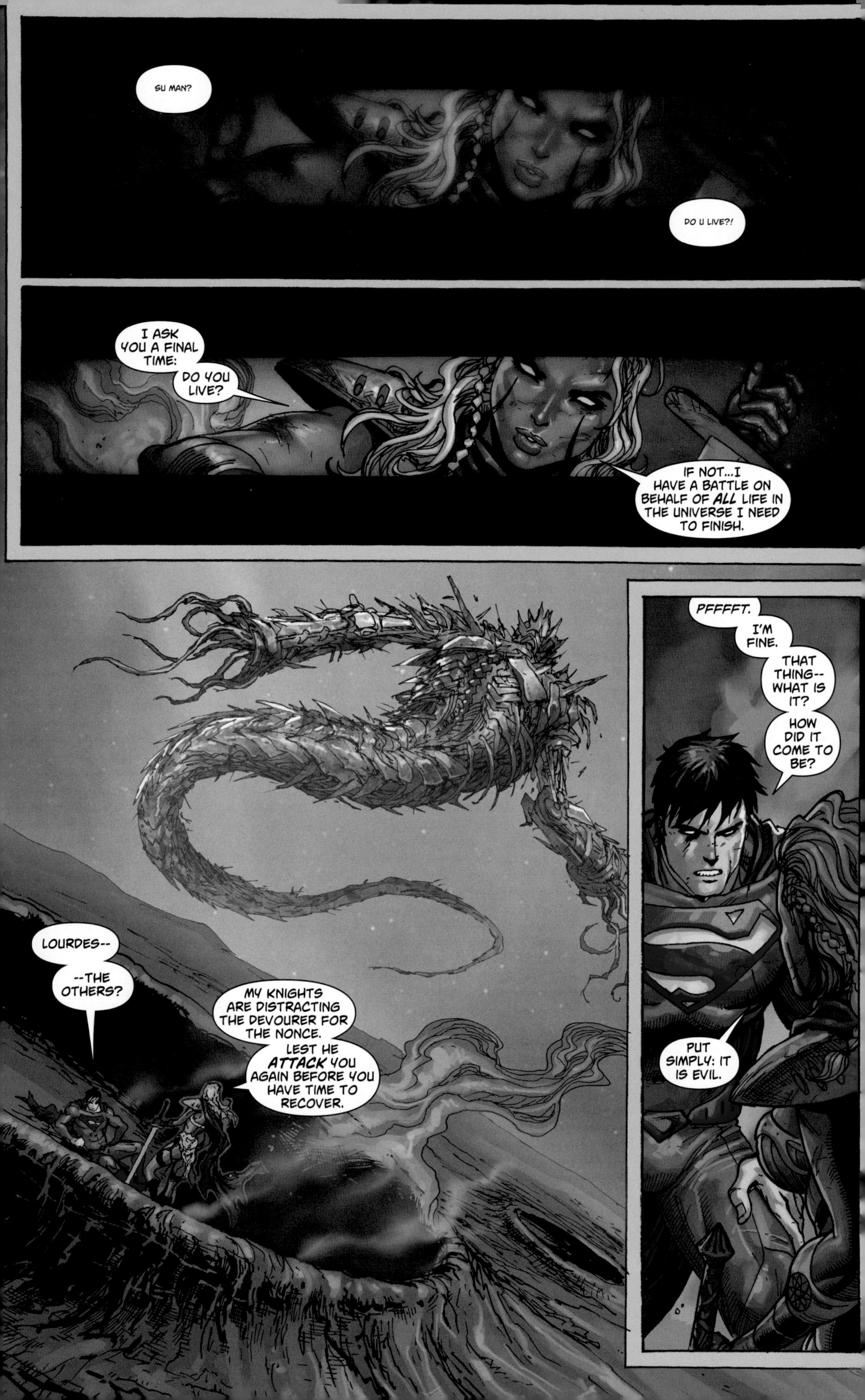
SU MAN?
DO U LIVE?!
I ASK YOU A FINAL TIME:
DO YOU LIVE?
IF NOT...I HAVE A BATTLE ON BEHALF OF ALL LIFE IN THE UNIVERSE I NEED TO FINISH.
PFFFFT.
I'M FINE.
THAT THING-- WHAT IS IT?
HOW DID IT COME TO BE?
PUT SIMPLY: IT IS EVIL.
LOURDES--
--THE OTHERS?
MY KNIGHTS ARE DISTRACTING THE DEVOURER FOR THE NONCE.
LEST HE ATTACK YOU AGAIN BEFORE YOU HAVE TIME TO RECOVER.

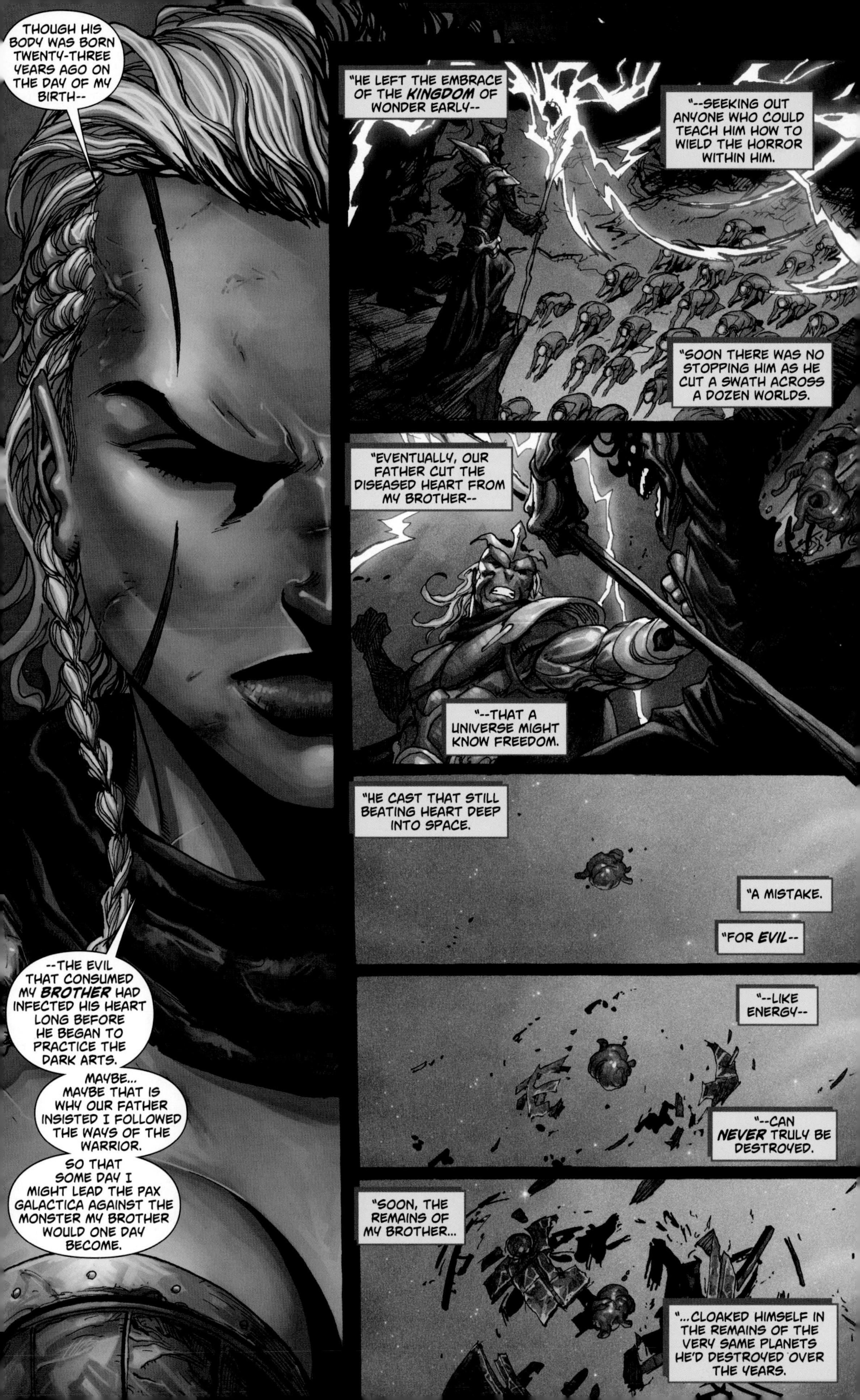
THOUGH HIS BODY WAS BORN TWENTY-THREE YEARS AGO ON THE DAY OF MY BIRTH--
"HE LEFT THE EMBRACE OF THE KINGDOM OF WONDER EARLY--
"--SEEKING OUT ANYONE WHO COULD TEACH HIM HOW TO WIELD THE HORROR WITHIN HIM.
"SOON THERE WAS NO STOPPING HIM AS HE CUT A SWATH ACROSS A DOZEN WORLDS.
"EVENTUALLY, OUR FATHER CUT THE DISEASED HEART FROM MY BROTHER--
"--THAT A UNIVERSE MIGHT KNOW FREEDOM.
"HE CAST THAT STILL BEATING HEART DEEP INTO SPACE.
"A MISTAKE.
"FOR EVIL--
"--LIKE ENERGY--
"--CAN NEVER TRULY BE DESTROYED.
"SOON, THE REMAINS OF MY BROTHER...
"...CLOAKED HIMSELF IN THE REMAINS OF THE VERY SAME PLANETS HE'D DESTROYED OVER THE YEARS.
--THE EVIL THAT CONSUMED MY BROTHER HAD INFECTED HIS HEART LONG BEFORE HE BEGAN TO PRACTICE THE DARK ARTS.
MAYBE... MAYBE THAT IS WHY OUR FATHER INSISTED I FOLLOWED THE WAYS OF THE WARRIOR.
SO THAT SOME DAY I MIGHT LEAD THE PAX GALACTICA AGAINST THE MONSTER MY BROTHER WOULD ONE DAY BECOME.

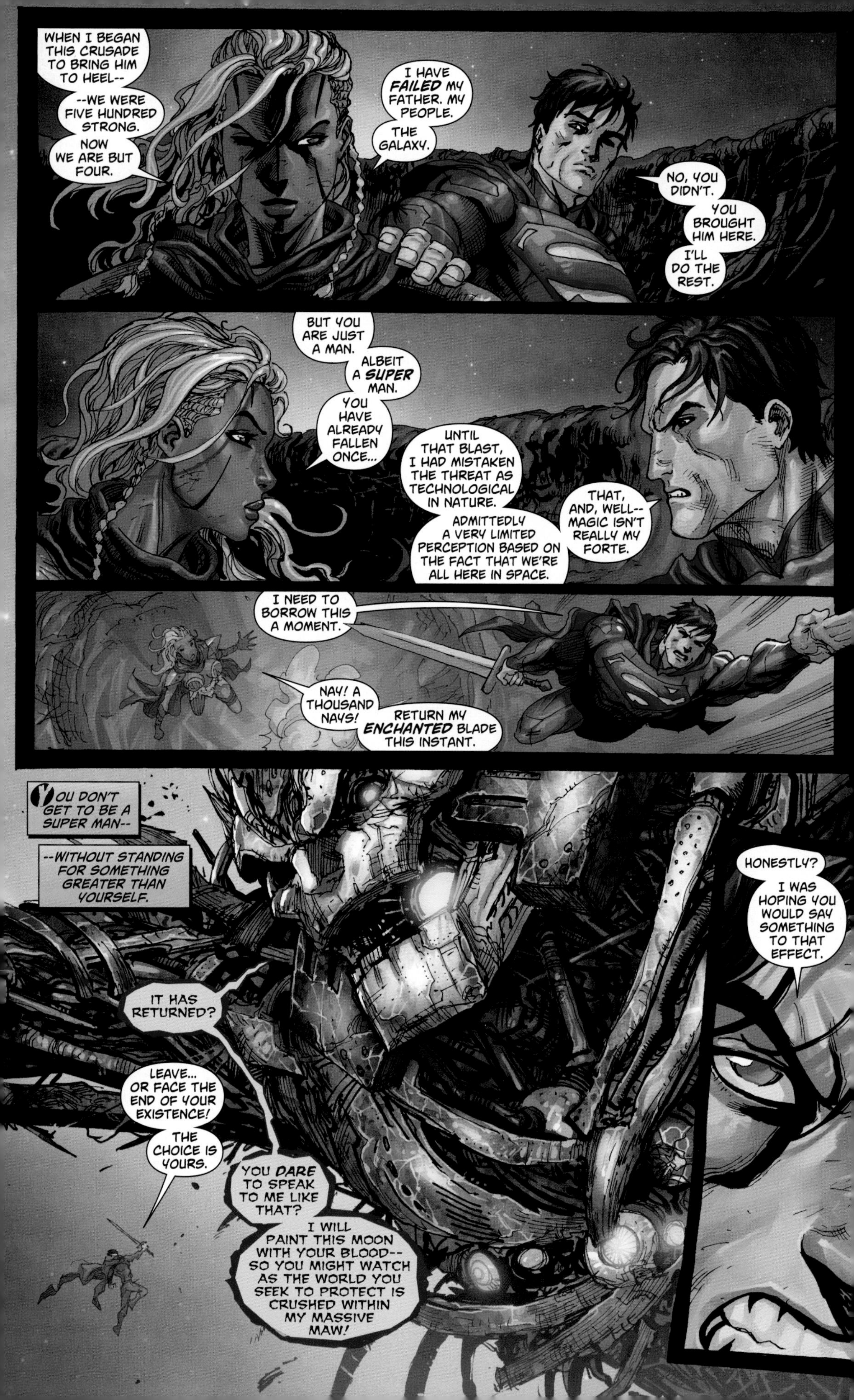

WHEN I BEGAN THIS CRUSADE TO BRING HIM TO HEEL--
--WE WERE FIVE HUNDRED STRONG.
NOW WE ARE BUT FOUR.
I HAVE FAILED MY FATHER. MY PEOPLE.
THE GALAXY.
NO, YOU DIDN'T.
YOU BROUGHT HIM HERE.
I'LL DO THE REST.
BUT YOU ARE JUST A MAN.
ALBEIT A SUPER MAN.
YOU HAVE ALREADY FALLEN ONCE...
UNTIL THAT BLAST, I HAD MISTAKEN THE THREAT AS TECHNOLOGICAL IN NATURE.
ADMITTEDLY A VERY LIMITED PERCEPTION BASED ON THE FACT THAT WE'RE ALL HERE IN SPACE.
THAT, AND, WELL-- MAGIC ISN'T REALLY MY FORTE.
I NEED TO BORROW THIS A MOMENT.
NAY! A THOUSAND NAYS!
RETURN MY ENCHANTED BLADE THIS INSTANT.
YOU DON'T GET TO BE A SUPER MAN--
--WITHOUT STANDING FOR SOMETHING GREATER THAN YOURSELF.
HONESTLY?
I WAS HOPING YOU WOULD SAY SOMETHING TO THAT EFFECT.
IT HAS RETURNED?
LEAVE... OR FACE THE END OF YOUR EXISTENCE!
THE CHOICE IS YOURS.
YOU DARE TO SPEAK TO ME LIKE THAT?
I WILL PAINT THIS MOON WITH YOUR BLOOD-- SO YOU MIGHT WATCH AS THE WORLD YOU SEEK TO PROTECT IS CRUSHED WITHIN MY MASSIVE MAW!

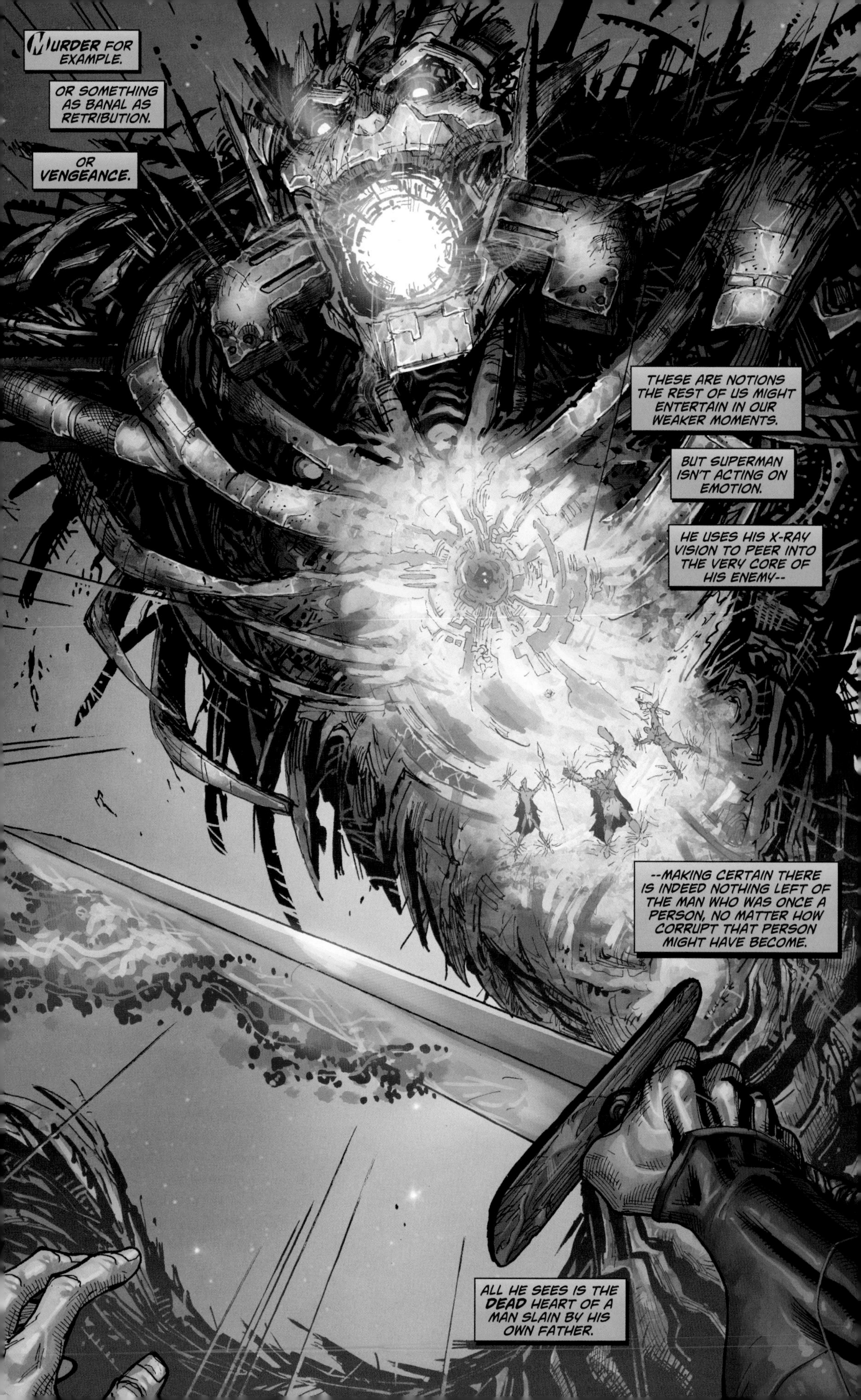
MURDER FOR EXAMPLE.
OR SOMETHING AS BANAL AS RETRIBUTION.
OR VENGEANCE.
THESE ARE NOTIONS THE REST OF US MIGHT ENTERTAIN IN OUR WEAKER MOMENTS.
BUT SUPERMAN ISN'T ACTING ON EMOTION.
HE USES HIS X-RAY VISION TO PEER INTO THE VERY CORE OF HIS ENEMY--
--MAKING CERTAIN THERE IS INDEED NOTHING LEFT OF THE MAN WHO WAS ONCE A PERSON, NO MATTER HOW CORRUPT THAT PERSON MIGHT HAVE BECOME.
ALL HE SEES IS THE DEAD HEART OF A MAN SLAIN BY HIS OWN FATHER.

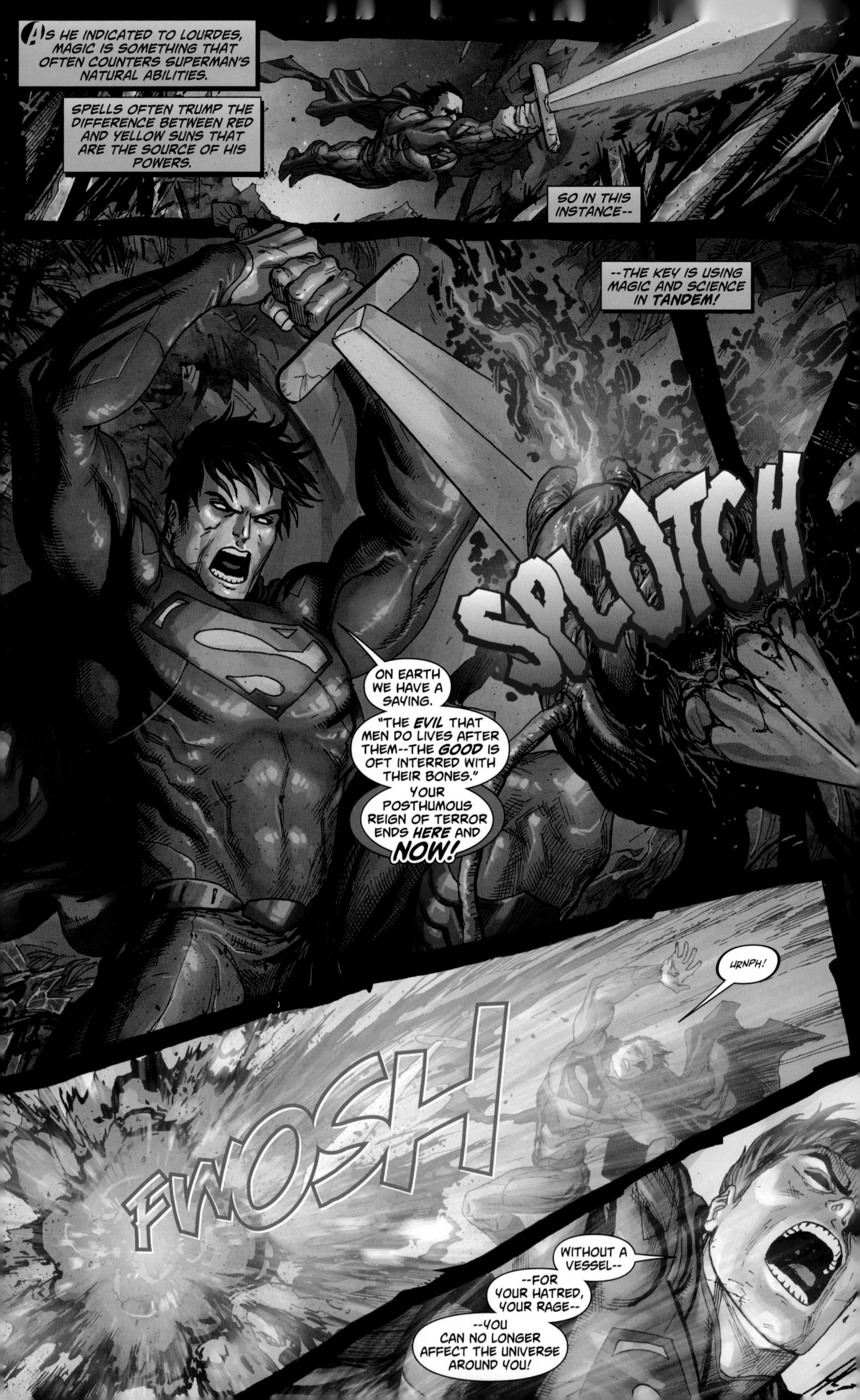
AS HE INDICATED TO LOURDES, MAGIC IS SOMETHING THAT OFTEN COUNTERS SUPERMAN'S NATURAL ABILITIES.
SPELLS OFTEN TRUMP THE DIFFERENCE BETWEEN RED AND YELLOW SUNS THAT ARE THE SOURCE OF HIS POWERS.
SO IN THIS INSTANCE--
--THE KEY IS USING MAGIC AND SCIENCE IN TANDEM!
SPLUTCH
ON EARTH WE HAVE A SAYING.
"THE EVIL THAT MEN DO LIVES AFTER THEM--THE GOOD IS OFT INTERRED WITH THEIR BONES."
YOUR POSTHUMOUS REIGN OF TERROR ENDS HERE AND NOW!
URNPH!
FWOSH
WITHOUT A VESSEL--
--FOR YOUR HATRED, YOUR RAGE--
--YOU CAN NO LONGER AFFECT THE UNIVERSE AROUND YOU!

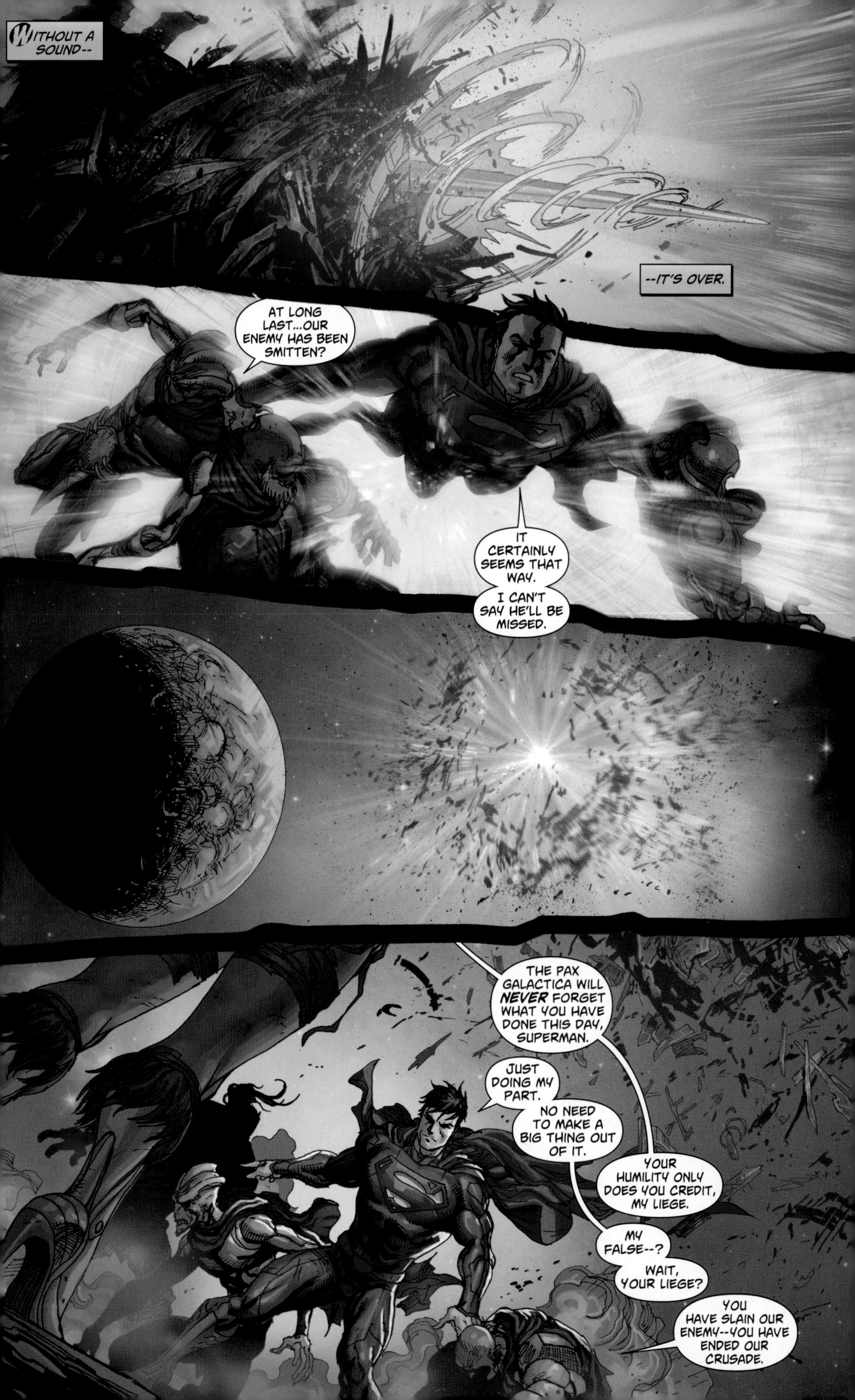
WITHOUT A SOUND--
--IT'S OVER.
AT LONG LAST...OUR ENEMY HAS BEEN SMITTEN?
IT CERTAINLY SEEMS THAT WAY.
I CAN'T SAY HE'LL BE MISSED.
THE PAX GALACTICA WILL **NEVER** FORGET WHAT YOU HAVE DONE THIS DAY, SUPERMAN.
JUST DOING MY PART.
NO NEED TO MAKE A BIG THING OUT OF IT.
YOUR HUMILITY ONLY DOES YOU CREDIT, MY LIEGE.
MY FALSE--?
WAIT, YOUR LIEGE?
YOU HAVE SLAIN OUR ENEMY--YOU HAVE ENDED OUR CRUSADE.

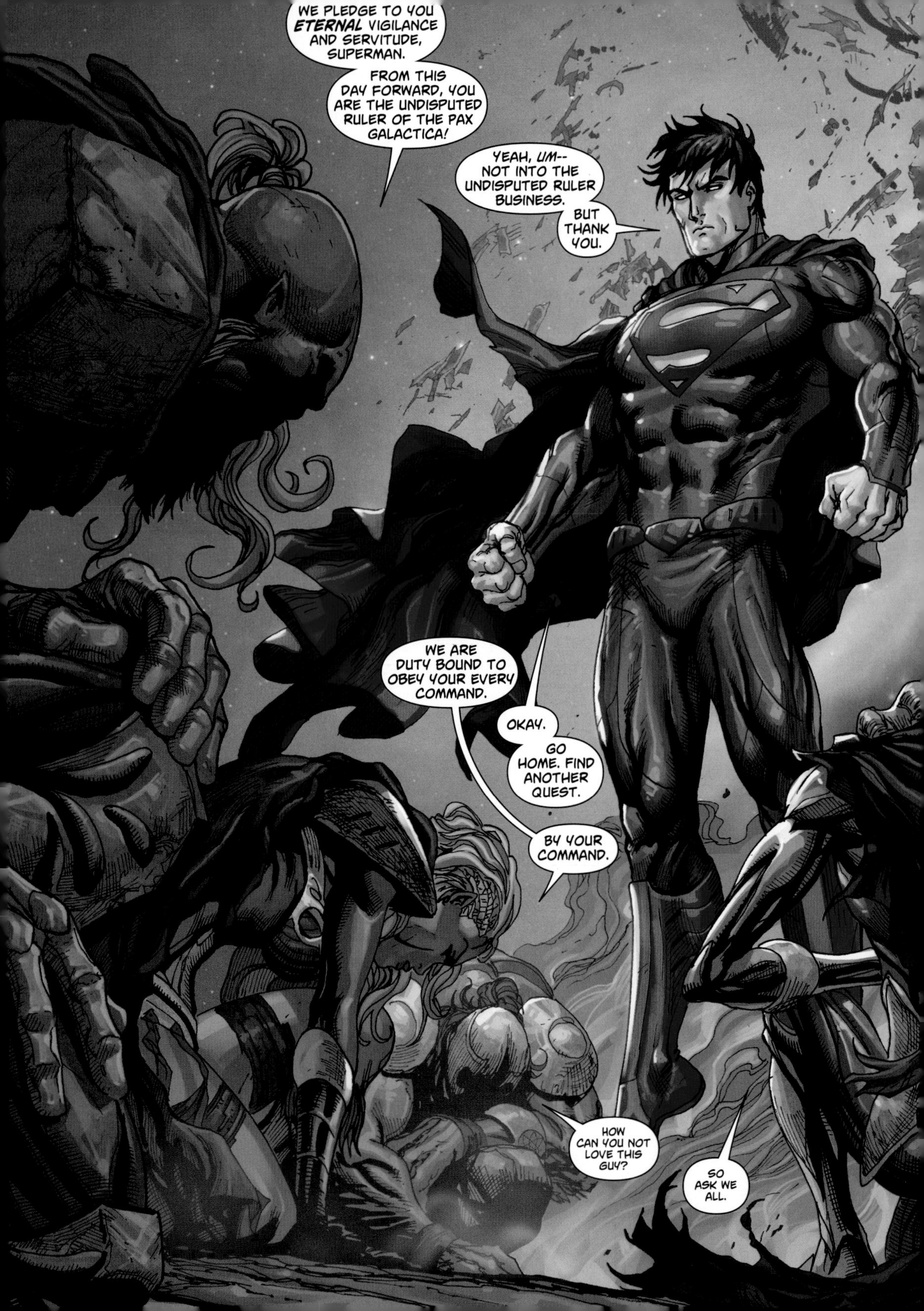

WE PLEDGE TO YOU ETERNAL VIGILANCE AND SERVITUDE, SUPERMAN.
FROM THIS DAY FORWARD, YOU ARE THE UNDISPUTED RULER OF THE PAX GALACTICA!
YEAH, UM-- NOT INTO THE UNDISPUTED RULER BUSINESS.
BUT THANK YOU.
WE ARE DUTY BOUND TO OBEY YOUR EVERY COMMAND.
OKAY.
GO HOME. FIND ANOTHER QUEST.
BY YOUR COMMAND.
HOW CAN YOU NOT LOVE THIS GUY?
SO ASK WE ALL.

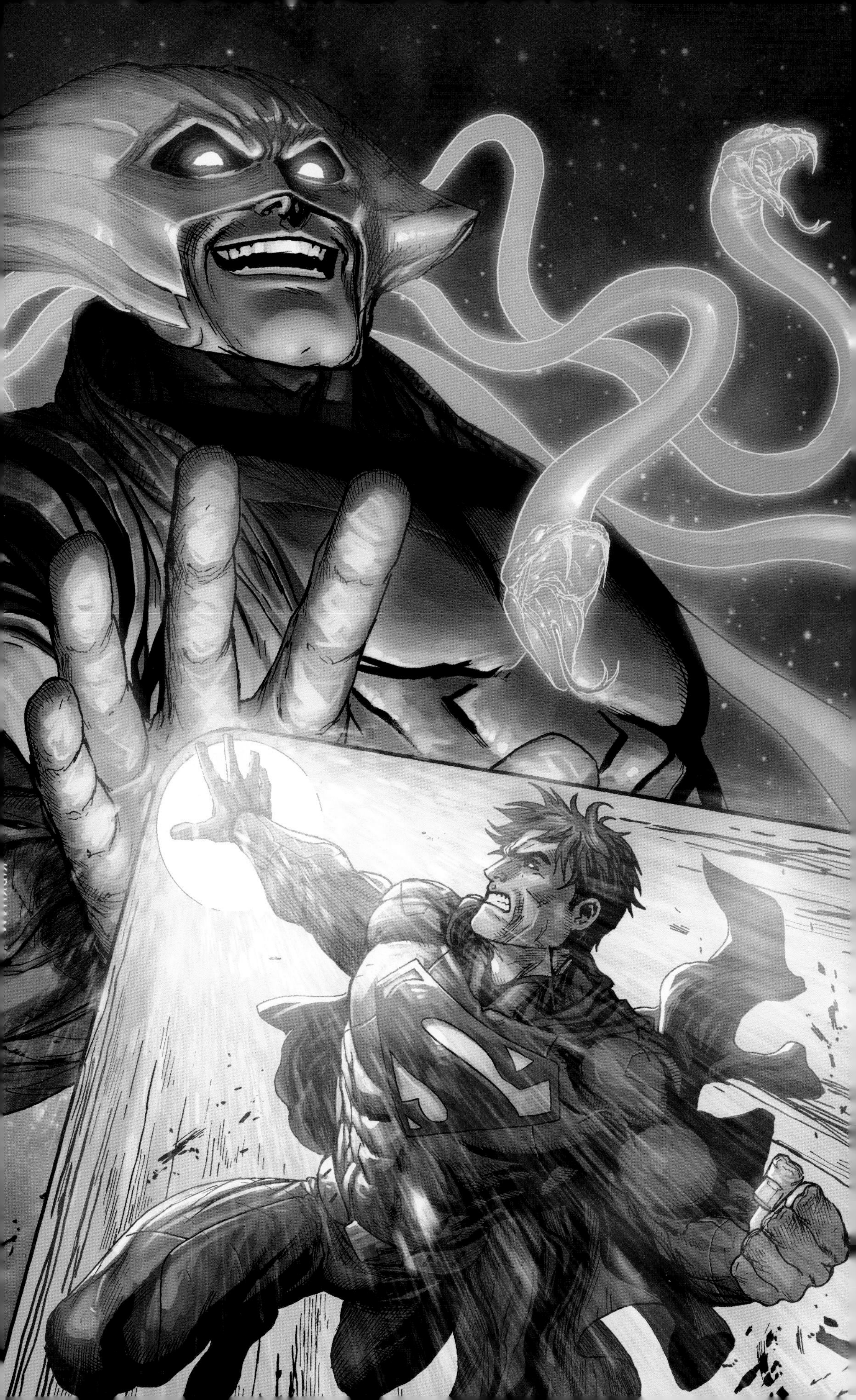

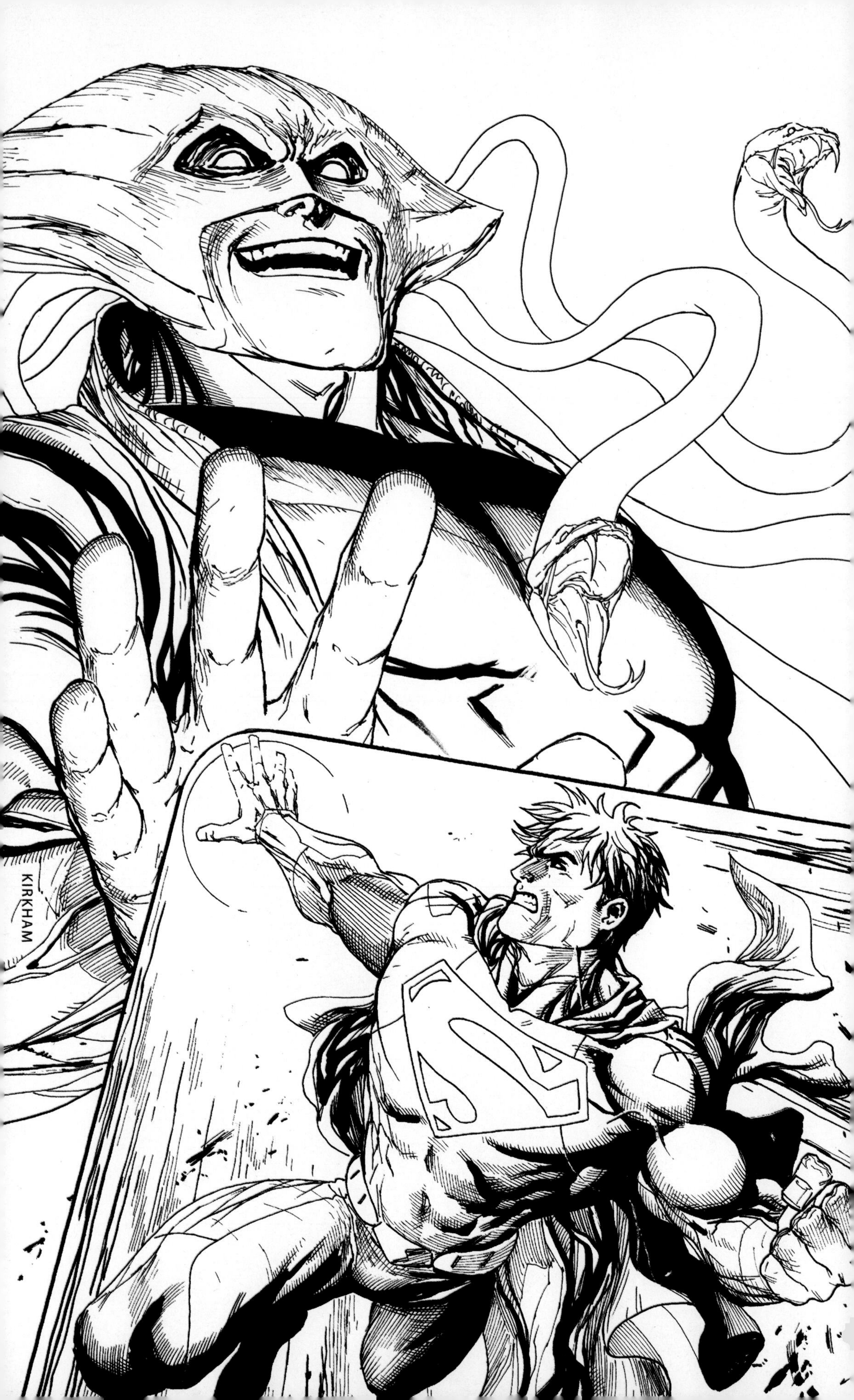
KIRKHAM

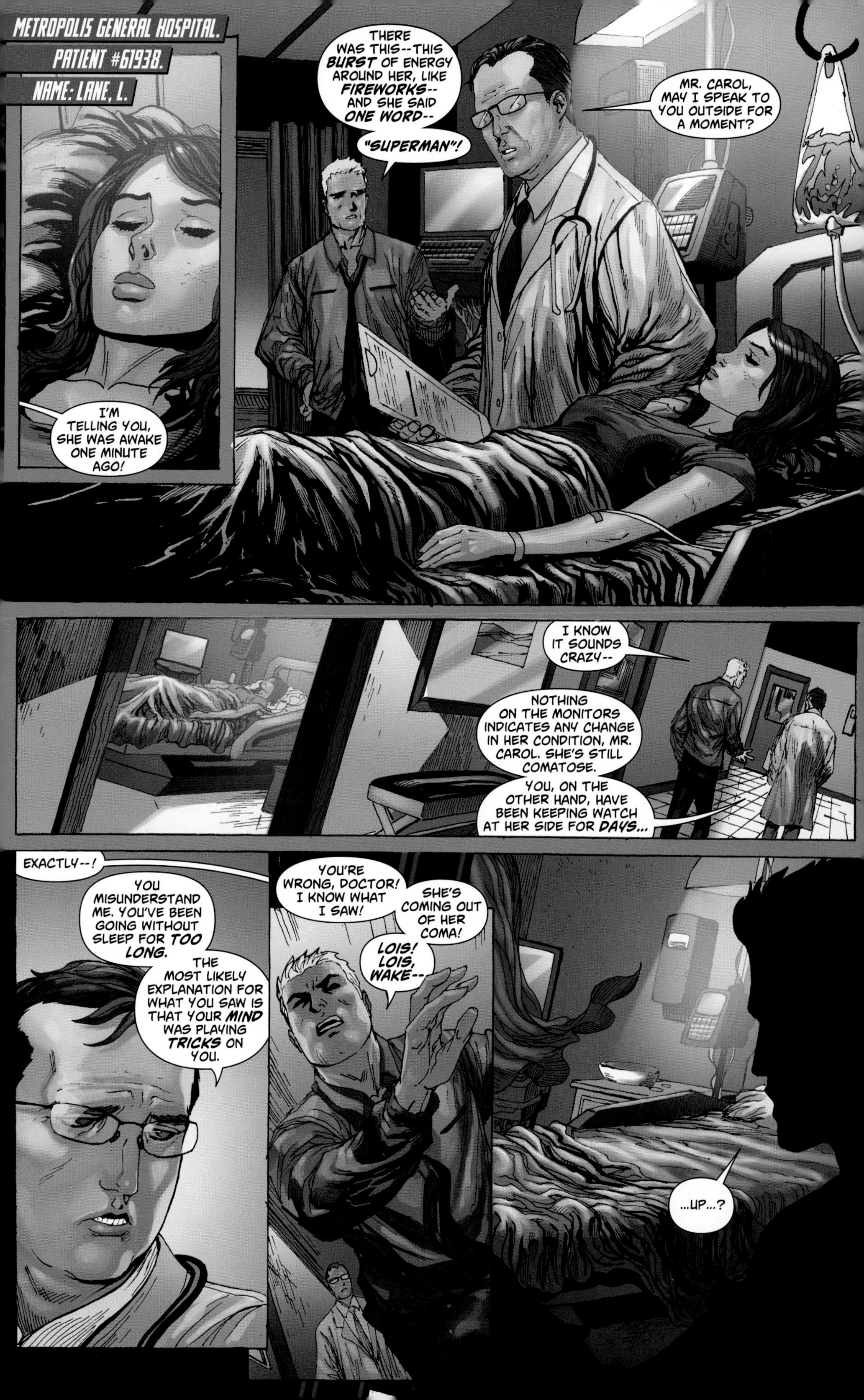
METROPOLIS GENERAL HOSPITAL.
PATIENT #61938.
NAME: LANE, L.
I'M TELLING YOU, SHE WAS AWAKE ONE MINUTE AGO!
THERE WAS THIS--THIS BURST OF ENERGY AROUND HER, LIKE FIREWORKS-- AND SHE SAID ONE WORD--
"SUPERMAN"!
MR. CAROL, MAY I SPEAK TO YOU OUTSIDE FOR A MOMENT?
I KNOW IT SOUNDS CRAZY--
NOTHING ON THE MONITORS INDICATES ANY CHANGE IN HER CONDITION, MR. CAROL. SHE'S STILL COMATOSE.
YOU, ON THE OTHER HAND, HAVE BEEN KEEPING WATCH AT HER SIDE FOR DAYS...
EXACTLY--!
YOU MISUNDERSTAND ME. YOU'VE BEEN GOING WITHOUT SLEEP FOR TOO LONG.
THE MOST LIKELY EXPLANATION FOR WHAT YOU SAW IS THAT YOUR MIND WAS PLAYING TRICKS ON YOU.
YOU'RE WRONG, DOCTOR! I KNOW WHAT I SAW!
SHE'S COMING OUT OF HER COMA!
LOIS! LOIS, WAKE--
...UP...?

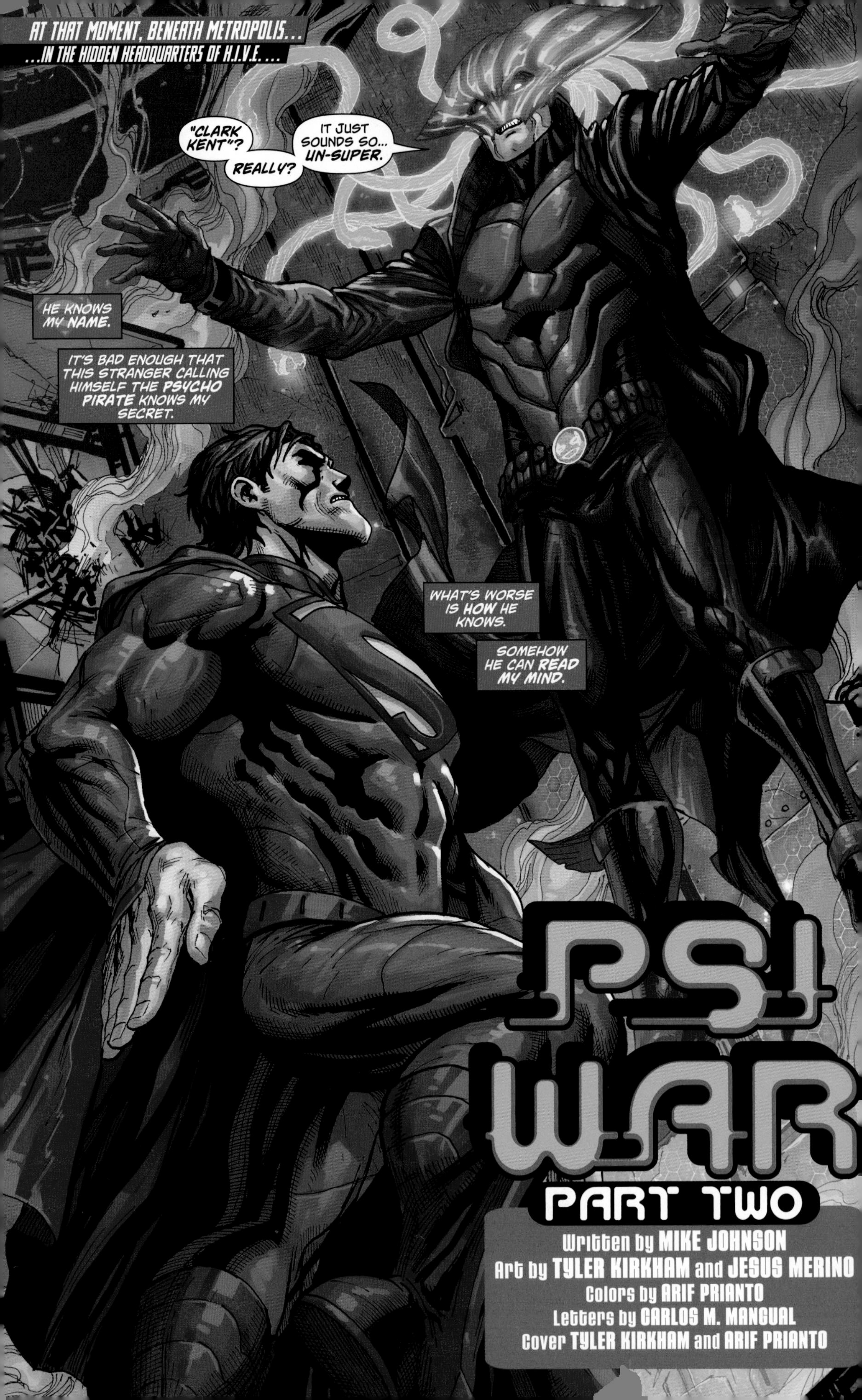
AT THAT MOMENT, BENEATH METROPOLIS...
...IN THE HIDDEN HEADQUARTERS OF H.I.V.E. ...
"CLARK KENT"? REALLY?
IT JUST SOUNDS SO... UN-SUPER.
HE KNOWS MY NAME.
IT'S BAD ENOUGH THAT THIS STRANGER CALLING HIMSELF THE PSYCHO PIRATE KNOWS MY SECRET.
WHAT'S WORSE IS HOW HE KNOWS.
SOMEHOW HE CAN READ MY MIND.
PSI WAR
PART TWO
Written by MIKE JOHNSON
Art by TYLER KIRKHAM and JESUS MERINO
Colors by ARIF PRIANTO
Letters by CARLOS M. MANGUAL
Cover TYLER KIRKHAM and ARIF PRIANTO

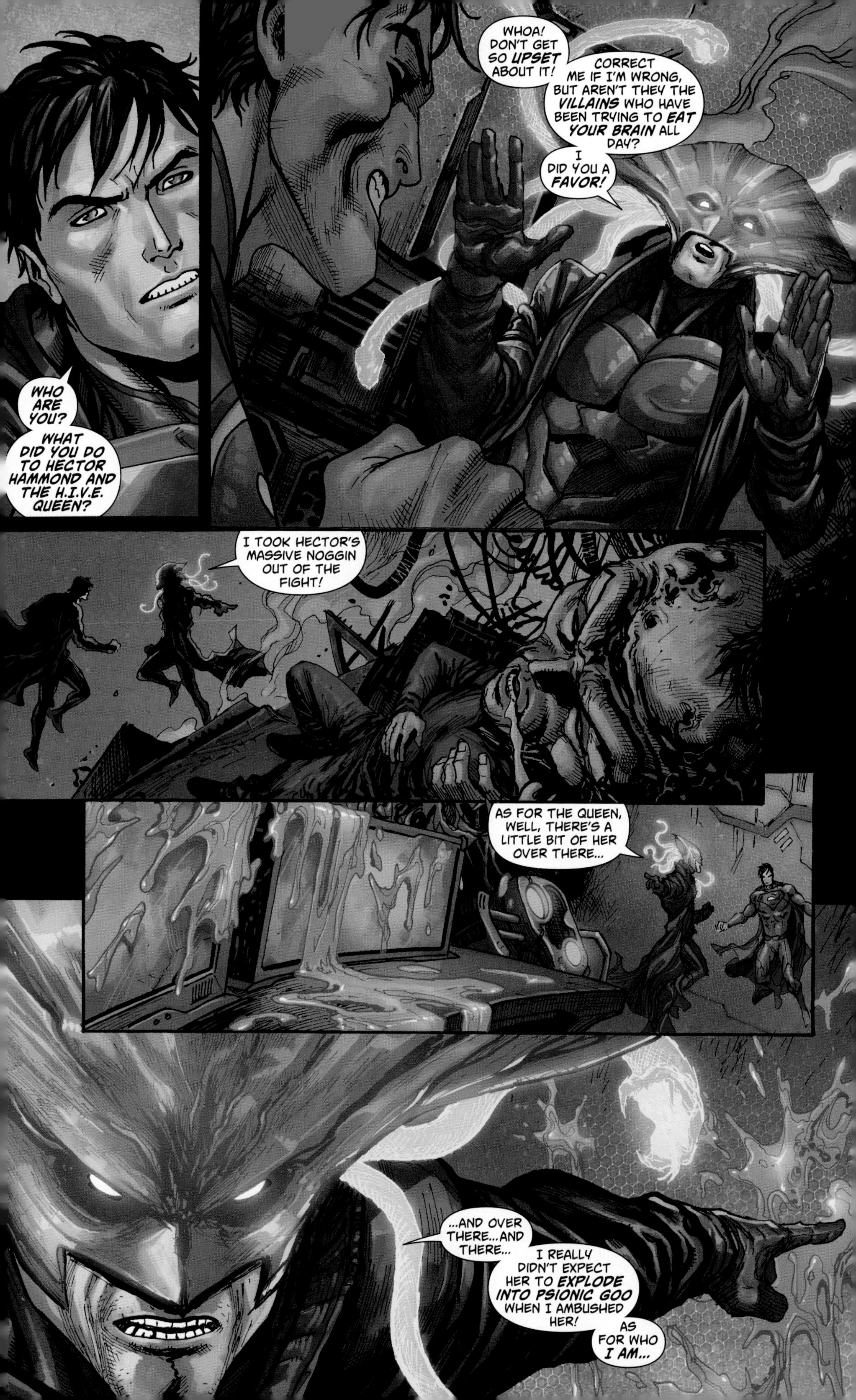
WHO ARE YOU?
WHAT DID YOU DO TO HECTOR HAMMOND AND THE H.I.V.E. QUEEN?
WHOA! DON'T GET SO UPSET ABOUT IT!
CORRECT ME IF I'M WRONG, BUT AREN'T THEY THE VILLAINS WHO HAVE BEEN TRYING TO EAT YOUR BRAIN ALL DAY?
I DID YOU A FAVOR!
I TOOK HECTOR'S MASSIVE NOGGIN OUT OF THE FIGHT!
AS FOR THE QUEEN, WELL, THERE'S A LITTLE BIT OF HER OVER THERE...
...AND OVER THERE...AND THERE...
I REALLY DIDN'T EXPECT HER TO EXPLODE INTO PSIONIC GOO WHEN I AMBUSHED HER!
AS FOR WHO I AM...

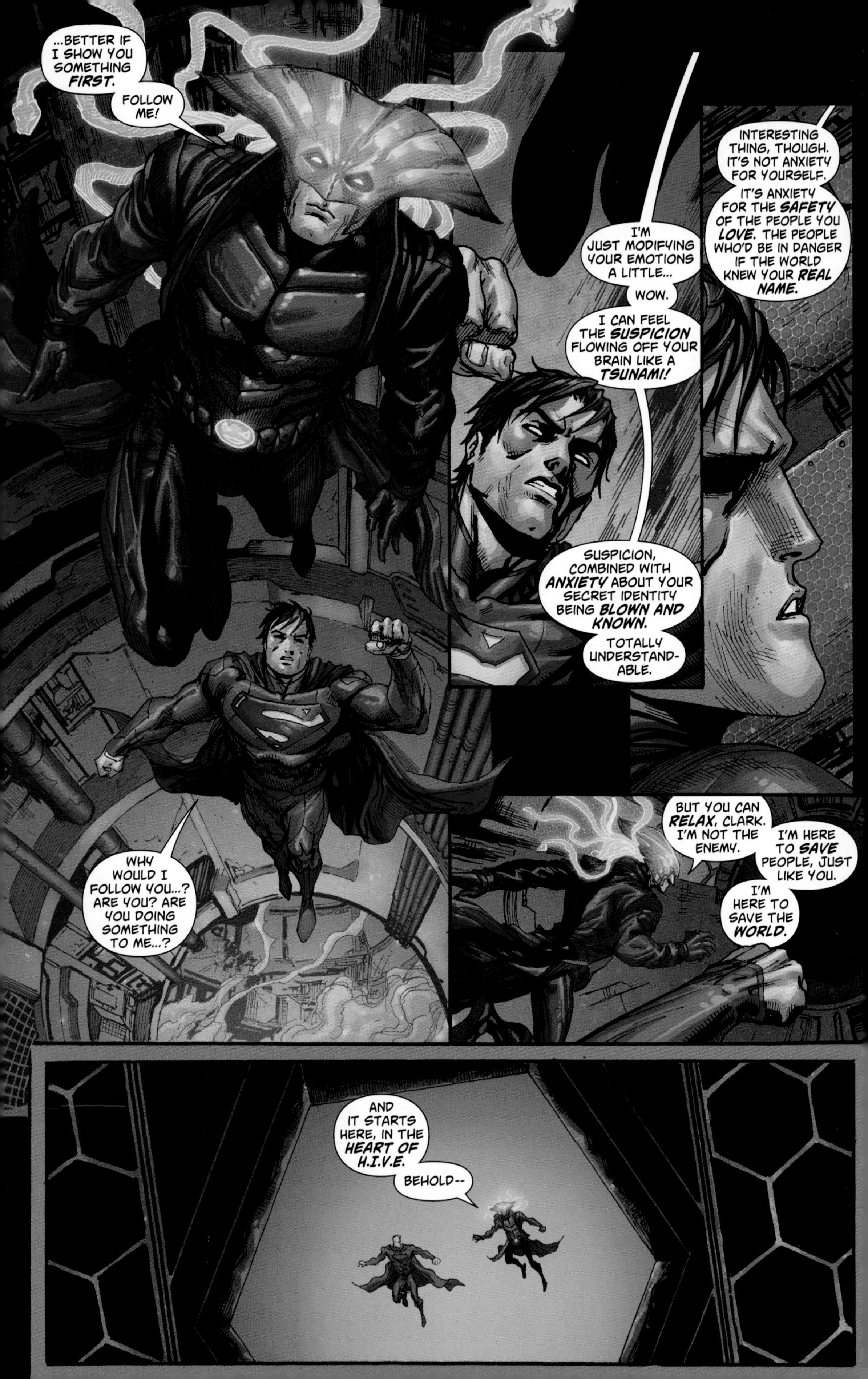

...BETTER IF I SHOW YOU SOMETHING FIRST.
FOLLOW ME!
WHY WOULD I FOLLOW YOU...? ARE YOU? ARE YOU DOING SOMETHING TO ME...?
I'M JUST MODIFYING YOUR EMOTIONS A LITTLE...
WOW.
I CAN FEEL THE SUSPICION FLOWING OFF YOUR BRAIN LIKE A TSUNAMI!
SUSPICION, COMBINED WITH ANXIETY ABOUT YOUR SECRET IDENTITY BEING BLOWN AND KNOWN.
TOTALLY UNDERSTAND-ABLE.
INTERESTING THING, THOUGH. IT'S NOT ANXIETY FOR YOURSELF.
IT'S ANXIETY FOR THE SAFETY OF THE PEOPLE YOU LOVE. THE PEOPLE WHO'D BE IN DANGER IF THE WORLD KNEW YOUR REAL NAME.
BUT YOU CAN RELAX, CLARK. I'M NOT THE ENEMY.
I'M HERE TO SAVE PEOPLE, JUST LIKE YOU.
I'M HERE TO SAVE THE WORLD.
AND IT STARTS HERE, IN THE HEART OF H.I.V.E.
BEHOLD--

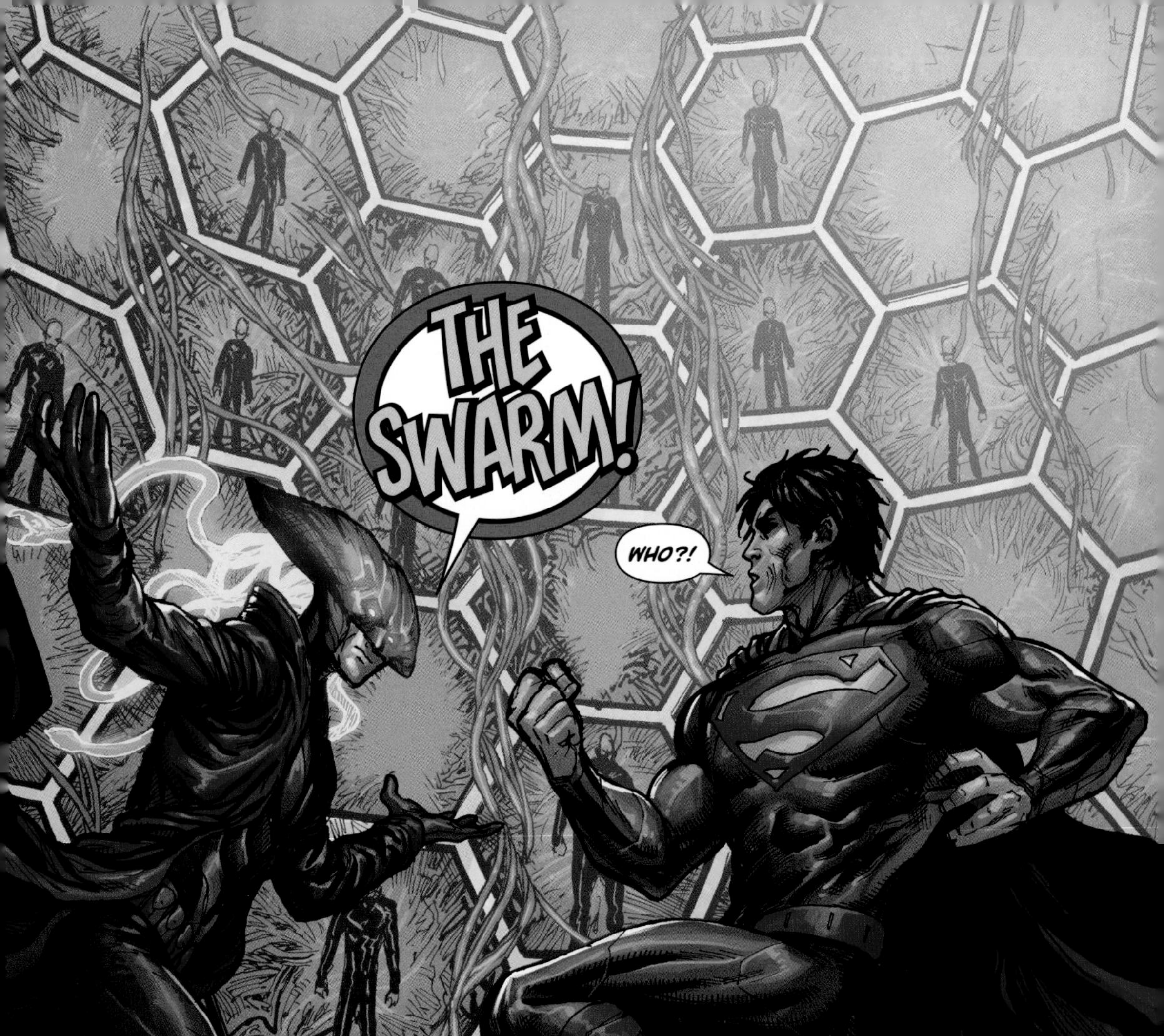
THE SWARM!
WHO?!

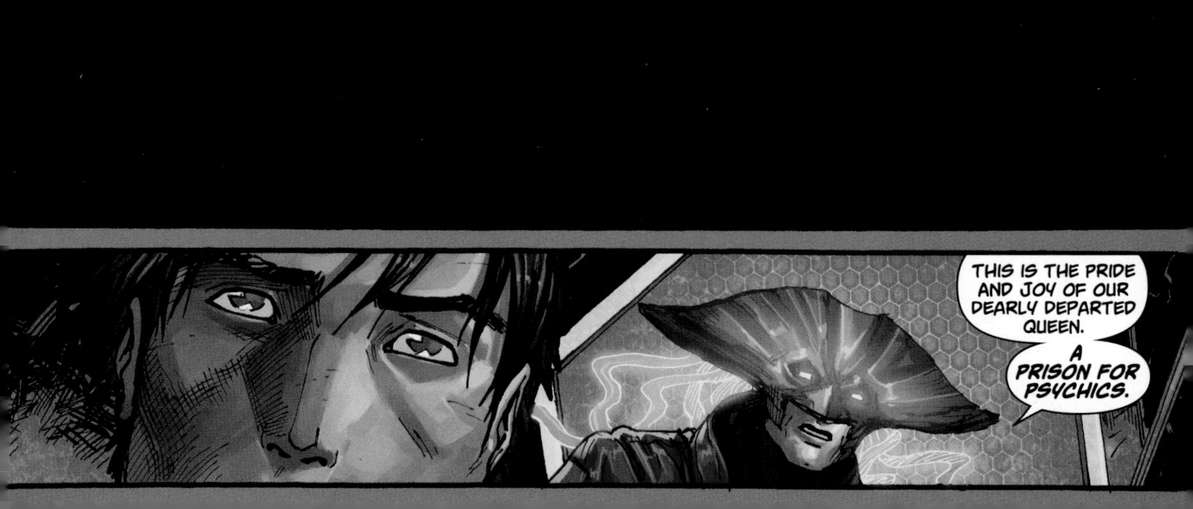
THIS IS THE PRIDE AND JOY OF OUR DEARLY DEPARTED QUEEN.
A PRISON FOR PSYCHICS.

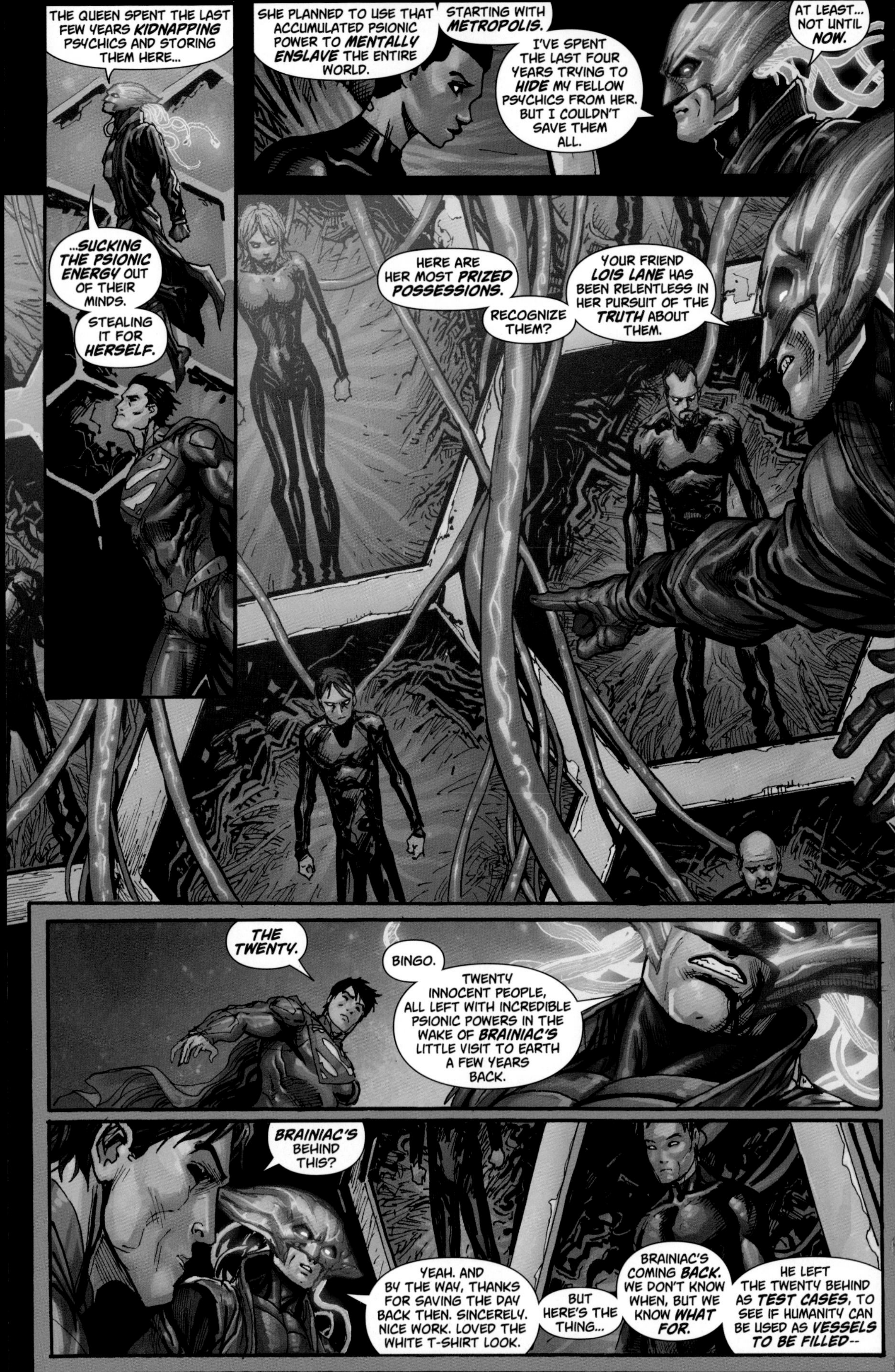
THE QUEEN SPENT THE LAST FEW YEARS KIDNAPPING PSYCHICS AND STORING THEM HERE...
SHE PLANNED TO USE THAT ACCUMULATED PSIONIC POWER TO MENTALLY ENSLAVE THE ENTIRE WORLD.
STARTING WITH METROPOLIS.
I'VE SPENT THE LAST FOUR YEARS TRYING TO HIDE MY FELLOW PSYCHICS FROM HER. BUT I COULDN'T SAVE THEM ALL.
AT LEAST... NOT UNTIL NOW.
...SUCKING THE PSIONIC ENERGY OUT OF THEIR MINDS.
STEALING IT FOR HERSELF.
HERE ARE HER MOST PRIZED POSSESSIONS.
RECOGNIZE THEM?
YOUR FRIEND LOIS LANE HAS BEEN RELENTLESS IN HER PURSUIT OF THE TRUTH ABOUT THEM.
THE TWENTY.
BINGO.
TWENTY INNOCENT PEOPLE, ALL LEFT WITH INCREDIBLE PSIONIC POWERS IN THE WAKE OF BRAINIAC'S LITTLE VISIT TO EARTH A FEW YEARS BACK.
BRAINIAC'S BEHIND THIS?
YEAH. AND BY THE WAY, THANKS FOR SAVING THE DAY BACK THEN. SINCERELY. NICE WORK. LOVED THE WHITE T-SHIRT LOOK.
BUT HERE'S THE THING...
BRAINIAC'S COMING BACK. WE DON'T KNOW WHEN, BUT WE KNOW WHAT FOR.
HE LEFT THE TWENTY BEHIND AS TEST CASES, TO SEE IF HUMANITY CAN BE USED AS VESSELS TO BE FILLED--

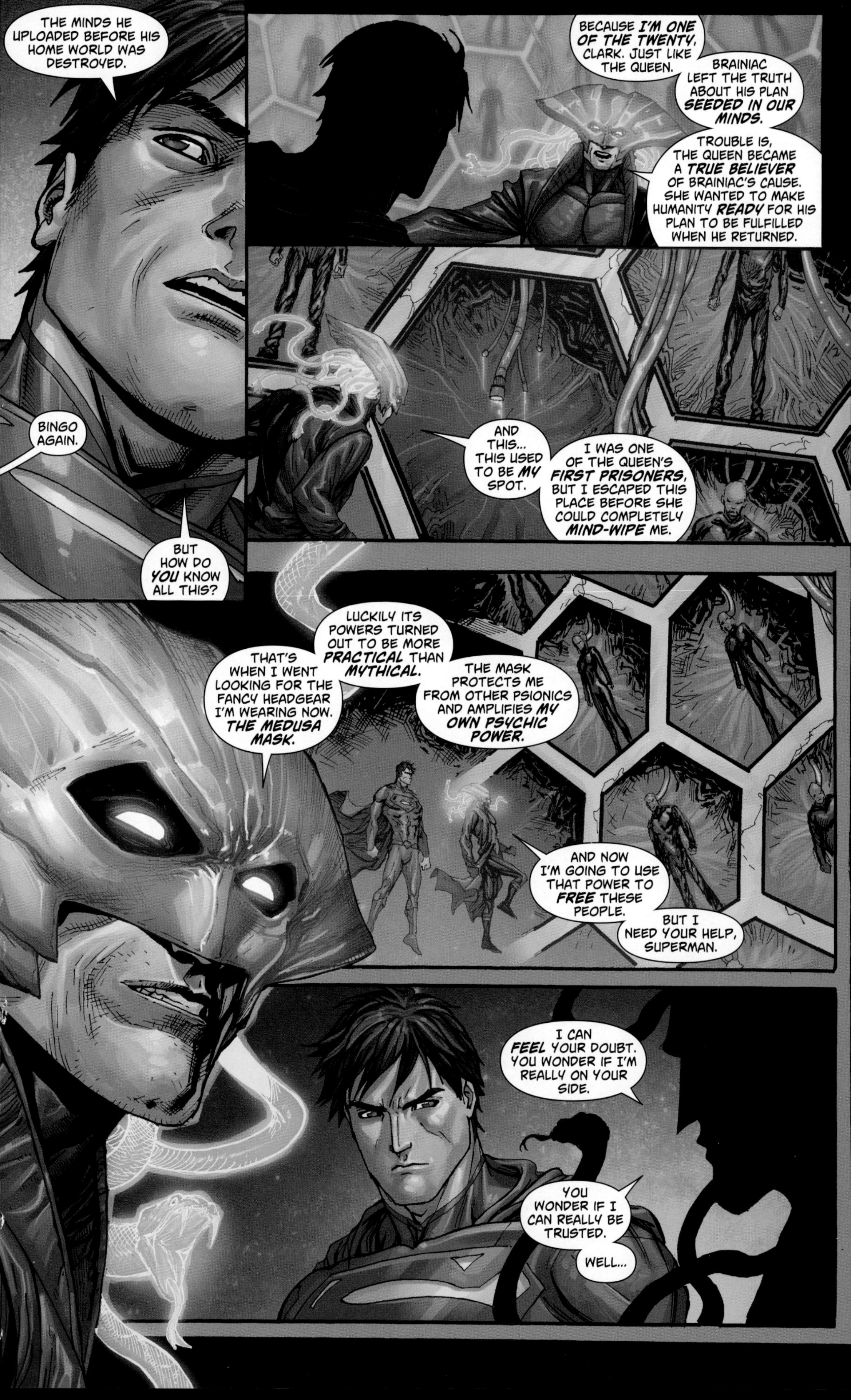
THE MINDS HE UPLOADED BEFORE HIS HOME WORLD WAS DESTROYED.
BECAUSE I'M ONE OF THE TWENTY, CLARK. JUST LIKE THE QUEEN.
BRAINIAC LEFT THE TRUTH ABOUT HIS PLAN SEEDED IN OUR MINDS.
TROUBLE IS, THE QUEEN BECAME A TRUE BELIEVER OF BRAINIAC'S CAUSE. SHE WANTED TO MAKE HUMANITY READY FOR HIS PLAN TO BE FULFILLED WHEN HE RETURNED.
BINGO AGAIN.
BUT HOW DO YOU KNOW ALL THIS?
AND THIS... THIS USED TO BE MY SPOT.
I WAS ONE OF THE QUEEN'S FIRST PRISONERS, BUT I ESCAPED THIS PLACE BEFORE SHE COULD COMPLETELY MIND-WIPE ME.
THAT'S WHEN I WENT LOOKING FOR THE FANCY HEADGEAR I'M WEARING NOW. THE MEDUSA MASK.
LUCKILY ITS POWERS TURNED OUT TO BE MORE PRACTICAL THAN MYTHICAL.
THE MASK PROTECTS ME FROM OTHER PSIONICS AND AMPLIFIES MY OWN PSYCHIC POWER.
AND NOW I'M GOING TO USE THAT POWER TO FREE THESE PEOPLE.
BUT I NEED YOUR HELP, SUPERMAN.
I CAN FEEL YOUR DOUBT. YOU WONDER IF I'M REALLY ON YOUR SIDE.
YOU WONDER IF I CAN REALLY BE TRUSTED.
WELL...

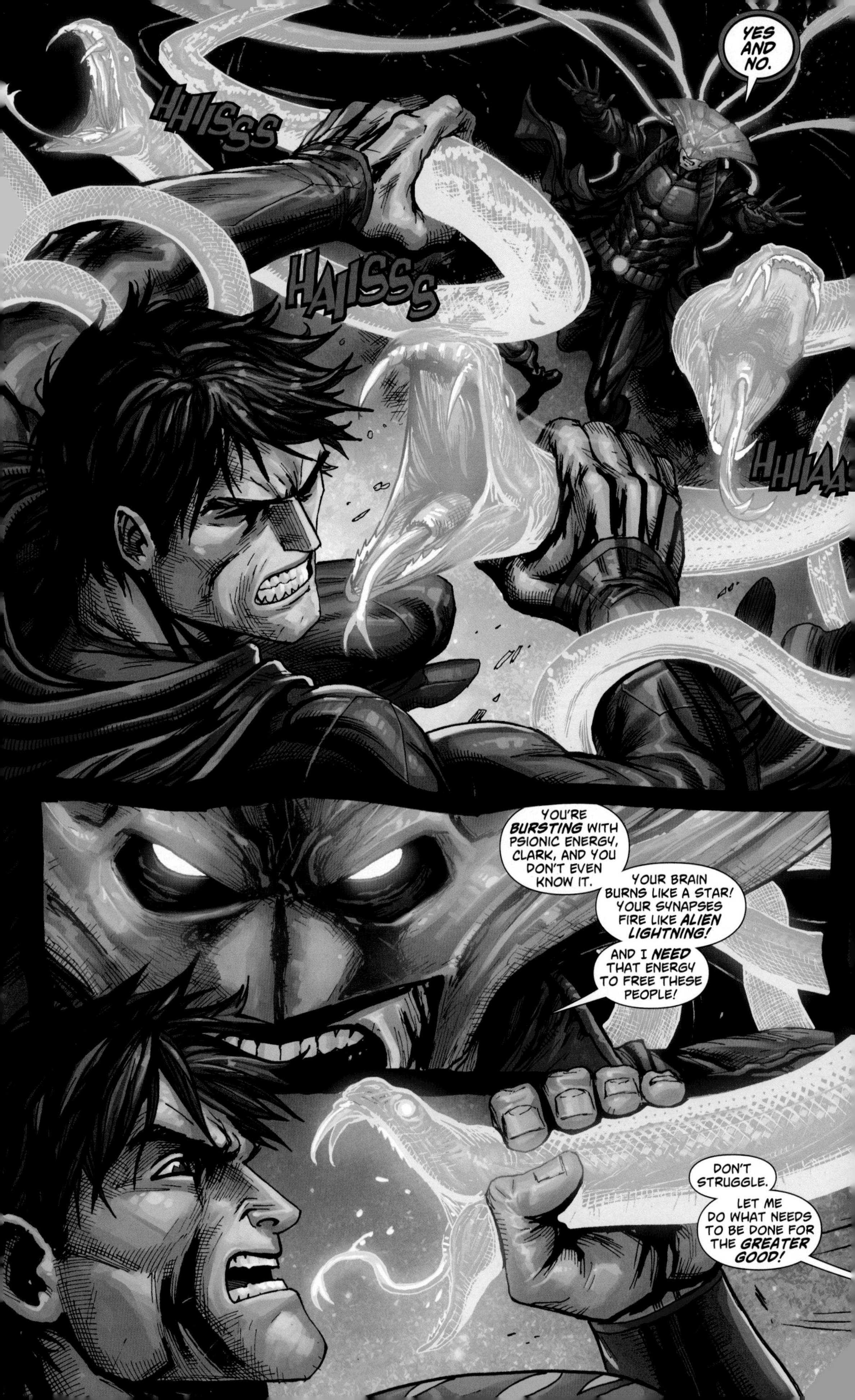
YES AND NO.
HHIISSS
HAIISSSS
HHIIAAS
YOU'RE BURSTING WITH PSIONIC ENERGY, CLARK, AND YOU DON'T EVEN KNOW IT.
YOUR BRAIN BURNS LIKE A STAR! YOUR SYNAPSES FIRE LIKE ALIEN LIGHTNING!
AND I NEED THAT ENERGY TO FREE THESE PEOPLE!
DON'T STRUGGLE.
LET ME DO WHAT NEEDS TO BE DONE FOR THE GREATER GOOD!

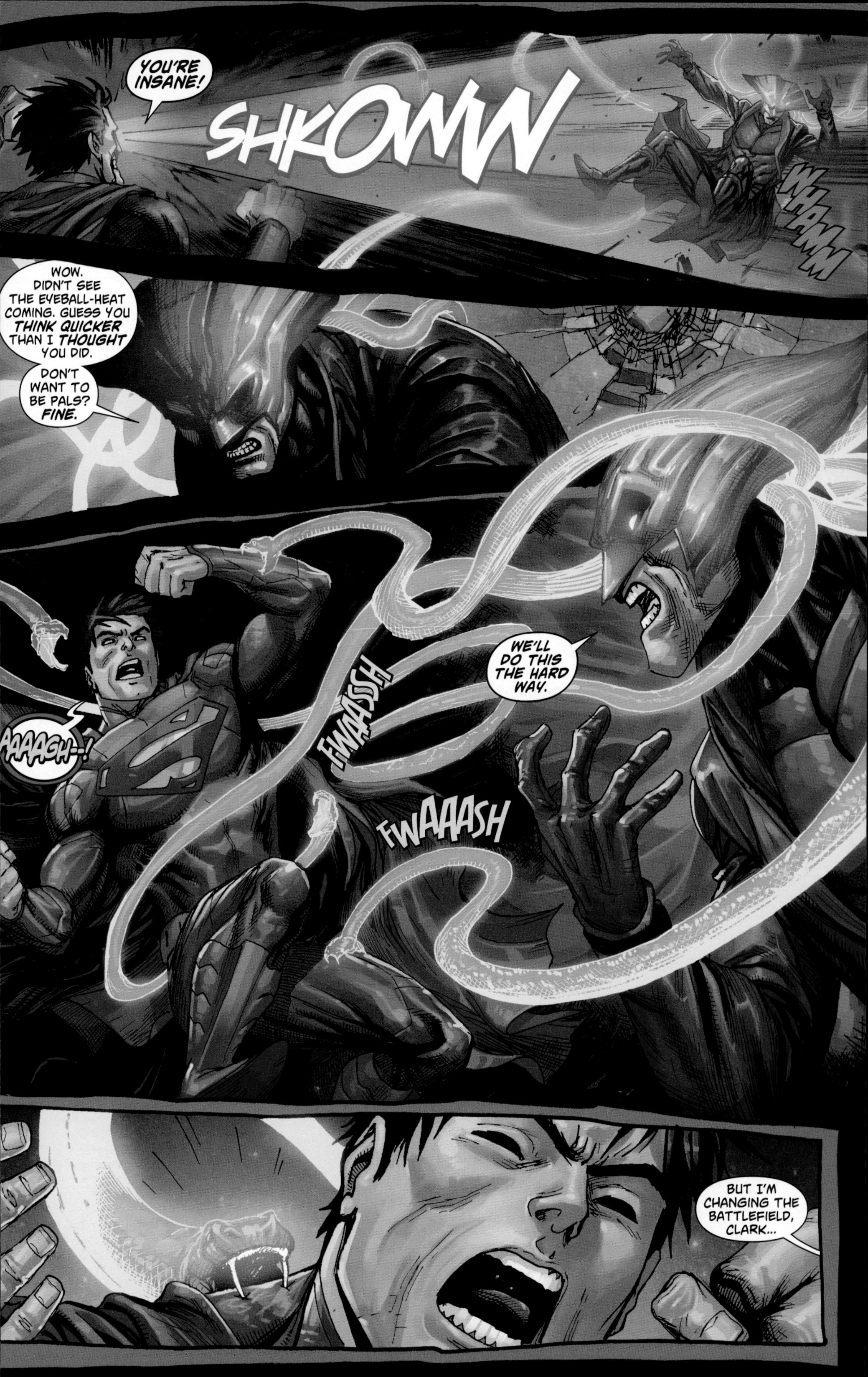
YOU'RE INSANE!
SHKOWW
WHAMM
WOW. DIDN'T SEE THE EYEBALL-HEAT COMING. GUESS YOU THINK QUICKER THAN I THOUGHT YOU DID.
DON'T WANT TO BE PALS? FINE.
WE'LL DO THIS THE HARD WAY.
AAAAGH--!
FWAASSH
FWAAASH
BUT I'M CHANGING THE BATTLEFIELD, CLARK...

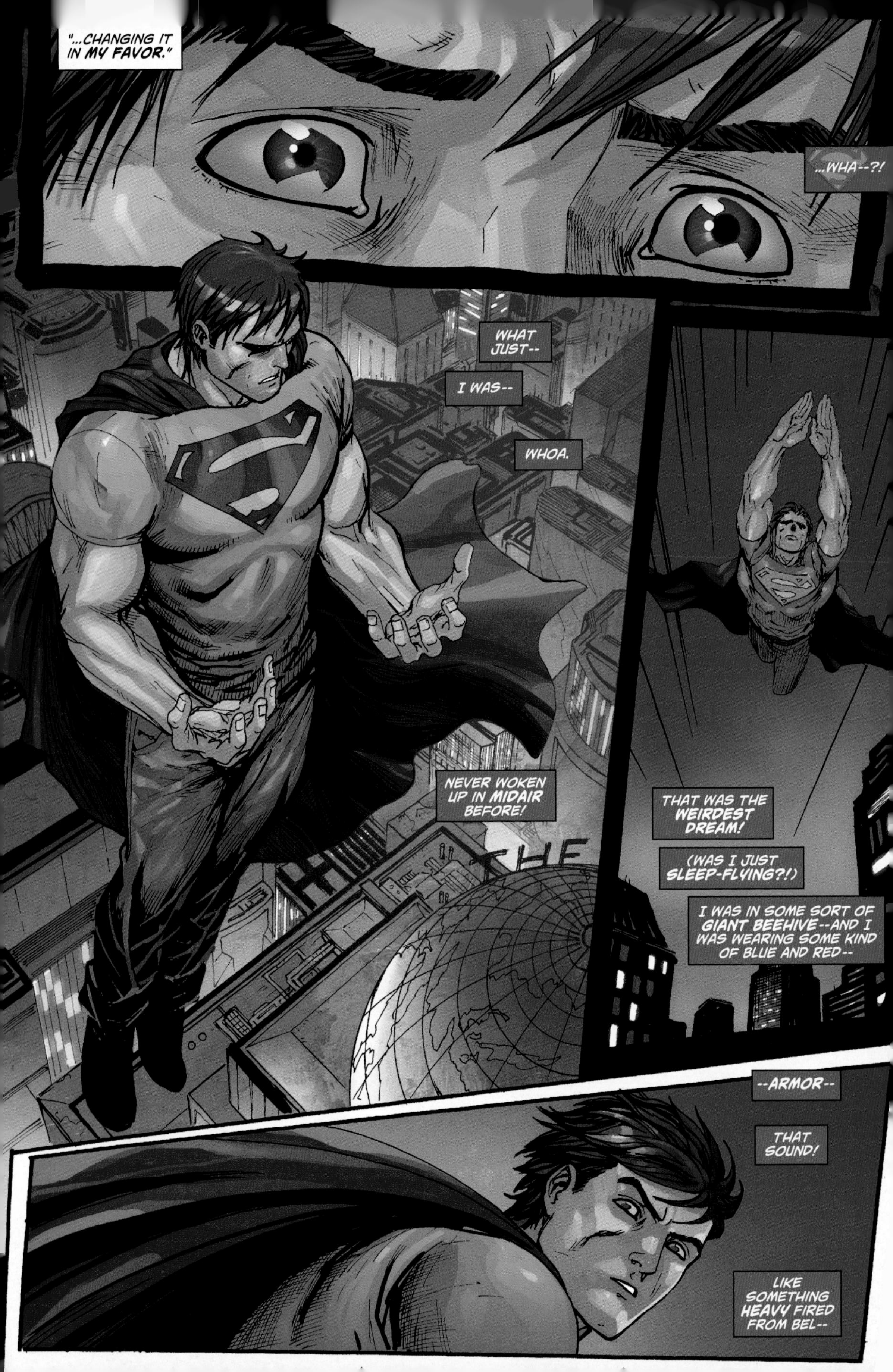

"...CHANGING IT IN MY FAVOR."
...WHA--?!
WHAT JUST--
I WAS--
WHOA.
NEVER WOKEN UP IN MIDAIR BEFORE!
THAT WAS THE WEIRDEST DREAM!
(WAS I JUST SLEEP-FLYING?!)
I WAS IN SOME SORT OF GIANT BEEHIVE--AND I WAS WEARING SOME KIND OF BLUE AND RED--
--ARMOR--
THAT SOUND!
LIKE SOMETHING HEAVY FIRED FROM BEL--

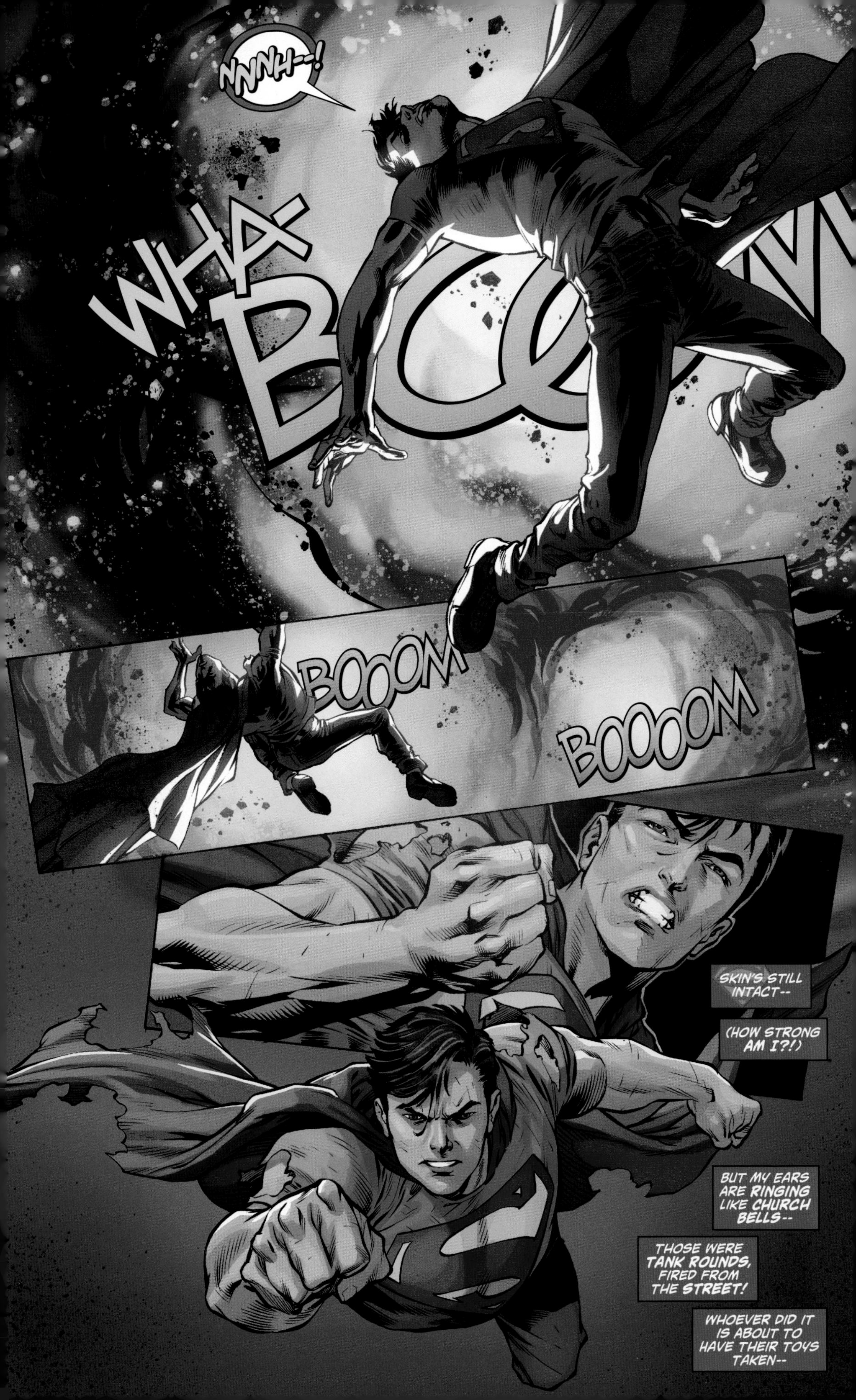
NNNH--!
WHA-
BOOM
BOOOM
BOOOOM
SKIN'S STILL INTACT--
(HOW STRONG AM I?!)
BUT MY EARS ARE RINGING LIKE CHURCH BELLS--
THOSE WERE TANK ROUNDS, FIRED FROM THE STREET!
WHOEVER DID IT IS ABOUT TO HAVE THEIR TOYS TAKEN--

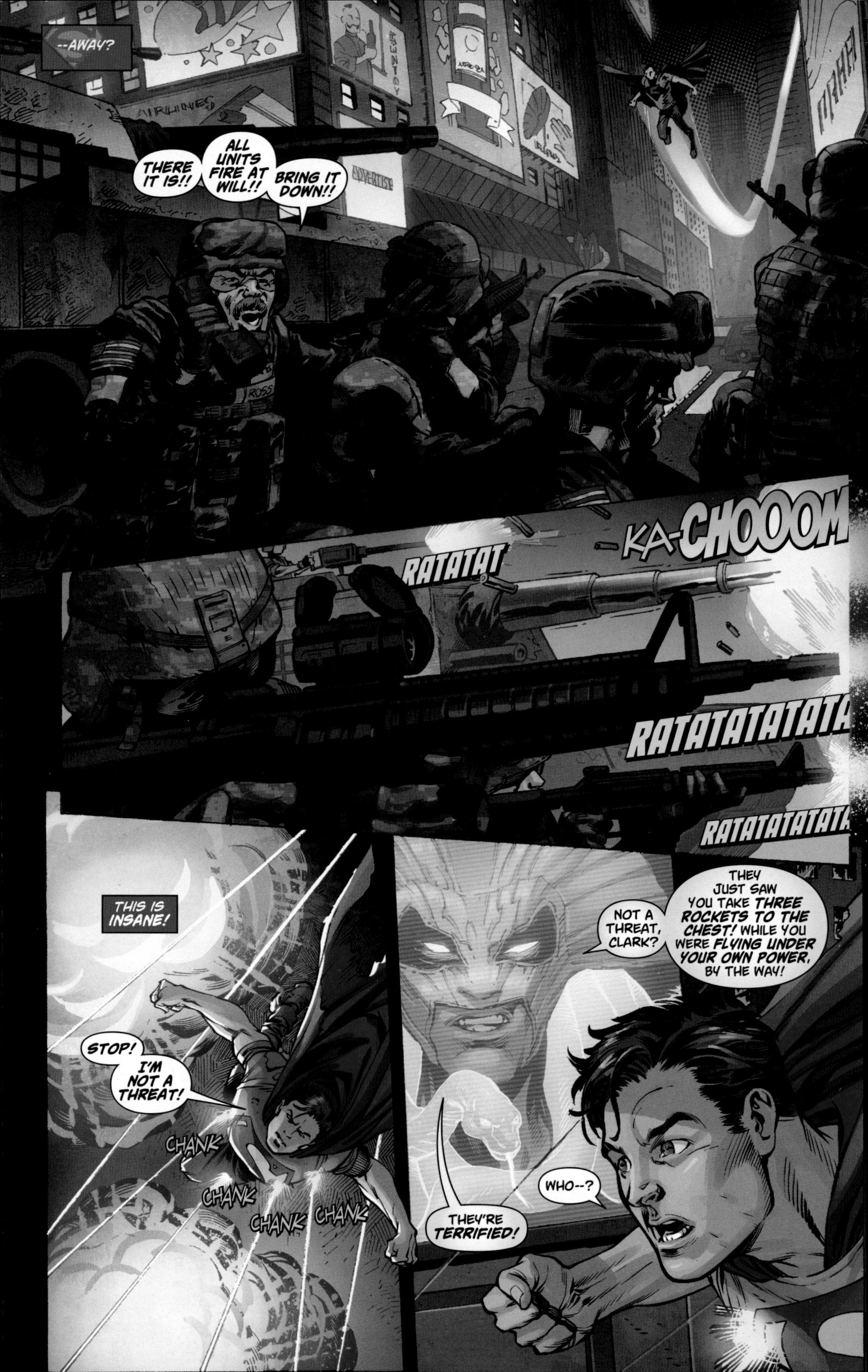
--AWAY?
THERE IT IS!!
ALL UNITS FIRE AT WILL!!
BRING IT DOWN!!
RATATAT
-KA-CHOOOM
RATATATATATA
RATATATATATA
THIS IS INSANE!
STOP! I'M NOT A THREAT!
CHANK
CHANK
CHANK CHANK
NOT A THREAT, CLARK?
THEY JUST SAW YOU TAKE THREE ROCKETS TO THE CHEST! WHILE YOU WERE FLYING UNDER YOUR OWN POWER, BY THE WAY!
WHO--?
THEY'RE TERRIFIED!

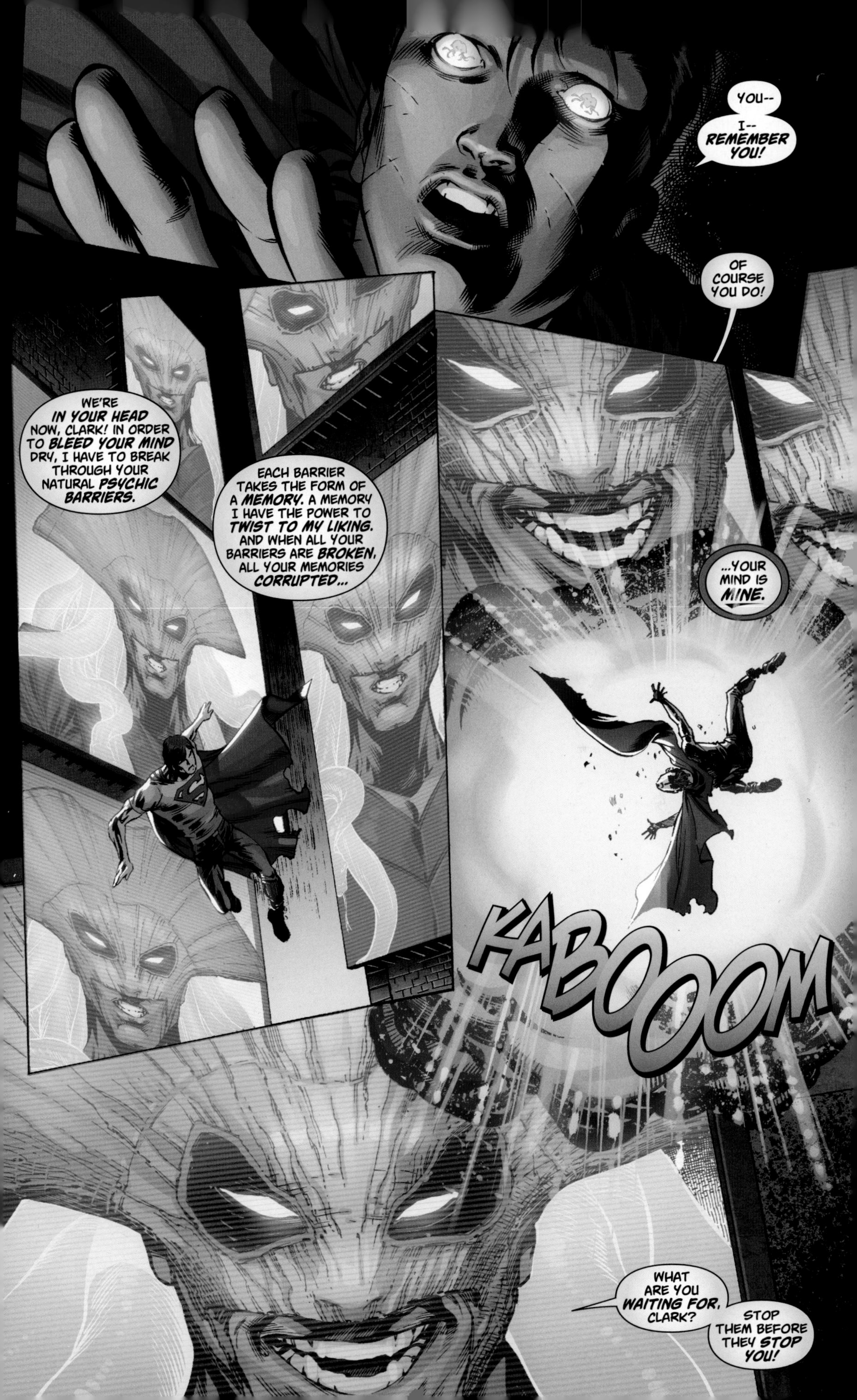
YOU--
I-- REMEMBER YOU!
OF COURSE YOU DO!
WE'RE IN YOUR HEAD NOW, CLARK! IN ORDER TO BLEED YOUR MIND DRY, I HAVE TO BREAK THROUGH YOUR NATURAL PSYCHIC BARRIERS.
EACH BARRIER TAKES THE FORM OF A MEMORY. A MEMORY I HAVE THE POWER TO TWIST TO MY LIKING. AND WHEN ALL YOUR BARRIERS ARE BROKEN, ALL YOUR MEMORIES CORRUPTED...
...YOUR MIND IS MINE.
KABOOOOM
WHAT ARE YOU WAITING FOR, CLARK?
STOP THEM BEFORE THEY STOP YOU!

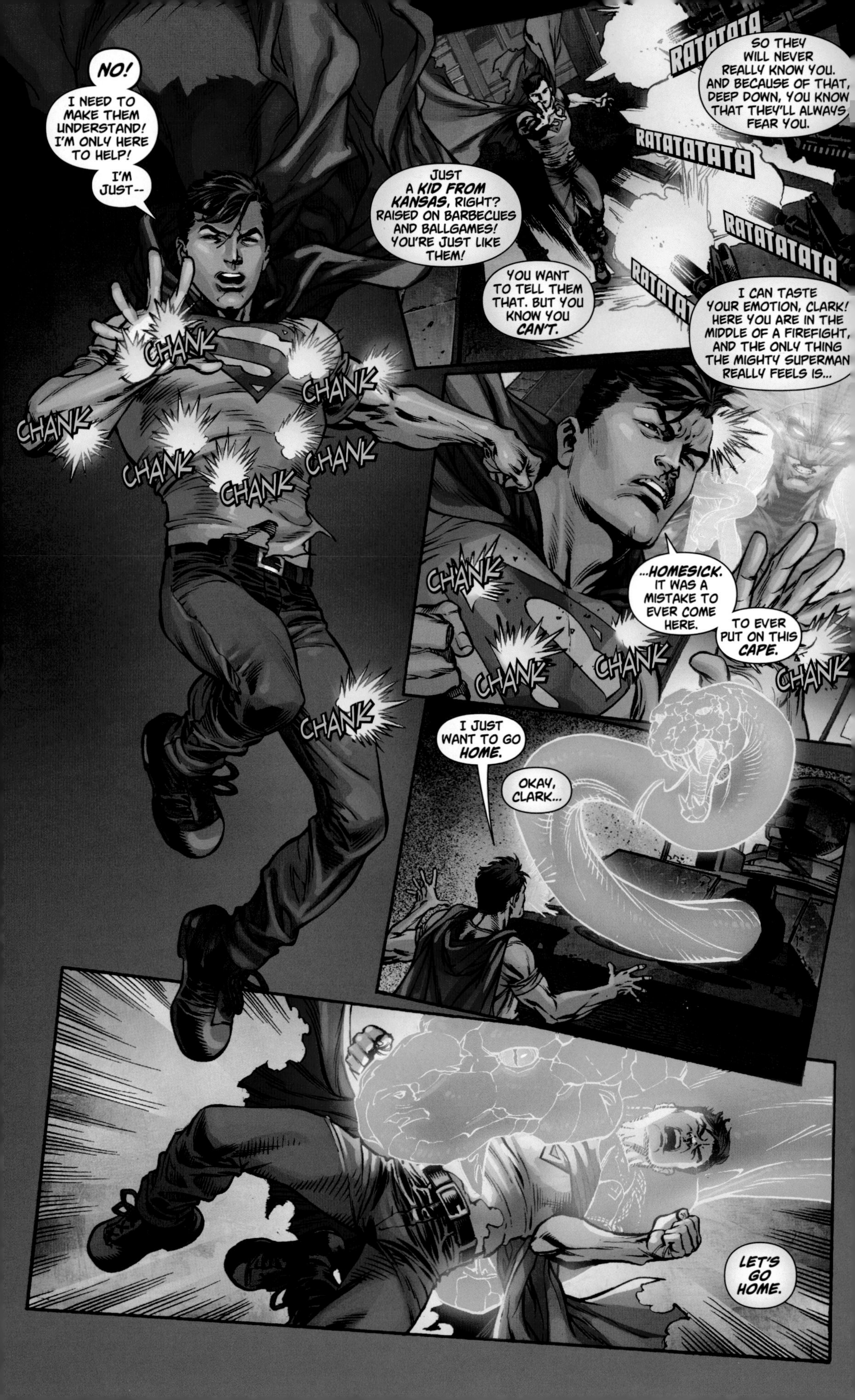

NO!
I NEED TO MAKE THEM UNDERSTAND! I'M ONLY HERE TO HELP!
I'M JUST--
RATATATA
SO THEY WILL NEVER REALLY KNOW YOU. AND BECAUSE OF THAT, DEEP DOWN, YOU KNOW THAT THEY'LL ALWAYS FEAR YOU.
RATATATATA
JUST A KID FROM KANSAS, RIGHT? RAISED ON BARBECUES AND BALLGAMES! YOU'RE JUST LIKE THEM!
YOU WANT TO TELL THEM THAT. BUT YOU KNOW YOU CAN'T.
RATATATATA
RATATATATA
I CAN TASTE YOUR EMOTION, CLARK! HERE YOU ARE IN THE MIDDLE OF A FIREFIGHT, AND THE ONLY THING THE MIGHTY SUPERMAN REALLY FEELS IS...
CHANK
CHANK
CHANK
CHANK
CHANK
CHANK
...HOMESICK. IT WAS A MISTAKE TO EVER COME HERE.
TO EVER PUT ON THIS CAPE.
CHANK
CHANK
CHANK
CHANK
CHANK
I JUST WANT TO GO HOME.
OKAY, CLARK...
LET'S GO HOME.

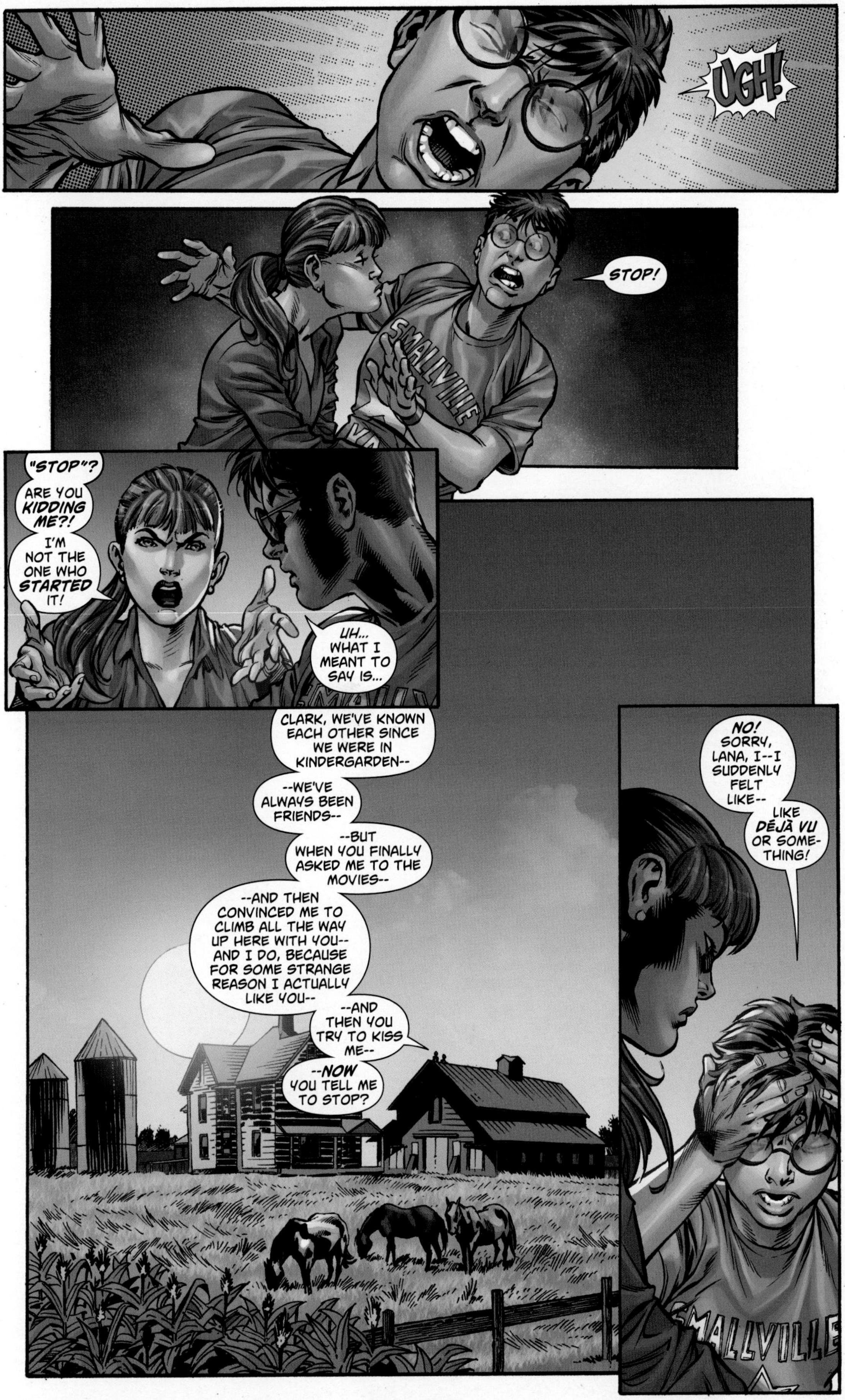
UGH!
STOP!
"STOP"?
ARE YOU KIDDING ME?!
I'M NOT THE ONE WHO STARTED IT!
UH... WHAT I MEANT TO SAY IS...
CLARK, WE'VE KNOWN EACH OTHER SINCE WE WERE IN KINDERGARDEN--
--WE'VE ALWAYS BEEN FRIENDS--
--BUT WHEN YOU FINALLY ASKED ME TO THE MOVIES--
--AND THEN CONVINCED ME TO CLIMB ALL THE WAY UP HERE WITH YOU-- AND I DO, BECAUSE FOR SOME STRANGE REASON I ACTUALLY LIKE YOU--
--AND THEN YOU TRY TO KISS ME--
--NOW YOU TELL ME TO STOP?
NO! SORRY, LANA, I--I SUDDENLY FELT LIKE--
LIKE DÉJÀ VU OR SOME-THING!

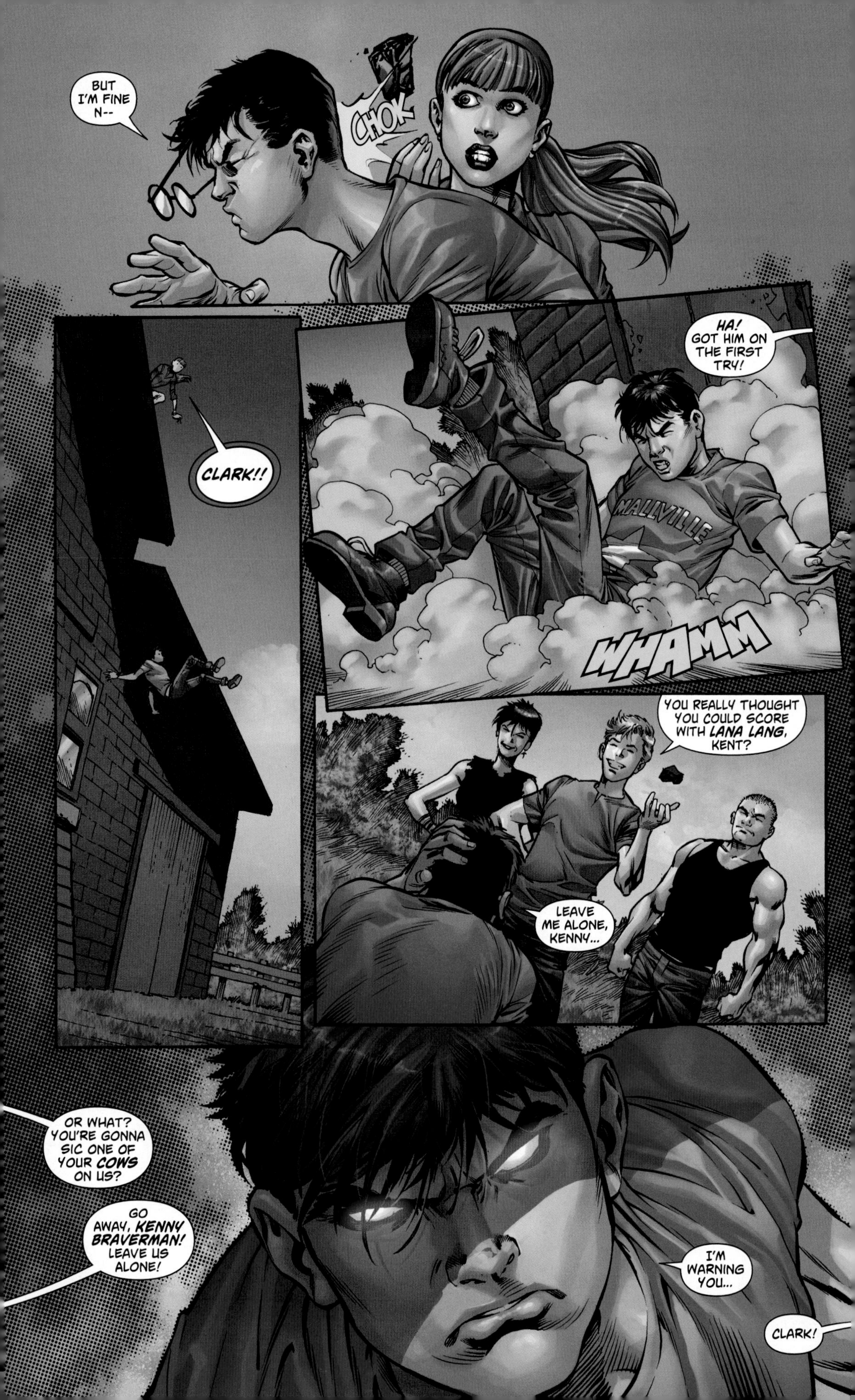
BUT I'M FINE N--
CHOK
CLARK!!
HA! GOT HIM ON THE FIRST TRY!
WHAMM
YOU REALLY THOUGHT YOU COULD SCORE WITH LANA LANG, KENT?
LEAVE ME ALONE, KENNY...
OR WHAT? YOU'RE GONNA SIC ONE OF YOUR COWS ON US?
GO AWAY, KENNY BRAVERMAN! LEAVE US ALONE!
I'M WARNING YOU...
CLARK!

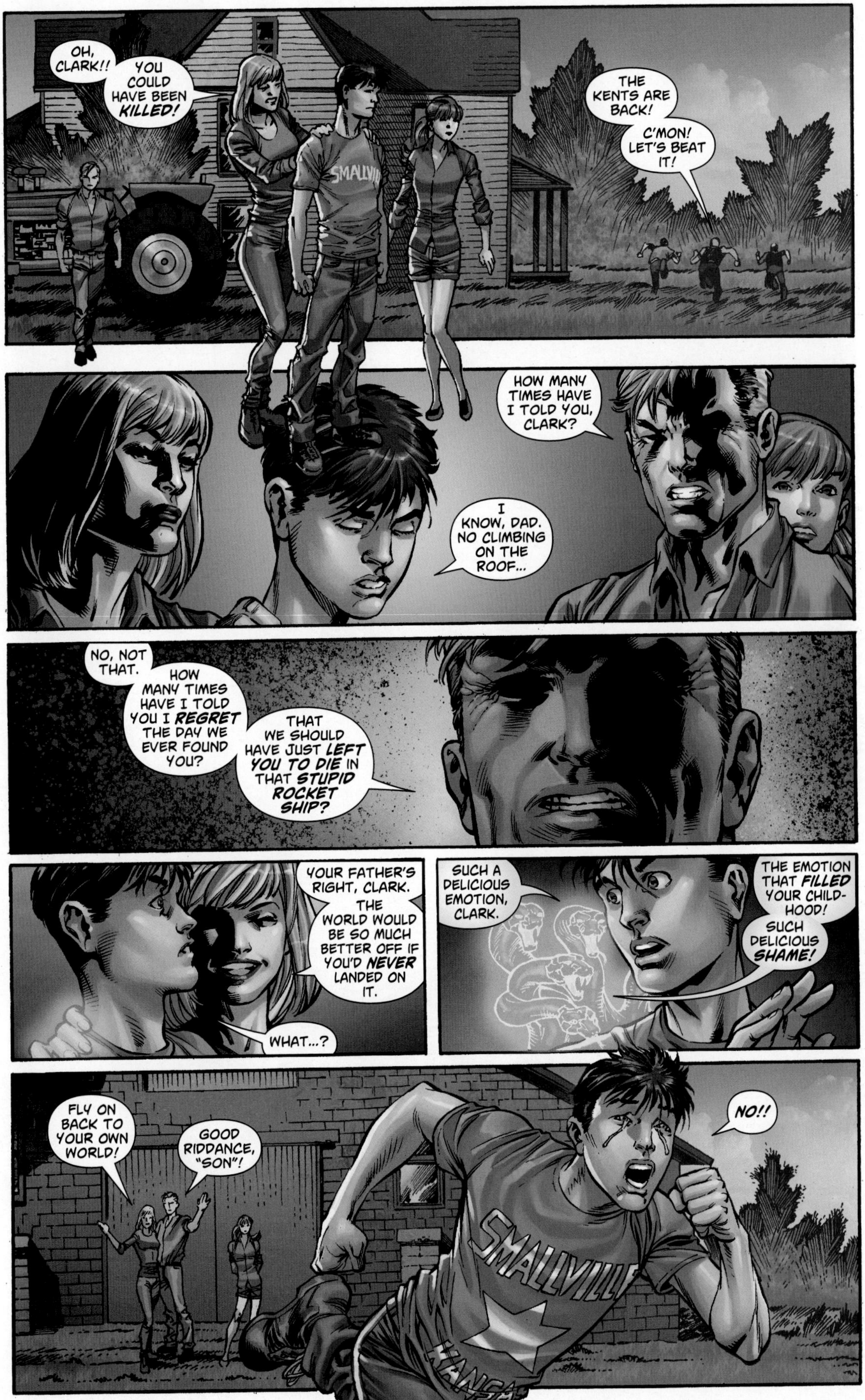
OH, CLARK!!
YOU COULD HAVE BEEN KILLED!
THE KENTS ARE BACK!
C'MON! LET'S BEAT IT!
SMALLVILLE
HOW MANY TIMES HAVE I TOLD YOU, CLARK?
I KNOW, DAD. NO CLIMBING ON THE ROOF...
NO, NOT THAT.
HOW MANY TIMES HAVE I TOLD YOU I REGRET THE DAY WE EVER FOUND YOU?
THAT WE SHOULD HAVE JUST LEFT YOU TO DIE IN THAT STUPID ROCKET SHIP?
YOUR FATHER'S RIGHT, CLARK.
THE WORLD WOULD BE SO MUCH BETTER OFF IF YOU'D NEVER LANDED ON IT.
WHAT...?
SUCH A DELICIOUS EMOTION, CLARK.
THE EMOTION THAT FILLED YOUR CHILDHOOD!
SUCH DELICIOUS SHAME!
FLY ON BACK TO YOUR OWN WORLD!
GOOD RIDDANCE, "SON"!
NO!!
SMALLVILLE

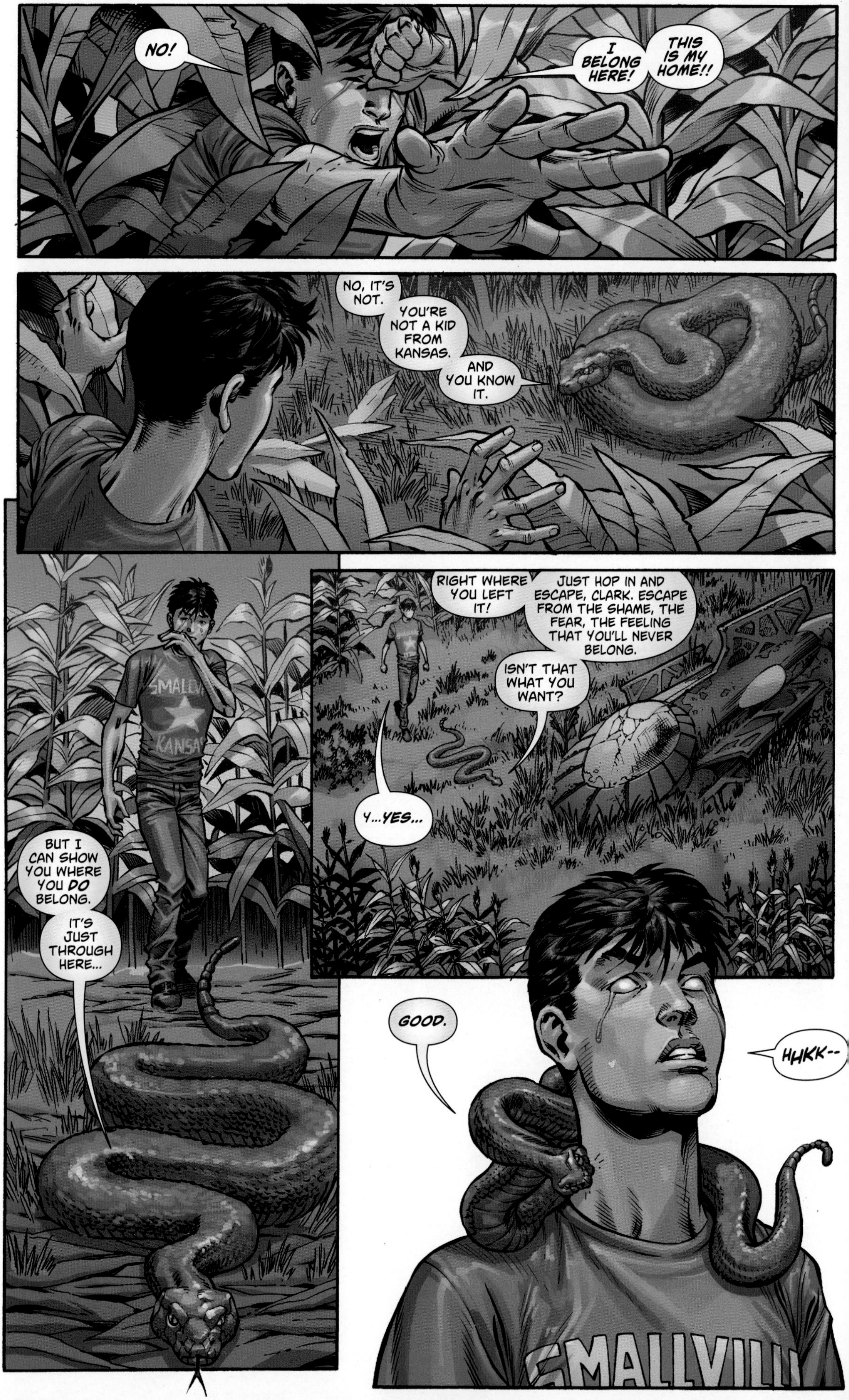
NO!
I BELONG HERE!
THIS IS MY HOME!!
NO, IT'S NOT.
YOU'RE NOT A KID FROM KANSAS.
AND YOU KNOW IT.
SMALLVILLE KANSAS
BUT I CAN SHOW YOU WHERE YOU *DO* BELONG.
IT'S JUST THROUGH HERE...
RIGHT WHERE YOU LEFT IT!
JUST HOP IN AND ESCAPE, CLARK. ESCAPE FROM THE SHAME, THE FEAR, THE FEELING THAT YOU'LL NEVER BELONG.
ISN'T THAT WHAT YOU WANT?
Y...*YES*...
GOOD.
HHKK--
SMALLVILL

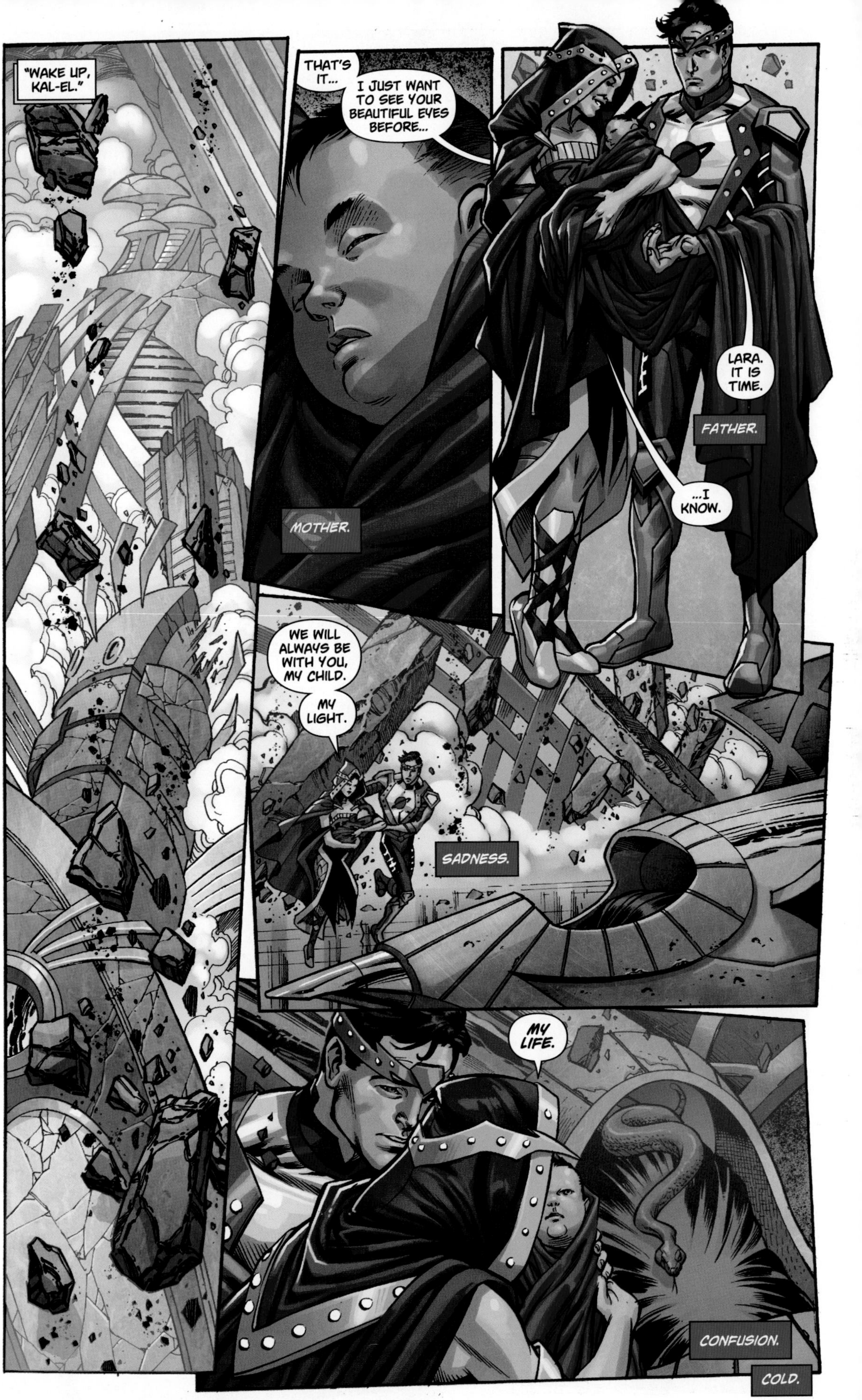
"WAKE UP, KAL-EL."
THAT'S IT...
I JUST WANT TO SEE YOUR BEAUTIFUL EYES BEFORE...
MOTHER.
LARA. IT IS TIME.
FATHER.
...I KNOW.
WE WILL ALWAYS BE WITH YOU, MY CHILD.
MY LIGHT.
SADNESS.
MY LIFE.
CONFUSION.
COLD.

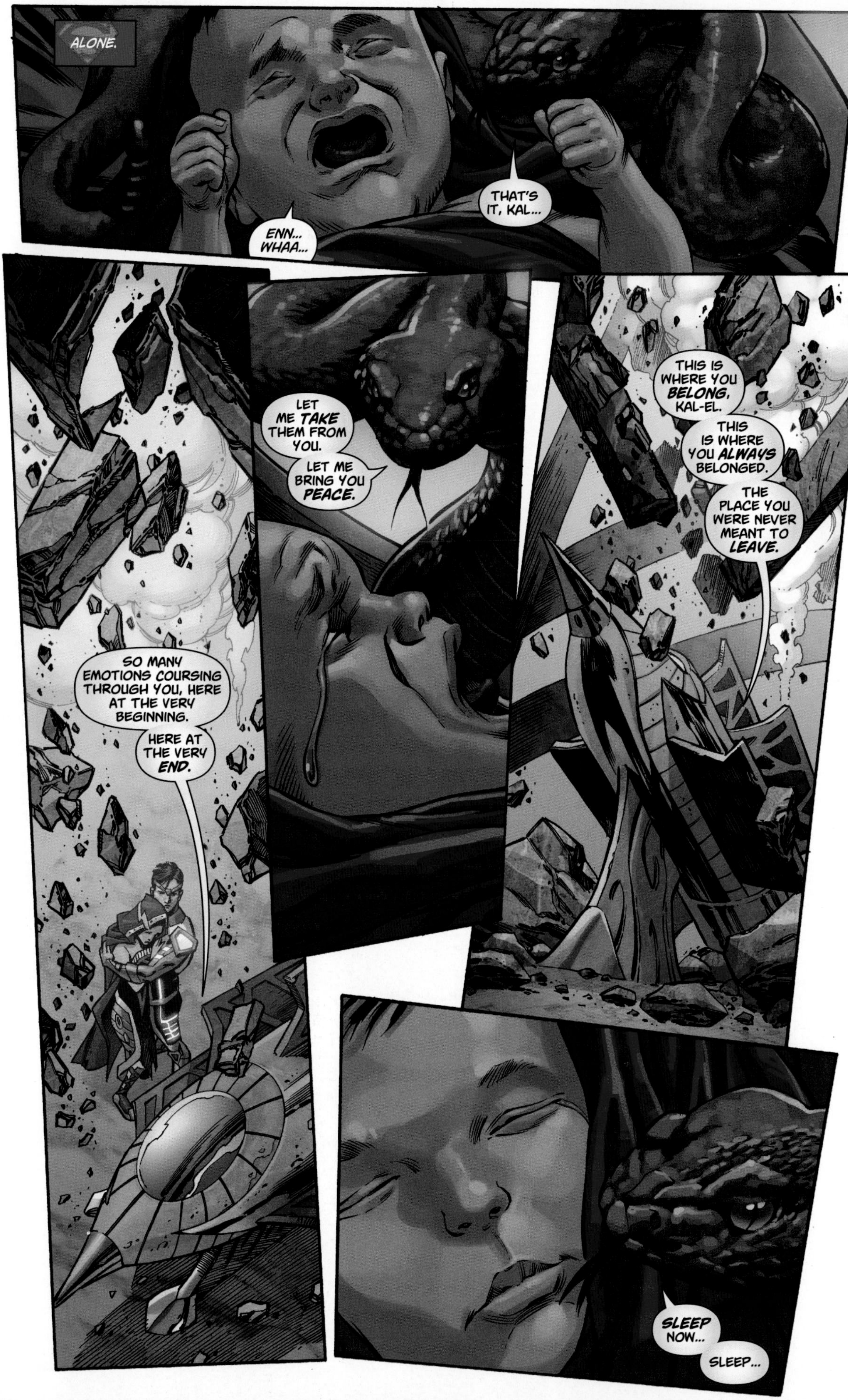
ALONE.
ENN... WHAA...
THAT'S IT, KAL...
SO MANY EMOTIONS COURSING THROUGH YOU, HERE AT THE VERY BEGINNING.
HERE AT THE VERY END.
LET ME TAKE THEM FROM YOU.
LET ME BRING YOU PEACE.
THIS IS WHERE YOU BELONG, KAL-EL.
THIS IS WHERE YOU ALWAYS BELONGED.
THE PLACE YOU WERE NEVER MEANT TO LEAVE.
SLEEP NOW...
SLEEP...

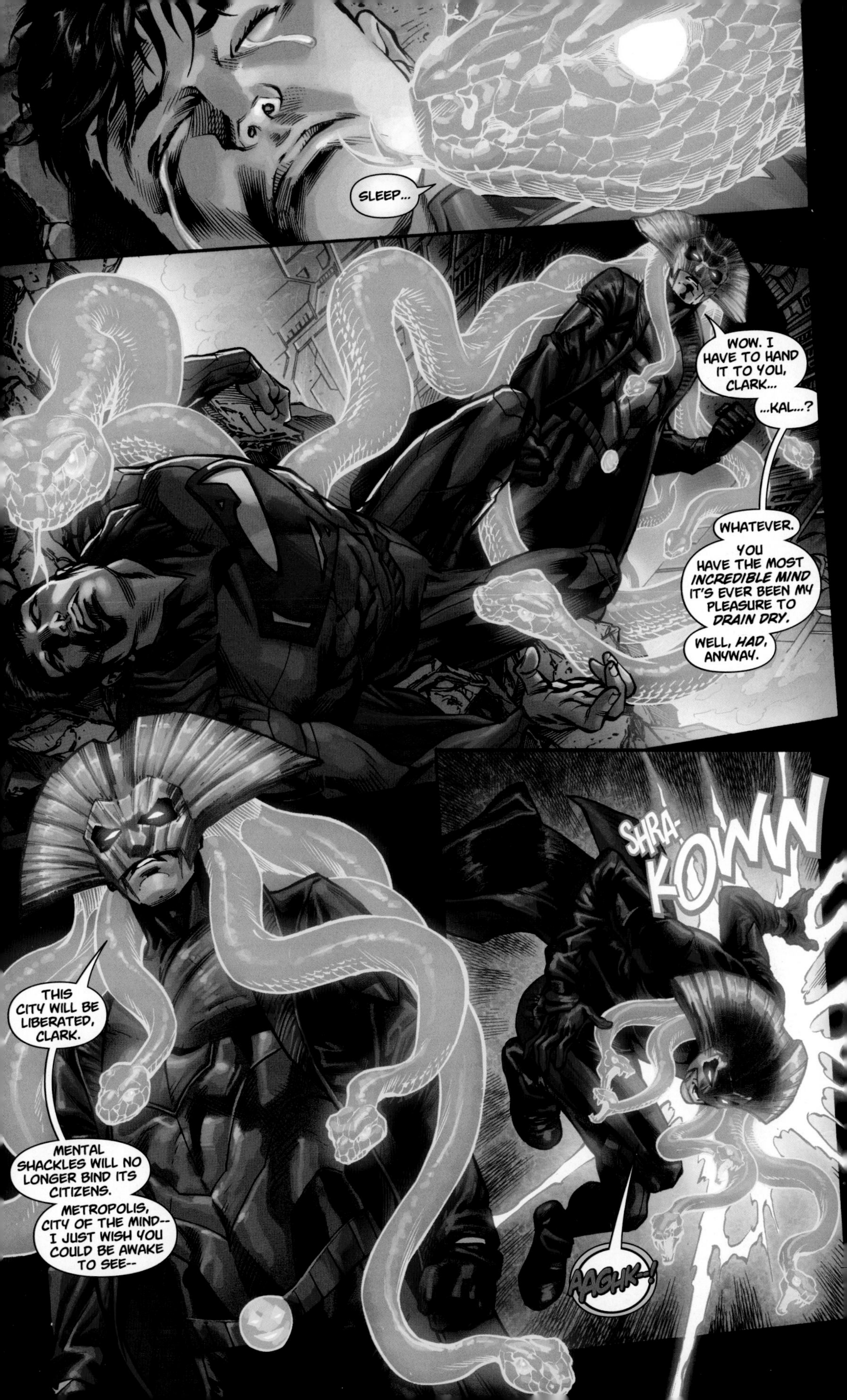
SLEEP...
WOW. I HAVE TO HAND IT TO YOU, CLARK...
...KAL...?
WHATEVER.
YOU HAVE THE MOST *INCREDIBLE MIND* IT'S EVER BEEN MY PLEASURE TO *DRAIN DRY.*
WELL, *HAD,* ANYWAY.
THIS CITY WILL BE LIBERATED, CLARK.
MENTAL SHACKLES WILL NO LONGER BIND ITS CITIZENS.
METROPOLIS, CITY OF THE MIND-- I JUST WISH YOU COULD BE AWAKE TO SEE--
SHRA-KOWW
AAGHK--!

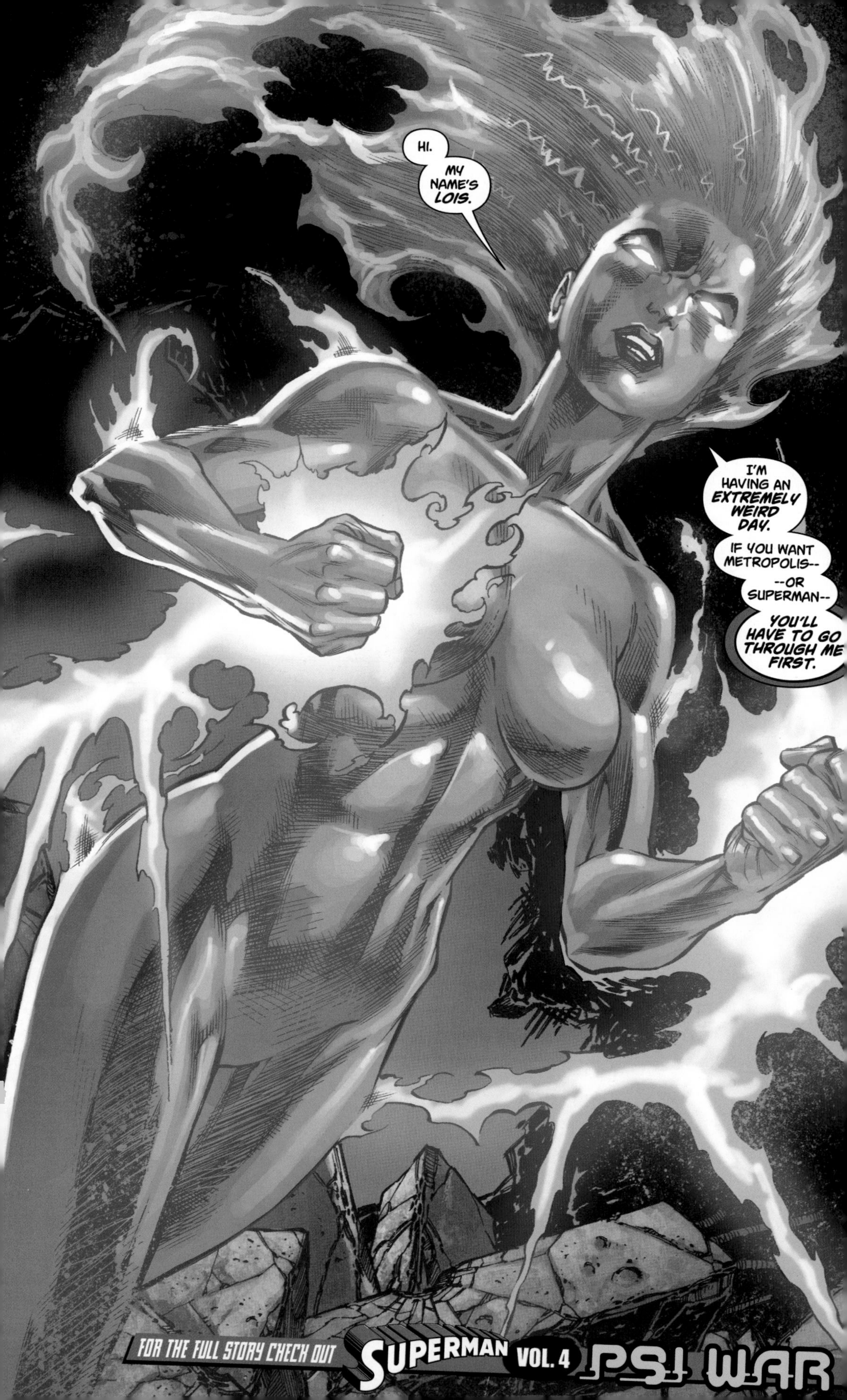
HI.
MY NAME'S LOIS.
I'M HAVING AN EXTREMELY WEIRD DAY.
IF YOU WANT METROPOLIS--
--OR SUPERMAN--
YOU'LL HAVE TO GO THROUGH ME FIRST.
FOR THE FULL STORY CHECK OUT SUPERMAN VOL. 4 PSI WAR

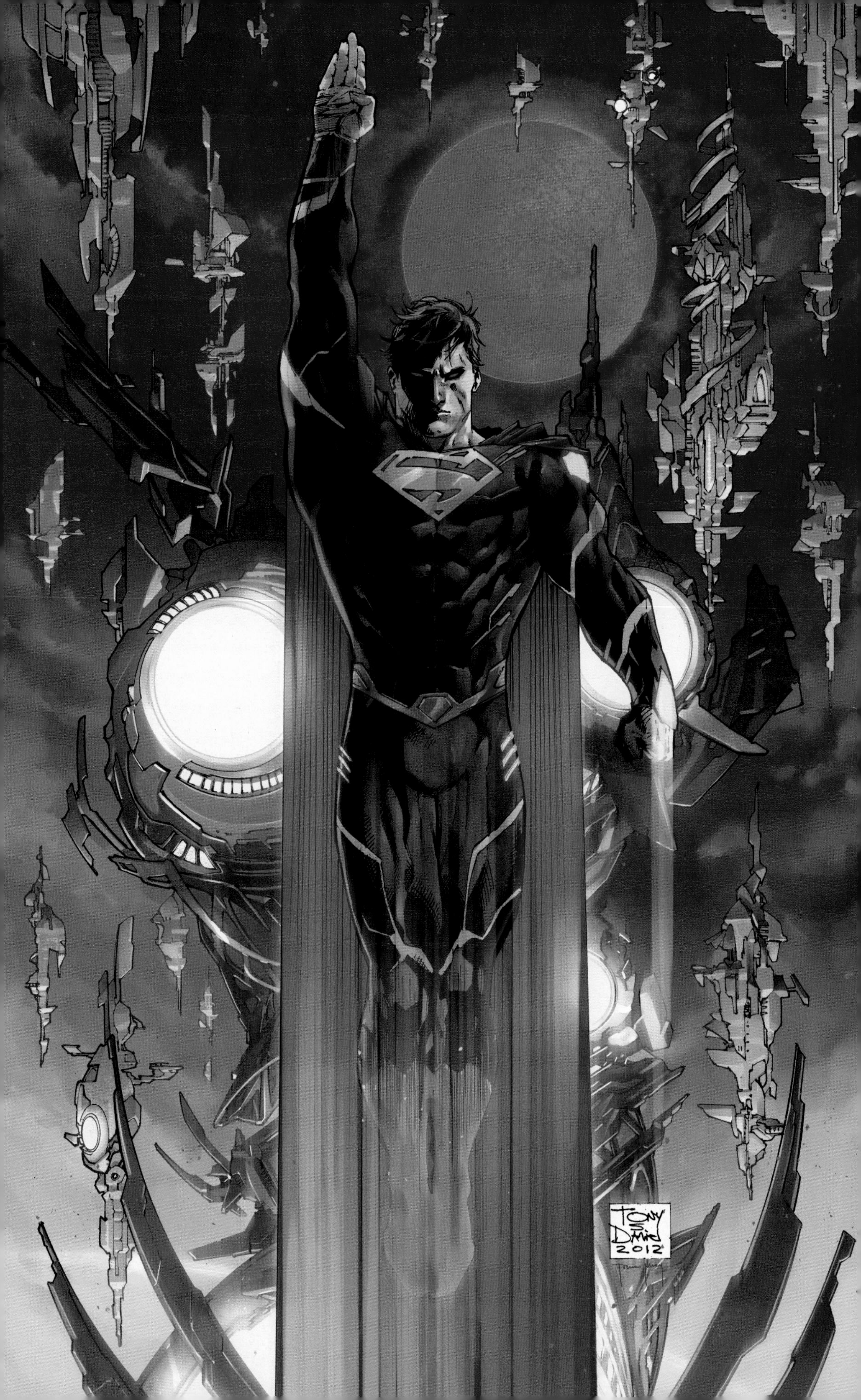
TONY S DANIEL 2012

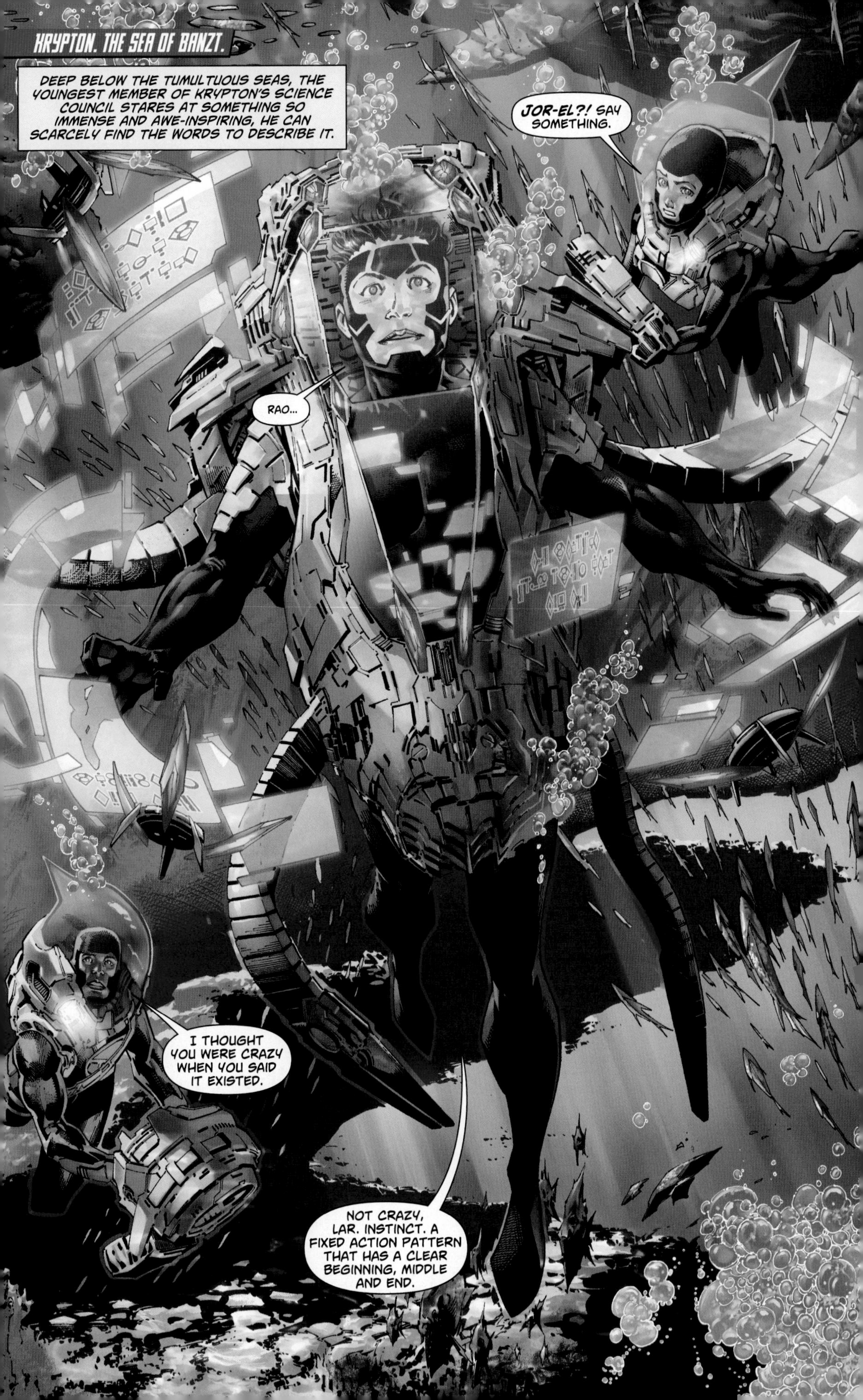

KRYPTON. THE SEA OF BANZT.
DEEP BELOW THE TUMULTUOUS SEAS, THE YOUNGEST MEMBER OF KRYPTON'S SCIENCE COUNCIL STARES AT SOMETHING SO IMMENSE AND AWE-INSPIRING, HE CAN SCARCELY FIND THE WORDS TO DESCRIBE IT.
JOR-EL?! SAY SOMETHING.
RAO...
I THOUGHT YOU WERE CRAZY WHEN YOU SAID IT EXISTED.
NOT CRAZY, LAR. INSTINCT. A FIXED ACTION PATTERN THAT HAS A CLEAR BEGINNING, MIDDLE AND END.

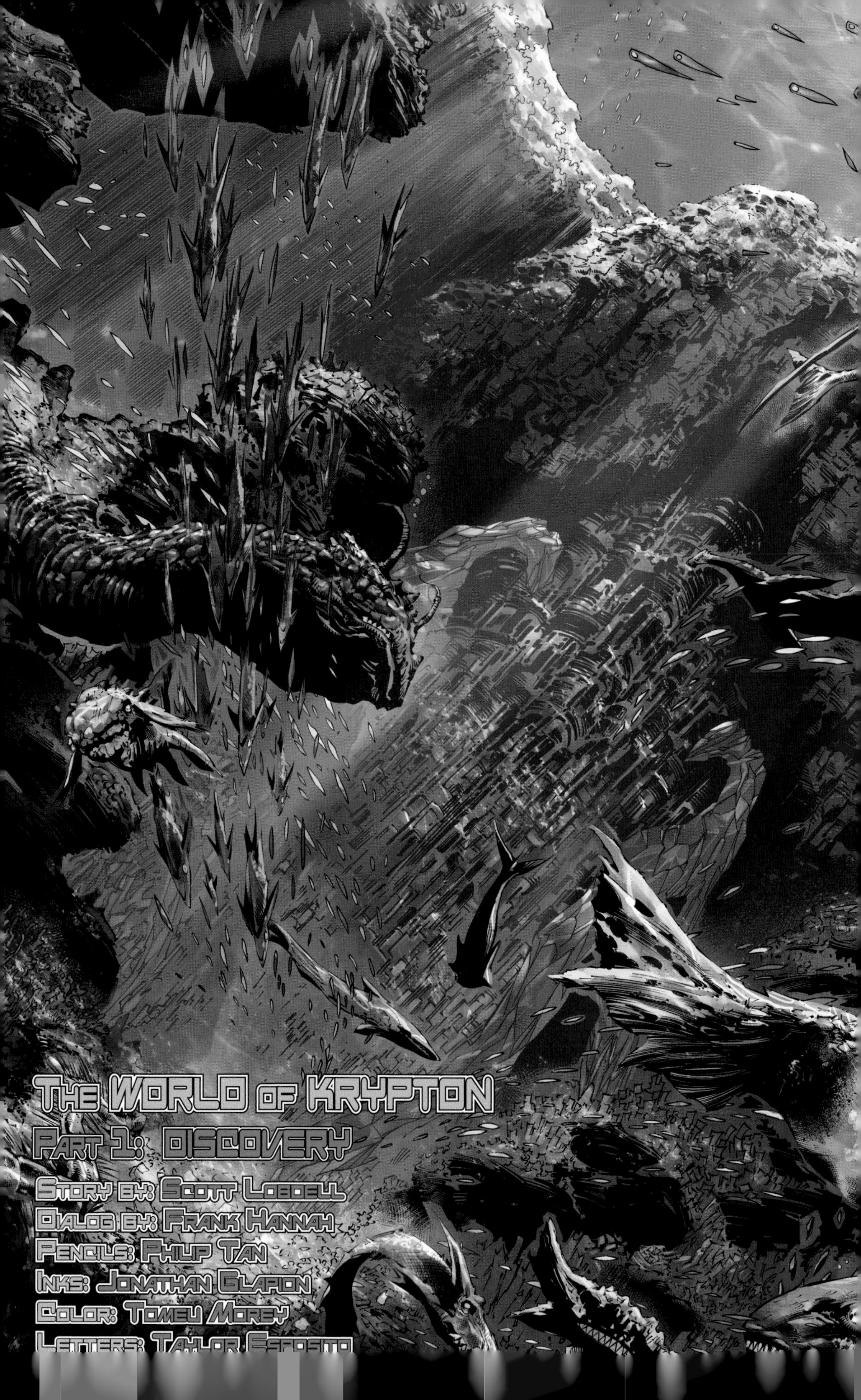
THE WORLD of KRYPTON
PART 1: DISCOVERY
STORY BY: SCOTT LOBDELL
DIALOG BY: FRANK HANNAH
PENCILS: PHILIP TAN
INKS: JONATHAN GLAPION
COLOR: TOMEU MOREY
LETTERS: TAYLOR ESPOSITO

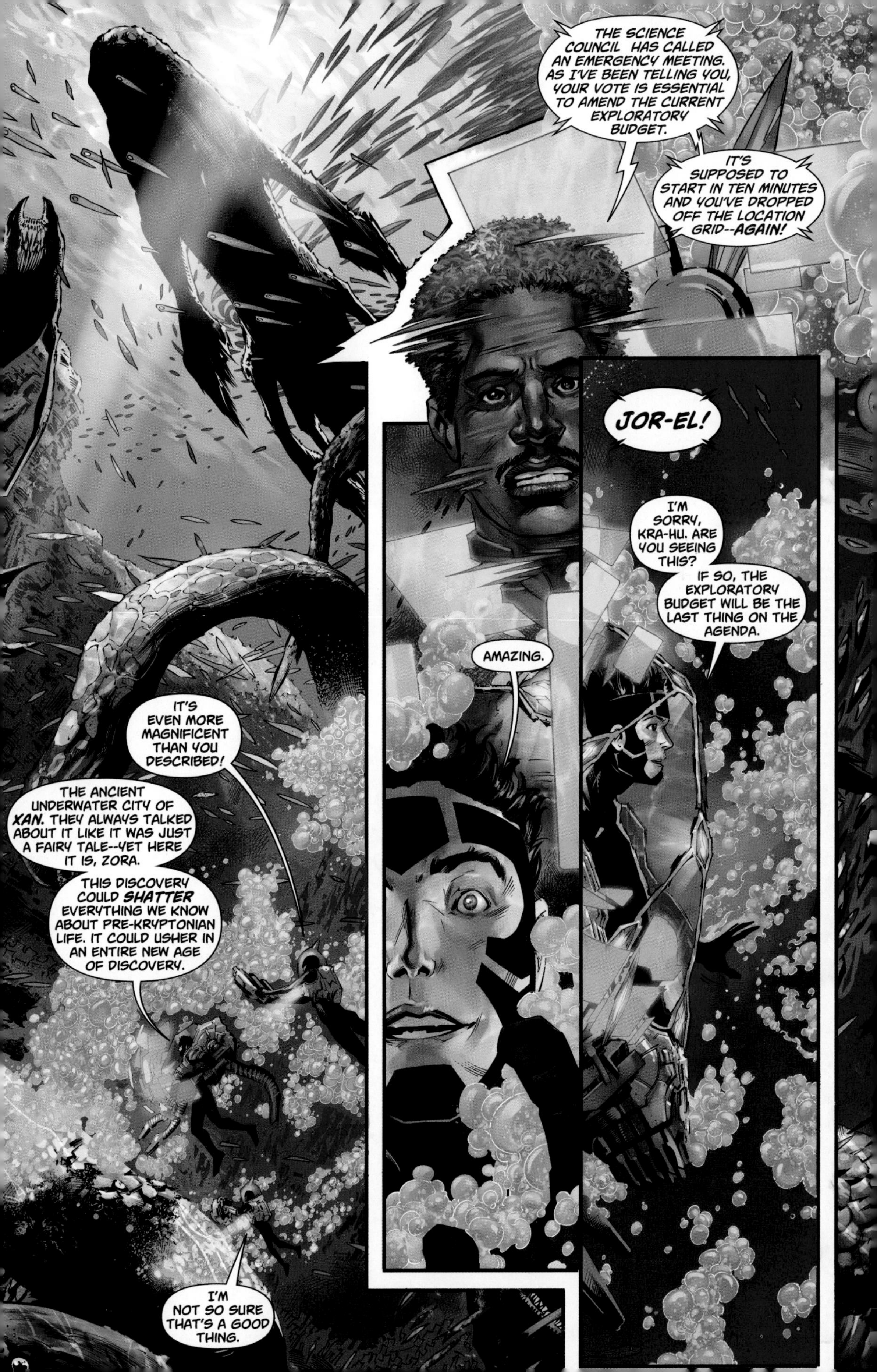
THE SCIENCE COUNCIL HAS CALLED AN EMERGENCY MEETING. AS I'VE BEEN TELLING YOU, YOUR VOTE IS ESSENTIAL TO AMEND THE CURRENT EXPLORATORY BUDGET.
IT'S SUPPOSED TO START IN TEN MINUTES AND YOU'VE DROPPED OFF THE LOCATION GRID--AGAIN!
JOR-EL!
I'M SORRY, KRA-HU. ARE YOU SEEING THIS?
IF SO, THE EXPLORATORY BUDGET WILL BE THE LAST THING ON THE AGENDA.
AMAZING.
IT'S EVEN MORE MAGNIFICENT THAN YOU DESCRIBED!
THE ANCIENT UNDERWATER CITY OF XAN. THEY ALWAYS TALKED ABOUT IT LIKE IT WAS JUST A FAIRY TALE--YET HERE IT IS, ZORA.
THIS DISCOVERY COULD SHATTER EVERYTHING WE KNOW ABOUT PRE-KRYPTONIAN LIFE. IT COULD USHER IN AN ENTIRE NEW AGE OF DISCOVERY.
I'M NOT SO SURE THAT'S A GOOD THING.

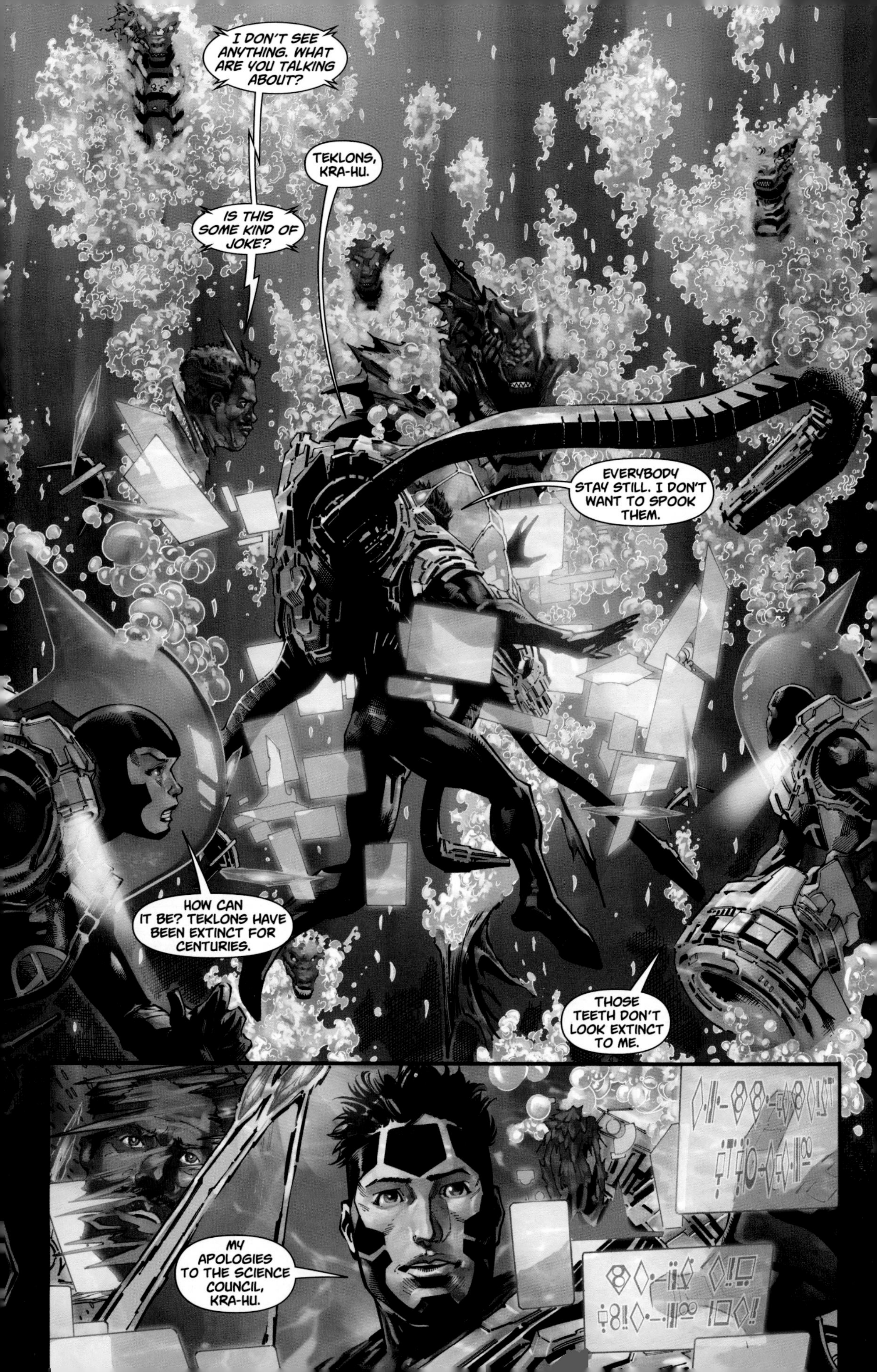
I DON'T SEE ANYTHING. WHAT ARE YOU TALKING ABOUT?
TEKLONS, KRA-HU.
IS THIS SOME KIND OF JOKE?
EVERYBODY STAY STILL. I DON'T WANT TO SPOOK THEM.
HOW CAN IT BE? TEKLONS HAVE BEEN EXTINCT FOR CENTURIES.
THOSE TEETH DON'T LOOK EXTINCT TO ME.
MY APOLOGIES TO THE SCIENCE COUNCIL, KRA-HU.

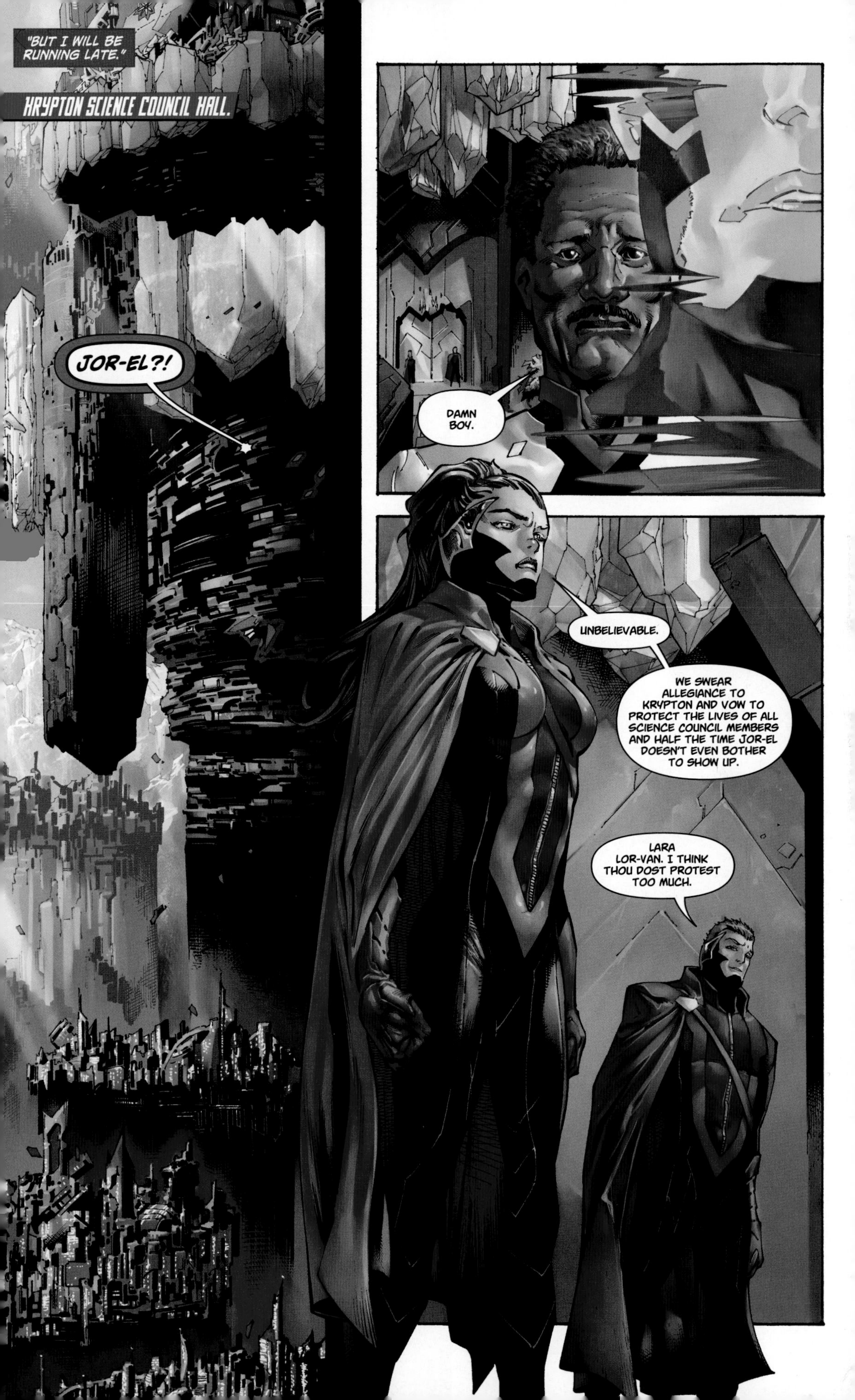
"BUT I WILL BE RUNNING LATE."
KRYPTON SCIENCE COUNCIL HALL.
JOR-EL?!
DAMN BOY.
UNBELIEVABLE.
WE SWEAR ALLEGIANCE TO KRYPTON AND VOW TO PROTECT THE LIVES OF ALL SCIENCE COUNCIL MEMBERS AND HALF THE TIME JOR-EL DOESN'T EVEN BOTHER TO SHOW UP.
LARA LOR-VAN. I THINK THOU DOST PROTEST TOO MUCH.

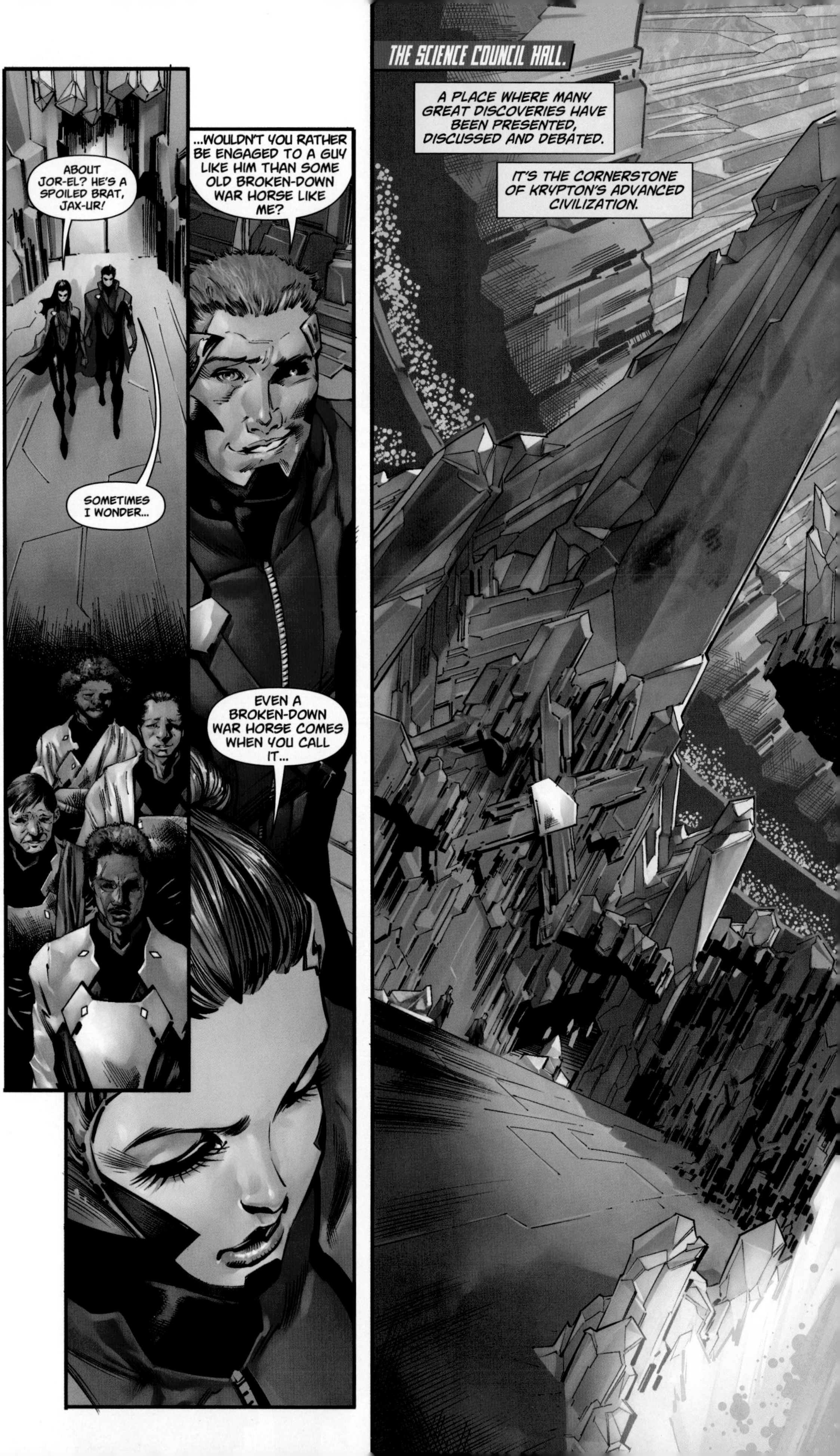
ABOUT JOR-EL? HE'S A SPOILED BRAT, JAX-UR!
...WOULDN'T YOU RATHER BE ENGAGED TO A GUY LIKE HIM THAN SOME OLD BROKEN-DOWN WAR HORSE LIKE ME?
SOMETIMES I WONDER...
EVEN A BROKEN-DOWN WAR HORSE COMES WHEN YOU CALL IT...
THE SCIENCE COUNCIL HALL.
A PLACE WHERE MANY GREAT DISCOVERIES HAVE BEEN PRESENTED, DISCUSSED AND DEBATED.
IT'S THE CORNERSTONE OF KRYPTON'S ADVANCED CIVILIZATION.

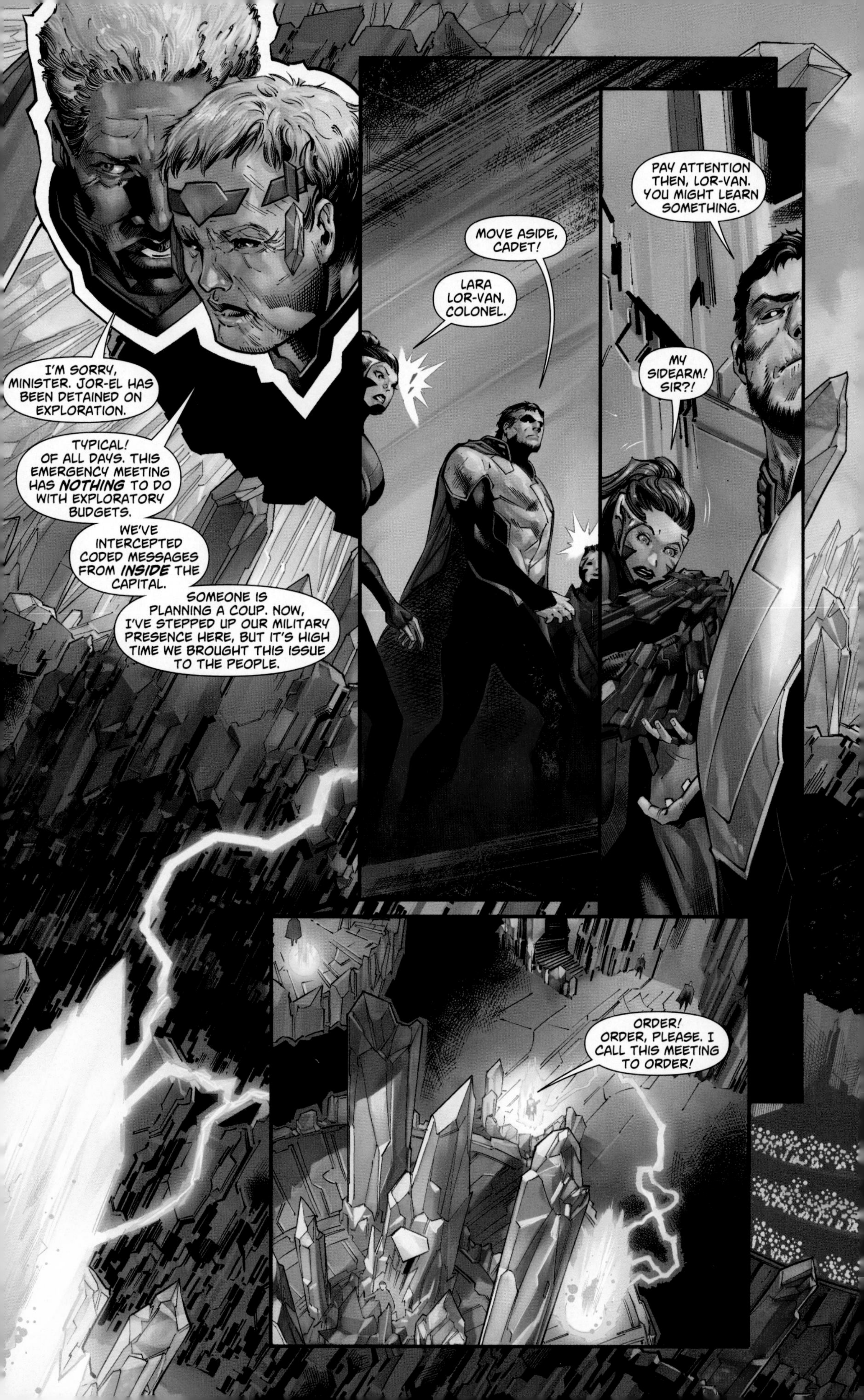

I'M SORRY, MINISTER. JOR-EL HAS BEEN DETAINED ON EXPLORATION.
TYPICAL! OF ALL DAYS. THIS EMERGENCY MEETING HAS NOTHING TO DO WITH EXPLORATORY BUDGETS.
WE'VE INTERCEPTED CODED MESSAGES FROM INSIDE THE CAPITAL.
SOMEONE IS PLANNING A COUP. NOW, I'VE STEPPED UP OUR MILITARY PRESENCE HERE, BUT IT'S HIGH TIME WE BROUGHT THIS ISSUE TO THE PEOPLE.
MOVE ASIDE, CADET!
LARA LOR-VAN, COLONEL.
!
PAY ATTENTION THEN, LOR-VAN. YOU MIGHT LEARN SOMETHING.
MY SIDEARM! SIR?!
ORDER! ORDER, PLEASE. I CALL THIS MEETING TO ORDER!

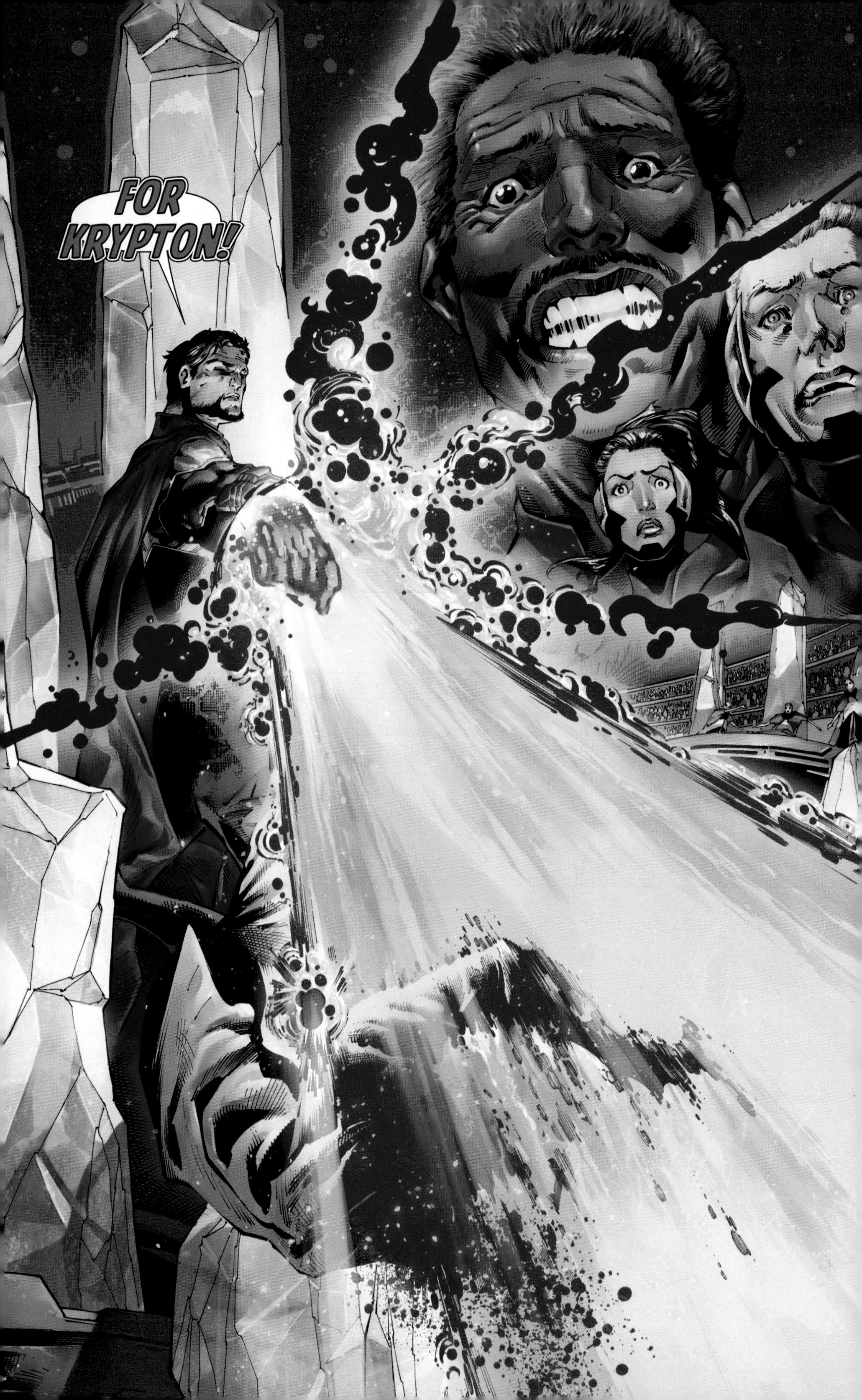
FOR KRYPTON!

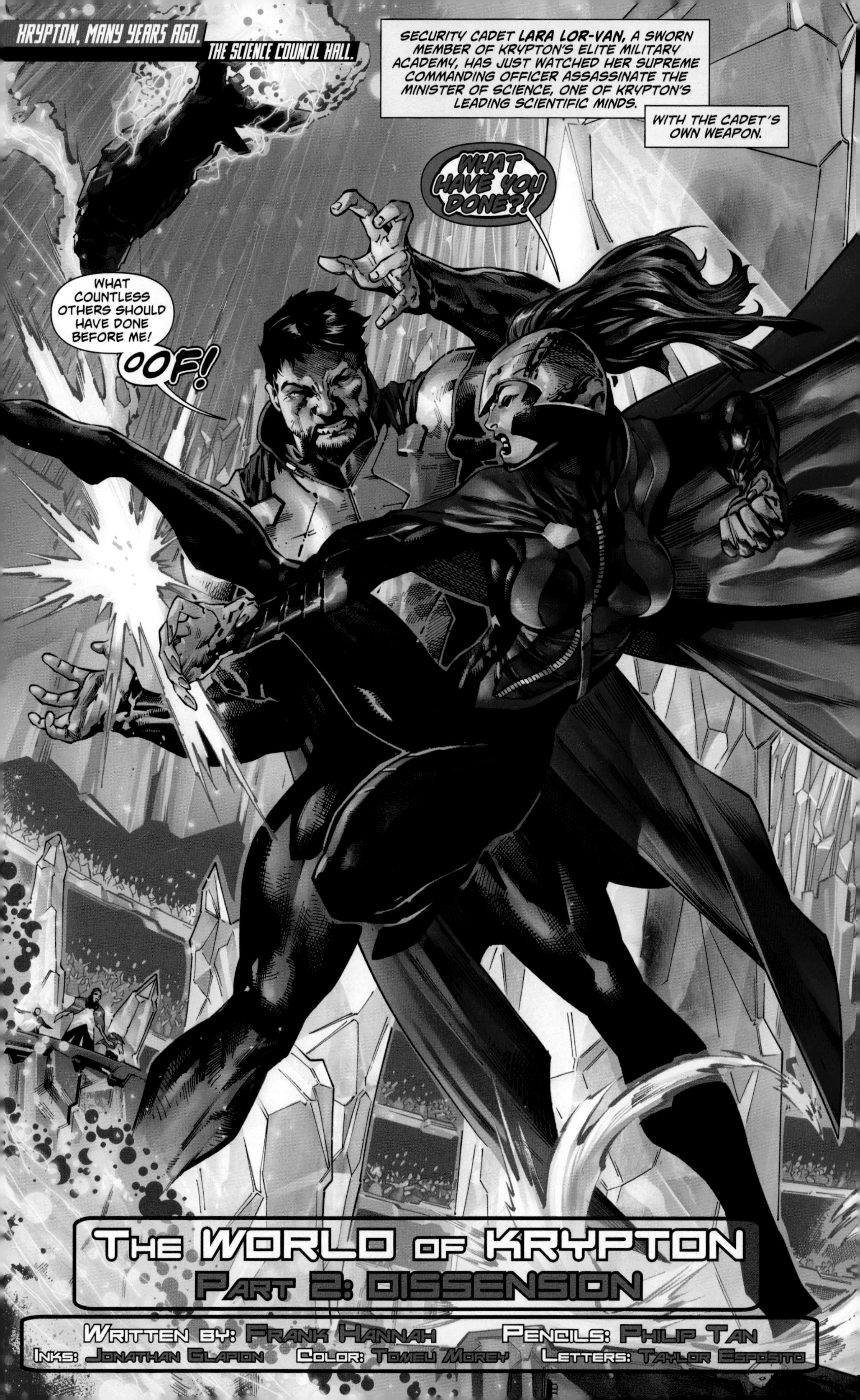
KRYPTON, MANY YEARS AGO.
THE SCIENCE COUNCIL HALL.
SECURITY CADET LARA LOR-VAN, A SWORN MEMBER OF KRYPTON'S ELITE MILITARY ACADEMY, HAS JUST WATCHED HER SUPREME COMMANDING OFFICER ASSASSINATE THE MINISTER OF SCIENCE, ONE OF KRYPTON'S LEADING SCIENTIFIC MINDS.
WITH THE CADET'S OWN WEAPON.
WHAT HAVE YOU DONE?!
WHAT COUNTLESS OTHERS SHOULD HAVE DONE BEFORE ME!
OOF!
THE WORLD OF KRYPTON
PART 2: DISSENSION
WRITTEN BY: FRANK HANNAH PENCILS: PHILIP TAN
INKS: JONATHAN GLAPION COLOR: TOMEU MOREY LETTERS: TAYLOR ESPOSITO

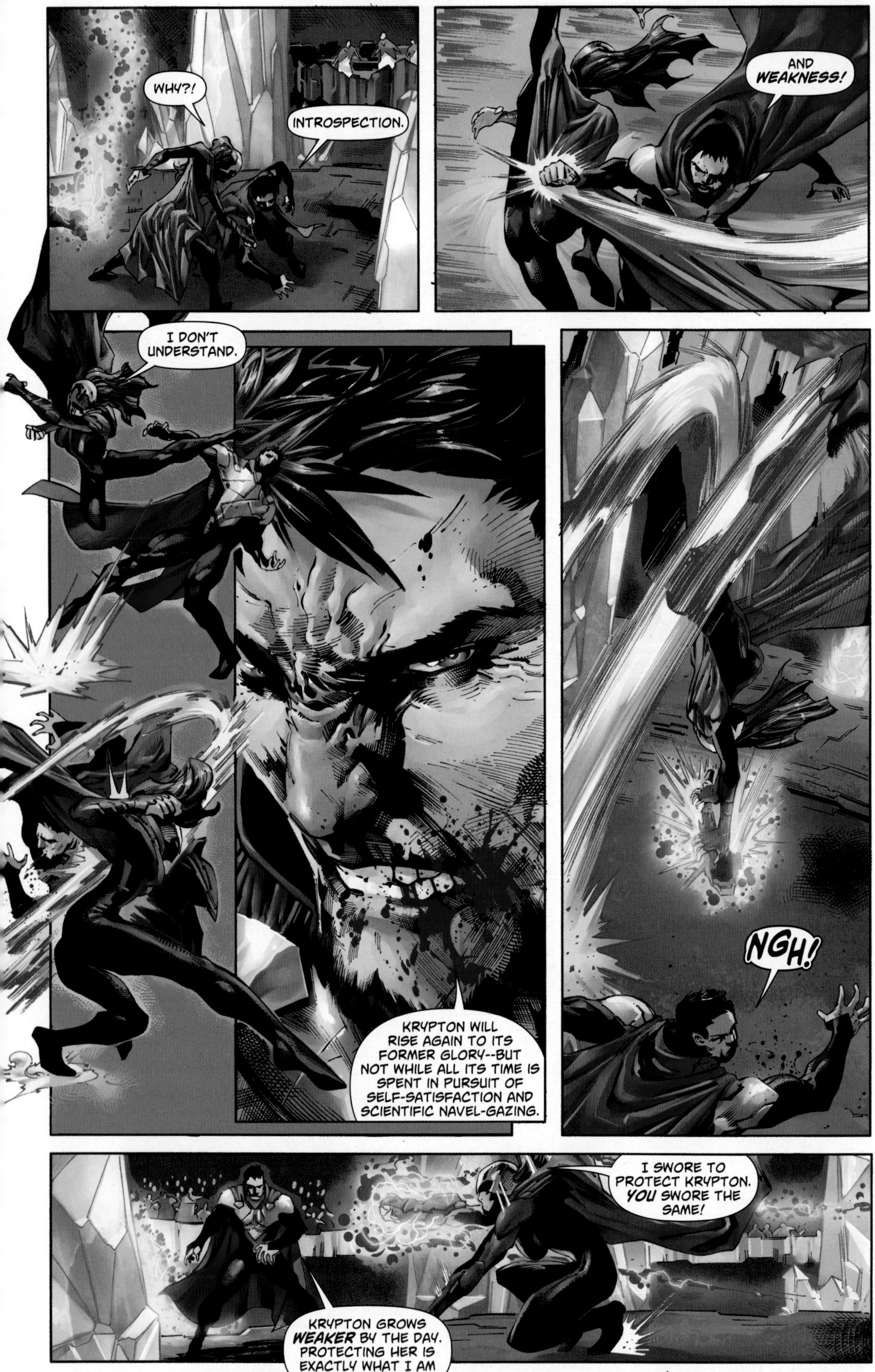
WHY?!
INTROSPECTION.
AND WEAKNESS!
I DON'T UNDERSTAND.
KRYPTON WILL RISE AGAIN TO ITS FORMER GLORY--BUT NOT WHILE ALL ITS TIME IS SPENT IN PURSUIT OF SELF-SATISFACTION AND SCIENTIFIC NAVEL-GAZING.
NGH!
I SWORE TO PROTECT KRYPTON. YOU SWORE THE SAME!
KRYPTON GROWS WEAKER BY THE DAY. PROTECTING HER IS EXACTLY WHAT I AM TRYING TO DO.

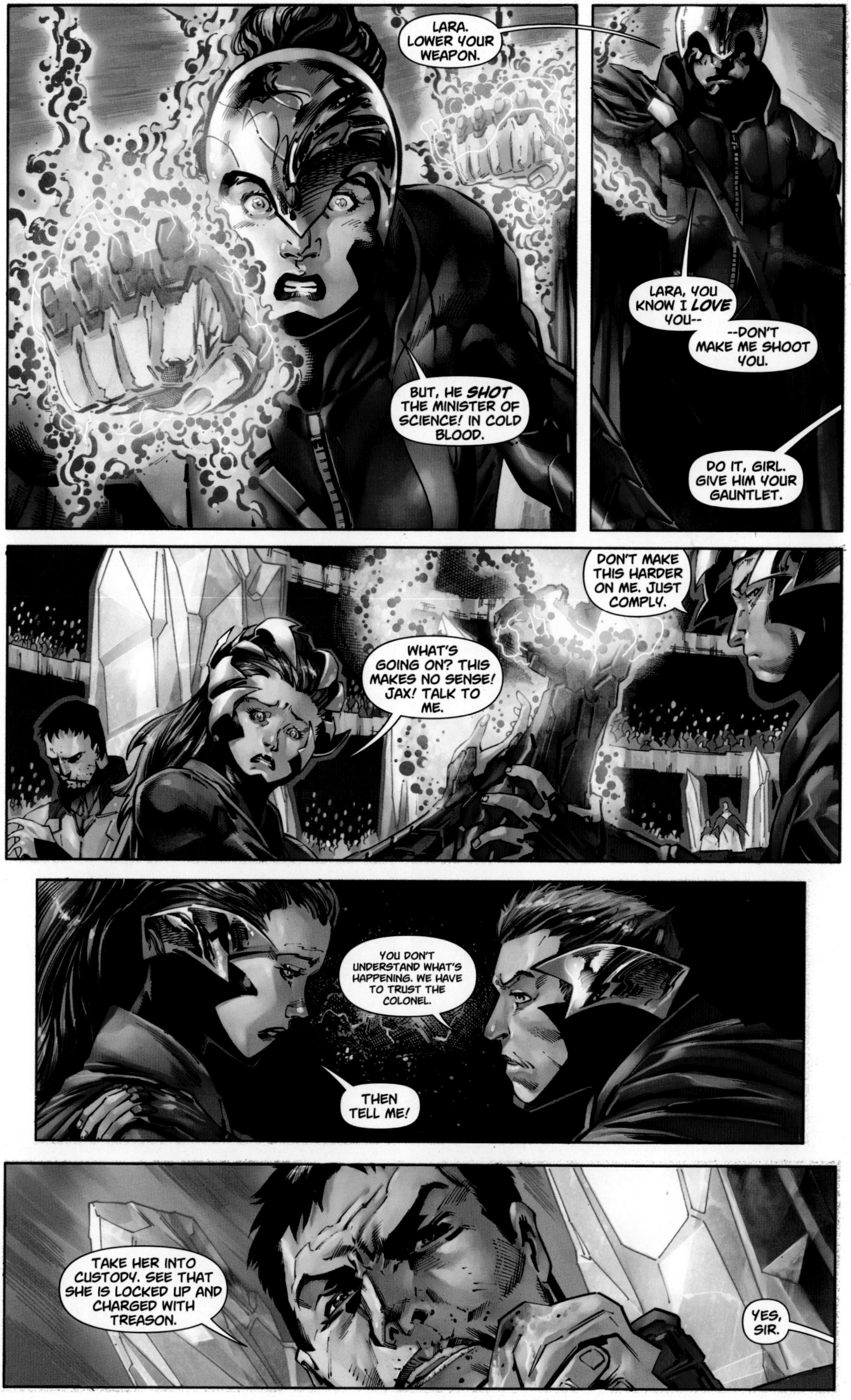
LARA. LOWER YOUR WEAPON.
BUT, HE SHOT THE MINISTER OF SCIENCE! IN COLD BLOOD.
LARA, YOU KNOW I LOVE YOU--
--DON'T MAKE ME SHOOT YOU.
DO IT, GIRL. GIVE HIM YOUR GAUNTLET.
DON'T MAKE THIS HARDER ON ME. JUST COMPLY.
WHAT'S GOING ON? THIS MAKES NO SENSE! JAX! TALK TO ME.
YOU DON'T UNDERSTAND WHAT'S HAPPENING. WE HAVE TO TRUST THE COLONEL.
THEN TELL ME!
TAKE HER INTO CUSTODY. SEE THAT SHE IS LOCKED UP AND CHARGED WITH TREASON.
YES, SIR.

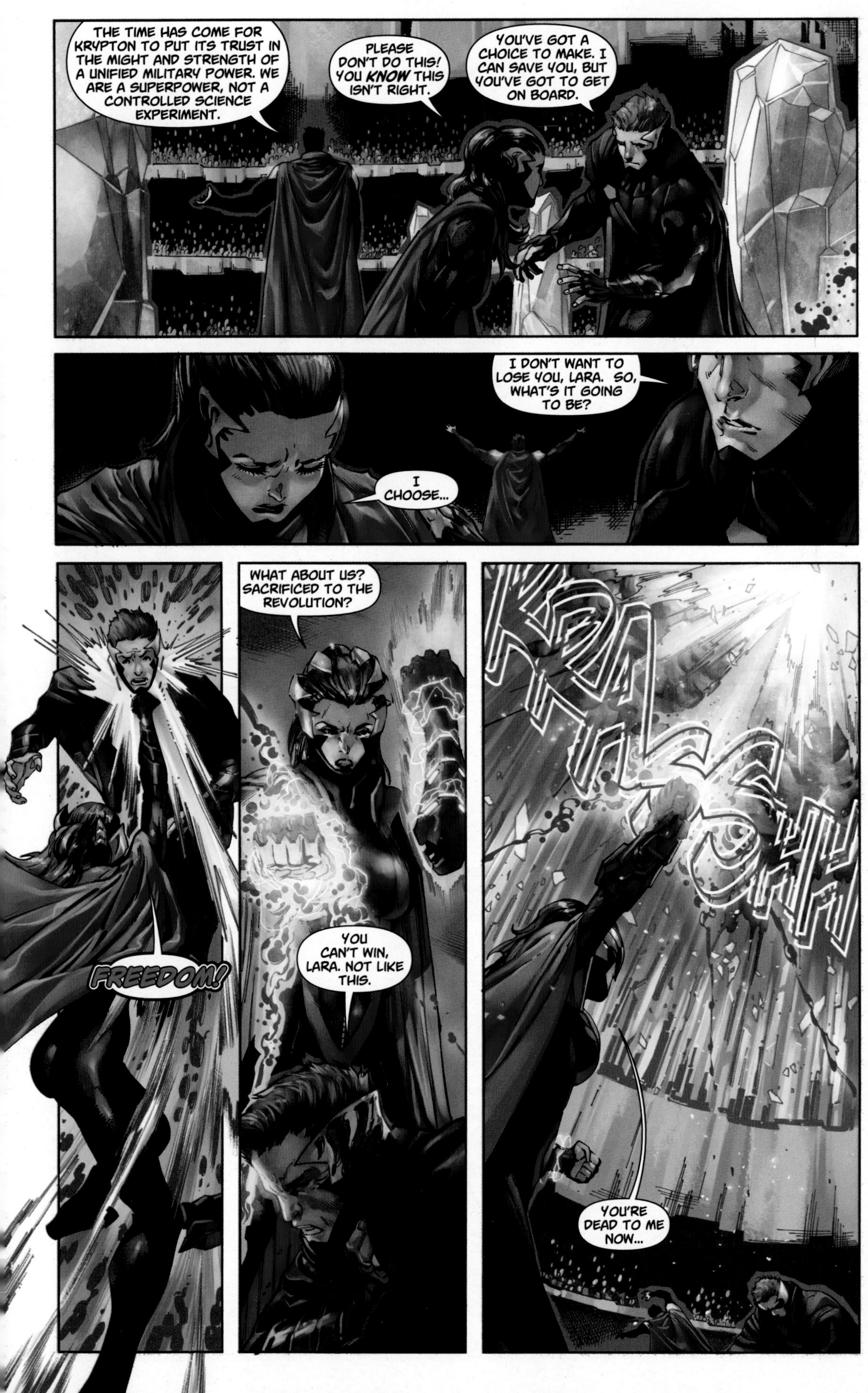
THE TIME HAS COME FOR KRYPTON TO PUT ITS TRUST IN THE MIGHT AND STRENGTH OF A UNIFIED MILITARY POWER. WE ARE A SUPERPOWER, NOT A CONTROLLED SCIENCE EXPERIMENT.
PLEASE DON'T DO THIS! YOU KNOW THIS ISN'T RIGHT.
YOU'VE GOT A CHOICE TO MAKE. I CAN SAVE YOU, BUT YOU'VE GOT TO GET ON BOARD.
I DON'T WANT TO LOSE YOU, LARA. SO, WHAT'S IT GOING TO BE?
I CHOOSE...
FREEDOM!
WHAT ABOUT US? SACRIFICED TO THE REVOLUTION?
YOU CAN'T WIN, LARA. NOT LIKE THIS.
YOU'RE DEAD TO ME NOW...

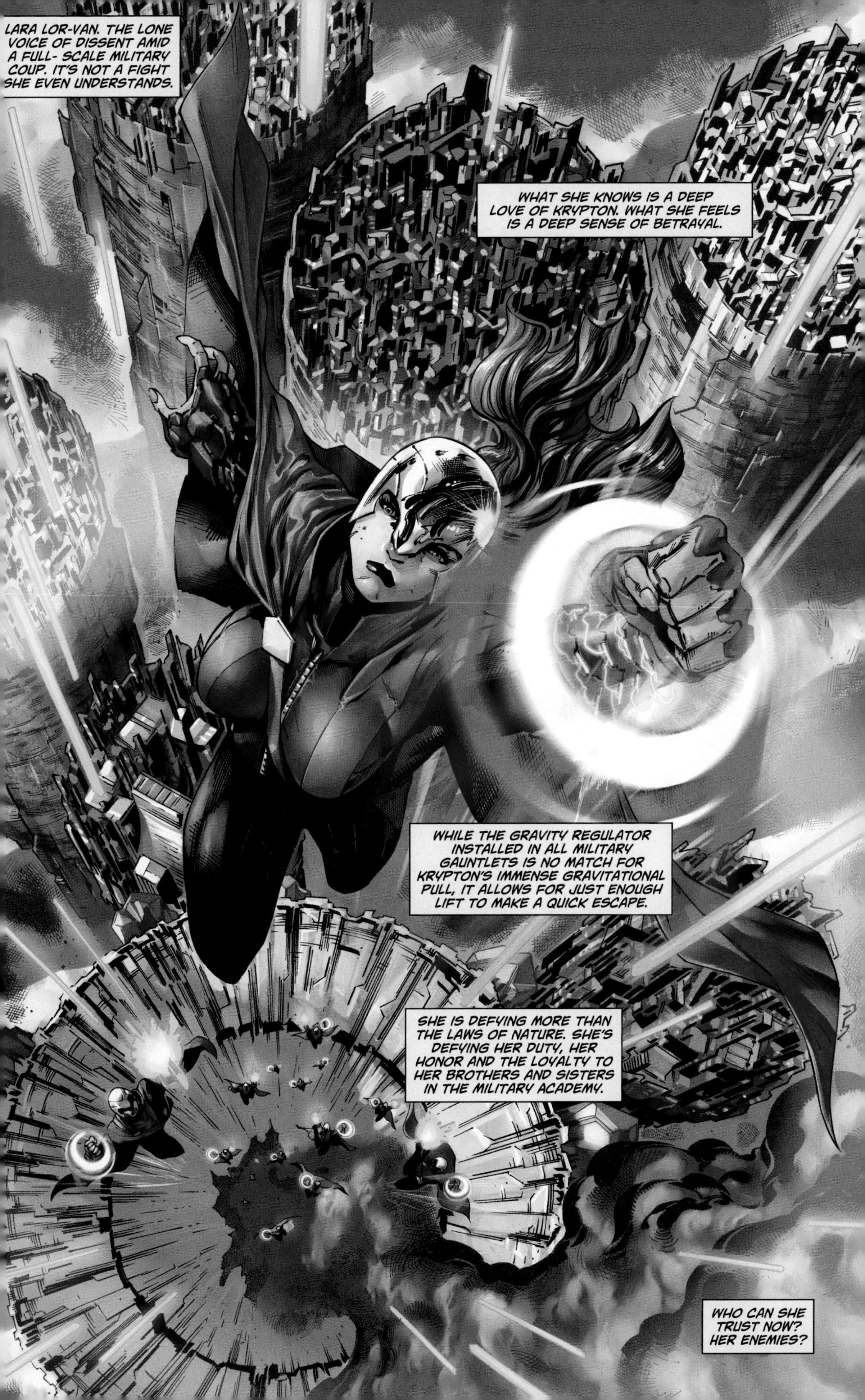
LARA LOR-VAN. THE LONE VOICE OF DISSENT AMID A FULL- SCALE MILITARY COUP. IT'S NOT A FIGHT SHE EVEN UNDERSTANDS.
WHAT SHE KNOWS IS A DEEP LOVE OF KRYPTON. WHAT SHE FEELS IS A DEEP SENSE OF BETRAYAL.
WHILE THE GRAVITY REGULATOR INSTALLED IN ALL MILITARY GAUNTLETS IS NO MATCH FOR KRYPTON'S IMMENSE GRAVITATIONAL PULL, IT ALLOWS FOR JUST ENOUGH LIFT TO MAKE A QUICK ESCAPE.
SHE IS DEFYING MORE THAN THE LAWS OF NATURE. SHE'S DEFYING HER DUTY, HER HONOR AND THE LOYALTY TO HER BROTHERS AND SISTERS IN THE MILITARY ACADEMY.
WHO CAN SHE TRUST NOW? HER ENEMIES?

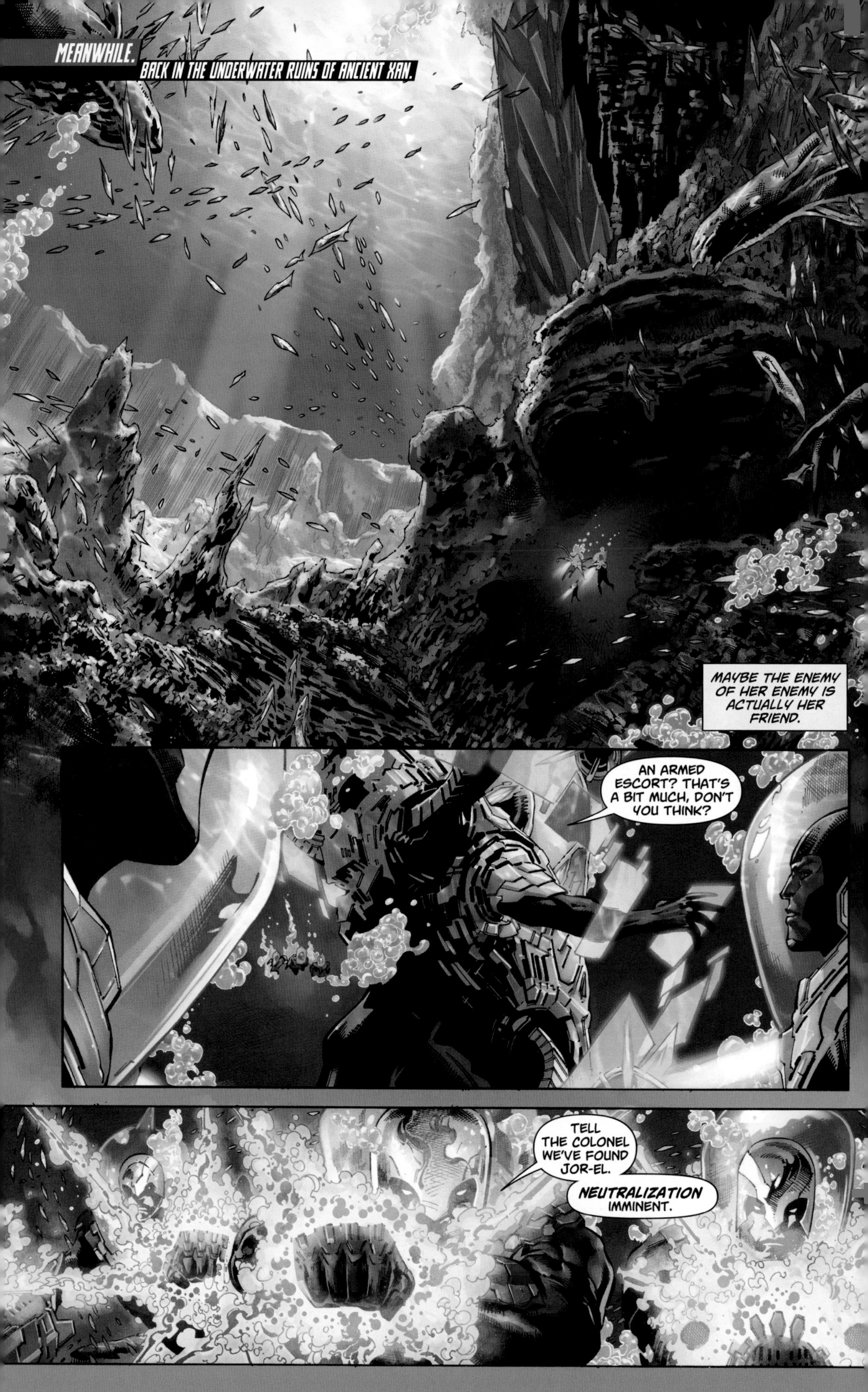
MEANWHILE.
BACK IN THE UNDERWATER RUINS OF ANCIENT XAN.
MAYBE THE ENEMY OF HER ENEMY IS ACTUALLY HER FRIEND.
AN ARMED ESCORT? THAT'S A BIT MUCH, DON'T YOU THINK?
TELL THE COLONEL WE'VE FOUND JOR-EL.
NEUTRALIZATION IMMINENT.

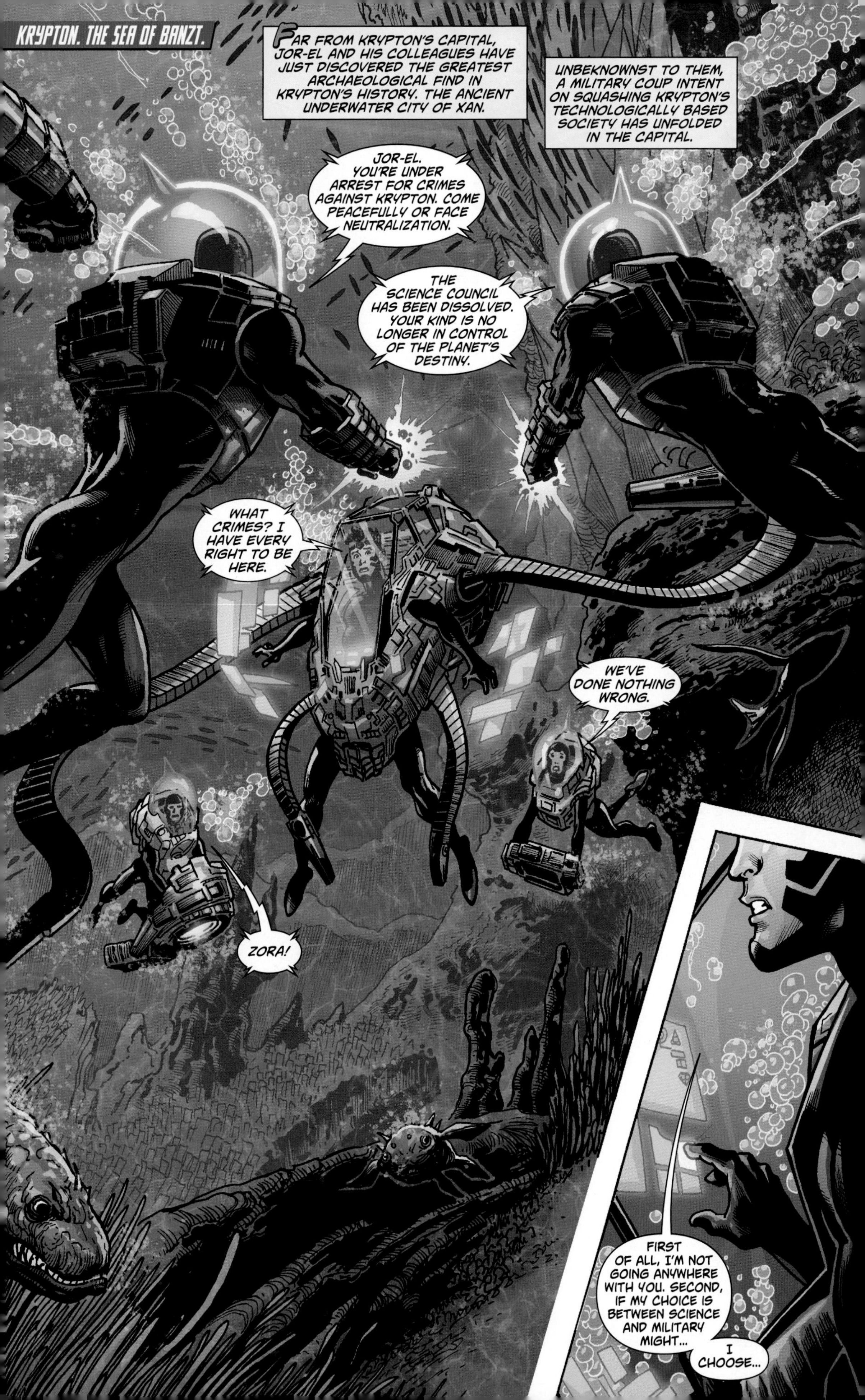
KRYPTON. THE SEA OF BANZT.
FAR FROM KRYPTON'S CAPITAL, JOR-EL AND HIS COLLEAGUES HAVE JUST DISCOVERED THE GREATEST ARCHAEOLOGICAL FIND IN KRYPTON'S HISTORY. THE ANCIENT UNDERWATER CITY OF XAN.
UNBEKNOWNST TO THEM, A MILITARY COUP INTENT ON SQUASHING KRYPTON'S TECHNOLOGICALLY BASED SOCIETY HAS UNFOLDED IN THE CAPITAL.
JOR-EL. YOU'RE UNDER ARREST FOR CRIMES AGAINST KRYPTON. COME PEACEFULLY OR FACE NEUTRALIZATION.
THE SCIENCE COUNCIL HAS BEEN DISSOLVED. YOUR KIND IS NO LONGER IN CONTROL OF THE PLANET'S DESTINY.
WHAT CRIMES? I HAVE EVERY RIGHT TO BE HERE.
WE'VE DONE NOTHING WRONG.
ZORA!
FIRST OF ALL, I'M NOT GOING ANYWHERE WITH YOU. SECOND, IF MY CHOICE IS BETWEEN SCIENCE AND MILITARY MIGHT...
I CHOOSE...

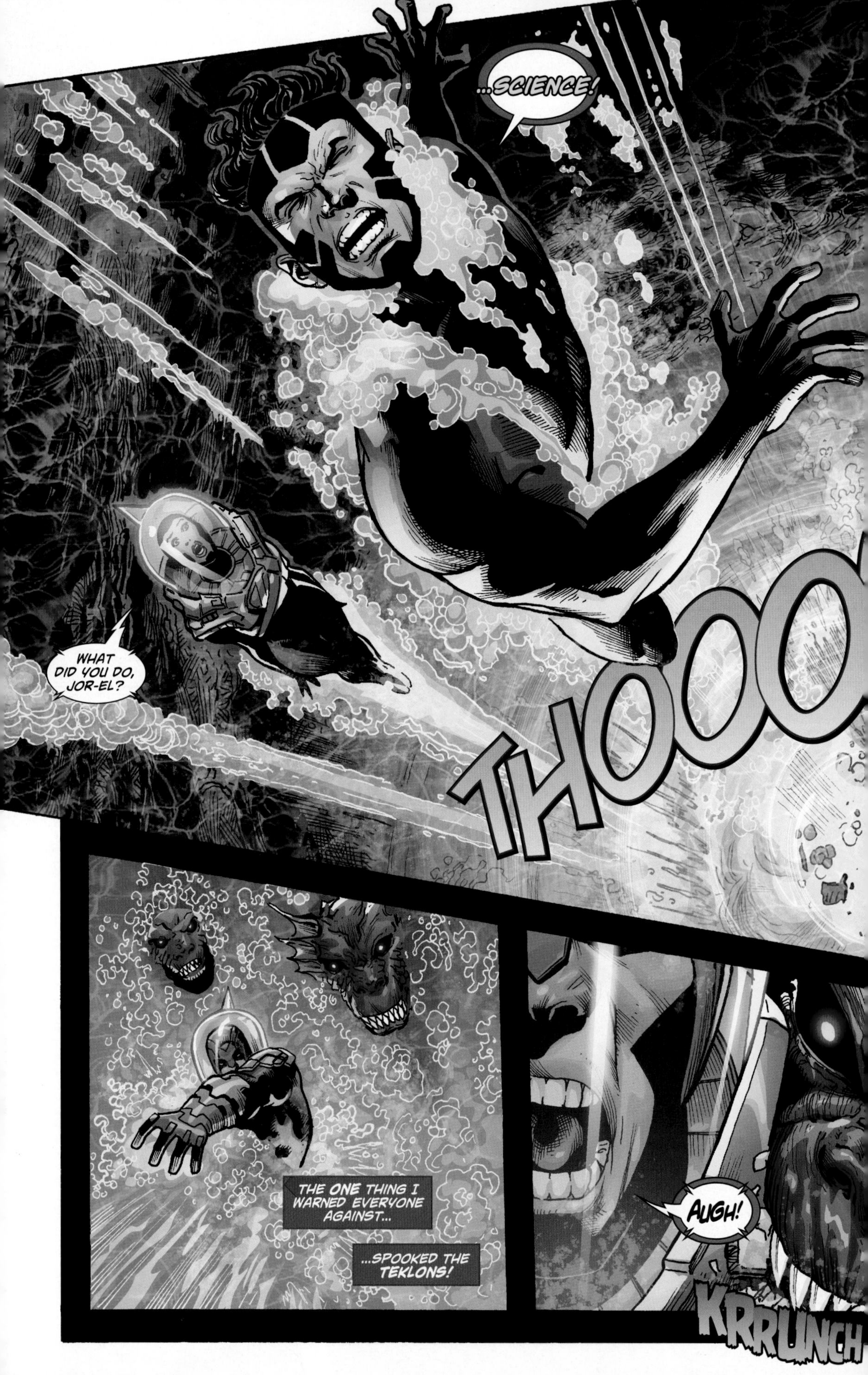
...SCIENCE!
WHAT DID YOU DO, JOR-EL?
THOOOO
THE ONE THING I WARNED EVERYONE AGAINST...
...SPOOKED THE TEKLONS!
AUGH!
KRRUNCH

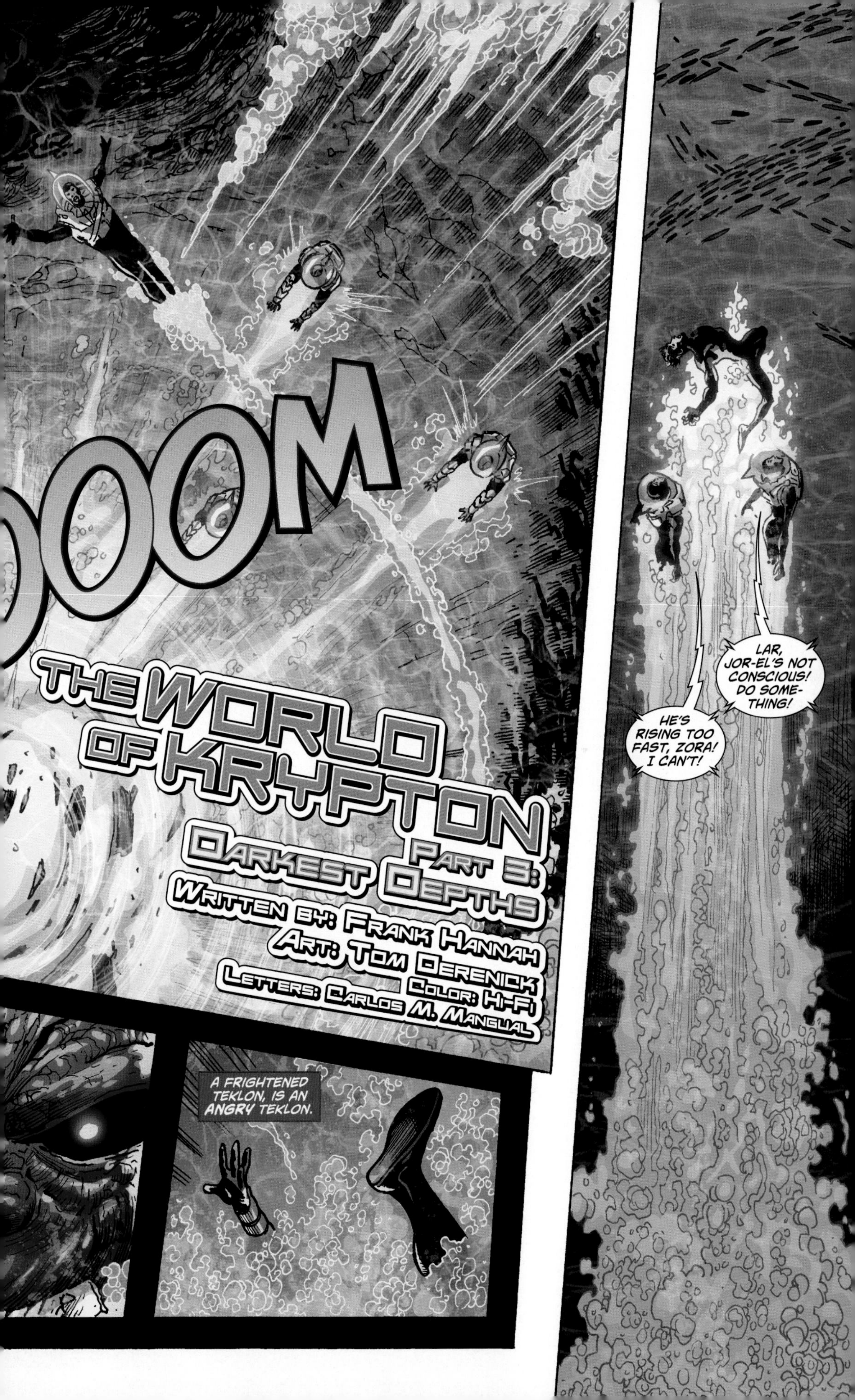
OOOM
THE WORLD OF KRYPTON
PART 3: DARKEST DEPTHS
WRITTEN BY: FRANK HANNAH
ART: TOM DERENICK
COLOR: HI-FI
LETTERS: CARLOS M. MANGUAL
A FRIGHTENED TEKLON, IS AN ANGRY TEKLON.
LAR, JOR-EL'S NOT CONSCIOUS! DO SOME-THING!
HE'S RISING TOO FAST, ZORA! I CAN'T!

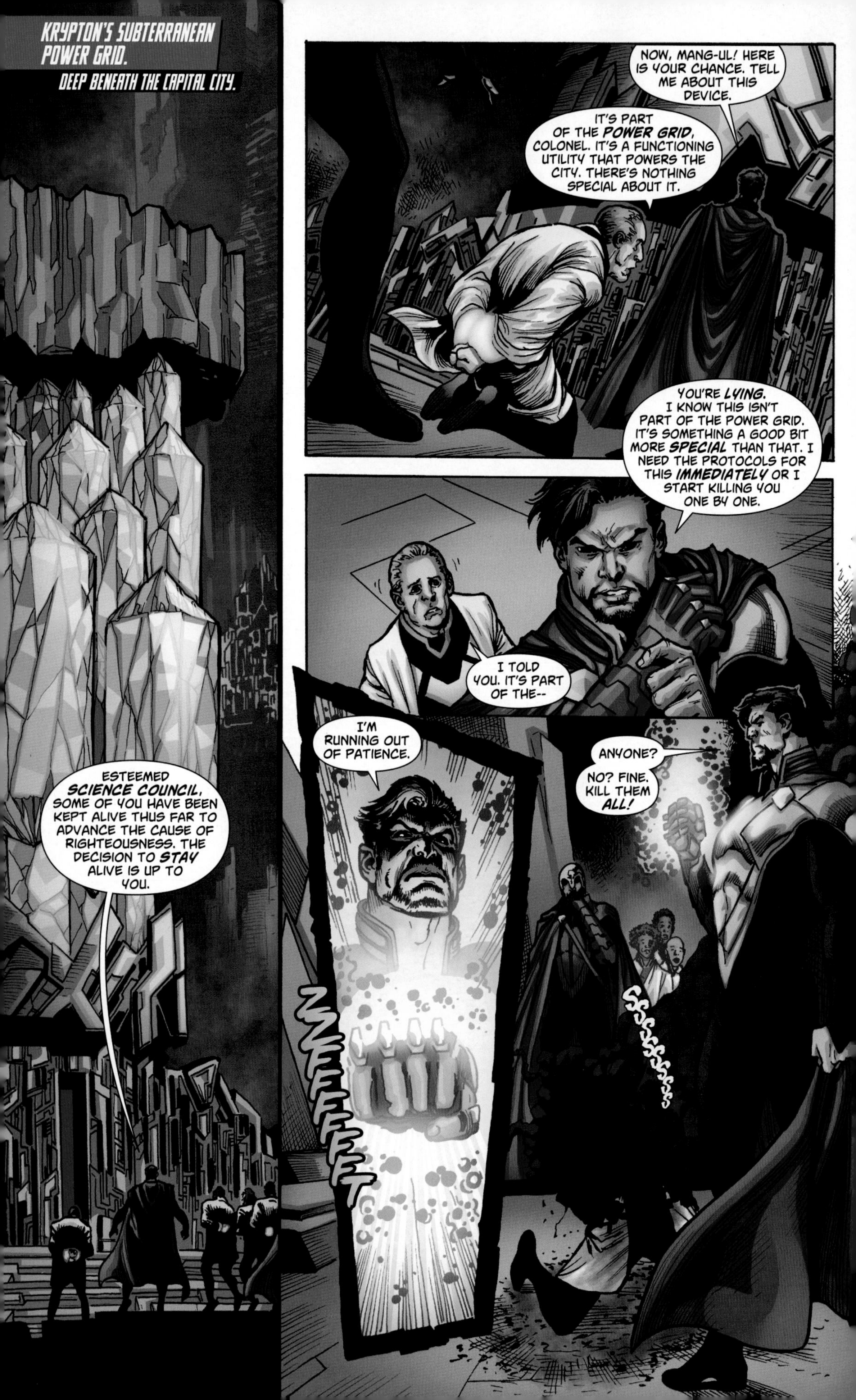

KRYPTON'S SUBTERRANEAN POWER GRID.
DEEP BENEATH THE CAPITAL CITY.
ESTEEMED SCIENCE COUNCIL, SOME OF YOU HAVE BEEN KEPT ALIVE THUS FAR TO ADVANCE THE CAUSE OF RIGHTEOUSNESS. THE DECISION TO STAY ALIVE IS UP TO YOU.
NOW, MANG-UL! HERE IS YOUR CHANCE. TELL ME ABOUT THIS DEVICE.
IT'S PART OF THE POWER GRID, COLONEL. IT'S A FUNCTIONING UTILITY THAT POWERS THE CITY. THERE'S NOTHING SPECIAL ABOUT IT.
YOU'RE LYING. I KNOW THIS ISN'T PART OF THE POWER GRID. IT'S SOMETHING A GOOD BIT MORE SPECIAL THAN THAT. I NEED THE PROTOCOLS FOR THIS IMMEDIATELY OR I START KILLING YOU ONE BY ONE.
I TOLD YOU. IT'S PART OF THE--
I'M RUNNING OUT OF PATIENCE.
ZZFFFFFFT
ANYONE?
NO? FINE. KILL THEM ALL!
SSSSSSSSS

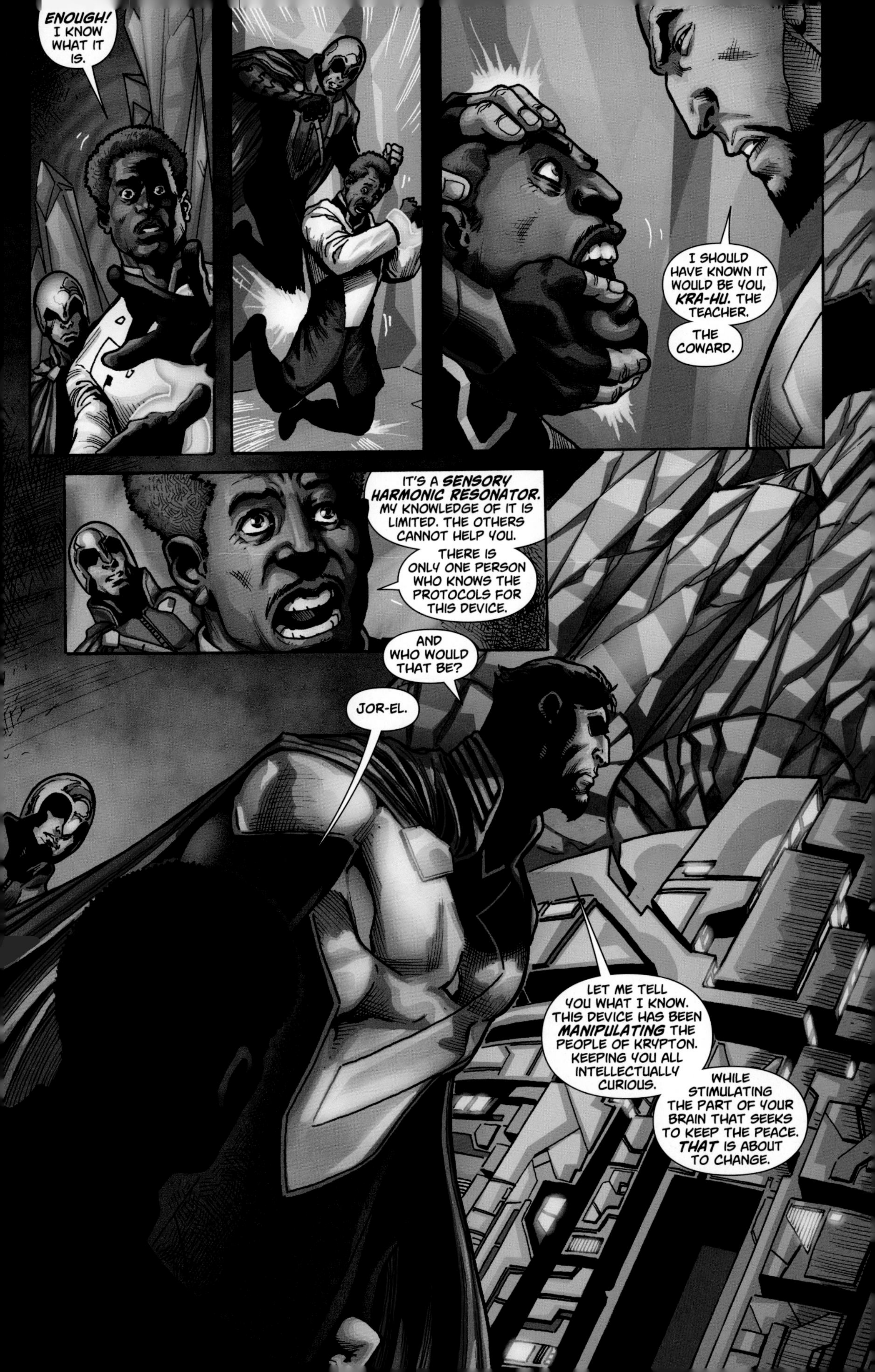
ENOUGH! I KNOW WHAT IT IS.
I SHOULD HAVE KNOWN IT WOULD BE YOU, KRA-HU. THE TEACHER.
THE COWARD.
IT'S A SENSORY HARMONIC RESONATOR. MY KNOWLEDGE OF IT IS LIMITED. THE OTHERS CANNOT HELP YOU.
THERE IS ONLY ONE PERSON WHO KNOWS THE PROTOCOLS FOR THIS DEVICE.
AND WHO WOULD THAT BE?
JOR-EL.
LET ME TELL YOU WHAT I KNOW. THIS DEVICE HAS BEEN MANIPULATING THE PEOPLE OF KRYPTON. KEEPING YOU ALL INTELLECTUALLY CURIOUS.
WHILE STIMULATING THE PART OF YOUR BRAIN THAT SEEKS TO KEEP THE PEACE. THAT IS ABOUT TO CHANGE.

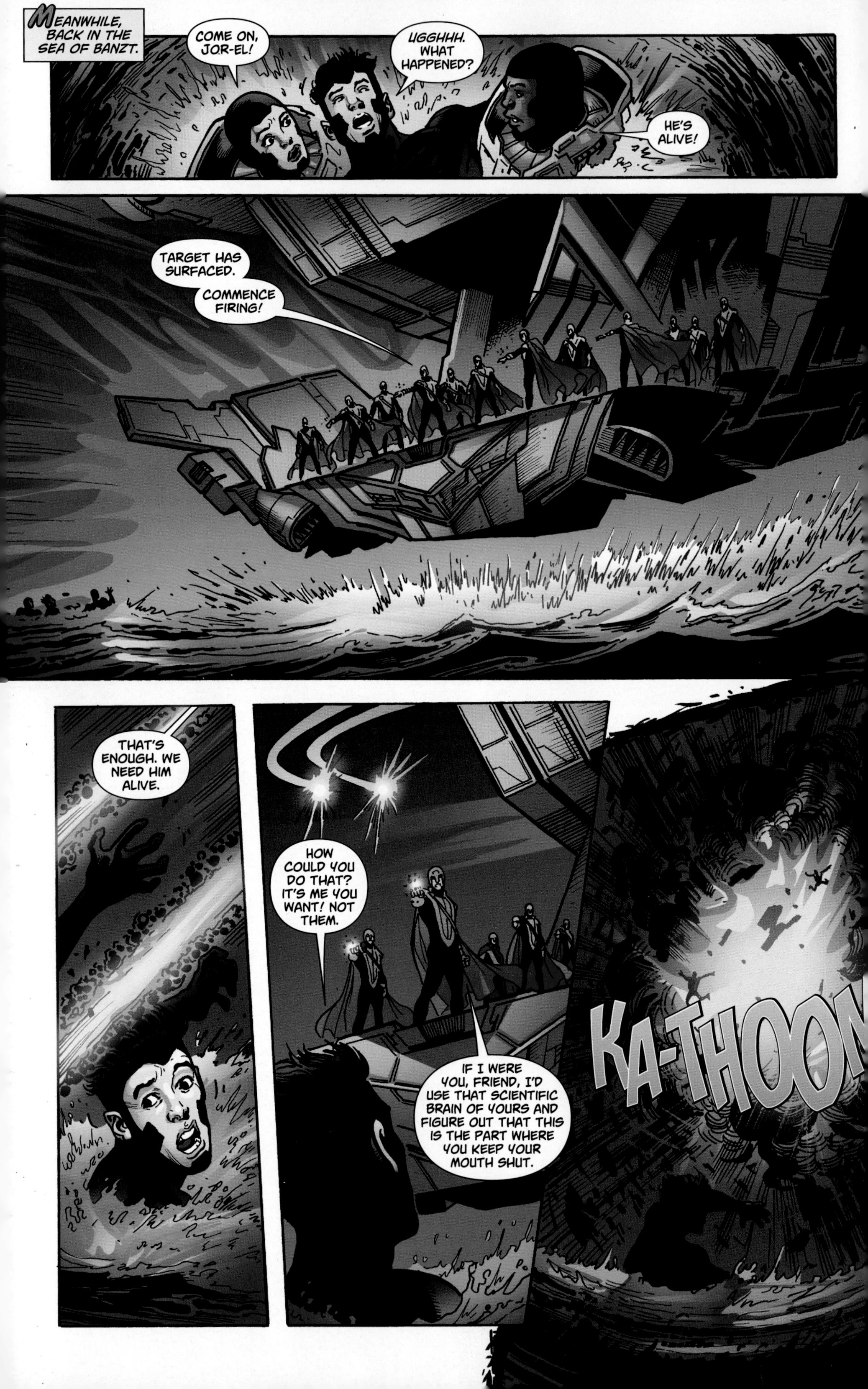
MEANWHILE, BACK IN THE SEA OF BANZT.
COME ON, JOR-EL!
UGGHHH. WHAT HAPPENED?
HE'S ALIVE!
TARGET HAS SURFACED.
COMMENCE FIRING!
THAT'S ENOUGH. WE NEED HIM ALIVE.
HOW COULD YOU DO THAT? IT'S ME YOU WANT! NOT THEM.
IF I WERE YOU, FRIEND, I'D USE THAT SCIENTIFIC BRAIN OF YOURS AND FIGURE OUT THAT THIS IS THE PART WHERE YOU KEEP YOUR MOUTH SHUT.
KA-THOOM

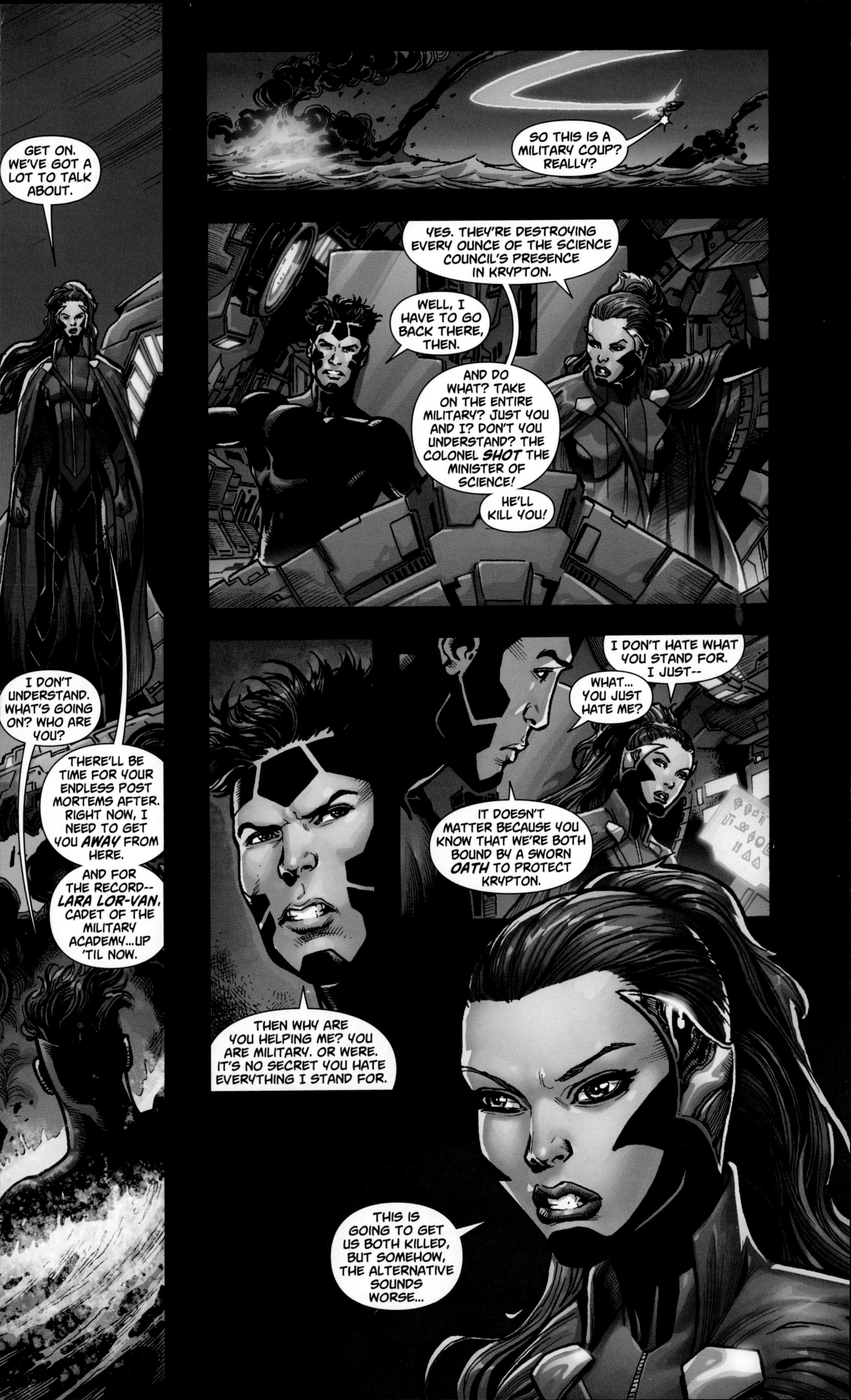
GET ON. WE'VE GOT A LOT TO TALK ABOUT.
SO THIS IS A MILITARY COUP? REALLY?
YES. THEY'RE DESTROYING EVERY OUNCE OF THE SCIENCE COUNCIL'S PRESENCE IN KRYPTON.
WELL, I HAVE TO GO BACK THERE, THEN.
AND DO WHAT? TAKE ON THE ENTIRE MILITARY? JUST YOU AND I? DON'T YOU UNDERSTAND? THE COLONEL SHOT THE MINISTER OF SCIENCE!
HE'LL KILL YOU!
I DON'T UNDERSTAND. WHAT'S GOING ON? WHO ARE YOU?
THERE'LL BE TIME FOR YOUR ENDLESS POST MORTEMS AFTER. RIGHT NOW, I NEED TO GET YOU AWAY FROM HERE.
AND FOR THE RECORD-- LARA LOR-VAN, CADET OF THE MILITARY ACADEMY...UP 'TIL NOW.
THEN WHY ARE YOU HELPING ME? YOU ARE MILITARY. OR WERE. IT'S NO SECRET YOU HATE EVERYTHING I STAND FOR.
I DON'T HATE WHAT YOU STAND FOR. I JUST--
WHAT... YOU JUST HATE ME?
IT DOESN'T MATTER BECAUSE YOU KNOW THAT WE'RE BOTH BOUND BY A SWORN OATH TO PROTECT KRYPTON.
THIS IS GOING TO GET US BOTH KILLED, BUT SOMEHOW, THE ALTERNATIVE SOUNDS WORSE...

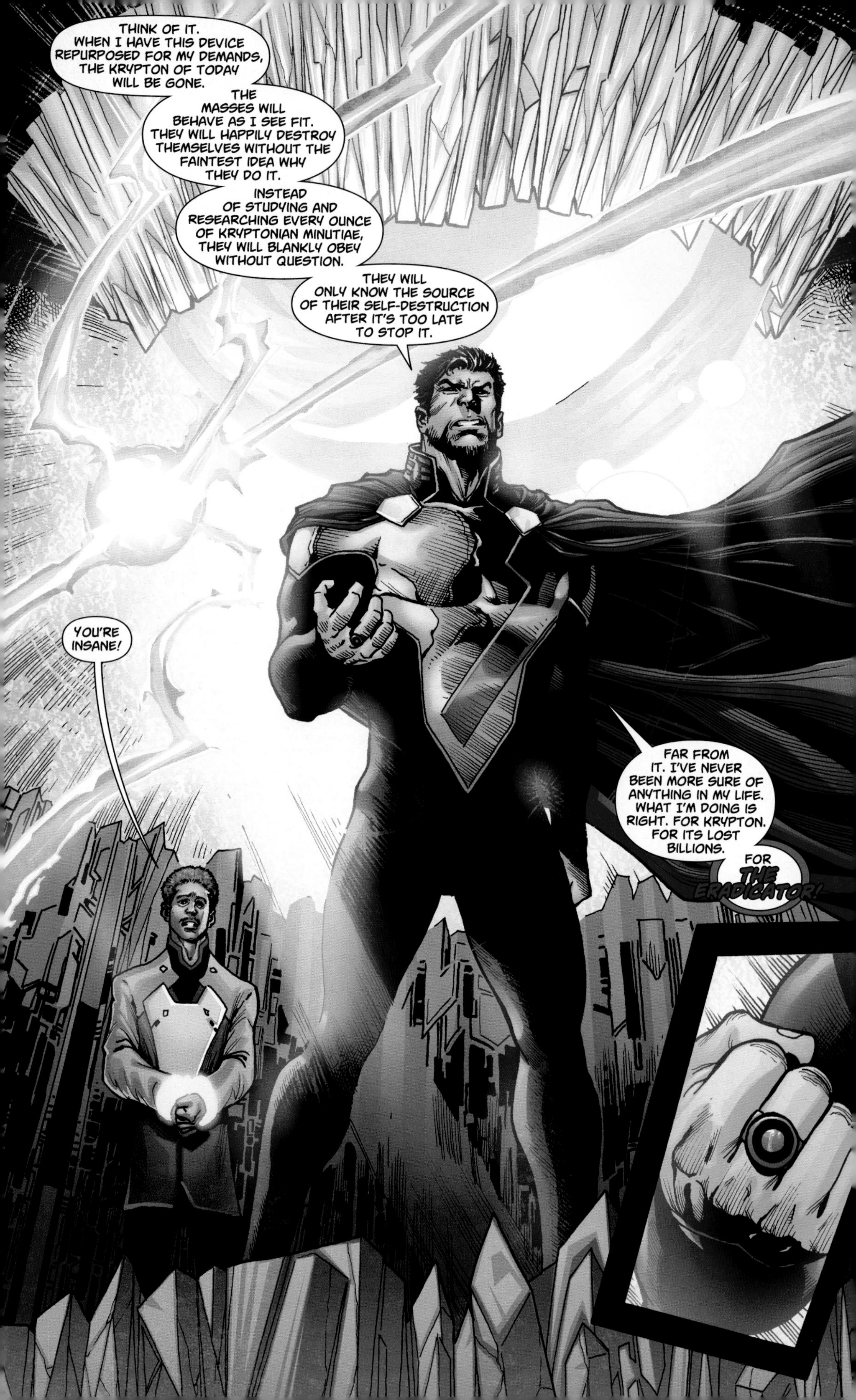
THINK OF IT. WHEN I HAVE THIS DEVICE REPURPOSED FOR MY DEMANDS, THE KRYPTON OF TODAY WILL BE GONE.
THE MASSES WILL BEHAVE AS I SEE FIT. THEY WILL HAPPILY DESTROY THEMSELVES WITHOUT THE FAINTEST IDEA WHY THEY DO IT.
INSTEAD OF STUDYING AND RESEARCHING EVERY OUNCE OF KRYPTONIAN MINUTIAE, THEY WILL BLANKLY OBEY WITHOUT QUESTION.
THEY WILL ONLY KNOW THE SOURCE OF THEIR SELF-DESTRUCTION AFTER IT'S TOO LATE TO STOP IT.
YOU'RE INSANE!
FAR FROM IT. I'VE NEVER BEEN MORE SURE OF ANYTHING IN MY LIFE. WHAT I'M DOING IS RIGHT. FOR KRYPTON. FOR ITS LOST BILLIONS.
FOR THE ERADICATOR!

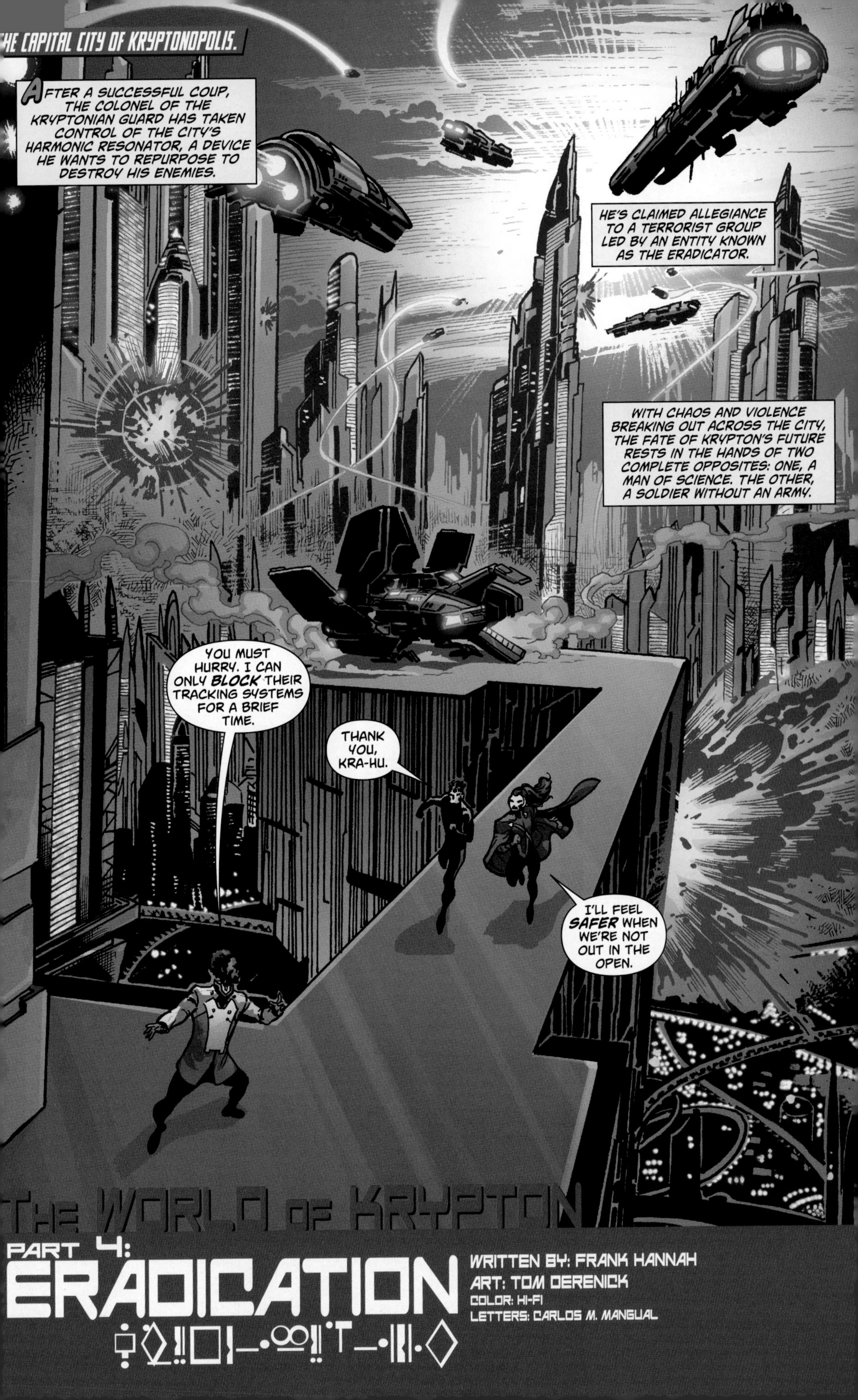

THE CAPITAL CITY OF KRYPTONOPOLIS.
AFTER A SUCCESSFUL COUP, THE COLONEL OF THE KRYPTONIAN GUARD HAS TAKEN CONTROL OF THE CITY'S HARMONIC RESONATOR, A DEVICE HE WANTS TO REPURPOSE TO DESTROY HIS ENEMIES.
HE'S CLAIMED ALLEGIANCE TO A TERRORIST GROUP LED BY AN ENTITY KNOWN AS THE ERADICATOR.
WITH CHAOS AND VIOLENCE BREAKING OUT ACROSS THE CITY, THE FATE OF KRYPTON'S FUTURE RESTS IN THE HANDS OF TWO COMPLETE OPPOSITES: ONE, A MAN OF SCIENCE. THE OTHER, A SOLDIER WITHOUT AN ARMY.
YOU MUST HURRY. I CAN ONLY BLOCK THEIR TRACKING SYSTEMS FOR A BRIEF TIME.
THANK YOU, KRA-HU.
I'LL FEEL SAFER WHEN WE'RE NOT OUT IN THE OPEN.
THE WORLD OF KRYPTON
PART 4:
ERADICATION
WRITTEN BY: FRANK HANNAH
ART: TOM DERENICK
COLOR: HI-FI
LETTERS: CARLOS M. MANGUAL

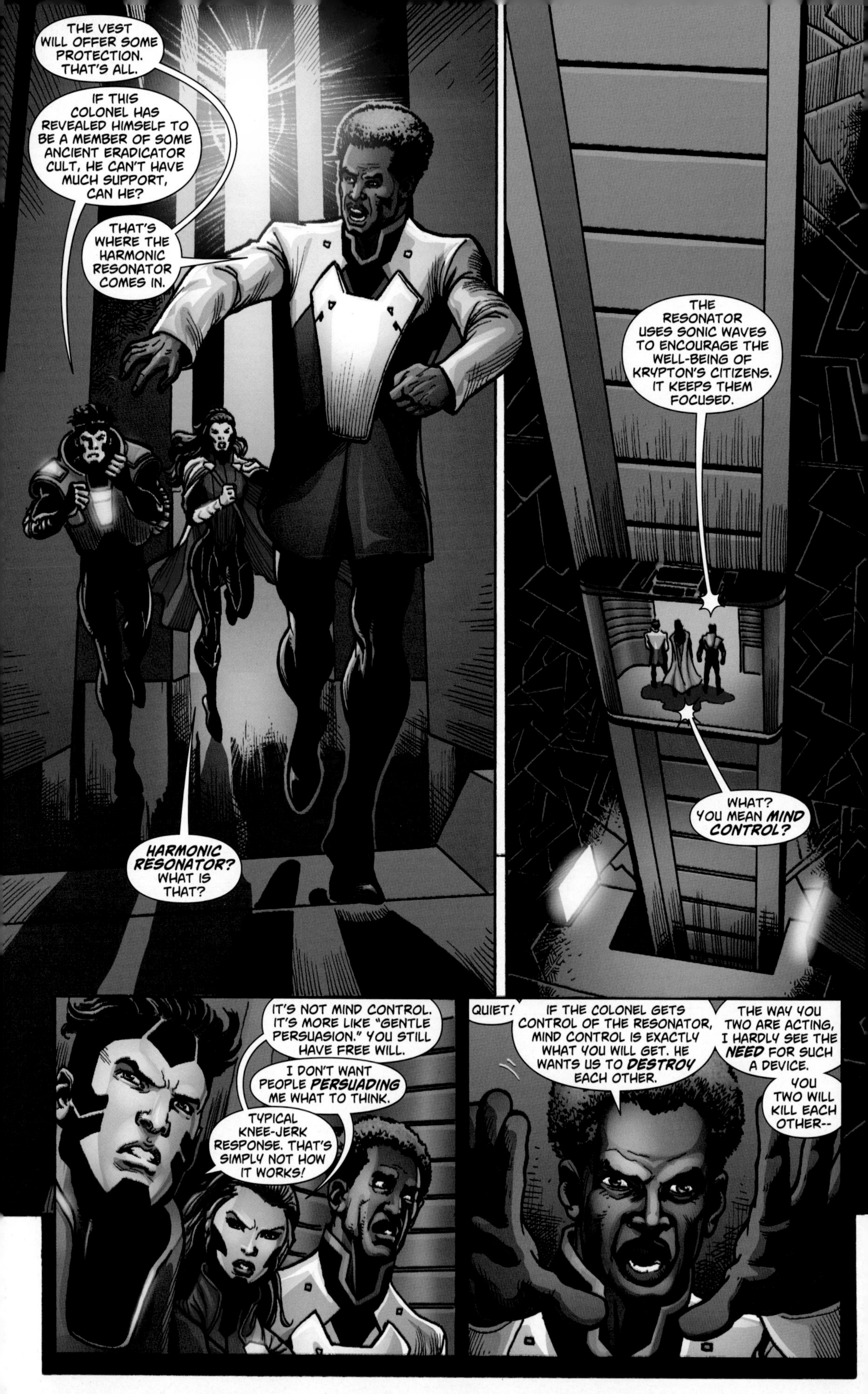

THE VEST WILL OFFER SOME PROTECTION. THAT'S ALL.
IF THIS COLONEL HAS REVEALED HIMSELF TO BE A MEMBER OF SOME ANCIENT ERADICATOR CULT, HE CAN'T HAVE MUCH SUPPORT, CAN HE?
THAT'S WHERE THE HARMONIC RESONATOR COMES IN.
HARMONIC RESONATOR? WHAT IS THAT?
THE RESONATOR USES SONIC WAVES TO ENCOURAGE THE WELL-BEING OF KRYPTON'S CITIZENS. IT KEEPS THEM FOCUSED.
WHAT? YOU MEAN MIND CONTROL?
IT'S NOT MIND CONTROL. IT'S MORE LIKE "GENTLE PERSUASION." YOU STILL HAVE FREE WILL.
I DON'T WANT PEOPLE PERSUADING ME WHAT TO THINK.
TYPICAL KNEE-JERK RESPONSE. THAT'S SIMPLY NOT HOW IT WORKS!
QUIET!
IF THE COLONEL GETS CONTROL OF THE RESONATOR, MIND CONTROL IS EXACTLY WHAT YOU WILL GET. HE WANTS US TO DESTROY EACH OTHER.
THE WAY YOU TWO ARE ACTING, I HARDLY SEE THE NEED FOR SUCH A DEVICE.
YOU TWO WILL KILL EACH OTHER--

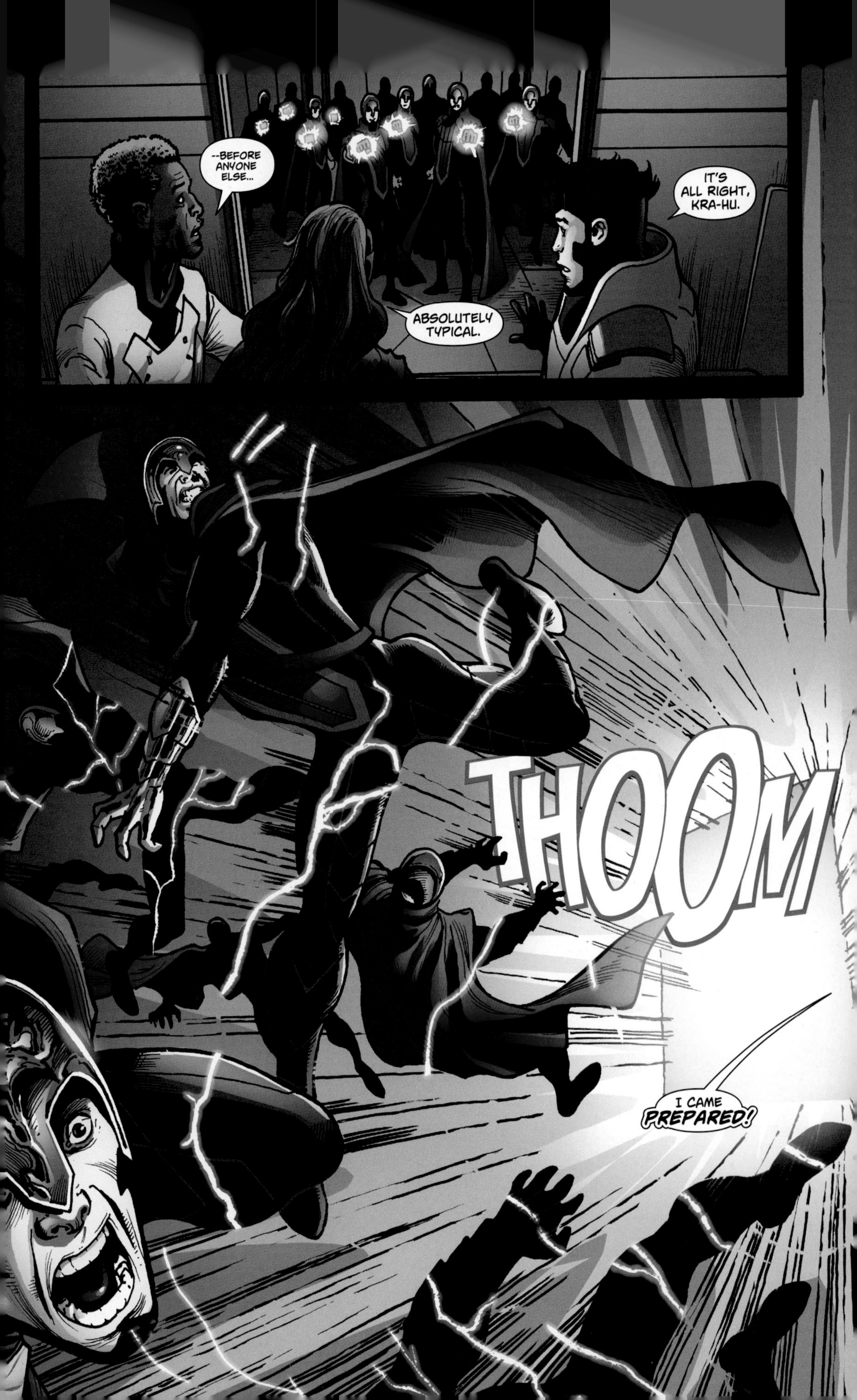
--BEFORE ANYONE ELSE...
IT'S ALL RIGHT, KRA-HU.
ABSOLUTELY TYPICAL.
THOOM
I CAME PREPARED!

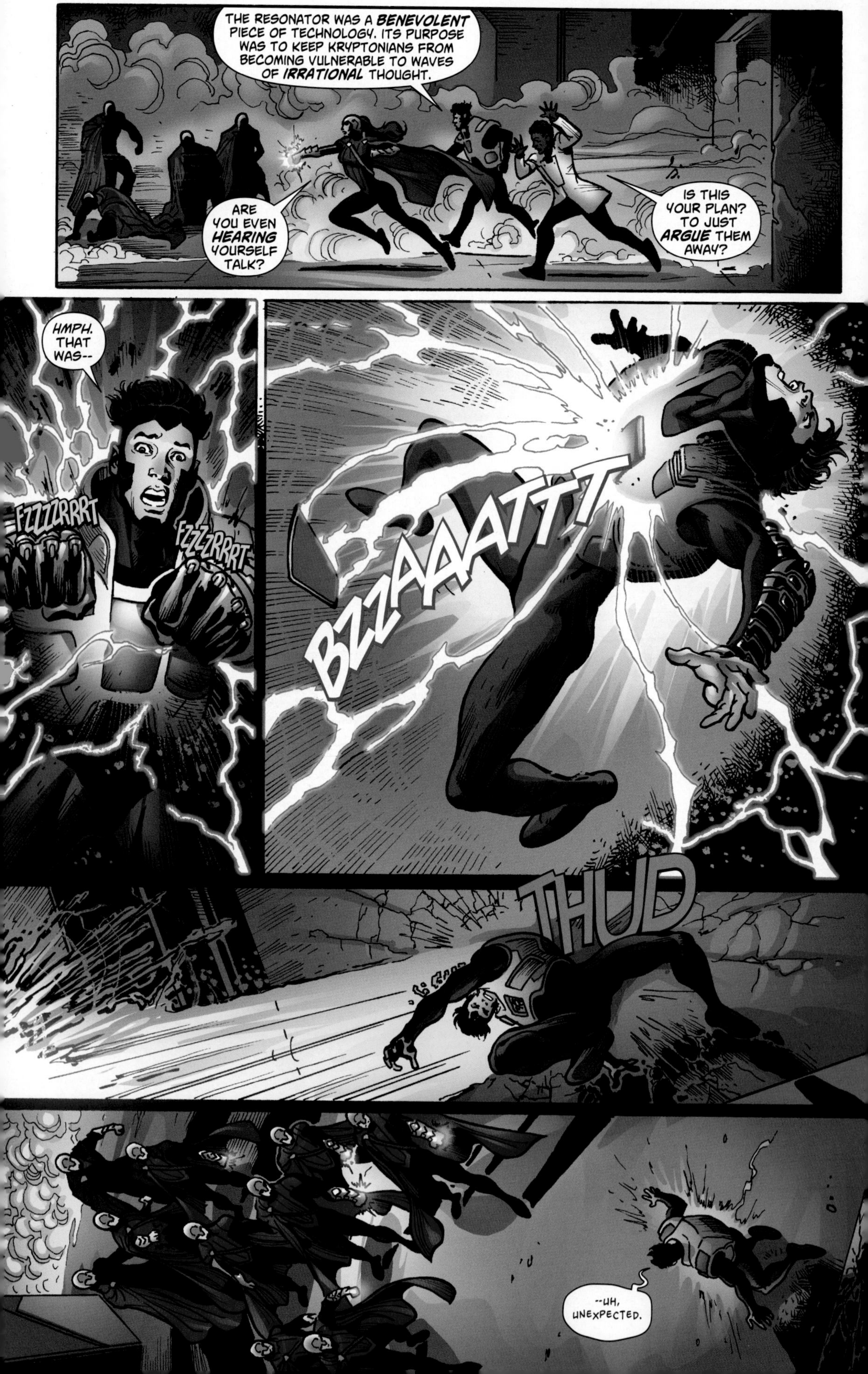
THE RESONATOR WAS A BENEVOLENT PIECE OF TECHNOLOGY. ITS PURPOSE WAS TO KEEP KRYPTONIANS FROM BECOMING VULNERABLE TO WAVES OF IRRATIONAL THOUGHT.
ARE YOU EVEN HEARING YOURSELF TALK?
IS THIS YOUR PLAN? TO JUST ARGUE THEM AWAY?
HMPH. THAT WAS--
FZZZZRRRT
FZZZZRRRT
BZZAAAATTT
THUD
--UH, UNEXPECTED.

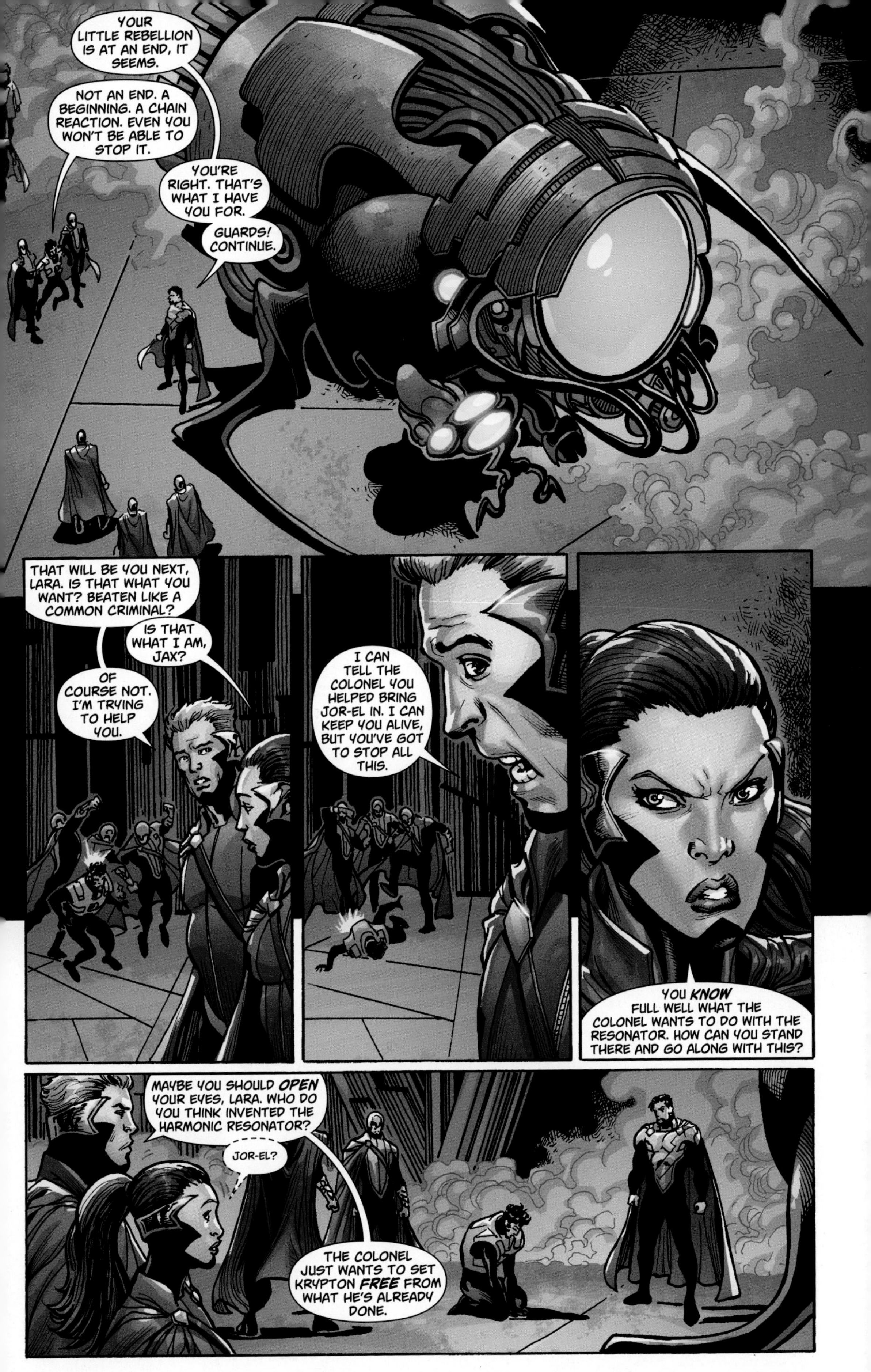
YOUR LITTLE REBELLION IS AT AN END, IT SEEMS.
NOT AN END. A BEGINNING. A CHAIN REACTION. EVEN YOU WON'T BE ABLE TO STOP IT.
YOU'RE RIGHT. THAT'S WHAT I HAVE YOU FOR.
GUARDS! CONTINUE.
THAT WILL BE YOU NEXT, LARA. IS THAT WHAT YOU WANT? BEATEN LIKE A COMMON CRIMINAL?
IS THAT WHAT I AM, JAX?
OF COURSE NOT. I'M TRYING TO HELP YOU.
I CAN TELL THE COLONEL YOU HELPED BRING JOR-EL IN. I CAN KEEP YOU ALIVE, BUT YOU'VE GOT TO STOP ALL THIS.
YOU KNOW FULL WELL WHAT THE COLONEL WANTS TO DO WITH THE RESONATOR. HOW CAN YOU STAND THERE AND GO ALONG WITH THIS?
MAYBE YOU SHOULD OPEN YOUR EYES, LARA. WHO DO YOU THINK INVENTED THE HARMONIC RESONATOR?
JOR-EL?
THE COLONEL JUST WANTS TO SET KRYPTON FREE FROM WHAT HE'S ALREADY DONE.

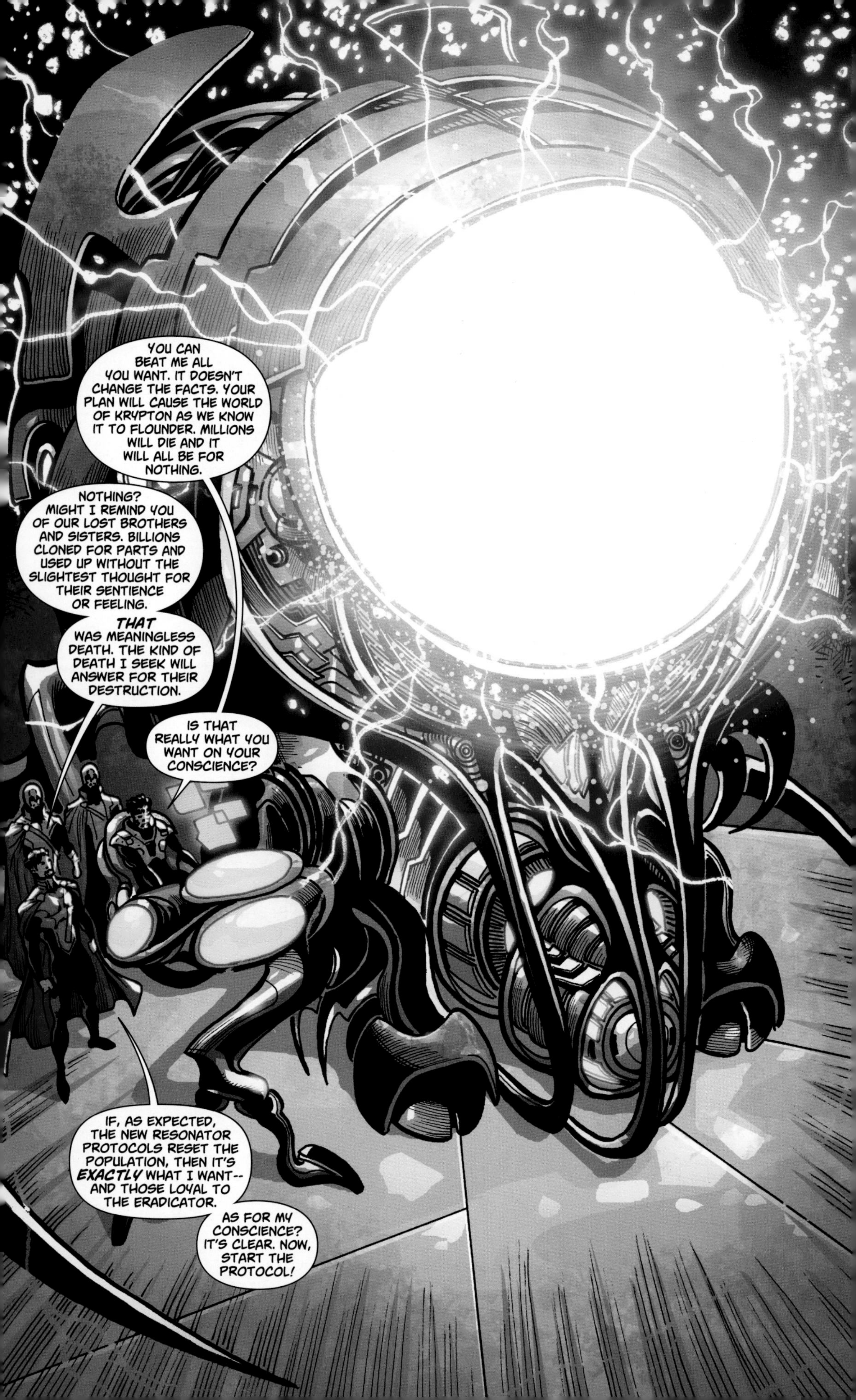
YOU CAN BEAT ME ALL YOU WANT. IT DOESN'T CHANGE THE FACTS. YOUR PLAN WILL CAUSE THE WORLD OF KRYPTON AS WE KNOW IT TO FLOUNDER. MILLIONS WILL DIE AND IT WILL ALL BE FOR NOTHING.
NOTHING? MIGHT I REMIND YOU OF OUR LOST BROTHERS AND SISTERS. BILLIONS CLONED FOR PARTS AND USED UP WITHOUT THE SLIGHTEST THOUGHT FOR THEIR SENTIENCE OR FEELING.
THAT WAS MEANINGLESS DEATH. THE KIND OF DEATH I SEEK WILL ANSWER FOR THEIR DESTRUCTION.
IS THAT REALLY WHAT YOU WANT ON YOUR CONSCIENCE?
IF, AS EXPECTED, THE NEW RESONATOR PROTOCOLS RESET THE POPULATION, THEN IT'S EXACTLY WHAT I WANT-- AND THOSE LOYAL TO THE ERADICATOR.
AS FOR MY CONSCIENCE? IT'S CLEAR. NOW, START THE PROTOCOL!

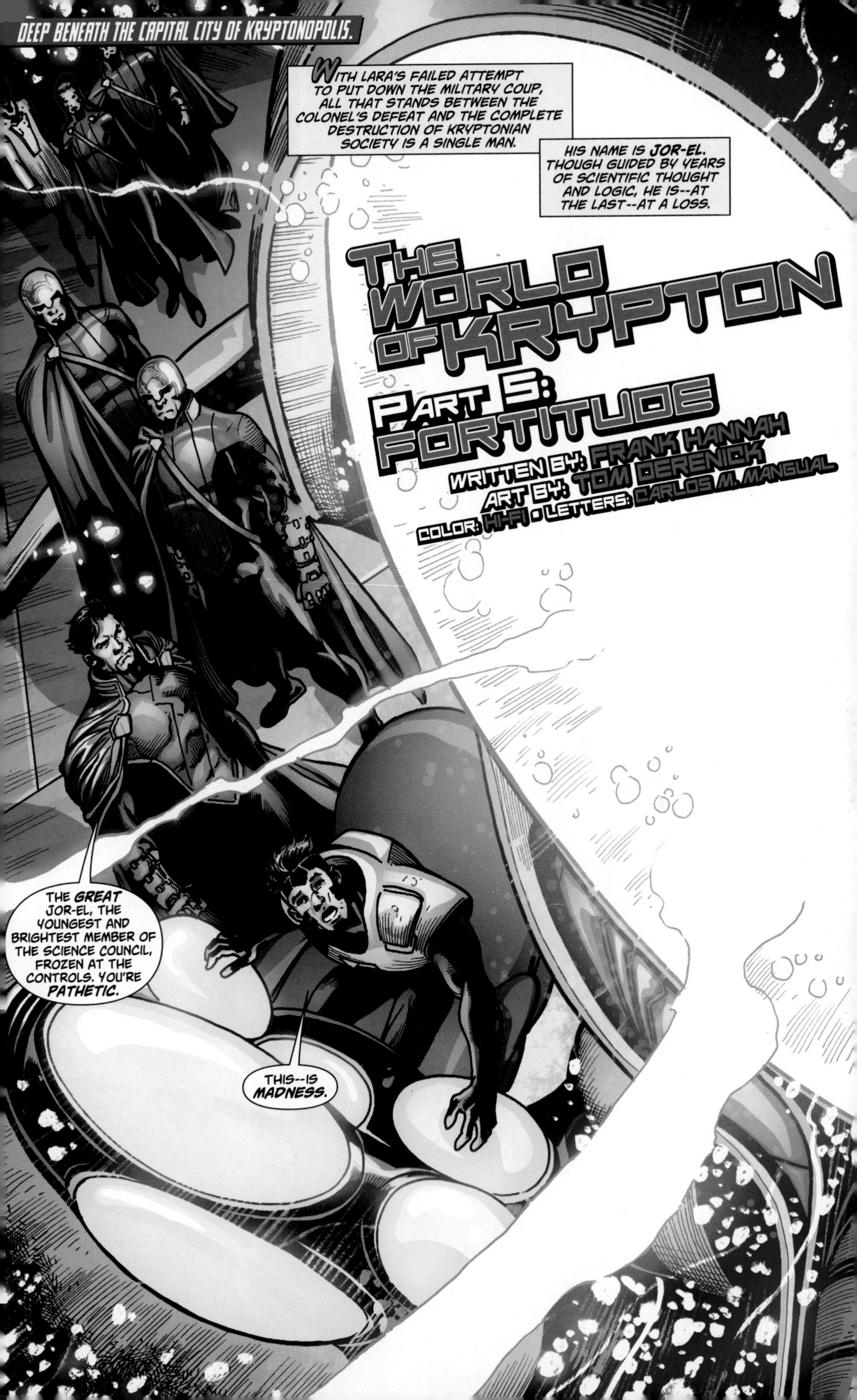
DEEP BENEATH THE CAPITAL CITY OF KRYPTONOPOLIS.
WITH LARA'S FAILED ATTEMPT TO PUT DOWN THE MILITARY COUP, ALL THAT STANDS BETWEEN THE COLONEL'S DEFEAT AND THE COMPLETE DESTRUCTION OF KRYPTONIAN SOCIETY IS A SINGLE MAN.
HIS NAME IS JOR-EL. THOUGH GUIDED BY YEARS OF SCIENTIFIC THOUGHT AND LOGIC, HE IS--AT THE LAST--AT A LOSS.
THE WORLD OF KRYPTON
PART 5: FORTITUDE
WRITTEN BY: FRANK HANNAH
ART BY: TOM DERENICK
COLOR: HI-FI • LETTERS: CARLOS M. MANGUAL
THE GREAT JOR-EL, THE YOUNGEST AND BRIGHTEST MEMBER OF THE SCIENCE COUNCIL, FROZEN AT THE CONTROLS. YOU'RE PATHETIC.
THIS--IS MADNESS.

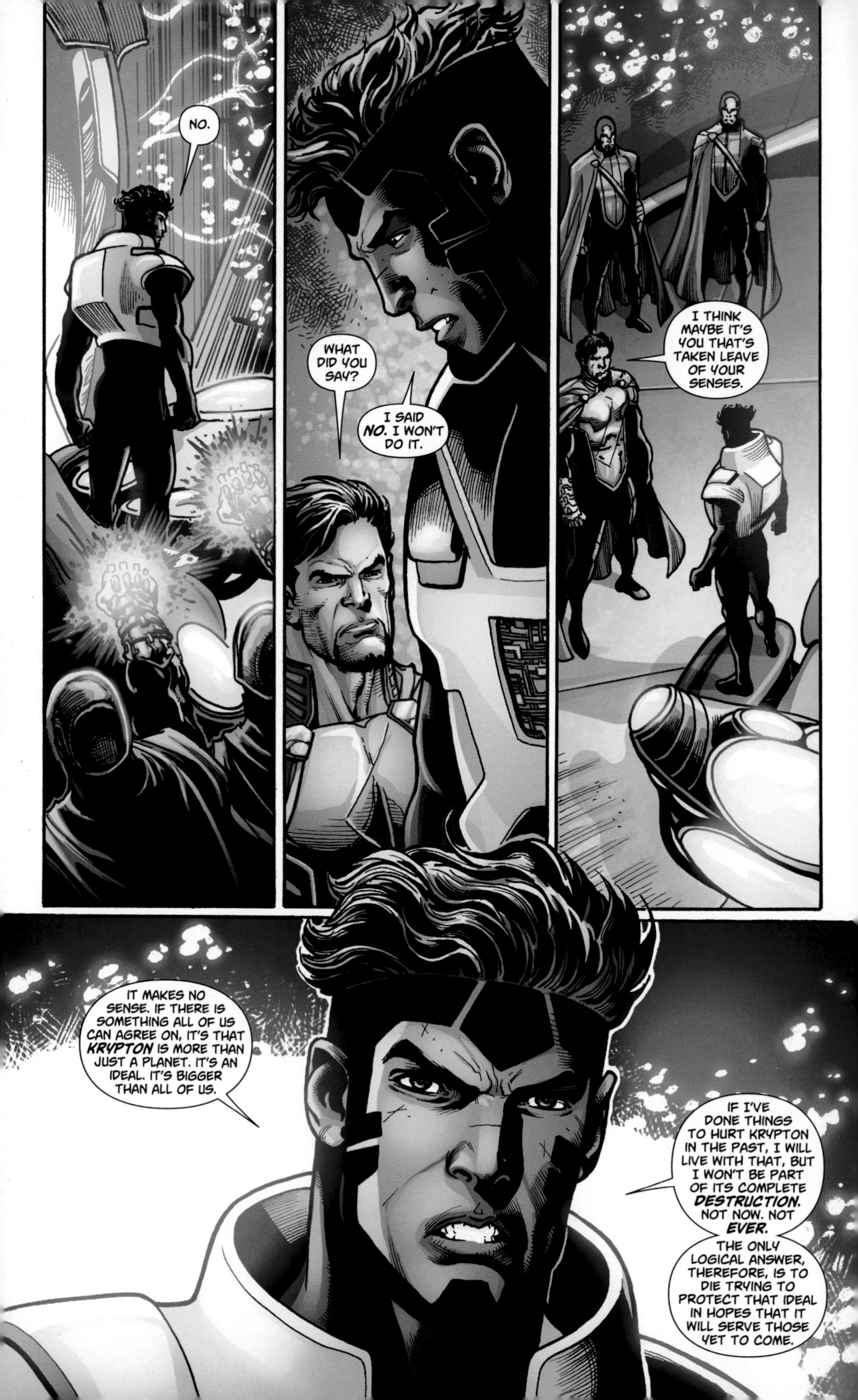
NO.
WHAT DID YOU SAY?
I SAID NO. I WON'T DO IT.
I THINK MAYBE IT'S YOU THAT'S TAKEN LEAVE OF YOUR SENSES.
IT MAKES NO SENSE. IF THERE IS SOMETHING ALL OF US CAN AGREE ON, IT'S THAT KRYPTON IS MORE THAN JUST A PLANET. IT'S AN IDEAL. IT'S BIGGER THAN ALL OF US.
IF I'VE DONE THINGS TO HURT KRYPTON IN THE PAST, I WILL LIVE WITH THAT, BUT I WON'T BE PART OF ITS COMPLETE DESTRUCTION. NOT NOW. NOT EVER.
THE ONLY LOGICAL ANSWER, THEREFORE, IS TO DIE TRYING TO PROTECT THAT IDEAL IN HOPES THAT IT WILL SERVE THOSE YET TO COME.

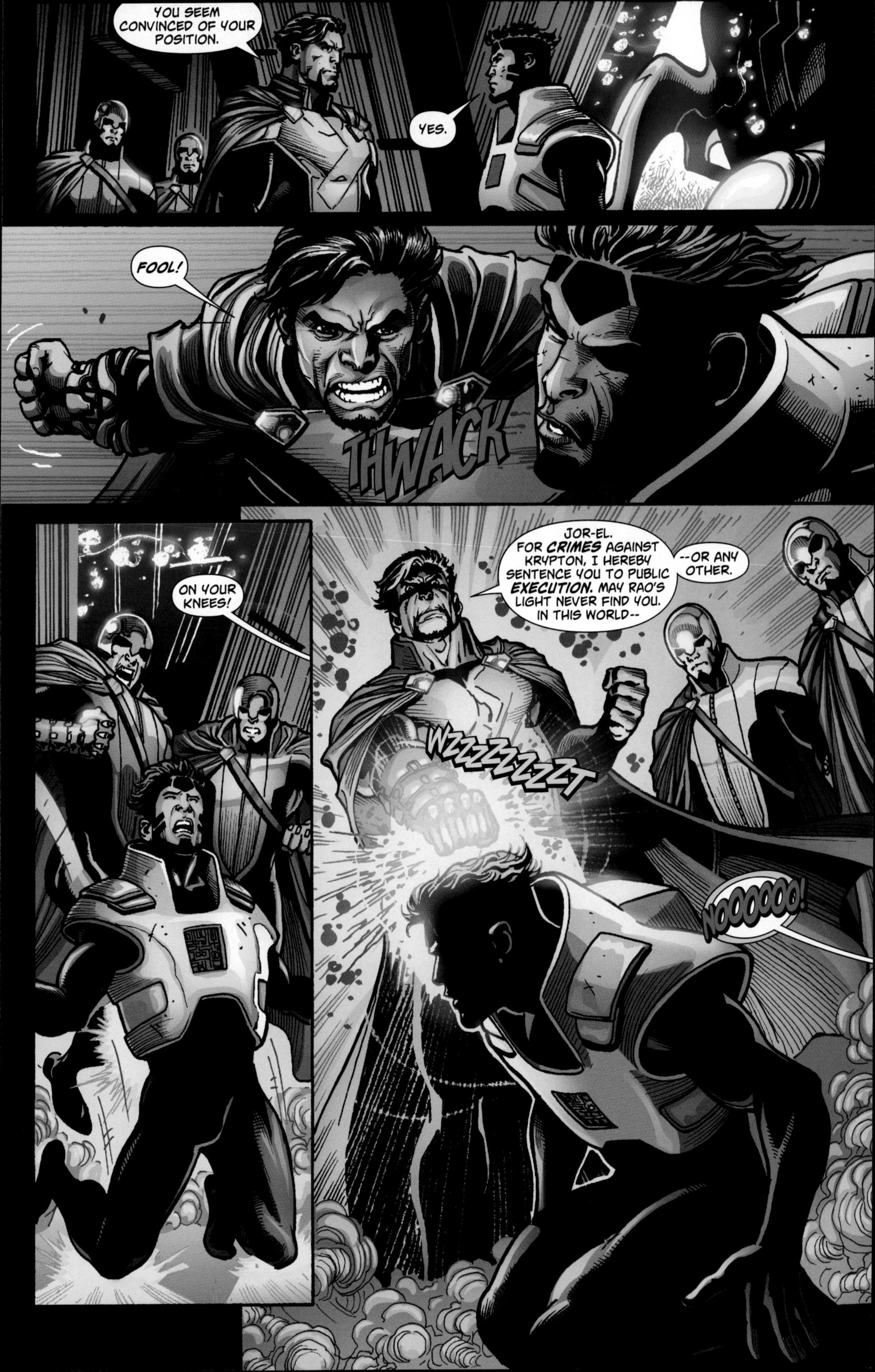
YOU SEEM CONVINCED OF YOUR POSITION.
YES.
FOOL!
THWACK
ON YOUR KNEES!
JOR-EL. FOR CRIMES AGAINST KRYPTON, I HEREBY SENTENCE YOU TO PUBLIC EXECUTION. MAY RAO'S LIGHT NEVER FIND YOU. IN THIS WORLD--
--OR ANY OTHER.
WZZZZZZZZT
NOOOOOO!

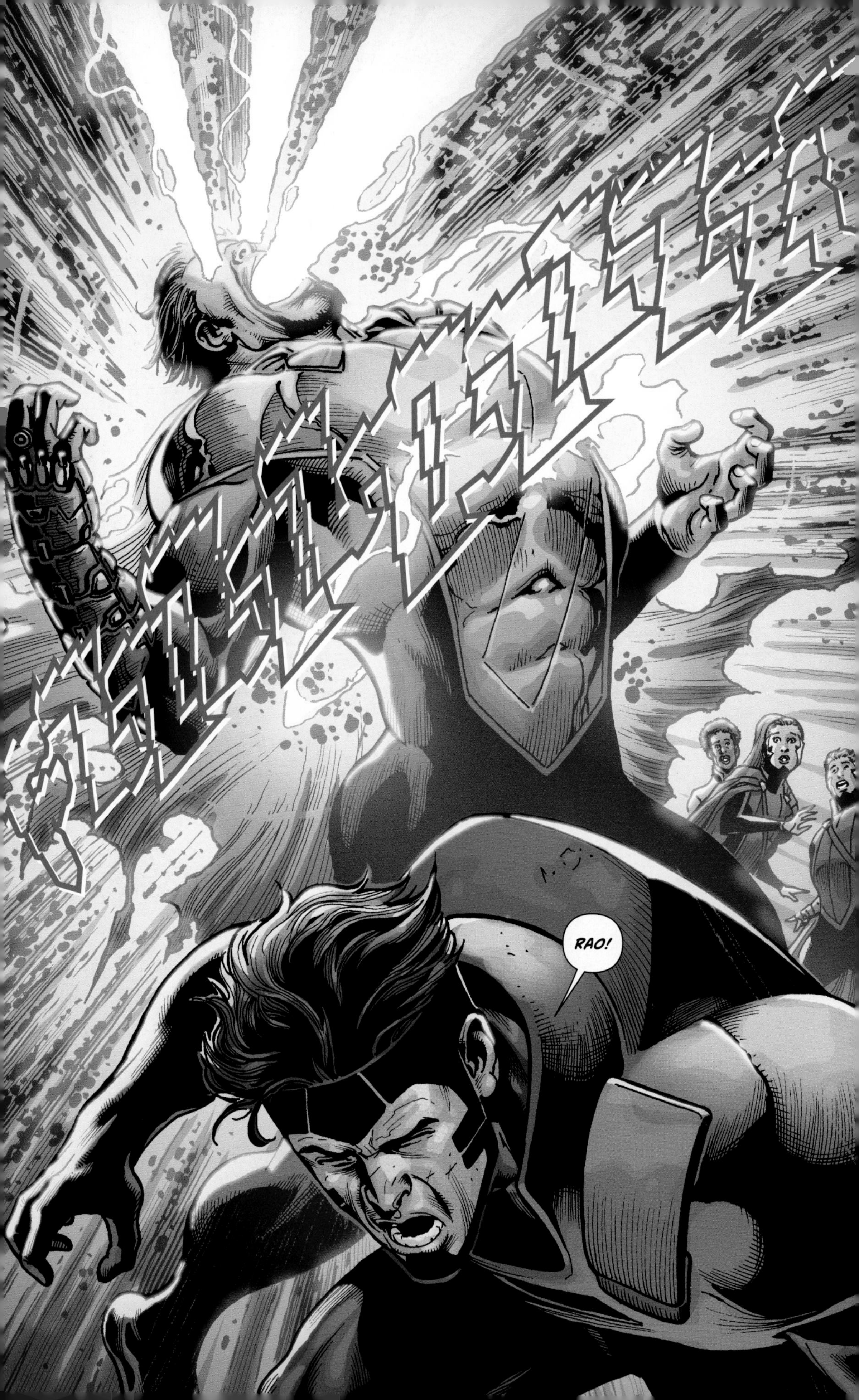
RAO!

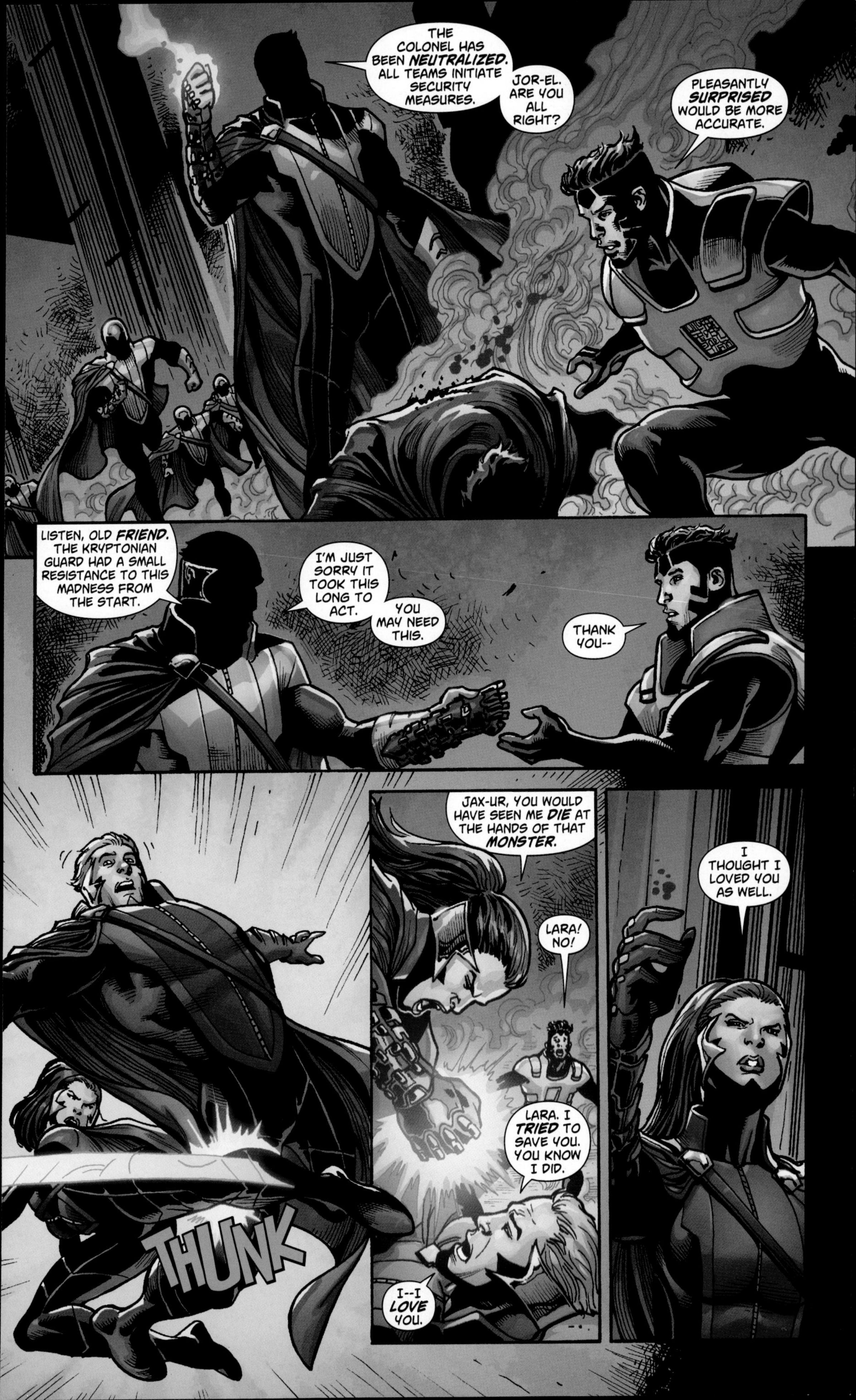
THE COLONEL HAS BEEN NEUTRALIZED. ALL TEAMS INITIATE SECURITY MEASURES.
JOR-EL. ARE YOU ALL RIGHT?
PLEASANTLY SURPRISED WOULD BE MORE ACCURATE.
LISTEN, OLD FRIEND. THE KRYPTONIAN GUARD HAD A SMALL RESISTANCE TO THIS MADNESS FROM THE START.
I'M JUST SORRY IT TOOK THIS LONG TO ACT.
YOU MAY NEED THIS.
THANK YOU--
THUNK
JAX-UR, YOU WOULD HAVE SEEN ME DIE AT THE HANDS OF THAT MONSTER.
LARA! NO!
LARA. I TRIED TO SAVE YOU. YOU KNOW I DID.
I--I LOVE YOU.
I THOUGHT I LOVED YOU AS WELL.

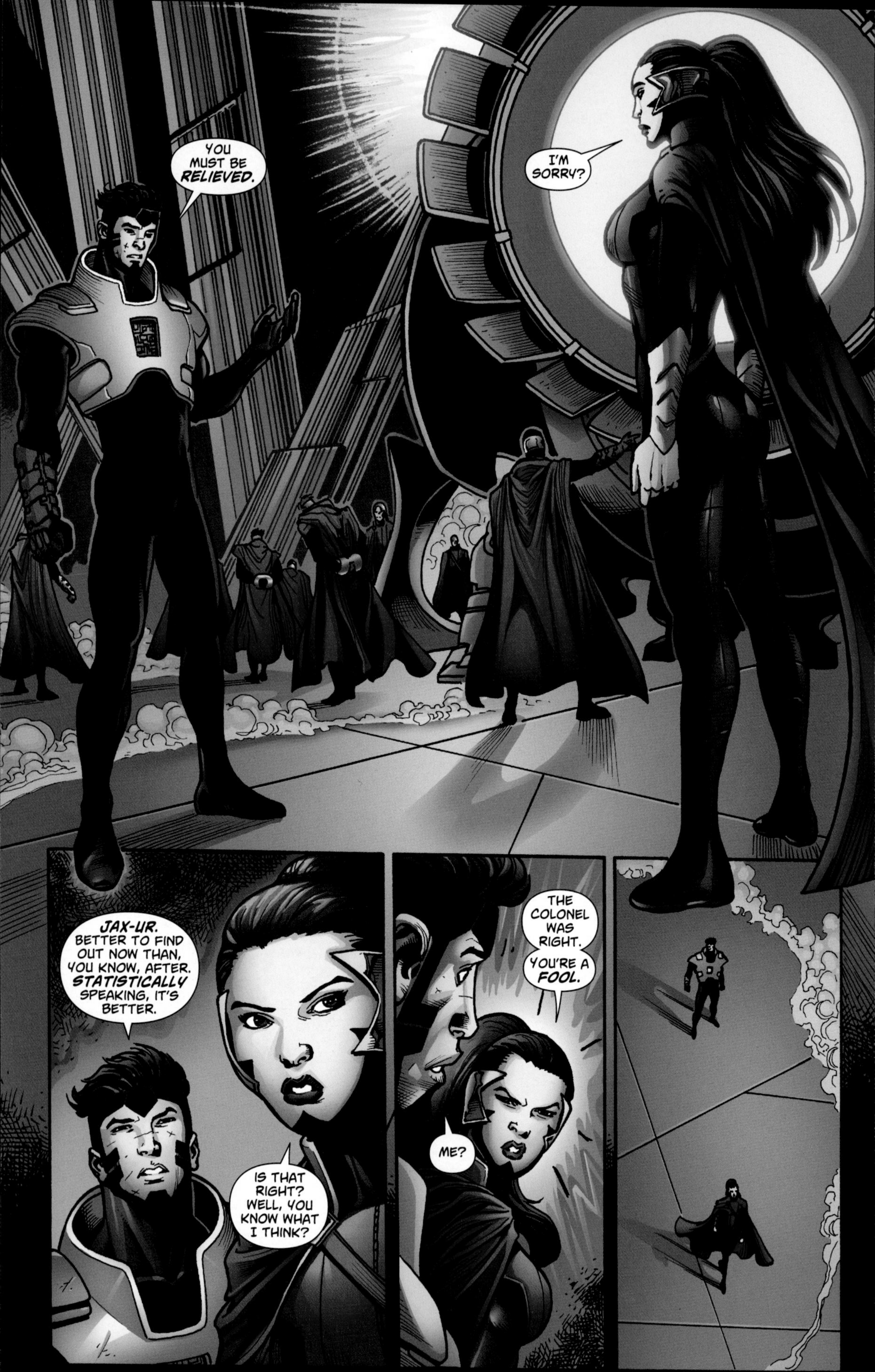
YOU MUST BE RELIEVED.
I'M SORRY?
JAX-UR. BETTER TO FIND OUT NOW THAN, YOU KNOW, AFTER. STATISTICALLY SPEAKING, IT'S BETTER.
IS THAT RIGHT? WELL, YOU KNOW WHAT I THINK?
THE COLONEL WAS RIGHT.
YOU'RE A FOOL.
ME?

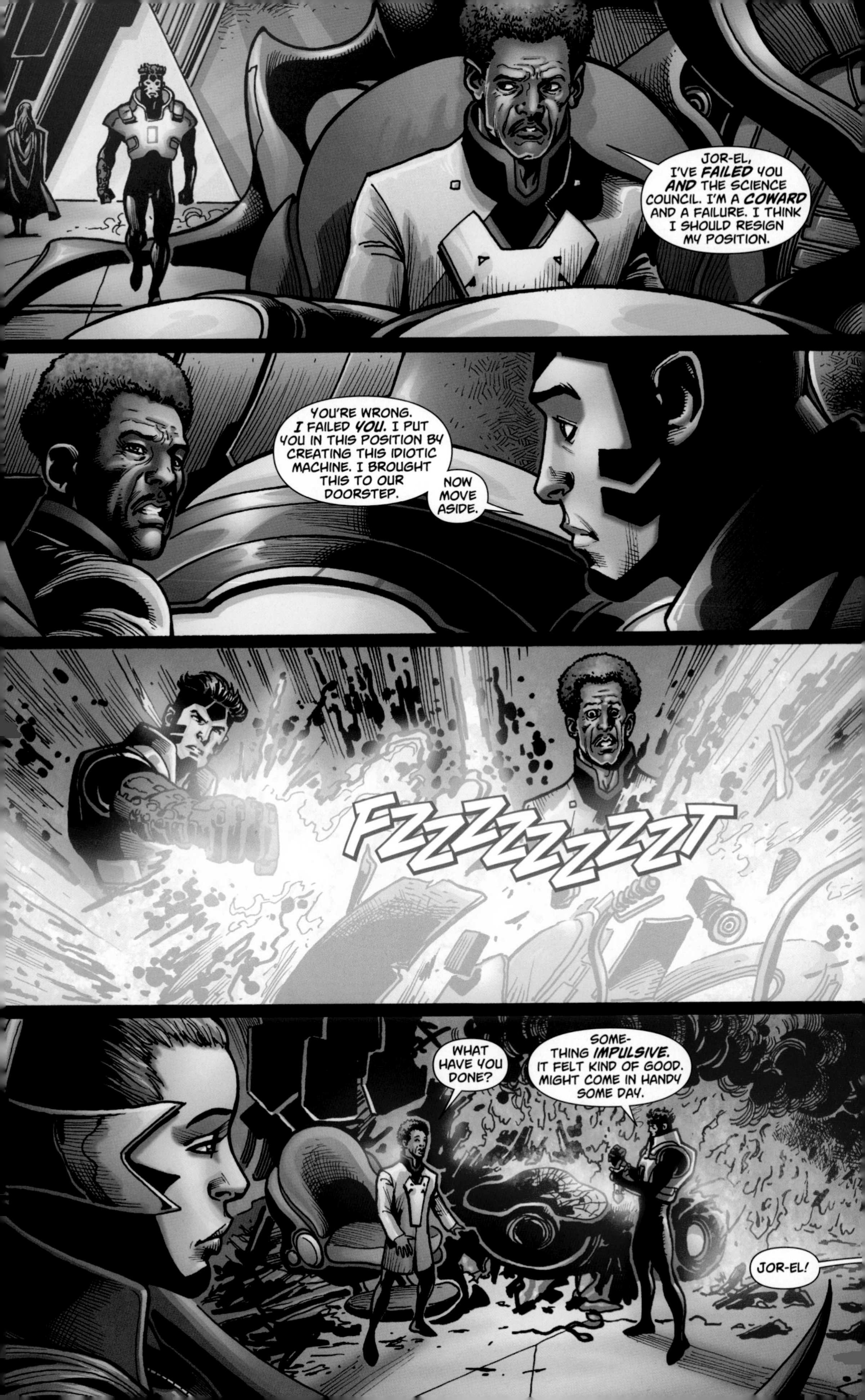
JOR-EL, I'VE FAILED YOU AND THE SCIENCE COUNCIL. I'M A COWARD AND A FAILURE. I THINK I SHOULD RESIGN MY POSITION.
YOU'RE WRONG. I FAILED YOU. I PUT YOU IN THIS POSITION BY CREATING THIS IDIOTIC MACHINE. I BROUGHT THIS TO OUR DOORSTEP.
NOW MOVE ASIDE.
FZZZZZZZZT
WHAT HAVE YOU DONE?
SOME-THING IMPULSIVE. IT FELT KIND OF GOOD. MIGHT COME IN HANDY SOME DAY.
JOR-EL!

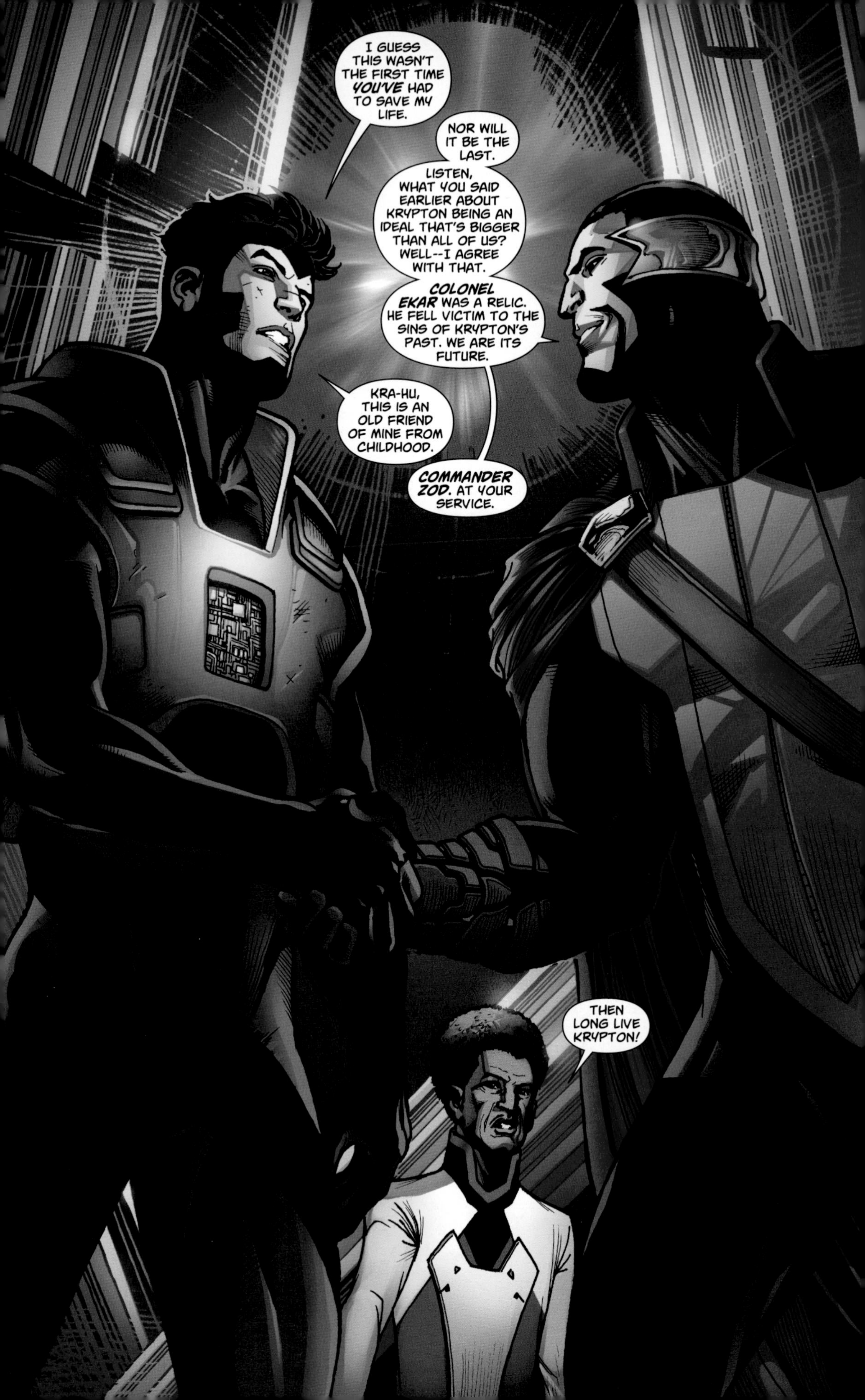
I GUESS THIS WASN'T THE FIRST TIME *YOU'VE* HAD TO SAVE MY LIFE.
NOR WILL IT BE THE LAST.
LISTEN, WHAT YOU SAID EARLIER ABOUT KRYPTON BEING AN IDEAL THAT'S BIGGER THAN ALL OF US? WELL--I AGREE WITH THAT.
COLONEL EKAR WAS A RELIC. HE FELL VICTIM TO THE SINS OF KRYPTON'S PAST. WE ARE ITS FUTURE.
KRA-HU, THIS IS AN OLD FRIEND OF MINE FROM CHILDHOOD.
COMMANDER ZOD. AT YOUR SERVICE.
THEN LONG LIVE KRYPTON!

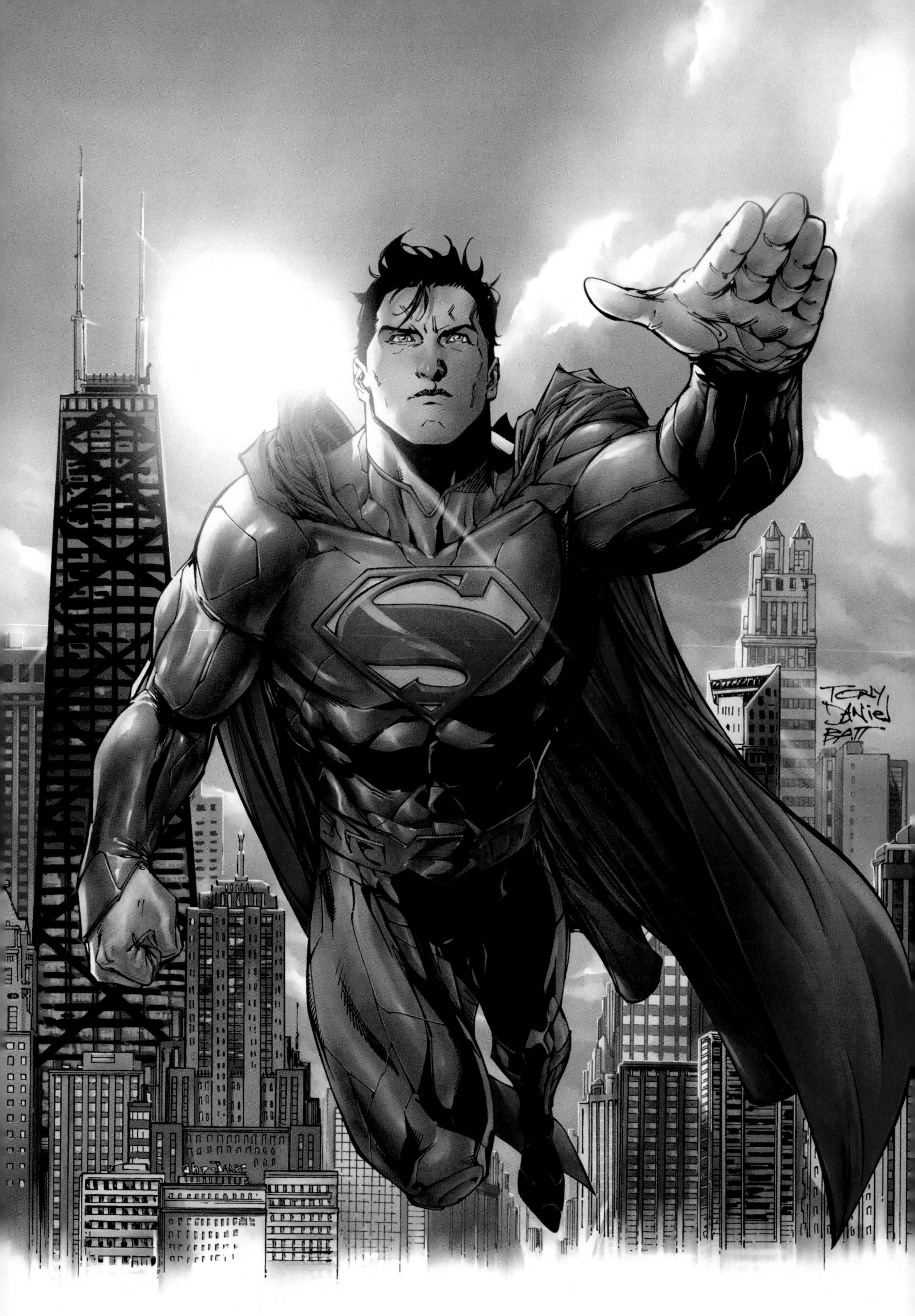
TONY DANIEL BATT

ACTION COMICS #19 CHICAGO COMIC & ENTERTAINMENT EXPO
VARIANT COVER BY TONY S. DANIEL, BATT & TOMEU MOREY

ACTION COMICS #19
FULL FOLD-OUT COVER BY TONY S. DANIEL, BATT & TOMEU MOREY

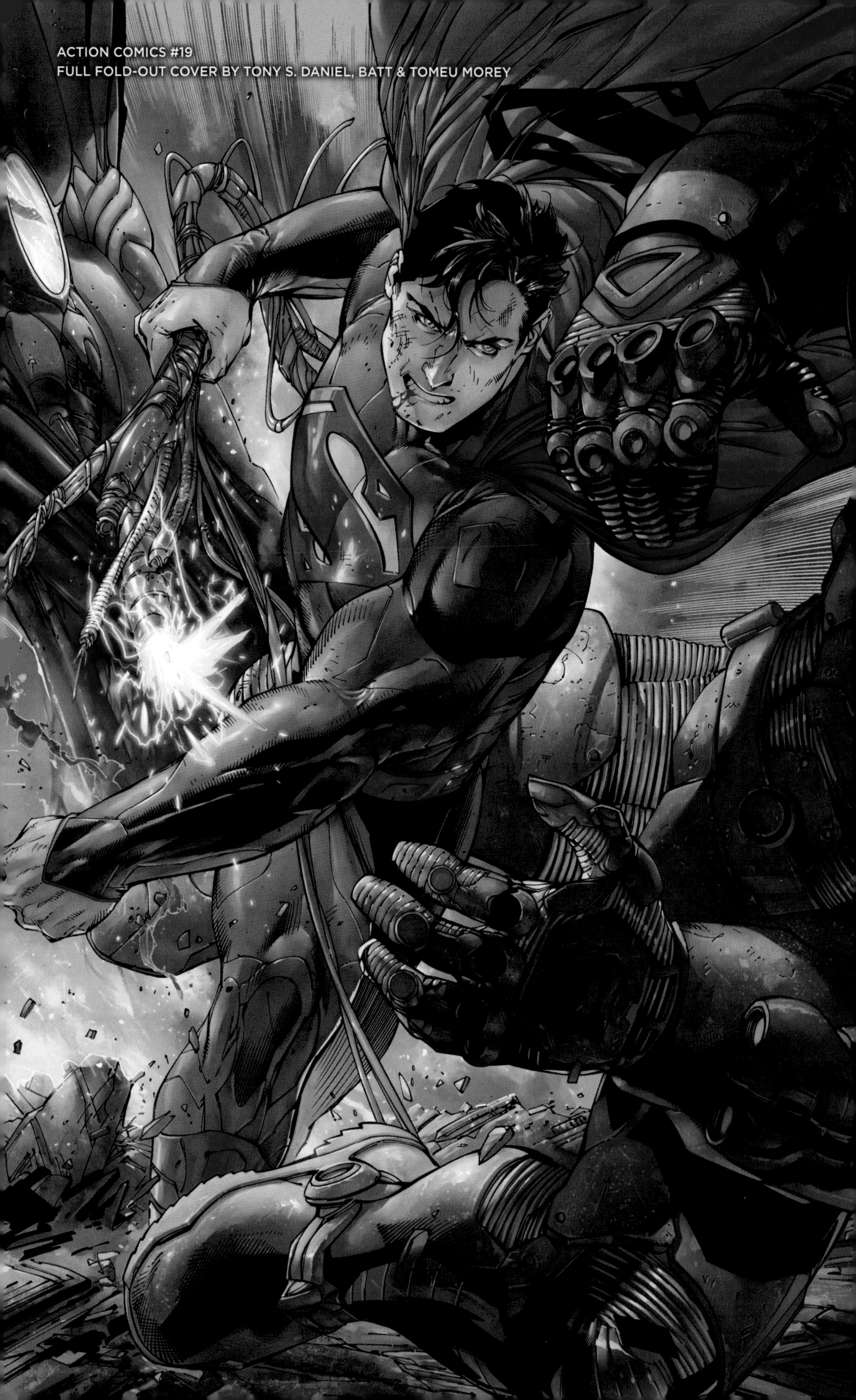

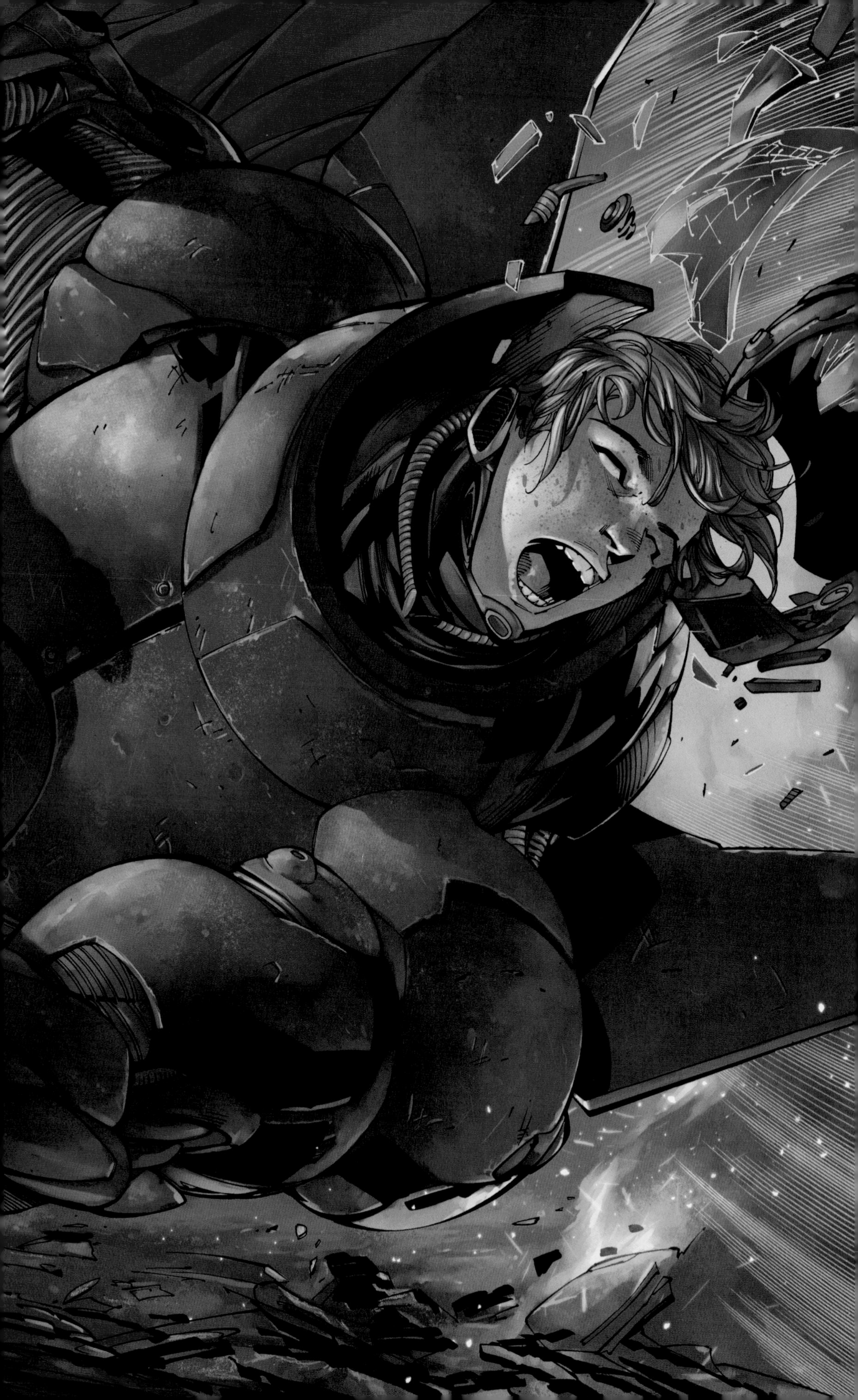

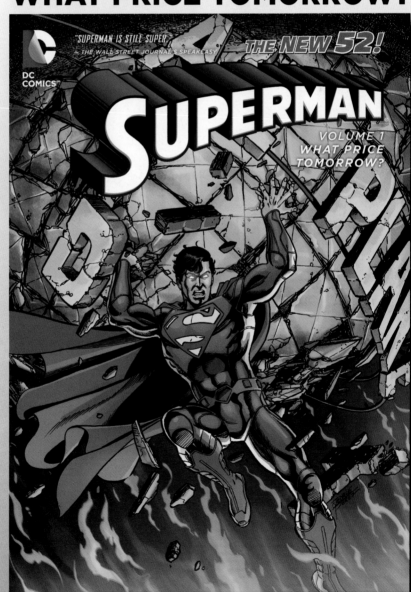

DC
COMICS™

START AT THE BEGINNING!

SUPERMAN VOLUME 1:
WHAT PRICE TOMORROW?

SUPERMAN VOL. 2:
SECRETS & LIES

SUPERMAN VOL. 3:
FURY AT WORLD'S
END

SUPERMAN:
H'EL ON EARTH

GEORGE **PÉREZ**   JESÚS **MERINO**   NICOLA **SCOTT**

DC COMICS™

"Writer Geoff Johns and artist Jim Lee toss you–and their heroes–into the action from the very start and don't put on the brakes. DC's über-creative team craft an inviting world for those who are trying out a comic for the first time. Lee's art is stunning."—USA TODAY

"A fun ride."—IGN

START AT THE BEGINNING!

JUSTICE LEAGUE VOLUME 1: ORIGIN

GEOFF JOHNS and JIM LEE

DC COMICS™
THE NEW 52!
JUSTICE LEAGUE
VOLUME 1 ORIGIN
"WRITTEN BY GEOFF JOHNS, WITH ART BY THE GODLY JIM LEE, JUSTICE LEAGUE IS A MUST READ."
– COMPLEX MAGAZINE
GEOFF JOHNS JIM LEE SCOTT WILLIAMS

JUSTICE LEAGUE VOL. 2: THE VILLAIN'S JOURNEY

THE NEW 52!
JUSTICE LEAGUE
GEOFF JOHNS JIM LEE SCOTT WILLIAMS

JUSTICE LEAGUE VOL. 3: THRONE OF ATLANTIS

THE NEW 52!
JUSTICE LEAGUE
GEOFF JOHNS IVAN REIS PAUL PELLETIER TONY S. DANIEL

JUSTICE LEAGUE OF AMERICA VOL. 1: WORLD'S MOST DANGEROUS

THE NEW 52!
JUSTICE LEAGUE OF AMERICA
GEOFF JOHNS DAVID FINCH BRETT BOOTH DOUG MAHNKE

"It's an exciting time to be a Batman fan, and Daniel is a large reason why."
—IGN.com

"Entertaining...Everything still shimmers and moves under Daniel's pen."
—Comic Book Resources

FROM THE WRITER/ARTIST OF *DETECTIVE COMICS*
TONY S. DANIEL

BATMAN: R.I.P.

with GRANT MORRISON

**BATMAN:
LIFE AFTER DEATH**

**BATMAN: BATTLE FOR
THE COWL**

"Clear storytelling at its best. It's an intriguing concept and easy to grasp."
—THE NEW YORK TIMES

"Azzarello is rebuilding the mythology of Wonder Woman."
–MAXIM

START AT THE BEGINNING!

WONDER WOMAN VOLUME 1: BLOOD

**MR. TERRIFIC
VOLUME 1:
MIND GAMES**

**BLUE BEETLE
VOLUME 1:
METAMORPHOSIS**

**THE FURY OF FIRESTORM:
THE NUCLEAR MEN
VOLUME 1:
GOD PARTICLE**

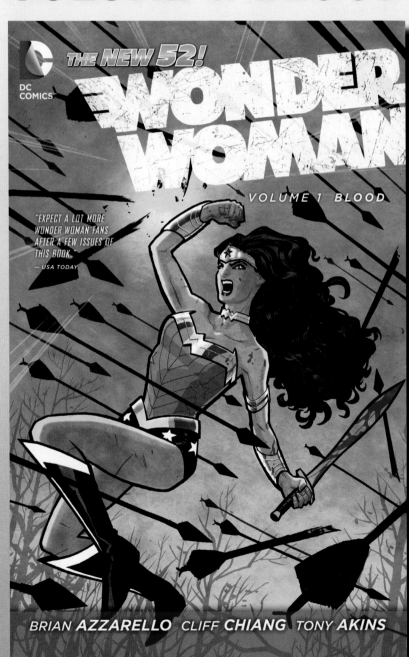